SEMEIA 90–91

THE BIBLE IN ASIAN AMERICA

Guest Editor: Tat-siong Benny Liew
Board Editor: Gale A. Yee

© 2002
by the Society of Biblical Literature

Published by
THE SOCIETY OF BIBLICAL LITERATURE
825 Houston Mill Road
Atlanta, GA 30329

Printed in the United States of America
on acid-free paper

CONTENTS

Contributors to This Issue v

Introduction: Whose Bible? Which (Asian) America?
        Tat-siong Benny Liew 1

PART I: READING THE BIBLE IN ASIAN AMERICA

1. From Babel to Pentecost: Finding a Home in the Belly of the Empire
        Eleazar S. Fernandez 29

2. Resident Aliens of the Diaspora: 1 Peter and Chinese Protestants in San Francisco
        Russell G. Moy 51

3. Uriah the Hittite: A (Con)Text of Struggle for Identity
        Uriah (Yong-Hwan) Kim..69

4. Home as Memory, Metaphor, and Promise in Asian/Pacific American Religious Experience
        Rachel A. R. Bundang 87

5. Shifts in Reading the Bible: Hermeneutical Moves among Asian Americans
        Roy I. Sano 105

6. Multiplicity and Judges 19: Constructing a Queer Asian Pacific American Biblical Hermeneutic
        Patrick S. Cheng 119

7. The Accidents of Being and the Politics of Identity: Biblical Images of Adoption and Asian Adoptees in America
        Mary F. Foskett 135

8. My Father Has No Children: Reflections on a *Hapa* Identity toward a Hermeneutic of Particularity
        Henry W. Rietz 145

PART II: READING READINGS OF THE BIBLE IN ASIAN AMERICA

9. The "Hidden Manna" That Sustains: Reading Revelation 2:17 in Joy Kogawa's *Obasan*
        Jane Naomi Iwamura..161

10. America Seen Through a Different Lens: The Bible
    in the Works of Yoshiko Uchida
    Fumitaka Matsuoka 181

11. Writing New and Joyful Songs: Con-Versing with Joy Kogawa
    Tat-siong Benny Liew 195

12. Evangelical and Mainline Teachings on Asian American Identity
    Russell Jeung..211

13. The Scandal of the "Model Minority" Mind? The Bible
    and Second-Generation Asian American Evangelicals
    Antony W. Alumkal..237

14. Second-Generation Chinese Evangelical Use of the
    Bible in Identity Discourse in North America
    Timothy Tseng 251

15. Hermeneutics and Asian American Preaching
    Eunjoo Mary Kim..269

16. Biblical Themes for Pastoral Care Revisited: An Asian
    American Rereading of a Classic Pastoral Care Text
    Peter Yuichi Clark 291

17. "The Bible Tells Me to Hate Myself": The Crisis in
    Asian American Spiritual Leadership
    Leng Leroy Lim...315

PART III: RESPONSE

18. At the Tables of an Asian American Banquet
    Jung Ha Kim 325

CONTRIBUTORS TO THIS ISSUE

Antony W. Alumkal
Iliff School of Theology
2201 South University Blvd.
Denver, CO 80210
aalumkal@iliff.edu

Rachel A. R. Bundang
(Union Theological Seminary [NY])
90 La Salle Street, #13-C
New York, NY 10027
Rab60@columbia.edu

Patrick S. Cheng
(Union Theological Seminary [NY])
3041 Broadway at Reinhold Niebuhr
    Place
New York, NY 10027
psc@post.harvard.edu

Peter Yuichi Clark
Department of Chaplaincy Services
Alta Bates Summit Medical Center
2450 Ashby Avenue
Berkeley, CA 94705-2067
pyclark@earthlink.net

Eleazar S. Fernandez
United Theological Seminary of the
    Twin Cities
3000 Fifth Street NW
New Brighton, MN 55112
Efernandez@UnitedSeminary-
MN.org

Mary F. Foskett
Department of Religion
Wake Forest University
POB 7212
Winston-Salem, NC 27109-7212
foskettm@wfu.edu

Jane Naomi Iwamura
School of Religion and the Program
in American Studies and Ethnicity
University of Southern California
3501 Trousdale Parkway
THH 328
Los Angeles, CA 90265-0355
iwamura@usc.edu

Russell M. Jeung
Department of Sociology
Foothill College
12345 El Monte Road
Los Altos Hills, CA 94022-4599
rj09207@tiptoe.fhda.edu

Eunjoo Mary Kim
Iliff School of Theology
2201 South University Blvd.
Denver, CO 80210
Ekim@Iliff.edu

Jung Ha Kim
Department of Sociology
Georgia State University
University Plaza
Atlanta, GA 30303
socjhk@panther.gsu.edu

Uriah (Yong-Hwan) Kim
(Pacific School of Religion)
2508 Benvenue Avenue, #202
Berkeley, CA 94704
yonghwan@earthlink.net

Tat-siong Benny Liew
Chicago Theological Seminary
5757 South University Avenue
Chicago, IL 60637
bliew@ctschicago.edu

Leng Leroy Lim
(Harvard Business School)
92 Rogers Avenue, #2
Somerville, MA 02144
LengLim@post.harvard.edu

Fumitaka Matsuoka
Pacific School of Religion
1798 Scenic Avenue
Berkeley, CA 94709
fmatsuoka@psr.edu

Russell G. Moy
Church Divinity School of the Pacific
2451 Ridge Road
Berkeley, CA 94709
rmoy@gabriel.cdsp.edu

Henry W. Rietz
Department of Religious Studies
Grinnell College
Grinnell, IA 50112-1690
Rietz@grinnell.edu

Roy I. Sano
Pacific School of Religion
1798 Scenic Avenue
Berkeley, CA 94709
bishoprsano@earthlink.net

Timothy Tseng
American Baptist Seminary of the West
2606 Dwight Way
Berkeley, CA 94704
ttseng@absw.edu

INTRODUCTION:
WHOSE BIBLE? WHICH (ASIAN) AMERICA?

Tat-siong Benny Liew
Chicago Theological Seminary

My Chinese husband ... told me one day that he thought the stories in the Bible were more like Chinese than American stories, and added: "If you had not told me what you have about it, I should say that it was composed by the Chinese." (Sui Sin Far: 78)

This citation begins Russell G. Moy's contribution to this volume on "The Bible in Asian America." Sui Sin Far (or Edith Maude Eaton), a Eurasian, is to "our" knowledge the first published writer of what "we" call today Asian American literature.[1] Originally written in the late nineteenth century, these quoted lines tell "us" not only of the Bible's place in America but also that Asian Americans have been reading and writing about the Bible for a long time. Despite its long history, this is (over a century since Sui Sin Far) the first time that an academic journal on biblical studies has devoted an entire issue—indeed, a double issue—to exploring this subject. In this "introduction," I would like to provide some rationale for this volume, point out some of the contents and challenges presented within, and propose several possible directions for future explorations.

THE WHAT-FORS

On one level, readers may read this volume as an attempt to "bridge" biblical studies and Asian American studies. The "bridging" of these two disciplines should seem logical to many, given the increasing number of Asian Americans in biblical studies[2] and the emergent interest in religion

---

[1] For a short but helpful introduction to Sui Sin Far, see Amy Ling and Annette White-Parks. For a book-length treatment of her life, work, and legacy, see White-Parks.

[2] According to statistics of the Association of Theological Schools in the United States and Canada (ATS), the number of full-time faculty members at ATS schools who are Asian American has increased from 51 in 1991 to 119 in 2000. In terms of percentage of all full-time faculty members at ATS schools, Asian American is also the only racial/ethnic minority group whose percentage has increased more than a fraction of a percentage point from 1996 to 2000. In terms of student enrollment in what ATS classifies as "advanced theological research" (Th.M./M.Th./S.T.M./Th.D./Ph.D.), Asian American is by far the largest minority group, with its number

within Asian American studies.[3] I would like to suggest, however, two additional reasons for this interdisciplinary endeavor.

In my opinion, interdisciplinary studies make special sense for Asian Americans once "we" realize that the same language or concepts are being used to patrol boundaries of academic disciplines and those of the nation-state (David Palumbo-Liu; Liew, 2001a:326–28). With emphasis on "origins" and "purity," gatekeepers of both geographical and intellectual space insist that "trespassers" and/or "transplants" will lead only to pollution, confusion, and destruction. Perceived to be perennially illegitimate "border-crossers" and thus perceptive to the oppressive power dynamics of most boundary constructions, Asian American biblical scholars should at least be open to the possibilities of interdisciplinary biblical studies in general and its "bridging" with Asian American studies in particular. This is especially the case if current practices of biblical studies do not meet the needs of Asian Americans (Kwok Pui-lan: 69–71). "We" need new interdisciplinary studies of the Bible that question current practices and imagine how biblical studies can be practiced differently.

What about people within Asian American studies? Why should they be interested in crossing this "bridge"? "We" should remember that as part of ethnic studies, Asian American studies have been interdisciplinary since the beginning, and thus been the targets of much disciplinary gaze (that is, "disciplinary" in Michel Foucault's double sense). More explicitly, "we" should remember that Asian American studies started in the 1960s as part of the Third World students' strike for changes in admission policies and curriculum designs (Keith Osajima: 59).[4] While the demand regarding admission policies had to do with increasing enrollment of students of color, the dispute regarding curriculum designs revolved around several issues: raising the number of faculty of color, incorporating ethnic histories and perspectives in course contents, and connecting with communities to make the classroom sociopolitically relevant. In other words, Asian American

---

rising from 475 in 1996 to 510 in 2000 (in contrast, the number of African Americans, the second largest minority group, has hovered around the high 200s in the same time span). Since ATS does not provide any figures on the basis of disciplinary distribution, I have to assume that the figures are equally representative of all theological disciplines. I have tried to get some statistics from the Society of Biblical Literature, but have not been successful. I must thank Bill Myers of ATS for providing me with the above statistics.

[3] In my mind, this is best evidenced by the formation of the Asian and Pacific Americans and Religion Research Initiative (APARRI) in 1999, and the Institute for Leadership Development and Study of Pacific and Asian North American Religion (PANA) in 2000. Since then, there is a growing list of publications on religion and Asian Americans; see, for example, David K. Yoo, 1999a; Fenggang Yang, 1999; Pyong Gap Min and Jung Ha Kim; and Paul R. Spickard and Jane Naomi Iwamura. For a recent review essay on this emerging emphasis, see Yang, 2000.

[4] Interpretive histories of the Asian American studies movement can be found in William Wei: 11–43, 132–61; and David L. Eng, 2001:208–11.

studies have always aimed to be inclusive in terms of both personnel ("who gets to teach, learn and participate") and programs ("what gets taught"; Stephen H. Sumida and Sau-ling Cynthia Wong: 4). I would argue that this inclusive ethos should imply an openness to religious and/or theological studies (and by extension, biblical studies), despite an understandable hesitation out of (1) a commitment to an anti-authority and anti-establishment tradition of the Asian American movement; and (2) a concern over accusations of mixing church and state.[5] Indeed, I contend that Asian Americanists should welcome this "crossover" in light of the recent lament over their own "professionalization," which refers to a disappearing radical politics as well as a shrinking interdisciplinary workspace (Michael Omi and Dana Takagi: xiii). The "cross-addressing" that this volume promotes will provide a new and emerging interdisciplinary workspace. In addition, it has the potential, as I think this volume illustrates, to help foreground Asian American studies as (radical) cultural politics. Considering the "cultural capital" that the Bible assumes in the U.S., biblical studies are very much a part of its (multi)cultural context and contest, notwithstanding the rhetoric about "church-and-state separation" (Liew, 1999:16–21).

While contributions to this volume do demonstrate the permeability between biblical studies and Asian American studies, I am in the final analysis personally not satisfied with the "bridging" language. Despite the popular understanding of Asian Americans as "bridge builders" (Aihwa Ong: 132–34, 169–70), the idea of a "bridge" seems to imply a "soft call for interdisciplinarity—that bane of serious scholarship that both keeps the disciplines in place (just use two!) and justifies not amateurism but superficiality" (Paul A. Bové: 305).[6] If Bové's language of "abandoning" disciplines seems too extreme, I would at least prefer the term "*trans-disciplinarity*," with the prefix denoting "both moving through space or across lines, as well as changing the nature of something" (Ong: 4).[7] That is

---

[5] These are the reasons given by L. Ling-Chi Wang, professor of Asian American studies at the University of California, Berkeley, to account for the lack of dialogue between Asian American studies and religious/theological studies during a panel discussion in the APARRI 2001 Conference ("Religion and Public Life in Pacific and Asian North America," University of California at Berkeley, August 9, 2001).

[6] In fact, an influential Asian American magazine was named *Bridge*; for a retelling of its history, see Wei: 112–23. The idea that this volume brings together "two" fields of study is at best simplistic. As I have already intimated, Asian American studies are themselves a multi-disciplinary *bricolage*. Biblical studies have also intersected with, to name just the obvious, the study of history, cultural anthropology, and literature. In other words, this project is not a dialectical project in the Hegelian sense, but a dialogical one in a Bakhtinian sense.

[7] Note that although Ong is talking about her understanding of transnationalism rather than that of transdisciplinarity, her own anthropological work is from my perspective no less transdisciplinary.

to say, if interdisciplinarity risks a benign understanding of inclusion, transdisciplinarity represents a dynamic explosion in the sense of a transgression and a transformation.[8] Transdisciplinarity questions assumed understandings and challenges accepted practices of an established discipline. As I begin to describe the contours and contents of this volume, I hope to delineate its transgressive and transformative aspects.

THE WHATS AND SO-WHATS

Continuing the tradition of Asian American studies, this volume raises the question of personnel participation. This question is not just about admitting and acknowledging Asian Americans as biblical scholars. Neither is it just about accepting Asian American studies as a rightful repertoire of reference by Asian American biblical scholars. As significant as these two steps are, this volume seeks to push a little further. Will biblical scholars be open to biblical interpretation by Asian Americans who do not even identify themselves as biblical scholars? Out of all the contributors to this volume, only four are "technically" speaking "specialists" of the Bible (Mary F. Foskett, Uriah [Yong Hwan] Kim, Henry W. Rietz, and myself).[9] Yet there is, as Jacques Derrida points out and proves in practice, a long tradition of biblical interpretation by continental philosophers (1995:23, 48–49).[10] And as the citation of Sui Sin Far shows, the Bible has always been read and referred to by Asian Americans in different fields. Within the pages of this volume, readers will find Asian American scholars

---

[8] I am well aware that the desirability of what I call transdisciplinary studies is still being debated heatedly today. I also have to admit that while I am an unashamed advocate of such studies, I do understand and share the concerns that such studies may turn out to be overwhelmingly burdensome and/or pointlessly shallow. For a helpful and enlightening example of this debate, see Charles Bernheimer.

[9] While it was intentional on my part to solicit involvement from people outside the discipline of biblical studies, the actual coming together of the present participants was in many ways coincidental. Many participants came by word of mouth, by people recommending people. I would like to take this opportunity to thank especially King-kok Cheung, Susan Koshy, Jeffrey Kah-Jin Kuan, Rachel C. Lee, Michael Omi, and Roshni Rustomji for the recommendations that they have taken the time to make behind the scene. If this reads like the operation of *quanxi* (relations or connections) that William Safire (1996) has found to be so typical and so offensive of many Asian and Asian American circles, let me point out that the "good-old-boy-network" has also had a long history within so-called "Western" practices.

[10] I am grateful to my colleague at Chicago Theological Seminary, Theodore W. Jennings Jr., for highlighting these pages in a course that we co-taught, and for constantly reminding me that "the Bible is too important to be left only in the hands of biblical scholars." Admittedly, Derrida's focus here is on readings of the Bible that bracket the question of revelatory events. Intended or not, I nonetheless think that his comments point also to important and influential readings of the Bible by people who are, "technically" speaking, not biblical scholars.

who have been trained as historians, rhetoricians, sociologists, and theologians (both constructive and pastoral), as well as Asian American scholars who are in the midst of career and academic transitions—including one queer ordained clergyperson who is now a graduate student at Harvard Business School, and one queer graduate of Harvard Law School who is now a seminary student and a practicing minister—writing about the Bible and its reading. Immediately chastising these nonwhite and nonbiblical scholars for not knowing "our" field and its *modus operandi* would effectually, of course, control what kind of questions one may or may not ask of the Bible and delegitimate what "outsiders" may have to say about the Bible and its reading. In this train of thought, I think it is worth quoting at length what the Japanese Canadian writer, Joy Kogawa, has to say about the operation of "standards":

> Yet just let us get a little too close—let us stub our toes on the line of privilege—and then watch the reaction from even your most liberal do-gooders. If we don't get our facts exactly right, you whites say, "Look, look, she made a mistake on the third line." You look for errors in our remarks rather than for the truth beyond our errors. And that too is racism. We're all trapped in it.... Every one of us lives and breathes in structures of racism from the moment we're born. We're caged in standards controlled by people of privilege—standards of truth and goodness, standards of excellence, standards of beauty which are standards of privilege through and through, and those are the bars that deny our specific realities and lock us out of even your most anti-racist institutions. (226)

Rather than eliminating all standards or all talks regarding standards, I am evoking the endless need to question *for what* and *for whom* standards are working. A blind and rigid stance on "standards" might rob biblical studies of the possibility that an "unprofessional" approach to and reading of the Bible may actually help advance knowledge and thinking (Bové: 302). By now, many biblical scholars are willing to incorporate other disciplines in their reading of the Bible, but that is not the same as inviting scholars from other disciplines to write about Bible reading. In my mind at least, this volume not only disputes the claim of monopoly that Anglo Americans may make of the Bible but also disallows biblical scholars from monopolizing biblical interpretation.

Does this shift in personnel translate into changes in the practice of biblical studies? While much scholarship within Asian American studies seeks to dispute the erasure of Asian American presence,[11] and African American

---

[11] For example, both Yoo (1999b:1–2) and Eng (2001:35–37) use the Promontory Summit photograph as a point to depart into their respective work on Asian American religions and

readings of the Bible can wrestle with the question "[w]ould or should the agenda of the study of the Bible ... necessarily be focused around the identification of Africans as biblical characters" (Vincent L. Wimbush: 2), essays in the first section of this issue, "Reading the Bible in Asian America," tend to do something else. They tend to look at how the Bible, as a culturally embedded and culturally powerful (library of) text(s), constructs ethnic identities from majority and/or minority perspectives. For example, Eleazer S. Fernandez looks at how such constructions in Genesis 11 and Acts 2 involve a politics of exclusion and inclusion, while Rachel A. R. Bundang scrutinizes Jer 29:4–23 to see if it sheds any light on diasporic existence. That is not to say, of course, that the long history of ethnic erasure suffered by Asian Americans (both textual and physical) does not play a role in these essays. It is interesting to note in that regard that both U. Kim and Patrick S. Cheng have chosen to focus their critical attention on a little-known victim character within a well-known biblical passage: respectively, Uriah the Hittite in the tangle between David and Bathsheba (2 Samuel 11), and the unnamed concubine in the parallel text to the so-called "sodomy" text of Genesis 19 (Judges 19). These critical practices to re-member a seemingly slight scapegoat character are, I would argue, inseparable from the vitrifying and vilifying violence within Asian American experiences. As Roy I. Sano shows in his essay on the hermeneutical shifts that he himself and other Asian Americans went through in reading the Bible, contexts and experiences influence both what "we" read and how "we" read. Analyzing how the Bible ascribes ethnic identities with political and disciplinary purposes, U. Kim and Cheng also help "us" think through and unpack how the dominant culture manages "us" textually and politically with certain Asian American identities (Darrell Y. Hamamoto; Robert G. Lee). A poetics of (re)presentation is often paradoxically coupled with a politics of elimination.

The essay that comes closest to "finding" Asian Americans in the Bible is, in my view, Moy's. Beginning with Sui Sin Far's statement that Chinese (Americans) could be the composers as well as the characters of the Bible, Moy proceeds to make two rather bold claims. First, Moy claims that the Chinese Protestants of nineteenth-century San Francisco may help illuminate the sociopolitical context of the New Testament letter, 1 Peter. Is Moy suggesting here that Asian Americans are the modern-day representatives of 1 Peter's community, and thus indirectly disputing Ambrose Bierce's late-nineteenth-century claim that "there was nothing about Chinamen [sic]

Asian American masculinity. The Promontory Summit photograph, which commemorates the completion of the Transcontinental Railroad (1869), shows no Asian American faces, although the Transcontinental Railroad was in many ways built on the exploitation of Chinese immigrant laborers.

in the New Testament" (451–52)? Or is he implying that Asian Americans can teach "us" something about the Bible that others cannot? Second, Moy makes the even bolder claim that with the organization of the *Zhengdaohui*, these newcomers to Christianity actually lived out the vision of 1 Peter. To say that one has "practiced" scriptures is certainly a daring declaration, but one must remember that throughout his essay, Moy has never even bothered to argue or suggest that this minority community in the U.S. had paid any special attention to 1 Peter.[12] Is he then insinuating that these people understood scriptures, in fact "fulfilled" scriptures, without needing to read them?

If the essays in the section "Reading the Bible in Asian America" help re-vision biblical studies to particular foci (including particular literary characters) with a sharp political edge, they also help re-mind "us" that revisionist scholarship within Asian American studies is not without its own blind spots. Cheng's essay is, after all, concerned to help bring to visibility the queer population within Asian America. Likewise, Foskett—herself an adoptee who has also recently adopted a child from Vietnam—looks at adoption imageries in the Bible (Exodus 1–2 and Romans 8–9) and reminds "us" all of another group that is often overlooked within Asian American studies: children adopted from Asia by white families in the U.S. There is yet a third such group that comes into the picture of this volume. Featuring his *hapa* identity, Rietz brings up the increasing number of bi- or multiracial persons within Asian America (as does Sano, though this concern is not the core of his essay). Significantly, these three groups of "often-forgotten" people raise an issue that has much to do with the past and the future of Asian America. Their presence presents both the tensions and relations between biological reproduction and cultural reproduction, that is, the possibility and reality of community that is based on something other than (full) "blood." Eng, in his recent work on queerness and masculinity, is certainly correct that this tension and relation between what Edward Said calls "filiation" and "affiliation" (1983:17) have a long history within Asian America that goes all the way back to the proliferation of "paper sons" (2001:190).[13] At the same time, one must not forget that this question has to do with more than just tradition. As Werner Sollors has helped identify, the reality and

---

[12] Note that in Moy's (re)telling, 1 Peter was never mentioned specifically by the Chinese Protestants of nineteenth-century San Francisco. In fact, Moy seems to emphasize the contrary: for many in that community, reading the Bible had more to do with learning the English language than with learning its teachings.

[13] "Paper sons" became a way for many Chinese to get around the exclusion policy that limited their entry into the U.S. for sixty years (1882–1943). For a fascinating story of this phenomenon, see Chin and Chin.

possibility of the U.S. as a national community hinge on—to use the vocabulary of Derrida (2001:45)—the "irreconcilable but indissociable" emphases on consent and descent. Along with some pioneering Asian Americanists (Eng and Alice Y. Hom; Teresa Williams-Leon and Cynthia L. Nakashima), contributors to this first section of the volume point out both the magnitude and the urgency of this matter, which is inseparable from the needs and situations of the three neglected groups mentioned above.

The ways personnel changes may shift the practice of biblical studies become, in my opinion, even more pronounced in the second section of this volume, "Reading Readings of the Bible in Asian America." In contrast to the first section that attempts to read or interpret the Bible itself, this second section is basically made up of ethnographic readings of how the Bible is read or understood by writers of Asian American literature or persons associated with Asian American churches, be they religious educators, preachers, pastoral counselors, or local church members. In other words, the emphasis shifts from readers reading in the first section to reading readers in the second.[14] While this type of ethnographic readings or reading ethnographies is unusual within biblical studies (and thus may well be viewed as "experimental" at best or "secondhand" at worst), I think there are at least four good reasons for such an endeavor. First, in one of the first anthologies on Asian American studies of religions, Yoo suggests that "real" religious actions should be found in the "fringes" instead of the "mainstream," meaning "in the everyday lives of people and their engagement with material circumstances" (1999a:3). Although I am reluctant to say that understandings of the Bible by biblical scholars are "unreal" or "less real," I do think that *Semeia* should/ could provide the space to explore other understandings that exist in equally real ways along the fringes, or even way outside the confines, of "our" guild. Did biblical scholar Wayne A. Meeks not argue almost twenty years ago that New Testament scriptures were written *for* and used *by* "ordinary Christians," and thus it was imperative that "we" tried to understand the "ordinary Christian" world (2)? While Meeks's project has to do with "ordinary Christians" of the first century, I think his argument is nevertheless applicable to studies devoted to "ordinary Christians" of the contemporary world.[15] Second, as many (postmodern)

---

[14] That is not to say that the boundary or division between the two sections is solid and rigid. For example, the essays by Moy and Timothy Tseng could easily fit within either section.

[15] See also Mary McClintock Fulkerson: 197; and Jon D. Levenson: 106–26, although Levenson speaks out of a context and a concern much different from my own. Levenson is urging biblical scholars not to isolate their own work from the interpretations of religious communities out of the context of historical-critical criticism (particularly its claim of objectivity and neutrality), and he seems to do so out of a concern to uphold the religious canon (in light of his affirmation of canonical criticism). I will have more to say about the question of canon later.

ethnographers are talking about the relationship between ethnography and reading (Jonathan Boyarin; James Clifford; Marjorie Garber, Rebecca L. Walkowitz and Paul B. Franklin), ethnographic readings or reading ethnographies, starting with Janice A. Radway's reading of how romances are read by "ordinary" female readers (1991), are becoming part of the larger world of literary/cultural studies (Radway, 1999; Erin Smith; Amy Frykholm).[16] Third, this type of readings facilitates a cooperation or a crossing between literary and sociological analysis, which have been deemed as both—to play on Derrida's earlier play on words—"irreconcilable and dissociable" by some (Omi and Takagi: xi–xv; Judith Butler, John Guillory, and Kendall Thomas: xi–xii). Last but not least, these ethnographic readings of readings provide a way to recover one of the original emphases of Asian American studies: reconnection with communities.

In what ways does this second section challenge Asian American studies? Its first three contributions (Iwamura's; Fumitaka Matsuoka's; and mine) have to do with the use of the Bible in Asian American literature. Almost twenty years ago, the Canadian literary critic Northrop Frye suggested that one could not understand literature of the Western world without knowledge of the Bible, what he called the "Great Code." While Asian *American* literature is not devoid of biblical allusions and citations (again, as evidenced by the citation of Sui Sin Far), most scholars of Asian American literature have surprisingly continued to (dis)miss the role of the Bible.[17] For example, a couple of critics (Laura Hyun Yi Kang: 41–42; Walter K. Lew) have attempted to help track the intertextual linkages of Theresa Hak Kyung Cha's multilayered text, *Dictee,* but both have somehow managed to overlook the Bible even when Matt 4:1–11 is cited in its entirety (Cha: 52–53). What "we" have in this section has no doubt only scratched the surface of studying the intersection between the Bible and Asian American literature. Iwamura, Matsuoka, and I have ended up looking at only two Japanese

---

[16] I am indebted to Radway for alerting me to the work of Smith and Frykholm and for introducing me to Frykholm. I am grateful to Frykholm for her willingness to share her work and for teaching me the methodological importance of audience studies for ethnographies of readings.

[17] An exception is King-kok Cheung's reading of Kogawa's *Obasan* (1993). In fact, this particular essay and the general scholarship of Cheung are in many ways inspirational and influential to how I conceptualize this issue on the Bible in Asian America. Let me also note that my reference to Frye here should not be taken as my wholehearted endorsement of Frye's approach to reading literature. After all, there are various approaches of reading, and intertexts can be limitless in width as well as depth (the Bible itself may go back to other ancient texts, and such textual trails can become an endless tail or tale). My interest lies in pointing out the glaring inconsistencies of those who do choose to read intertextually, and how their practice may end up denying Asian American literature as *American* literature, or denying the Bible as a significant intertext of Asian America.

writers of North America (Kogawa and Yoshiko Uchida), but as my references to Sui Sin Far and Cha show, use of the Bible in Asian American literature is far more pervasive. Neither is the use of the Bible in Asian American literature the only way to explore this complex intersection. Jeffrey Kah-Jin Kuan, for example, has attempted to use Amy Tan's *Kitchen God's Wife* as a lens to illuminate his own reading of the book of Job in the Hebrew Bible.

Let me spend some time highlighting three challenging issues raised in this second section of the volume. The first one has to do with the issue of (ethnic) identity.[18] If the essays of the first section, as well as Peter Yuichi Clark's essay in the second, demonstrate how (ethnic) identity helps one read (biblical) texts from particular perspectives and with particular foci (including the ascription of [ethnic] identity in texts), the ethnographic readings or reading ethnographies of the second section show that (ethnic) identity is also formed in the process of reading. That is to say, there is certain circularity involved in the interaction between identity and interpretation. Identity does not only influence reading, but reading also influences identity (Ken Stone, 1997). "Reading Readings of the Bible in Asian America" further illustrates the complexity, indeed the contradictions, within the process of (ethnic) identity formation. (Ethnic) identity is complicated because it is not some essentialized thing that just exists inside a person (as the popular expression "simply be myself" or "go find myself" implies), nor is it something that can be freely chosen. Instead, (ethnic) identity is historically motivated as well as sociopolitically particular.[19] One's (ethnic) identity is always already (in)formed and inhibited by myriads of larger existing structures.

Russell Jeung's ethnographic research of two pan-Asian American churches, for example, suggests that webs of institutional logic (mainline or evangelical Protestant) affect one's reading of the Bible, which in turn affects one's ethnic identity as an Asian American. If there is always a social logic at

---

[18] One should remember that the theoretical link between interpretation and identity is not only because of the emphasis on the reader that comes with reader-response criticism, but also very much a part of the continental (or more specifically, German) tradition of philosophical hermeneutics that Eunjoo Mary Kim refers to in her contribution to this volume. I am referring, of course, to the way Martin Heidegger and Hans-Georg Gadamer present and understand hermeneutics as an ontological issue. See Gerald L. Bruns: 2–10.

[19] Since identity and experience are often intertwined and mutually constitutive, see also the problematization of experience in Joan W. Scott. In this regard, this volume differs from Wimbush, who makes experience the unproblematic center of African American readings of the Bible (12). I agree with Said's lament about "an impoverishing politics of knowledge [that is] based only upon the assertion and reassertion of identity, [which is] an ultimately uninteresting alternation of presence and absence" (1993:310). Note also the way Rietz, in the first section, problematizes identity, but then proceeds to reinscribe experience as the basis of his interpretation. Both identity and experience are social constructions; as such, they not only engineer interpretation but also entail interpretation.

work, then the view that "religion is something private" is actually not private at all; neither are the privatistic and pietistic emphases of evangelical Christianity. Antony W. Alumkal's essay seems to support Jeung's point. According to Alumkal, Asian American evangelicals who excel in many rigorous academic pursuits can ironically be quite unquestioning and complacent with their reading and understanding of the Bible. While their essays do not deny the operation of institutional logic in reading practice and (ethnic) identity formation, Tseng and E. Kim end up, I think, providing further nuance to the point made by Jeung and Alumkal. Tseng, a self-identified evangelical who is concerned to bring out the complexity of Asian American evangelicalism and to break out of what he calls its "assimilationist and orientalist" way of reading the Bible, proposes a re-identification of the Hebraic Christian characters in Acts 6:1–7 as Anglo American Christians. Moving beyond the usual identification of those characters as Chinese-speaking pastors of Chinese American churches (in other words, what is dictated by traditional institutional logic), this rereading will, in Tseng's estimation, (in)form a new Chinese American evangelical identity that can engage in the discourse on race. If Tseng's article reveals an Asian American evangelical who has broken out of its dominant institutional logic, E. Kim's research on Korean American Presbyterian (that is, mainline Protestant) preaching betrays an "invasive" evangelical emphasis on (material) "blessing" (see also Yoo, 1996:xiii). For Tseng and E. Kim, then, neither mainline Asian American churches nor evangelical Asian American churches are as monolithic as Jeung's essay seems to suggest.[20] Both the religious and the ethnic identity of Asian Americans appear to be porous, fluid, and ambivalent. As Sano's essay in the first section makes clear, there are contesting and conflicting factors in/forming "our" interpretations and "our" identities as Asian Americans.[21] If the circularity between identity and interpretation underlines the importance of reading as a site of struggle for (ethnic) identity, I think the complexity and contradictions of identity formation point to the prospect of ever-evolving reading practices, as well as suggest many unexpected twists and turns when it comes to affiliation within and without Asian America.

---

[20] Part of the dynamics may have to do with Tseng's point that Chinese American churches have been historically and fiercely independent. Moy's retelling of the *Zhengdaohui* reminds us, of course, that this "independence" is itself inseparable from the racism that Chinese American Christians encounter in society in general, and in Christian denominations in particular. It also remains to be seen whether the difference between Jeung, on one hand, and Tseng and E. Kim, on the other, may have anything to do with the differences between pan-Asian American congregations (in the case of Jeung) and ethnic-specific churches (in the case of Tseng and E. Kim).

[21] I am using the word "in/form" here to communicate the double sense that Asian American identities are informed by various structural logics, and in formation as a process.

Biological reproduction and cultural reproduction are, as I mention earlier, heterogeneous even if they are often tightly hinged.

In addition to the issue of (ethnic) identity and interpretation, this second section also raises questions about the concept of sacred texts. While there may be a difference in degrees, all three contributions that explore the use of the Bible in Asian American literature (Iwamura's; Matsuoka's; and mine) present a rather ambivalent attitude toward the Bible. This ambivalence may well be related to the ambiguous traditions within the Bible itself. Several essays in the first section have pointed out, for example, that the Bible does not say one and the same thing regarding difference (Fernandez's juxtaposition of Babel and Pentecost), adoption (Foskett's juxtaposition of Exodus 1–2 and Romans 8–9), and purity (Sano's juxtaposition of Ruth and Leviticus). As Derrida asks regarding what he calls the "Abrahamic" heritage on forgiveness (a topic that is related to Sano's inquiry about reconciliation and redemption), "What does it mean to inherit when the heritage includes an injunction at once double and contradictory?" (2001:35).

What it seems to mean to many Asian Americans is that the Bible has been a weapon both *for* and *against* "us." I would further argue that many Anglo Americans have the same ambivalence toward this library of books. As Moy's essay recounts, while white Christians at San Francisco in the nineteenth century were eager to teach the Bible to the Chinese, they were also reluctant to let the Chinese study the Bible without white presence. Likewise, in Monica Sone's *Nisei Daughter*, when Japanese Americans were forced into internment camps after Pearl Harbor, they were forbidden to keep with them even their Japanese Bibles, translations that were no doubt facilitated by the work of white missionaries.

> Later, we were ordered to turn in all literature printed in Japanese. Mother went to the central receiving station to plead with the young man. "I have a few things, but they're not dangerous, I assure you. Why does the government want to take away the little I have left?"
> The Nisei explained patiently, "No one is taking them away from you, Oba-san. They'll be returned to you eventually. Now what have you there?"
> Mother smiled. "A Bible. Pray tell me, what's so dangerous about it?"
> The Nisei threw his arms up. "If it's printed in Japanese, I must have it. What else?" (188; see also 154–56)

In the presence of this can(n)on that both helps and hurts, Sano suggests in the first section that the solution lies in using functional methods (meaning the space created by redaction and canonical criticism for Sano) to identify a contextual and thus constantly changing "functional canon" within the "orthodox canon." In a related but also dissimilar fashion, You-Leng Leroy Lim in the second section takes a more radical stance and states that the well-being of Asian American Christian communities has little to do with the Bible or finding the "proper" "exegetical" method(s). Instead, Lim proposes that one should focus on the cultivation of a pragmatic spiritual leadership, an example of which is provided by the way Lim's predecessor used the Exodus story to interpret the wartime internment experiences of his Japanese American parishioners.

This suggests to me that Lim's biblical hermeneutics is one that centers on task rather than on text or technique. It is important to point out that Lim's focus on leadership does not end up eliminating hermeneutics. To the contrary, his own attempt to explicate what he means by "good" leadership underscores the indispensability, and thus the importance, of interpretation. After all, terms such as "pragmatic," "spiritual," and "good" may mean different things to different people. If I may take the liberty to conflate Lim's essay with my interview of Kogawa in the same section of this volume, whether an interpretation of a biblical text "works" (Lim's emphasis) to bring about "well-being" and "love" (Kogawa's criteria to adjudicate competing interpretations) is something that is itself subject to different interpretations. Why? Because people will advocate a different interpretation of the same biblical text in accordance with their different interpretations of what the words "works," "well-being," or "love" mean (Georgia Warnke). If this sounds like a post-structuralist cliché of how signifier differs and defers endlessly from a signified, let me arrest its flow to prevent one ultimate question (as opposed to the Ultimate Question with capital letters) from slipping and sliding away from "our" attention. My question is: Why do Asian Americans, given their ambivalence about the Bible, continue to embrace the concept of sacred texts without greater effort to interrogate or interpret the meaning of this concept?[22] In addition to talking about what the words of a biblical text mean and do, should "interpreting scriptures" not also take on the task of exploring the meaning of the very word "scriptures"?[23] According to Louis Althusser:

> Left to itself, a spontaneous (technical) practice produces only the "theory" it needs as a means to produce the end assigned to it: this "theory" is never more than the reflection of this end, uncriticized, unknown, in its means of realization, that is, it is a by-product of the reflection of the technical practice's end on its means. A "theory" which does not question the end whose by-product it is remains a prisoner of this end and of the "realities" which have imposed it as an end. (171)

---

[22] Incidentally, Wimbush raises a similar question in his introduction to the volume on African Americans and the Bible (14–16).

[23] I personally do not think that biblical scholars have given enough effort on the concept of sacred texts and the related concept of scriptural authority. For a couple of recent examples that do make such an attempt from different feminist perspectives, see Sandra M. Schneiders, and Mary Ann Tolbert.

If so, then Lim and others are right to suggest in this section of the volume that biblical interpretation must go beyond the focus on techniques of reading texts ("what does this text mean?") to consider its task or end ("why am I reading this text?"). This latter question should, at least in my view, break the relative silence around the meaning of scripture and/or canon. The question of canon formation is, of course, not unrelated to that of identity formation (Eng, 1998). In like manner, the question of content is inseparable from that of form.[24] The third issue that I want to highlight from this second section of the volume is that this section contains a couple of pieces that challenge the traditional form of academic essays within the discipline of biblical studies. My own contribution is in the form of an interview. Although interview is not an uncommon form within Asian American studies (Cheung, 2000; Ruth Y. Hsu)—and is in fact widespread in the larger world of literary/cultural studies (Imre Salusinszky; Gayatri Chakravorty Spivak; Peter Osborne; Trinh T. Minh-ha; Gloria E. Anzaldúa; Donna J. Haraway)—it is indeed a rarity, if not an exception, within biblical studies.[25] Then there is Lim's essay, which comes without any footnotes or bibliographical entries and reads more like a piece of creative prose. In the last few years, there have been a few isolated incidents of such a breakout in form.[26] Maybe this second section will facilitate a discussion, if not the practice, of this experimental version of "form criticism" in biblical studies.

THE NOW-WHATS

By providing the contours and challenges of this volume, I hope I have managed to manifest that the experimentation of this transdisciplinary project is not to be ornamental, but political. Both U. Kim and Cheng point out in their essays, for example, that the ascription of ethnic identity by the powerful results in the deaths of many, from Uriah the Hittite and the unnamed concubine in the Bible to Vincent Chin and unnamed queer Asian Americans in (real) life. As hinted by Alumkal, the so-called "model minority" stereotypifies Asian Americans as excellent with the sciences rather

---

[24] Interestingly enough, Wei has consistently characterized the *Amerasia Journal*, arguably the flagship journal of Asian American studies, as "scholarly (though not necessarily conventional)" (125, 129).

[25] Not to be neglected is, of course, the politics of the form of interview, particularly its implicit ideology of authenticity. For a helpful discussion of this politics, and how interviews with authors are parts of textual "afterlife" that do *not* settle meaning, see Trinh: 4–5, 247–52. To the best of my knowledge, I can think of only three interview pieces within biblical studies; they all appear in the same journal, and they are all by Alich Bach (1997a; 1997b; 1998).

[26] The most recognizable representative of this is arguably Roland Boer. See, for example, Boer, 1997, 2001. See also Liew, 2001b:182–83.

than humanities, not to mention religions. If religion is ever mentioned in the same breath with Asian Americans, what gets talked about is generally the "pagan" or "exotic" traditions like Confucianism, Buddhism, or Hinduism (Yoo, 1996:xvii). With this published volume on Asian Americans and the Bible of the dominant Judeo-Christian tradition(s), the so-called "white man's book" is no longer (if indeed it ever was) in the sole possession of white hands.[27] While this volume does contain an element of what the Bible may have to say about Asian America, I think its greater value lies in what Asian Americans ("biblical scholars" or not) have to say about the Bible. To participate in the political resistance of Asian America, contributors to this volume move out of their various assigned places to remember and dream with ingenuity, intelligence, and passionate interests.[28]

With the completion of this volume, the project on the Bible in Asian America has just begun. Let me then attempt to delineate some directions for the future. I hope to see more intentional interventions at the intersections (see also Kwame Anthony Appiah and Henry Louis Gates Jr.: 1). I personally understand the genitive in Cheng's hermeneutics *of* multiplicity in both a subjective and an objective sense. That is to say, there is a multiplicity in the interpretive process, as well as a multiplicity in the identity or power relations that one seeks to interpret.[29] Therefore, "we" need a multi-focal reading that examines multiple intersections. Many, if not most, of the contributions to this project have looked at only the intersection between race and religion. However, as Eng argues by pointing to the limitation to mainly "femininized" occupations (like restaurants and laundry shops), as well as the formation of

---

[27] In addition to contesting, borrowing Kent A. Ono's term (71), the "ethnic monopolizing" of the Bible, talking about the Bible in Asian America also serves to deconstruct Samuel P. Huntington's frighteningly popular and grossly simplistic orientalist divide between "Eastern" and "Western" civilizations, a divide that Huntington distills in religious terms by equating "Eastern" civilization as "Islamic-Confucian." Derrida has also contended that globalization (definitely a theme and a concern of Huntington's book) should be more adequately called "globalatinisation," because of the global impact of Roman Christianity despite the claim of secularization (2001:32). For a helpful analysis of Huntington's thesis, see Ong: 185–213.

[28] In his own transdisciplinary work, Eng has recently used a psychoanalytic lens to talk about the importance of memory and dreamwork for Asian American political resistance (2001:52–89). Interestingly enough, both have been emphasized within this volume (memory by Bundang in the first section, and dream by Kogawa in my interview with her in the second).

[29] The idea of a multiplicity of identity, or a multiplicity of self, is also related to the transdisciplinarity that I am attempting to argue for. Is there room in our understanding that one person can be a biblical scholar as well as a scholar of Asian American studies? Why can a person not be a sociologist and a biblical scholar at the same time? Or have we been so compartmentalized, or departmentalized, that "one-thing-at-a-time" has become the only way of being and reading? Likewise, one should not fail to relate Jeung's argument about institutional logic and identity formation, or Lim's comment about the regime(s) of truth in operation within the guild or the academy of biblical scholars, to our identity as biblical scholars.

an imposed bachelor society in the history of Chinese America, the racialization and marginalization of Asian Americans often involve a simultaneous gendering and a simultaneous sexualizing process (2001:15–19).[30] To cite the most obvious example, Moy's concern with race and religion but neglect of gender results in a disturbing silence about both the household code in 1 Pet 2:18–3:7 and the all-male membership of the *Zhengdaohui*.[31]

Another influential item in "our" investigation of intersections is class, which has become increasingly heterogeneous in Asian America since 1965 (Lane Ryo Hirabayashi, 1998a:5; Ong: 169–74). For Sau-ling Cynthia Wong, class difference is crucial to the transnational emphasis within much of recent Asian American studies (14–15). Transnationalism and global capital have been the subjects of much cutting-edge scholarship and are of particular relevance to Asian America (Arif Dirlik; Eng, 2001:32–33, 204–207, 211–15). Contributions to this volume do not, however, give these two issues enough attention. Instead, contributions have basically focused on cultural nationalism and "our" spatial entitlement to the U.S. as Asian Americans. I hope to see more focus on how the use and understanding of the Bible are related to transnationalism and the global economy. Several Asian American scholars (in terms of race and ethnicity, if not in terms of academic discipline) have begun to explore the role of religion within the development of transnationalism and the global economy. Whether one agrees with his views or not, Tu Weiming has argued that Confucian values are foundational to "the rise of industrial East Asia" within the global economy (1998; 2000). Ong, in her book on "flexible citizenship," has also commented on the role of Islam in Malaysia's entry into global capitalism (204–5, 216, 226–29); and Rey Chow has just completed a book-length manuscript entitled, *The Protestant Ethnic and the Spirit of Capitalism* (forthcoming). These pioneer works point towards a promising direction of possibilities for those who are interested in the Bible, particularly in light of (1) what E. Kim in this volume identifies as the theme of (material) "blessing" in

---

[30] Like many other scholars in Asian American studies, Eng leaves out the role of religion in this process of racialization and marginalization that he has otherwise so acutely analyzed. As Moy's essay points out, "heathen Chinese" was one of the most popular labels given out by the white society (see also Liew, 2001a:320–21). I also cannot help but notice from Moy's essay the parallel rhetoric that has been used to marginalize nineteenth-century Chinese immigrants and contemporary queers.

[31] Rather than denouncing the patriarchal tendencies of Asian cultures, I think it is important that gender oppression within Asian America be studied in the context of racial oppression of Asians in America (David Leiwei Li: 61). I also wonder, given Moy's thesis that the *Zhengdaohui* lived out the vision of 1 Peter, if it were possible to do a sociohistorical study of the association (including both its internal and external power dynamics) to help illuminate the implications of 1 Peter, particularly in light of the letter's emphasis on being a "model minority" and its emphasis on the household code (2:11–3:22). In other words, may the *Zhengdaohui* illuminate not just the sociopolitical *context* of 1 Peter as Moy claims, but also its potential sociopolitical *consequences*?

much of Korean American hermeneutics and homiletics; and (2) what Rudy V. Busto has called the evangelical "gospel of model minority."

Finally, I hope future scholarship on the Bible in Asian America will proceed to problematize or further nuance every term that makes up the title of this project. I have already mentioned the need to investigate the concept of canon. "We" should also remember that the Bible, or what Sano calls "the orthodox canon," is different for Catholics and Protestants within Christendom. "We" should further recognize that this "orthodox canon" (howsoever defined) is not the only sacred text in Asian America, nor is it the only sacred text for *bona fide* biblical scholars (as Rietz's essay on the Dead Sea Scrolls in this issue shows). Given the repeated and favorable references to religious syncretism within Asian America in "our" volume (especially by Sano, Kogawa in my interview with her, and Lim), I envision future studies that will not only cover the other sacred texts of Asian America but also explore how many Asian Americans manage to interpret them and the Bible in light of each other.

What about the "Asian" in Asian America (Sumida and Wong: 3–4)? While I am proud of the diversity represented in this issue (in terms of ethnicity, geographical location, and nativity), I am wary that no Southeast Asian American or Pacific Islander is being represented. Their future participation will no doubt greatly enhance what "we" can learn and make of both the Bible and Asian America. In addition, the adoptee population featured by Foskett and the mixed racial population by Rietz confront "us" once again with the question if by "*Asian* American," "we" are talking about blood or culture, or both. How one answers that question will, of course, result in a different conception of *Asian* America. One must also remember in this regard that the blurring line between Asians and Asian Americans is one of the by-products of the transnational global economy. What one means by Asians and Asian Americans can no longer be assumed or fastened; instead, both need to be probed, investigated, and made anew.

I think the last term of the title, "America," needs to be problematized in at least three ways. First, I hope future scholarship on the Bible and Asian America will compare and contrast "our" use and understanding of the Bible with not only Anglo Americans (as Clark does explicitly in part 2, but implicitly as well by all the contributors) but also African Americans, Latino/Latina Americans, and Native Americans (as E. Kim advocates briefly in the second section, and as I have tried to do tentatively in this "introduction").[32] Bringing different ethnic Americas into dialogue is important

---

[32] I must thank Gale Yee for suggesting that I take into account Wimbush's essay in my own introduction. For an example within Asian American studies that advocates a shift from the "racial dyad" of Anglo/Asian America to other America-s, see Gary Y. Okihiro: 29–31.

because of the roots that Asian American studies have in the Third World students' strike and "our" placement as the "middle minority" (rather than "model minority") in the U.S. (Jonathan H. Turner and Edna Bonacich; Richard J. Jensen and Cara J. Abeyta). As Rietz's essay implies, specificity and particularity cannot be erased or covered over if "we" want to establish any meaningful kind of community or solidarity.[33] Bringing in an-other minority group will also displace the Anglo/Asian binarism, as well as disrupt the suffocating burdens of authenticity ("*Only* Asian Americans *really know* Asian America, and *only* African Americans *really know* African America") and representation ("Asian Americans can *only* talk about Asian America, and African Americans *only* about African America") that the majority places on minorities. In other words, it helps "us" create a third space, as well as claim an identity but not be confined to it (Liew, 2001a:311–16). Second, I hope "we" will remember that the U.S. is not America, as the inclusion of Japanese Canadian author, Kogawa, in this volume should have reminded "us."[34] Finally, I hope "we" will also remember that there are also an abundance of Asians in Central and South America (Akemi Kikumura-Yano). As Madhulika S. Khandelwal points out, bringing up Asians in Central and South America can help "us" re-cognize, for instance, that not all Asians in the U.S. today came from Asia, and thus the inadequacy of "simple formulas" and set assumptions (119). The same is true of my call here to further nuance the title of "our" issue. Considering the different sacred texts, as well as the diversities within Asian America, the U.S., and the Americas, should "we" from now on not be talking about the Bible-*s* in Asian America-*s* instead? Confronting "us" with the multiple particularities (to conflate Cheng's and Rietz's terminologies) that are present at each single moment, this plurality compels "us" to keep s(h)ifting rather than solidifying boundaries, whether academic or ethnic.

The What-Ifs

Let me admit that I have one big anxiety about this volume. What if the title of this issue means that it will only be read by Asian Americans? In other words, my anxiety has to do with what Chow has helpfully identified as the dilemma of the ethnic label, or the "vicious cycle of discriminatory

---

[33] As evidenced by the subtitle of Hirabayashi's edited volume (1998b), questions of community are becoming increasingly complex as Asian America becomes more diverse. For examples of related discussions about similar challenges within the context of feminism, see Biddy Martin and Chandra Talpade Mohanty; and Catherine Keller: 215–22.

[34] In my view, how the name for a continent becomes equated with that of a country is well worth one's pondering.

practice" (2000a:2–3). If one erases the ethnic label, ethnic Asians in (North) America will once again be invisible. If one puts in the ethnic label to gain visibility, the one with the ethnic label runs the risk of being immediately categorized, dismissed as "special interest," and placed on the shelf. I can only hope that this will not be the case.

I have another anxiety regarding the expectation of those who do read the volume (Asian American or not). What if they expect to find within these pages a definition of Asian America(n),[35] or a definite delineation of *the* Asian American biblical hermeneutics? To deal with my own anxiety over a potentially disappointed readership, let me be clear that in reading through this issue, one will not find who the Asian American is, nor will one find an essentialized reading strategy among Asian Americans. In this regard, I think a group project is still one of the best ways to diffuse the burden of representation. I also think that the essays in this volume will support my contention that identity, interpretation, and interpersonal coalition are all fashioned more by specific sociopolitical and economic differences within different historical moments, and less by either biological or cultural differences. Rather than definitions, what I offer in this volume are the diversity, the complexity, and the creativity of Asian America. As Trinh puts it, the richness of Asian America makes it necessary that I serve both as its host and its guest (22). What I have found here have been engaging and energizing for me. And I do hope that this will also be true for all of its readers, despite what one may expect to find and not find here.

The Thank-Yous

In addition to those who participated directly (the contributors and respondents) and indirectly (many of whom I have tried to acknowledge in various footnotes), I want to thank the Wabash Center of Teaching and Learning in Theology and Religion for awarding me a summer grant to work on this project. I am also grateful to Dr. Dow Edgerton, Academic Dean at Chicago Theological Seminary, for providing me with the necessary funding to secure the editorial assistance of Mr. Wil Brant.

Finally, I want to thank my four-year-old son, Aaron Taylor Liew, for what he told me on two separate occasions when I tried to explain to him this "project" that had taken me away from so many of our "play times" together. First, he told me, "Dad, the Bible is *not* from America"; and then,

---

[35] Sumida and Wong have recently suggested that Asian America(n) be understood as an "analytic category" rather than as a category of identity; see Sumida and Wong: 7n5.

"Dad, everybody knows something, but nobody can know everything." I hope I will never forget to remember these two important reminders. It is to you, Aaron, and your generation of Asian Americans that I dedicate this volume.

Works Cited

Althusser, Louis
 1979 *For Marx*. Trans. Ben Brewster. New York: Verso.

Anzaldúa, Gloria E.
 2000 *Interviews/Entrevistas*. Ed. AnaLouise Keating. New York: Routledge.

Appiah, Kwame Anthony, and Henry Louis Gates Jr.
 1995 "Editors' Introduction: Multiplying Identities." Pp. 1–6 in *Identities*. Ed. Kwame Anthony Appiah and Henry Louis Gates Jr. Chicago: University of Chicago Press.

Bach, Alice
 1997a "Mieke Bal: An Interview." *Biblicon* 1:61–66.

 1997b "Daniel Boyarin: An Interview." *Biblicon* 2:61–66.

 1998 "Elisabeth Schüssler Fiorenza: An Interview." *Biblicon* 3:27–44.

Bernheimer, Charles, ed.
 1995 *Comparative Literature in the Age of Multiculturalism*. Baltimore: Johns Hopkins University Press.

Bierce, Ambrose
 1946 "The Haunted Valley." Pp. 451–60 in *The Collected Writings of Ambrose Bierce*. New York: Citadel. [Orig. 1870]

Boer, Roland
 1997 *Novel Histories: The Fiction of Biblical Criticism*. Playing the Texts 2. Sheffield: Sheffield Academic Press.

 2001 "Yahweh As Top: A Lost Targum." Pp. 75–105 in Stone, 2001.

Bové, Paul A.
 2000 "Afterword: The Possibilities of Abandonment." Pp. 301–15 in Chow, 2000a.

Boyarin, Jonathan
 1994 *The Ethnography of Reading*. Berkeley and Los Angeles: University of California Press.

Bruns, Gerald L.
 1992 *Hermeneutics Ancient and Modern*. New Haven, Conn.: Yale University Press.

Busto, Rudy
    1999   "The Gospel according to the Model Minority?: Hazarding an Interpretation of Asian American Evangelical College Students." Pp. 169–87 in Yoo, 1999b.

Butler, Judith, John Guillory, and Kendall Thomas
    2000   "Preface." Pp. viii–xii in *What's Left of Theory? New Work on the Politics of Literary Theory*. Ed. Judith Butler, John Guillory, and Kendall Thomas. New York: Routledge.

Cha, Theresa Hak Kyung
    1995   *Dictee*. Berkeley: Third Woman.

Cheung, King-kok
    1993   "Attentive Silence: *Obasan*." Pp. 126–67 in *Articulate Silence: Hisaye Yamamoto, Maxine Hong Kingston, Joy Kogawa*. Ithaca, N.Y.: Cornell University Press.

Cheung, King-kok, ed.
    2000   *Words Matter: Conversations with Asian American Writers*. Honolulu: University of Hawai'i Press.

Chin, Tung Pok, with Winifred C. Chin
    2000   *Paper Son: One Man's Story*. Philadelphia: Temple University Press.

Chow, Rey
    2000a   "Introduction: On Chineseness As a Theoretical Problem." Pp. 1–25 in Chow, 2000b.

    Forthcoming   *The Protestant Ethnic and the Spirit of Capitalism*. New York: Columbia University Press.

Chow, Rey, ed.
    2000b   *Modern Chinese Literary and Cultural Studies in the Age of Theory: Reimagining a Field*. Durham, N.C.: Duke University Press.

Clifford, James
    1988   *The Predicament of Culture: Twentieth-Century Ethnography, Literature, and Art*. Cambridge: Harvard University Press.

Derrida, Jacques
    1995   *The Gift of Death*. Trans. David Wills. Chicago: University of Chicago Press.

    2001   *On Cosmopolitanism and Forgiveness*. Trans. Mark Dooley and Michael Hughes. New York: Routledge.

Dirlik, Arif
    1996   "Asians on the Rim: Transnational Capital and Local Community in the Making of Contemporary Asian America." *Amerasia Journal* 22:1–24.

Eng, David L.
    1998   "Queer/Asian American/Canons." Pp. 13–23 in Hirabayashi, 1998b.

2001 *Racial Castration: Managing Masculinity in Asian America.* Durham, N.C.: Duke University Press.

Eng, David L., and Alice Y. Hom, eds.
1998 *Q & A: Queer in Asian America.* Philadelphia: Temple University Press.

Frye, Northrop
1982 *The Great Code: The Bible and Literature.* Toronto: Academic.

Frykholm, Amy
2001 "Reading the Rapture: Christian Fiction and the Social Structure of Belief." Ph.D. diss., Duke University.

Garber, Marjorie, Rebecca L. Walkowitz, and Paul B. Franklin, eds.
1996 *Field Work: Sites in Literary and Cultural Studies.* New York: Routledge.

Hamamoto, Darrell Y.
1994 *Monitored Peril: Asian Americans and the Politics of TV Representation.* Minneapolis: University of Minnesota Press.

Haraway, Donna J.
2000 *How Like a Leaf: An Interview with Thyrza Nichols Goodeve.* New York: Routledge.

Hirabayashi, Lane Ryo
1998a "Introduction." Pp. 1–12 in Hirabayashi, 1998b.

Hirabayashi, Lane Ryo, ed.
1998b *Teaching Asian America: Diversity and the Problem of Community.* Lanham, Md.: Rowman & Littlefield.

Hsu, Ruth Y.
1996 "Conversation with Joy Kogawa." *Amerasia Journal* 22:199–216.

Huntington, Samuel P.
1996 *The Clash of Civilizations and the Remaking of World Order.* New York: Simon & Schuster.

Jensen, Richard J., and Cara J. Abeyta
1987 "The Minority in the Middle: Asian-American Dissent in the 1960s and 1970s." *Western Journal of Speech Communication* 51:404–16.

Kang, Laura Hyun Yi
2001 "*Dictee* by Theresa Hak Kyung Cha." Pp. 32–44 in Wong and Sumida.

Keller, Catherine
1996 *Apocalypse Now and Then: A Feminist Guide to the End of the World.* Boston: Beacon.

Khandelwal, Madhulika S.
1998 "Reflections on Diversity and Inclusion: South Asians and Asian American Studies." Pp. 111–22 in Hirabayashi, 1998b.

Kikumura-Yano, Akemi, ed.
  Forth-   *Encyclopedia of the Japanese in the Americas.* Walnut Creek, Calif.:
  coming   AltaMira.

Kogawa, Joy
  1992   *Itsuka.* New York: Anchor.

Kuan, Jeffrey Kah-Jin
  2000   "Reading Amy Tan Reading Job." Paper presented at the Society of Biblical Literature Annual Meeting (Asain and Asian-American Biblical Hermeneutics Group), Nashville, Tenn.

Kwok Pui-lan
  1998   "Jesus/the Native: Biblical Studies from a Postcolonial Perspective." Pp. 69–85 in Segovia and Tolbert.

Lee, Robert G.
  1999   *Orientals: Asian Americans in Popular Culture.* Philadelphia: Temple University Press.

Levenson, Jon D.
  1993   *The Hebrew Bible, the Old Testament, and Historical Criticism: Jews and Christians in Biblical Studies.* Louisville: Westminster/John Knox.

Lew, Walter K.
  1991   *Excerpts from: Dikte for Dictee.* Chongno Gu: Yeul Eum.

Li, David Leiwei
  1998   *Imagining the Nation: Asian American Literature and Cultural Consent.* Stanford, Calif.: Stanford University Press.

Liew, Tat-siong Benny
  1999   *Politics of Parousia: Reading Mark Inter(con)textually.* Leiden: Brill.

  2001a   "Reading with Yin Yang Eyes: Negotiating the Ideological Dilemma of a Chinese American Biblical Hermeneutics." *BibInt* 9:309–35.

  2001b   "(Cor)Responding: A Letter to the Editor." Pp. 182–92 in Stone, 2001.

Ling, Amy, and Annette White-Parks
  1995   "Introduction." Pp. 1–8 in Sui Sin Far.

Martin, Biddy, and Chandra Talpade Mohanty
  1986   "Feminist Politics: What's Home Got to Do with It?" Pp. 191–212 in *Feminist Studies/Critical Studies.* Ed. Teresa de Lauretis. Bloomington: Indiana University Press.

McClintock Fulkerson, Mary
  2000   "Practice." Pp. 189–98 in *Handbook of Postmodern Biblical Interpretation.* Ed. A. K. M. Adam. St. Louis: Chalice.

Meeks, Wayne A.
  1983   *The First Urban Christians: The Social World of the Apostle Paul.* New Haven, Conn.: Yale University Press.

Min, Pyong Gap, and Jung Ha Kim, eds.
    2001   *Religions in Asian America: Building Faith Communities.* Walnut Creek, Calif.: AltaMira.

Okihiro, Gary Y.
    1998   "Teaching Asian American History." Pp. 25–33 in Hirabayashi, 1998b.

Omi, Michael, and Dana Tagaki
    1995   "Thinking Theory in Asian American Studies." *Amerasia* 21:xi–xv.

Ong, Aihwa
    1999   *Flexible Citizenship: The Cultural Logics of Transnationality.* Durham, N.C.: Duke University Press.

Ono, Kent A.
    1995   "Re/signing 'Asian America': Rhetorical Problematics of Nation." *Amerasia Journal* 21:67–78.

Osajima, Keith
    1998   "Critical Pedagogy in Asian American Studies: Reflections on an Experiment in Teaching." Pp. 59–72 in Hirabayashi, 1998b.

Osborne, Peter, ed.
    1996   *A Critical Sense: Interviews with Intellectuals.* New York: Routledge.

Palumbo-Liu, David
    1995   "Theory and the Subject of Asian American Studies." *Amerasia Journal* 21:55–65.

Radway, Janice A.
    1991   *Reading the Romance: Women, Patriarchy, and Popular Literature.* Chapel Hill: University of North Carolina Press. [Orig. 1984]

    1999   *A Feeling for Books: The Book-of-the-Month Club, Literary Taste, and Middle-Class Desire.* Chapel Hill: University of North Carolina Press.

Safire, William
    1996   "Get Riady, Get Set . . . " *New York Times.* October 21: A17 column 2.

Said, Edward
    1983   *The World, the Text, and the Critic.* Cambridge: Harvard University Press.

    1993   "The Politics of Knowledge." Pp. 306–14 in *Race, Identity and Representation in Education.* Ed. Cameron McCarthy and Warren Crichlow. New York: Routledge.

Salusinszky, Imre
    1987   *Criticism in Society.* New York: Methuen.

Schneiders, Sandra M.
    1999   *The Revelatory Text: Interpreting the New Testament As Sacred Scripture.* 2d ed. Collegeville, Minn.: Liturgical.

Scott, Joan W.
    1992   "Experience." Pp. 22–40 in *Feminists Theorize the Political*. Ed. Judith Butler and Joan W. Scott. New York: Routledge.

Segovia, Fernando F., and Mary Ann Tolbert, eds.
    1998   *Teaching the Bible: The Discourse and Politics of Biblical Pedagogy*. Maryknoll, N.Y.: Orbis.

Smith, Erin
    2000   *Hard-Boiled: Working-Class Readers and Pulp Magazines*. Philadelphia: Temple University Press.

Sollors, Werner
    1986   *Beyond Ethnicity: Consent and Descent in American Culture*. New York: Oxford University Press.

Sone, Monica
    1979   *Nisei Daughter*. Seattle: University of Washington Press. [Orig. 1953]

Spickard, Paul R., and Jane Naomi Iwamura, eds.
    Forthcoming   *Revealing the Sacred in Asian and Pacific America*. New York: Routledge.

Spivak, Gayatri Chakravorty
    1990   *The Post-Colonial Critic: Interviews, Strategies, Dialogues*. Ed. Sarah Harasym. New York: Routledge.

Stone, Ken
    1997   "Biblical Interpretation As a Technology of the Self: Gay Men and the Ethics of Reading." *Semeia* 77:139–55.

Stone, Ken, ed.
    2001   *Queer Commentary and the Hebrew Bible*. Cleveland: Pilgrim.

Sui Sin Far
    1995   *Mrs. Spring Fragrance and Other Writings*. Ed. Amy Ling and Annette White-Parks. Urbana: University of Illinois Press.

Sumida, Stephen H., and Sau-ling Cynthia Wong
    2001   "Introduction." Pp. 1–9 in Wong and Sumida.

Tan, Amy
    1992   *Kitchen God's Wife*. New York: Ivy Books.

Tolbert, Mary Ann
    1998   "A New Teaching with Authority: A Re-evaluation of the Authority of the Bible." Pp. 168–89 in Segovia and Tolbert.

Trinh T. Minh-ha
    1999   *Cinema Interval*. New York: Routledge.

Tu Weiming
    1998   "The Rise of Industrial East Asia: The Role of Confucian Values." *Copenhagen Journal of Asian Studies* 13:81–97.

2000 "Implications of the Rise of 'Confucian' East Asia." *Dædalus: Journal of the American Academy of Arts and Sciences* 129:195–218.

Turner, Jonathan H., and Edna Bonacich
    1980 "Toward a Composite Theory of Middleman Minorities." *Ethnicity* 7:144–58.

Warnke, Georgia
    1993 *Justice and Interpretation*. Cambridge: MIT Press.

Wei, William
    1993 *The Asian American Movement*. Philadelphia: Temple University Press.

White-Parks, Annette
    1995 *Sui Sin Far/Edith Maude Eaton: A Literary Biography*. Urbana: University of Illinois Press.

Williams-Leon, Teresa, and Cynthia L. Nakashima, eds.
    2001 *The Sum of Our Parts: Mixed Heritage Asian Americans*. Philadelphia: Temple University Press.

Wimbush, Vincent L.
    2000 "Introduction: Reading Darkness, Reading Scriptures." Pp. 1–43 in *African Americans and the Bible: Sacred Texts and Social Textures*. Ed. Vincent L. Wimbush. New York: Continuum.

Wong, Sau-ling Cynthia
    1995 "Denationalization Reconsidered: Asian American Cultural Criticism at a Theoretical Crossroads." *Amerasia Journal* 21:1–27.

Wong, Sau-ling Cynthia, and Stephen H. Sumida, eds.
    2001 *A Resource Guide to Asian American Literature*. New York: Modern Language Association of America.

Yang, Fenggang
    1999 *Chinese Christians in America: Conversion, Assimilation, and Adhesive Identities*. University Park: Penn State University Press.

    2000 "The Growing Literature of Asian American Religions: A Review of the Field." *Journal of Asian American Studies* 3:251–56.

Yoo, David K.
    1996 "For Those Who Have Eyes to See: Religious Sightings in Asian America." *Amerasia Journal* 22:xiii–xxii.

    1999a "Introduction: Reframing the US Religious Landscape." Pp. 1–15 in Yoo, 1999b.

Yoo, David K., ed
    1999b *New Spiritual Homes: Religion and Asian Americans*. Honolulu: University of Hawai'i Press.

Part I

Reading the Bible in Asian America

FROM BABEL TO PENTECOST:
FINDING A HOME IN THE BELLY OF THE EMPIRE

Eleazar S. Fernandez
United Theological Seminary of the Twin Cities

ABSTRACT

As the title suggests, this essay interprets Babel and Pentecost in relation to the U.S. context, especially as seen through the struggle and dreams of Asian North Americans for a colorful and just society. Through a postcolonial critique of the myth of the tower of Babel, which is a countermyth to the *Enuma Elish* (the dominant Mesopotamian myth), the master narrative and other hegemonic practices of white capitalist United States are exposed and decentered in an attempt to give space for Asian North American narrative. If the myth of the tower of Babel is about hegemony and its various expressions, the Pentecost event points to a different way of thinking, dwelling, and acting. Pentecost presents to us a vision of what it means to live together in a pluralistic United States and how to construe power and organize society. This essay ends with a challenge to "conspire" with the Spirit, the primary agent in the Pentecost event, in order to forge a colorful and just tomorrow.

My hermeneutical naïveté has been shattered more than once, and intensely in recent years since I settled in the "land of the free and home of the brave" and started my teaching career. As a *pharmakon* for my hermeneutical naïveté, I turned to hermeneutics of suspicion in order to expose hegemonic practices and resurrect muted voices (Armour).[1] I became familiar with the writings of the masters of suspicion (Karl Marx, Sigmund Freud, Friedrich Nietzsche). As one concerned about exposing hegemonic discourses, I have given a considerable amount of my time and energy to dealing with epistemological concerns in my courses and writings. Yet, to my surprise, my suspicion has not been enough. Obviously, my hermeneutics of suspicion needs to be subjected to another hermeneutics of suspicion.

In thinking about my journey into the world of hermeneutics I am led back to my years in the Philippines. Like many of the early liberation theologians, I was attracted to the exodus narrative because of its explicit liberation theme. I was not bothered that within the exodus narrative is the

---

[1] *Pharmakon* can be a remedy or a poison. I intended it to be a cure for hermeneutical naïveté.

conquest of the Canaanites. What I cared for was that the Israelites—God's chosen people—finally got out of Egypt and acquired their own land. Of course, I knew about the conquest of the Canaanites, but I did not hear their cries. Their plight did not register in my brain as something worthy of serious attention.

My own encounter with the exodus narrative is not unique. I lifted up the same exodus narrative while teaching seminary students in the northern part of Myanmar (Burma) in 1998. With full intentionality I brought to their attention the plight of the Canaanites, but they, too, like myself, were so captive to the notion of "election" that the cries of the Canaanites did not matter. Whatever the Israelites did to the Canaanites was all right because they were God's "elect" or "chosen people." God was on the side of the Israelites, who were simply executing God's plan. The "chosen people" were right because Yahweh made them right.

Resonating with my hermeneutical encounter of the exodus narrative is my encounter with the myth of the tower of Babel. I now realize that my early reading of the myth of the tower of Babel was counterproductive to the aspirations of people of color in white America. I operated on the assumption of a homogenous culture and language, and I viewed multiple cultures and languages as God's means to confuse and punish people. Multiple languages lead to confusion: it is God's form of punishment. With recent developments in biblical hermeneutics and a change in my geographical and social location, I now see the myth of the tower of Babel in a different light. In this essay I am going to interpret this myth to cast light on the plight of Asian Americans who are struggling to find a home in the belly of a modern empire—the United States of America.

The Tower of Babel: Symbol of Imperial Praxis

J. Severino Croatto helps us situate the myth of the tower of Babel by making two negations: (1) it has nothing to do with the origin of the multiplication of languages; and (2) it has nothing to do with the creation of various peoples (204). After putting forward these two negations, Croatto says that we need to understand the text within its context of production, which is the Israelites' exilic experience in Babylon. Also important to note is that though the tower of Babel is a symbol of imperial praxis, the myth of the tower of Babel is a product of an exiled people designed to counter the founding myth of Mesopotamia, the *Enuma Elish*. In other words, the myth of the tower of Babel was produced and circulated by the exiled Israelites not to extol the Babylonian lords and the tower of Babel but, ironically, to subvert them.

From the ancient to the contemporary period, cities, buildings, and especially towers have embodied people's dreams and achievements. The ancient ziggurat and the modern-day Eiffel Tower, Toronto's CNN Tower, the Sears Tower, and the like are monuments of human dreams and aspirations. They testify to human prowess, ingenuity, intelligence, and mastery over nature. Rather than "passive architecture," these edifices are mythic in proportion and are purposely made to "stand out" from the rest of the landscape (Middleton and Walsh: 16).

The ancient city of Babylon and its tower of Babel testify to the power, grandeur, and achievement of the Babylonian Empire. Genesis 11:3–4 gives us an account of the magnificent Babylonian projects:

> And they said to one another, "Come, let us make bricks, and burn them thoroughly." And they had brick for stone, and bitumen for mortar. Then they said, "Come, let us build ourselves a city, and a tower with its top in the heavens, and let us make a name for ourselves; otherwise we shall be scattered abroad upon the face of the whole earth." (NRSV)

A close reading of the text reveals that two projects are mentioned here: a city and a tower with its top reaching to the heavens. By the standard of the time, the two projects were massive. They were not simple housing projects for the common city dwellers, but huge infrastructure projects that represented the highest Babylonian achievements of the time. We can imagine the enormous wealth as well as the engineering and architectural genius of the Babylonians.

But, like all other imperial projects, whether ancient or modern, the Babylonian projects were erected on the backs of others, especially the marginalized sectors of society. More particularly, the Babylonian Empire exploited the labor of the conquered and exiled population—the Israelites. Behind the grandeur of the Babylonian city and its tower was the exploited labor of the exiled Israelites. Similar to their experience in Egypt, the Israelites were conscripted for the construction of Babylonian projects.

As in any other projects that "stand out," something more is involved than the Babylonians' need for infrastructure. The myth suggests that the city and the tower of Babel were constructed beyond fulfilling the basic physical needs or "use value." Beyond the "use value" is the production, the selling, and consumption of "sign." We produce and consume "sign" perhaps more than we consume "use value." Whereas "use value" finds satisfaction, "sign" or "image" value has no satisfaction.

Builders of empires are after not only the "use value" of the infrastructure projects but also the "sign." We can glean from the text that what was constructed by the ancient Babylonians was not only the massive edifice but a "name" for themselves. More specifically, they were building the "name" of those who wield imperial power. The projects were for the perpetuation of the imperial "name" and social status.

The construction of the city and tower and, finally, a "name" made it possible for ancient Babylonians to speak of "settled life." This trinity—city, tower, and "name"—worked in systemic ways to guarantee the "settled life" of the Babylonians. This is very clear in Gen 11:4: "and let us make a name for ourselves; otherwise we shall be scattered abroad upon the face of the whole earth." While the tower is the dominant image, let us not forget that it is built as part of the city and as an edifice symbolizing the city. The tower represents the city, which is a mark of a "settled life."

But there is more to the tower of Babel than representing the city or a symbol of a "settled life." The tower symbolized the centralized power and organization that is the "guarantor" of the "settled life." It symbolized the surveillance mechanism of the Babylonian imperial power. It stood above the city to monitor the movements of the city dwellers. The tower is the eye of the monarchy to enforce order within the city.

Those who live a privileged life within the protection of the empire are likely to think that "settled life" is a matter of individual choice. But this is clearly not so for those who have experienced the precarious life of diaspora. "Settled life" is not simply a matter of individual choice, but a creation of power. In the case of ancient Babylonians, "settled life" was guaranteed by the imperial power that the tower of Babel symbolized.

When we see "settled life" as a creation of power, it explains why diaspora was the plight of ancient Israelites, comparable to the plight of marginalized peoples in our time. Conquered, colonized, and exploited, the Israelites were then dispersed. Dispersion usually follows after conquest and colonization. Many of the dispersed colonials end up as colonized minorities in the heart of the empire. As is evident with racial minorities in the U.S., the Israelites became colonized minorities in Babylon.

If centralized politics symbolized by the tower of Babel is the guarantor of the "settled life," the production of "name" is the cultural-ideological counterpart. The strength of the city is not only economic and political, but also cultural-ideological. No empire can survive in the long run by sheer exercise of political power. The "name," according to Croatto, functions as a cohesive cultural force (210–11). In other words, it possesses centripetal power that counters dispersion. Unity of language, which is a central category in the myth, is critical to centralized organization and cultural cohesion. Croatto writes:

> [U]nity of language is a fundamental factor in every concentration of power. All measures such as the homogenization of practices, the centralization of the decision-making power, and the imposition of the dominant ideology have need of a univocal linguistic code. (221)

The presence of different languages, from the Babylonian Empire's point of view, was a stumbling block to centralized power, cohesion, and progress. At worst, it was viewed as a hotbed for chaos and dispersion.

The Counterproject: The Destruction of the Tower of Babel

As I made clear in the previous section, the tower of Babel is a symbol of imperial praxis. When viewed from the perspective of the Babylonian Empire, it is an expression of the Babylonian achievement. But the myth of the tower of Babel is a countermyth, a myth produced by the exiled Israelites to counter the Mesopotamian myth (*Enuma Elish*) of the creation of Babylon. The myth of the tower of Babel tells us of Yahweh's counterproject, which is directed against the Babylonians and their god, Marduk.

A record of Yahweh's counterproject begins in Gen 11:6: "And the LORD said, 'Look, they are one people, and they have all one language; and this is only the beginning of what they will do; nothing that they propose to do will now be impossible for them'" (NRSV).

It is evident that Yahweh is worried about the Babylonian projects. The tone of the lines is very worrisome: "This is only the beginning of what they will do; nothing that they proposed to do will now be impossible for them."

These worrisome words express the orientation of Yahweh's counterproject. It is opposed to the megalomaniacal Babylonian projects. These excessive projects that rest on the backs of others must be undone to prevent similar projects from arising in the future. If not stopped at the opportune time, the Babylonian Empire will continue with its megalomaniacal projects.

The decisive step of the counterproject is found in Gen 11:7: "Come, let us go down, and confuse their language there, so that they will not understand one another's speech"; 11:8 follows: "So the LORD scattered them abroad from there over the face of all the earth, and they left off building the city" (NRSV). As a countermyth to the *Enuma Elish*, the myth of the tower of Babel confronts its adversary at the level of myth or worldview. Yahweh's counterproject, to use postmodern terminology, is an attempt to deconstruct the dominant metanarrative—the *Enuma Elish*. A countermyth is used to deconstruct the master narrative of the Babylonian Empire. The myth of the tower of Babel shows us that Yahweh is opposed to the Babylonian master narrative. There is no future to the empire; it will collapse in due time. The fate of the Israelites will also happen to the Babylonians.

In the beginning of this essay I said, along with Croatto, that the myth of the tower of Babel has nothing to do with the origin of language or with multiple languages as a form of God's punishment. When we study the text carefully, it is clear that Yahweh's counterproject is not directed at multiple languages. It does not even talk about multiple languages. Rather, Yahweh's project is directed against the univocal linguistic code of the Babylonian Empire, a code of centralized power and control.

Yahweh's counterproject strikes at the symbolic core of the empire's unity, its language. Its first line of attack is to confuse the communication line of the empire. With confused communication, no empire can stand.

Confused language eventually leads to dispersion. The possibility of this happening was dreaded by the Babylonians. Imperial Babylon knew that unity of language was crucial to its existence and that it must defend the unity of language at any cost.

The Making of the American Tower of Babel: The Grand Master Narrative

If Babylon had its myth—the *Enuma Elish*—the United States of America also has its founding myth. In order to critique this myth, I follow Enrique Dussel's lead by taking account of what he calls the "ethico-mythical nucleus," which often is expressed in symbolic-religious language (cited in Bonino: 50). By this Dussel means the self-understanding of a people regarding its origin and destiny.

The self-understanding of the white founders of the United States of America is encapsulated in the discourse of "chosen people" and "manifest destiny." It is the "manifest destiny" of the "chosen people" to become the new masters of the world. Philip Schaff illustrated this mindset: "The Anglo-Saxon and Anglo-American, of all modern races, possess the strongest national character and the one best fitted for universal domination" (cited in Marty: 17).

"The sense of special mission, so characteristic of British Christianity in its various forms," as pointed out by Robert Handy, "became a fundamental motif in American life, and was to be expressed in many ways, religious and secular, through the years" (8). In its most benevolent expression, this "manifest destiny" means the mission of spreading civilization, democracy, and science to the whole world.

In obedience to its "manifest destiny," the United States took the "errand to the wilderness" to spread the blessings of a "settled" life. It annexed western Florida in order to have access to the Gulf of Mexico (1810), and by 1853 it was able to acquire by various means Florida, Texas, Arizona, Nevada, Utah, New Mexico, California, and a good portion of Kansas, Colorado, Oklahoma, and Wyoming (González: 31–32). Not satisfied with these acquisitions, the master race sailed the Pacific Ocean and occupied the Philippines, Guam, Samoa, and annexed the Kingdom of Hawaii in 1898 despite the opposition of the Hawaiian people (Coffman).

Propelled by a sense of "manifest destiny," the expansionist move of the United States was even viewed by religious groups as providential and an opportune moment (*kairos*) for mission. To turn one's back on this precious opportunity was considered unpatriotic to the country and unfaithful to the gospel (Anderson). Even imperialism was viewed in a positive and religious sense by the expansionists.

This does not mean that there was no opposition to the expansionist thrust. There was an anti-imperialist movement with a group of eloquent personalities, including Mark Twain, Andrew Carnegie, William James, David Starr, Charles Eliot, Henry Rogers, Henry Van Dyke, former presidents Harrison and Cleveland, and others. But the expansionist tide was sweeping the country (Anderson: 283).

Intoxicated by the success of its imperialist projects and progress in various realms, the new nation took the name of the whole continent to itself. In the 1920s the name United States gave way to America. The United States is America. The people, notes Sharon Welch, "like the term 'America' precisely for its imperial suggestions of an intoxicating and irresistible identity windswept into coherence by the momentum of destiny" (3).

The current rhetoric may take a more secularist tone, but the myth of "manifest destiny" is much alive, and the religious discourse is not totally absent. Welch speaks of the American myth in terms of "the grand narrative of progress, American innocence, beneficence, global pre-eminence" (xvii). In both its domestic and foreign political-economic praxis, the United States has continued to live the myth of "manifest destiny." At the height of the Cold War, "manifest destiny" took the expression of fighting against the "godless" communists. The same myth was operative in the U.S. support of the Contras against the Sandinistas and other "murderous" regimes in Latin America, in the invasion of Grenada, Panama, Iraq, and most recently the intervention in Kosovo. Likewise, the myth is alive in the rhetoric of U.S. leadership on economic globalization, even as postcolonial and postmodern discourses have pointed to the emergence of various centers and voices.

It is in the light of the United States' "obedience" to its "manifest destiny" and in the context of its imperial projects, economic progress, global preeminence, beneficence, and pretensions of innocence that Asians found their way into America. Imperial powers, for various reasons, draw the subjugated and marginalized peoples not only into their orbit, but also into their heartlands. "Colonialism," as Robert Blauner puts it, "brings into its orbit a variety of groups, which it oppresses and exploits in differing degrees and fashions; the result is a complex structure of racial and ethnic division" (158). As people of various nationalities found their way into the imperial Babylon and Rome, many racial minorities also have found their way into the United States.

Asian Americans and the Construction of the American Tower of Babel

Congressman Norman Mineta observes that "when one hears Americans tell of the immigrants who built the nation, one is often led to believe that all our forbears came from Europe. When one hears stories about the pioneers going West to shape the land, the Asian immigrant is rarely mentioned" (Takaki, 1989:6). It is not only an act of historical oversight but an act of injustice against Asian Americans to speak of the building of the American nation while remaining silent about the labors of Asian Americans.

Crucial to the transformation of the United States into a booming economy, notes Takaki, is the entry of "strangers from different shores"—from China as well as Japan, Korea, the Philippines, and India (1989:23). The United States needed Asian labor to help build its economy, especially at the height of its westward expansion (across the Indian lands and Mexican territory to a new Pacific frontier). Asians provided an army of ready reserved "cheap labor" for the new empire. U.S. government and private companies ordered Asian labor as if it were a commodity. For example, the Davies Company sent a memorandum to another company acknowledging receipt of an order with this list: "bonemeal, canvas, Japanese laborers, macaroni, a chinaman" as well as "fertilizer, Filipinos" (Takaki, 1989:25). The list recalls the insights of Michel Foucault's work, *The Order of Things* (xv). From the order of things defined by U.S. economic growth, there is no distinction between macaroni and chinaman, or fertilizers and Filipinos.

The Chinese were among those first to participate in the building of the American empire. They named the land of their destination Tan Heung Shan or "Fragrant Sandalwood Hills"—the Hawaiian islands—and Gam Saan or "Gold Mountain"—California (Cao and Novas: 10; Takaki, 1989:31). In the Kingdom of Hawaii they worked for the booming sugar industry. The annexation of California in 1848 opened the floodgates for Asian labor. Aaron Palmer, a U.S. policy maker, recommended the importation of Chinese labor for the construction of the Transcontinental Railroad. By connecting Atlantic states to the western frontier, the fertile lands of California would be cultivated and San Francisco would become the "great emporium of our commerce on the Pacific" (Takaki, 1989:22).

Other Asians came in waves in response to the need for laborers to build America: Japanese (1880s), Filipinos (1900), Koreans (1903), and Indians (1907). Their first area of destination was Hawaii. Over 300,000 Asians entered the islands between 1850 and 1920. These hordes of laborers helped transform the sugar industry into a "King" industry and helped the Asian laborers earn income, while at the same time displacing the Native Hawaiians (Takaki, 1989:132).

There was, of course, another motive for the importation of various racial/ethnic groups. The ethnic diversity of laborers was used to prevent concerted action or strikes by one group. "Keep diversity of laborers," said a spokesperson for the sugar planters, "that is different nationalities, and thus prevent any concerted action in case of strikes, for there are few, if any cases of Japs, Chinese, and Portuguese entering into a strike as a unit" (Takaki, 1989:26). This strategy was used effectively by the planters, and it took years before these groups formed a coalition.

Later waves of Asian newcomers came to the mainland. Some remigrated from Hawaii to the mainland. These Asians found themselves employed as railroad workers, canners in Alaska, and farm workers. The Filipino "old timers," being small in physical stature, were given jobs that, from their Euro-American employers point of view, "fit" their physical feature: planting and harvesting asparagus, iceberg lettuce, spinach, strawberries, and sugar beets (Tuzon: 66). Asian Indians, often referred to as "Dark Caucasians," found jobs as railroad workers in the Northern Pacific Railways, lumber mills, and as fruit pickers in the orchards of California. Some of the early Koreans went to work in the copper mines of Utah, the coal mines of Colorado and Wyoming, and the railroads of Arizona. A few also found work in the Alaskan salmon cannery (Cao and Novas: 290).

The latest Asian group to arrive in America is from Southeast Asia. This group (Vietnamese, Hmong, Laotian, and Cambodian) began coming to the United States in the 1970s as "refugees" from the war-torn places of Asia. In comparison to the "immigrants," the circumstances of the "refugees" coming to the U.S. have made their adjustment even more difficult. But, in spite of difficulties, they are striving to make America home.

Asian newcomers have continued to contribute to the building of the American empire. While many continue to work in jobs that are poorly paid, other Asian Americans have found their niches in various fields. Asian American presence is more widespread in various walks of life than the limited opportunities of the earlier waves. Some have broken the glass ceiling of corporate America and made inroads in other fields of endeavor.[2] Whatever their jobs, the reality is that Asian Americans have helped build the "towers" of America, yet America has not given them their due recognition.

The America we know today is partly due to the labors of the early waves of Asians and the new generations of Asian Americans. Ironically, white workers consider Asian American labor as a threat, especially when these whites are experiencing economic misfortunes. "It's because of you motherfuckers that we're out of work," echoed the words of two white auto workers who killed Vincent Chin (a Chinese American) in 1982 in Detroit, Michigan (Karnow and Yoshihara: 47; Takaki, 1989:481; Cao and Novas: 53–54). Chin's only "crime" was that he was mistaken as

---

[2] For example, a few Filipino Americans have broken the glass ceiling: military (Major General Edward Soriano and Brigadier General Antonio Taguba of the Army), entrepreneurship (Diosdado Banatao and other Silicon Valley success stories), sports (Tiffany Roberts), journalism (Carlos Bulosan, Jessica Hagedorn, Byron Acohido, Alex Tizon), showbiz/entertainment (Paulo Montalban, Tia Carrere, Jocelyn Enriquez, Enrico Labayen), and the political arena (Gov. Benjamin Cayetano of Hawaii, Pete Fajardo of Carson City, California). See Barros; Guillermo, 1997; Schiff.

a Japanese and became the recipient of misguided anger against the Japanese auto manufacturers.[3]

Participation of Asian Americans in the economic sphere did not automatically include political participation. What is true of the Chinese experience is also true of other Asians. Asian Americans were "part of America's production process but not her body politic" (Takaki, 1987:28). It took a long struggle before the white-dominated society opened political participation to its racial minorities.

Hegomonic Practices: The American Project of Homogenization

E pluribus unum; from many one. Indeed, the one nation is composed of the many. But for the "founding fathers," the making of the many into one can only be accomplished through the "assimilation" of other races and cultures into the dominant white Euro-American race. The assimilationist vision is clearly one of uniformity. The "melting pot" model (amalgamation) seems a "progress" from the assimilation model in the sense that its vision is not uniformity but unity. Nevertheless, amalgamation, argues Andrew Sung Park, "still is amalgamation into the dominant race" (106). While the slogan *e pluribus unum* is the demographic reality and the political foundation of the United States, the operative worldview remains the same: the immigrants from various nations will one day be assimilated into the Euro-American mainstream.

In an effort to be accepted and successful in the United States, many Asian Americans tried to assimilate as quickly as possible. As the price of acceptance and success, many Asian Americans betrayed their "origins by shedding their pasts, their ethnicity—the language, customs, dress, culture of the old country" (Takaki, 1989:12). Some Asian American women even undergo surgery to remove "the slant" from their eyes (Williams: 184).

With the hope of mitigating racism, many Asian Americans view the church as a route and catalyst toward assimilation. Many Asian Americans, for whom (with the exception of Filipino Americans) Christianity is not the dominant religion, have become Christians. On their part, the churches have played an active role in the work of assimilation, even though it is also true

---

[3] It is not known to most people in the United States that American auto companies are investing in "foreign" auto companies themselves. Takaki notes that "General Motors owns 34 percent of Isuzu (which builds the Buick Opel), Ford 25 percent of Mazda (which makes transmissions for the Escort), and Chrysler 15 percent of Mitsubishi (which produces Colt and Charger)" (1989:483; also see Brecher and Costello: 18). GM and Toyota are engaged in a joint venture. GM also owns part of a Fiat subsidiary in the U.S., while Fiat owns 48 percent of Ford's Iveco Truck subsidiary. In Brazil and Argentina VW and Ford have a joint venture called Autolatina. And Nissan produces a VW in Japan.

that they have become a venue for the preservation of ethnic identities (Matsuoka, 1995:16).

But there is a disastrous irony here. The white race calls for "assimilation," but cannot really give the stamp of full acceptance to the other race because its dominance is predicated on the unassimilability of the other. It is saying in effect: We want you to be like us, but you cannot really be like us. "I have been four years in America," a Filipino immigrant in California said sadly, "and I am a stranger. It is not because I want to be. I have tried to be as 'American' as possible. I live like an American, eat like American, and dress the same, and yet everywhere I find Americans who remind me of the fact that I am a stranger" (Takaki, 1989:316).

Peter McLaren is helpful here, especially his critique of "whiteness" and the process of *engabachamiento* (whitening). With "whiteness" as the implacable norm, non-Anglo Americans undergo the process of *engabachamiento* and are forced to "act white" in order to succeed. But *engabachamiento*, says McLaren, is a "discursive relay of sorts—'white but not quite'" (250). There is an invitation to become "white," but the hierarchical difference is maintained because it is beneficial to the existing power arrangement. "Racism and the exploitation of peoples considered to be ontologically inferior to Euro-Americans," contends McLaren, "have always been historical allies to the white supremacist, capitalist, and patriarchal hegemony that characterizes the United States" (250).

After Babel: The Tottering Tower

The American tower is tottering. In their work *Downsizing the U.S.A.*, Thomas Naylor and William Willimon speak of urban America as a modern-day tower of Babel (48–75). The American tower of Babel is tottering with poverty, downsizing, criminality, drug abuse, violence, alcoholism, alienation, and meaninglessness. The "sweet dreams in America," to use Sharon Welch's book title, have soured for many and turned into nightmares for others. Welch adds to the list of signs of tottering American Babel: "the reality of downsizing, massive cuts in social services, absence of affordable housing, hopelessness, homelessness, violence, and anger: the anger of white males at women and minorities for getting their jobs, anger and violence of a marginalized urban underclass" (xvii).

Not surprisingly, criminality is on the rise. It has been pointed out by social scientists that there are at least five causes of urban crime: (1) poverty and inequality; (2) violence in the media; (3) breakdown of family and community; (4) inadequate criminal justice system; and (5) racism. Naylor and Willimon add a sixth cause: meaninglessness; the United States has the highest homicide rate in the world (66, 68).

To counter criminality, the United States is getting tough on crime. Not a coincidence, along with the zeal for tough law enforcement, is the rise of police brutalities. There are thirty-eight states that have resorted to capital punishment. Over 1.5 million people are incarcerated in the United States (Naylor and Willimon: 66).

When we look at this figure closer, there is a color and a class to the number. A high percentage of those in jail are African Americans and other minorities. The class factor is also present because the criminalized acts are those that are most likely to be committed by the lower strata, while "crimes at the top" do not even get into the criminal code (Bauman: 123–27). Jeffrey Reiman's book title hits the point: *The Rich Get Richer and the Poor Get Prison*.

Aside from being tough on crimes, affluent Americans protect and insulate themselves by barricading themselves in "fortress communities." Naylor and Willimon call these communities "privatopia." "Privatopia" is a "privatized artificial, utopian environment ... where master planning, homogenous population, and private governments offer the affluent a chance to escape from urban reality" (51). Many small governments have become allies in the making of these "privatopias" through zoning regulations on the pretext of local control and empowerment.

I would like to extend the metaphor of the modern-day tower of Babel to rural America. Anyone who is familiar with rural America in this epoch of globalization knows that it, too, is a tottering tower of Babel. The "Golden Age of Agriculture" (1980) turned into a "farm crisis" and spiraled into "rural crisis." Around 600,000 farm families lost their land in the 1980s, which paved the way for transnational agribusiness (Jung et al.: 100). There is unemployment, poverty, hopelessness, cynicism, anger, and a high rate of suicide in rural America.

When things are not going well, the stage is set for violence directed against the perceived authority and, as usual in history, the minorities. The potentially dangerous situation is put this way: "After God and country and neighbors desert you, what's left" (Davidson: 101)? The "rural crisis" has led to a disturbing turn with the increase in the growth of radical right and hate groups. The federal government and minority groups have become the target. Frequently, the target of the long-term rural residents' frustration is not the transnational agribusiness in their localities, but the newcomers who are mostly people of color, such as Hispanics, Africans, and other Asians, such as Hmong, Laotians, Cambodians, and Vietnamese (Amato).

Instead of a harmonious blending of contrasting themes, the United States is fast becoming a culture of adversarial relations. There is an ever-widening gap between the rich and poor, racial conflict, and culture wars of various sorts. The homogenization project of the empire is showing cracks because racial minorities have not been completely assimilated. Except for the Filipino Americans who are proud of their skill at blending, often at the expense of their empowerment, Chinese have their Chinatowns and Koreans their Koreatowns.

Many of the "self-evident truths" that the "founding fathers" proclaimed are not readily self-evident for many any longer. The "new order of the ages" (*e pluribus unum, annuit coeptis, novus ordo seculorum*) is full of discordant sour notes and, according to Fumitaka Matsuoka, "has included enough embarrassment since its inception—slavery, immigrant exclusion laws, and internment of its own citizens at the outbreak of World War II, to name a few" (1998:2).

Not Quite "After Babel": The Empire Strikes Back

We like to speak of "after" or "post" something, as in the case of Jeffrey Stout's *Ethics after Babel*. I do not think we are already "after Babel." The empire has been challenged, and there are cracks, but it is striking back. The empire is cunning and knows how to execute both brazen and sophisticated countermoves.

In a way we can say that significant breakthroughs have been made in our society. Ethnic and racial minorities are not only surviving; many of them are thriving even against major obstacles. Significant laws have passed to improve their status and situation. Some racial minorities have broken the glass ceiling, and their "success" stories have been told. Their "success" stories have been given media attention as a way of saying that the system really works for all, regardless of color, religion, gender, and sexual orientation.

On the other hand, the gains that we can lift up are not unambiguous. For every inch of "progress" made, new forces of closure that are more sophisticated appear or new realizations happen that offset the "progress," so that "progress," it seems to me, has only occurred against the measure of older forms. While every inch of victory needs to be celebrated to sustain us in the long and arduous journey, self-satisfaction can be self-delusion. Gloria Yamato's comment about racism can be applied to other forms of systemic evils as well: "Like a virus, it's hard to beat racism because by the time you come up with a cure, it's mutated to a 'new cure-resistant' form. One shot just won't get it" (91).

One shot will not kill the virus that has become cure-resistant or smarter; it is fighting back with renewed strength and greater ferocity, both subtle and brazen. It does not require much careful scrutiny to observe that there has been an increasing momentum toward what has been called "postmodernism of reaction" (Foster). I am referring in particular to those determined to turn the clock back and stay in the comfort of our old beliefs. In the world of intellectual discourse, Paul Lakeland classifies this kind of postmodern reaction under the umbrella of "nostalgic postmodernism."

Lakeland puts the neoconservative cultural critics Allan Bloom and Daniel Bell under this form of postmodern attitude (17).

We see the rise of "postmodernism of reaction" not only in rhetoric but also in various pieces of legislation and the rise of hate crimes and police brutalities against minorities. The *Filipinas* magazine calls the year 1999 "a bloody year for Asian Americans" (Eljera: 19). On August 10, 1999, Joseph Ileto, a Filipino American postman, was pumped with nine bullets by white supremacist Buford Furrow. A few months later, on April 28, 2000, another wave of hate-motivated murders against Asian Americans and other minorities hit Pittsburgh, Pennsylvania. This shooting rampage claimed the lives of an Asian Indian, a Vietnamese American, a Chinese American, an African American, and a Jewish American woman ("Wave of Hate Crime": 1). In an article about Joseph Ileto, Emil Guillermo painfully reminds us that "hate and ignorance die hard in the land of the free" (1999:32).

Constructing Counterprojects: The Praxis of Pentecost

There are cracks in the tower of Babel. The tower is tottering. While some wallow in affluence, others wallow in poverty. Dreams and "privatopia" for some, nightmares and ghettos for others. Adversarial relations and cultural wars are increasing in momentum. The "self-evident truths" of the "founding fathers" are not self-evident after all and are now heavily contested. The empire is striking back with more ferocity.

We are at a critical juncture that is fraught with both danger and promise for new possibilities. Either we entertain the breakdown of the totalizing aspirations of Babel's architects as an opening for new possibilities or we see it as a threat. The way we perceive this situation, whether as a threat or as an opportunity, will certainly shape the course of action we take. Matsuoka poses the issue theologically: "What does it mean to live out our faith in a time when basic patterns of human relationship seem to be under major reconstruction?" (1998:4).

The myth of the tower of Babel has been helpful in our reading of our situation. But for us to move on to the task of construction, we need another hermeneutic lens to complement the myth of the tower of Babel. The Pentecost event (Acts 2), I believe, provides us with the hermeneutic lens to move from deconstruction to construction of alternative ways of thinking, dwelling, and acting. It offers us a powerful vision that is counter to the vision of the tower of Babel: it is a vision that does not homogenize but allows the flourishing of various colors and narratives, a vision of the overcoming of division and the existence of communication, a vision of sharing what is on the table, and a vision of a society that builds and values the charisma of all members of the society.

If in the myth of the tower of Babel Yahweh is the active agent of the counterproject, in the Pentecost event the active agent is the Spirit (Acts 2:2–4). "The Spirit," says Jürgen Moltmann, "is more than just one of God's gifts among others; the Holy Spirit is the unrestricted presence of God in which our life wakes up, becomes wholly and entirely living, and is endowed with the energies of life" (10–11). This Spirit wakes up life in us, makes us alive, restores life to our rattling bones, and makes us committed to the preservation and renewal of life.

In the Pentecost event the people of various ethnicities felt the indwelling of the Spirit and something amazing happened (Acts 2:4–5). Through the power of the Spirit, the once-closeted believers came out to the open, broke their silence, let loose their stammering tongues, and went public with their vision (Acts 2:6–41). The Spirit gave them the courage and wisdom to name their pain and articulate their vision.

Veni, Creator Spiritus. Come, Creator Spirit. "Breathe" into the valley of the dry bones of our lives and society that we may experience life anew. Hebraic and Christian heritages speak of the Spirit as "breath" (Hebrew *ruach*; Greek *pneuma*; Latin *spiritus*). Spirit is synonymous with breath, for the Spirit gives life and without breath there is no life.

Bones dry up when the Spirit is absent. When there is a drought of the Spirit, individual and social lives dry up and the forces of death dominate the social landscape. Dried-up bones, chilly apathy, and psychic numbing are but a few of the manifestations of the drought of the Spirit in our times.

What is this life that is infused by the Spirit? What is this life that is lived under the impact or the indwelling of the Spirit? Is this life different from what we have here on earth now?

No! Living according to the Spirit, contrary to the notion that it snatches us away from this world, keeps us rooted into the world, to the earth. The new life that the Spirit brings is not different from this life here; rather, it is the power that makes our life here different (Acts 2:42–47). It is an earthly life lived differently while we have it. We may not be able to change the world as much as we desire to, but we continue to live differently while we have life, and we continue to live differently as if the future that calls us "to be" were already a present reality.

When the Spirit dwells in us, life wakes up. This indwelling awakens us to a heightened self and social sensitivity. The Spirit breaks through the indifference of our hearts, inner numbness, and emotional frigidity. With the Spirit rousing our vitality, we can cry out again, weep again, laugh and dance again. And, we can be outraged again, outraged at the wrongs being done against the whole of creation, and outraged because we care and because we hope. From calloused hearts of stone, we acquire the hearts of flesh, with undivided love for life and sharpened senses.

Contrary to common understanding, the Spirit is not shapeless. One of its shapes or embodiments is the creation and nurturance of covenanted communal relationship (Acts 2:42–47). Peter Hodgson points to this community-creating power of the Spirit: "God in the Spirit is God existing as community" (296). Caring relationship is an embodiment of the Spirit of God who first loved us. Loving God—the Spirit—means seeking an embodiment of this love in the most tangible and concrete ways. The Spirit became true to itself as a community-creating power in the Pentecost event.

The community that the Spirit builds is structured around the "charisma" of each member. The term "charisma" is derived from *charis* or *chairein,* which means gratuity or God's gift to a person (Boff: 154). Each member has one or more charisma. No member of the community is without charisma; there is no noncharismatic member. Each one occupies an important place in the community, and each one uses her or his charisma for the common good. The diverse charisma of the members are directed for the edification of the community. The apostle Paul "makes charisma the structuring element of the community" (Boff: 157; cf. Rom 12:4–8; 1 Corinthians 12–14). Charisma, which is a gift of the Spirit, offers a vision of how we may organize our society.

In accordance with the character of the Spirit, the community that the creative Spirit forms is one that is expressive of the inherent diversity of human life. There are diverse expressions and diverse gifts of the Spirit. The Spirit, in its concrete embodiment, expresses itself in various modes of being human, with different cultures and languages. Diversity is not something that is simply to be tolerated but to be affirmed, for it is an expression of the Spirit: it is life as such in its beauty and challenge. The Pentecost event points to this profound reality (Acts 2:1–13).

However, common interpretations of the Pentecost event fail to take seriously the multicultural message of the Pentecost event because they construe the speaking of different languages as a mere adjunct or a means to the proclamation of the universal gospel. There is fundamental theological flaw in this interpretation. It fails to realize that the universal gospel is not a pure essence, but a universal gospel only in so far as it is intrinsically embodied in specific media and contexts. Or, to put it differently, we cannot separate the media from the message. The message is embedded and embodied in the media. For the Pentecost event, the speaking of tongues is not a mere medium for the universal gospel but the gospel itself in its concrete expression. As Andrew Park interprets the Pentecost event: "We need ... to see that the event itself was the very content of the gospel, not its mere form. The occurrence denoted the understanding and accepting of other cultures" (Park: 130). The Pentecost event does not portray the presence of various languages as an event of confusion, but a new sense of communal experience and the possibility of rich communication amidst cultural and racial differences.

Matsuoka articulates well the points I have tried to express about the Pentecost vision. The challenge, according to Matsuoka, is to move past a climate of distrust and alienation and to articulate a vision of communal dwelling in which the dignity of each is affirmed. Moreover, we need to

> recover speech that permits communion with one another, to break bread together, a communion for which people so deeply yearn and we Christian confess to be our deeply held value.... Our society must move from the loss of speech across lines of difference and alienation to serious, covenantal conversation that fosters the root form of human relatedness: communion. (1998:4)

The Pentecost event confronts us with a choice. Which moral vision will be normative for us? Babel or Pentecost? We can put the alternatives in the stark way of Rudyard Kipling's famous line: "East is East, and West is West, and never the twain shall meet." Or, following the words of the invitation to the Lord's Supper: "People will come from east and west, and from north and south, and sit at the table of the kin(g)dom" (Wilbanks: 109; modification of "kin(g)dom" supplied).

The United States of America, with its multicultural demographic makeup, is faced with a hard and painful choice. Alice Walker, when asked whether California (a multiracial/ethnic society) represents the America of the future, replied: "If that's not the future reality of the United States, there won't be any United States, because that's who we are" (cited in Takaki, 1989:12). America's self-recognition and self-acceptance of its multicultural self is a crucial step in the journey toward a colorful tomorrow.

Although self-recognition of our multicultural self is a crucial step, it is only a beginning. The move toward a just and colorful tomorrow, argues McLaren, requires more than postmodern discursive suturing. Critique of images and representation is important, but it must go along with the struggle to alter the reigning socioeconomic arrangement. The call to multiculturalism, without altering the reigning social relations of production, remains captive to neoliberal hegemony.

The journey toward the realization of the promise of the Pentecost event is long and arduous. It is easy to be cynical, but cynicism is not the way of those who are empowered by the Pentecost experience. Even such a horrible experience as the "pillar of fire" that consumed South Central Los Angeles has rekindled a "fire of hope." In the horrible consuming fire is the horrifying presence of the Spirit, showing that unless we shove our idols of death into the "melting furnace" (not a "melting pot"), our future is bleak. We struggle to name the pain and the pervasiveness of the forces of closure, not because our situation is entirely hopeless, but because it is only in naming our pain that we can articulate our deepest joy and soaring hopes. It does not require much effort for those who are privileged to participate in the perpetuation of the system. All it takes is silence and inactivity. Yet, silence, in the face of privilege, is not after all a *mere* silence. To paraphrase the words of a theologian: silence is a lie when truth needs to be spoken (Comblin: 15). More than breaking our silence, letting loose our stammering tongues, and going public with our vision, we who have been empowered by the Spirit must be engaged in a conspiracy—a "conspiracy of goodness" (Messer: 148). The word *conspiracy* comes to us with a negative connotation. But when we analyze the word "conspire," it literally means "to breathe together." "Breath" as well as "breadth" (space) are words associated with the Spirit. To be empowered by the Spirit, then, is to "breathe together" with the Spirit, to conspire with the Spirit, to conspire with the community in creating "breathing spaces" (breadth)—spaces of freedom and spaces where people can experience healing and wholeness.

In our world divided by class, race, gender, religion, and ideologies, conspiracy with the Spirit has to take the form of shattering divisions or, following Donald Messer's metaphor, of moving fences. The church is a "community of fence movers" conspiring with the Spirit in breaking and shattering stereotypes and in moving fences of divisions (127–44).

A story may lend clarity to the point I am making here: As the story goes, soon after the devastation of the First World War, Quakers responded to the need of the impoverished people of Poland by distributing food and clothing. One relief worker contracted typhus and died within twenty-four hours. Only Roman Catholic cemeteries were present in the area, and canonical law forbade burying anyone not of that confession in consecrated ground. So the well-loved deceased relief worker was buried in a grave outside the fence of the cemetery. But during the night the villagers did something daring and radically liberating. They moved the fence of the cemetery to include the grave (Messer: 127).

What do fence movers do? Fence movers dare to dream, dare to hope, and dare to struggle in breaking idolatrous fences and dare to forge more inclusive communities. They are boundary crossers in the good sense, overcoming fences of race, class, and gender divisions. They dare to dream of a sustainable and colorful tomorrow. They are called to a mission—not mission impossible—of moving fences of exclusivism and division.

We who have experienced the indwelling of the Spirit and have been empowered by the vision of the Pentecost are faced with a daunting and momentous task. It is the task of conspiring with the Spirit of the Pentecost. It is only in conspiring with the Spirit and with each other that we can move past Babel and realize the promise of the Pentecost.

Works Consulted

Amato, Joseph
    1996   *To Call it Home: The New Immigrants of Southwestern Minnesota*. Marshall: Crossings.

Anderson, Gerald
    1969   "Providence and Politics behind Protestant Missionary Beginnings in the Philippines." Pp 279–300 in *Studies in Philippine Church History*. Ed. Gerald Anderson. Ithaca, N.Y.: Cornell University Press.

Armour, Ellen
    1999   *Deconstruction, Feminist Theology, and the Problem of Difference: Subverting the Race/Gender Divide*. Chicago: University of Chicago Press.

Barros, Ely
    1997   "The U.S. Army's First Filipino Generals." *Filipinas* (October): 27–28.

Bauman, Zygmunt
    1998   *Globalization: The Human Consequences*. New York: Columbia University Press.

Blauner, Robert
    1987   "Colonized and Immigrant Minorities." Pp. 149–60 in *From Different Shores: Perspective on Race and Ethnicity in America*. Ed. Ronald Takaki. New York: Oxford University Press.

Boff, Leonardo
    1986   *Church: Charisma and Power*. New York: Crossroad.

Bonino, José Miguez
    1983   *Towards a Christian Political Ethics*. Philadelphia: Fortress.

Brecher, Jeremy, and Tim Costello
    1998   *Global Village or Global Pillage: Economic Reconstruction from the Bottom Up*. Cambridge: South End.

Cao, Lan, and Himilce Novas
    1996   *Everything You Need to Know about Asian American History*. New York: Plume.

Coffman, Tom
    1998   *Nation Within: The Story of America's Annexation of the Nation of Hawai'i*. Kanehoe: Epicenter.

Comblin, José
    1979   *The Church and National Security State*. Maryknoll, N.Y.: Orbis.

Croatto, Severino J.
    1998   "A Reading of the Story of the Tower of Babel from the Perspective of Non-Identity." Pp. 203–23 in *Teaching the Bible: The Discourse and Politics*

of Biblical Pedagogy. Ed. Fernando Segovia and Mary Ann Tolbert. Maryknoll, N.Y.: Orbis.

Davidson, Osha Gray
    1990   *Broken Heartland: The Rise of America's Rural Ghetto.* New York: The Free Press.

Eljera, Bert
    1999   "A Bloody Year for Asian Americans." *Filipinas* (October): 19.

Foster, Hal
    1983   *The Anti-aesthetic: Essays on Postmodern Culture.* Port Townsend: Bay.

Foucault, Michel
    1973   *The Order of Things: An Archeology of the Human Sciences.* New York: Vintage Books.

González, Justo L.
    1990   *Mañana: Christian Theology from a Hispanic Perspective.* Nashville: Abingdon.

Guillermo, Emil
    1997   "Tiffany Roberts: Gold Mettle." *Filipinas* (March): 38–39, 41.

    1999   "What Joseph Ileto Stands For?" *Filipinas* (October): 32.

Handy, Robert
    1971   *A Christian America: Protestant Hopes and Historical Realities.* New York: Oxford University Press.

Hodgson, Peter
    1994   *Winds of the Spirit: A Constructive Christian Theology.* Louisville: Westminster/John Knox.

Jung, Shannon, et al.
    1998   *Rural Ministry: The Shape of the Renewal to Come.* Nashville: Abingdon.

Karnow, Stanley, and Nancy Yoshihara
    1992   *Asian Americans in Transition.* New York: The Asian Society.

Lakeland, Paul
    1997   *Postmodernity: Christian Identity in a Fragmented Age.* Minneapolis: Fortress.

Marty, Martin
    1970   *Righteous Empire.* New York: The Dial.

Matsuoka, Fumitaka
    1995   *Out of Silence: Emerging Themes in Asian American Churches.* Cleveland: United Church.

    1998   *The Color of Faith: Building Community in a Multicultural Society.* Cleveland: United Church.

McLaren, Peter
    1997   *Revolutionary Multiculturalism: Pedagogies of Dissent for the New Millennium.* Boulder, Colo.: Westview.

Messer, Donald
    1992   *Conspiracy of Goodness: Contemporary Images of Christian Mission.* Nashville: Abingdon.

Middleton, Richard J., and Brian Walsh
    1995   *Truth Is Stranger Than It Used to Be: Biblical Faith in a Postmodern Age.* Downers Grove, Ill.: InterVarsity Press.

Moltmann, Jürgen
    1997   *The Source of Life: The Holy Spirit and the Christian Life.* Minneapolis: Fortress.

Naylor, Thomas, and William Willimon
    1997   *Downsizing the U.S.A.* Grand Rapids, Mich.: Eerdmans.

Park, Andrew Sung
    1996   *Racial Conflict and Healing: An Asian American Theological Perspective.* Maryknoll, N.Y.: Orbis.

Reiman, Jeffrey
    1998   *The Rich Get Richer and the Poor Get Prison: Ideology, Class, and Criminal Justice.* Boston: Allyn & Bacon.

Schiff, Laura
    1997   "She's Just Drawn That Way." *Filipinas* (August): 38–42.

Stout, Jeffrey
    1988   *Ethics after Babel: The Language of Morals and Their Discontents.* Boston: Beacon.

Takaki, Ronald
    1987   "Reflections on Racial Patterns in America." Pp. 26–37 in *From Different Shores: Perspectives on Race and Ethnicity in America.* Ed. Ronald Takaki. New York: Oxford University Press.

    1989   *Strangers from a Different Shore: A History of Asian Americans.* New York: Penguin.

Tuzon, Brandy
    1996   "The War in Salinas." *Filipinas* (October): 66, 74.

"Wave of Hate Crimes Hits APAs in Pittsburgh."
    2000   *Asian American Press* xix no. 18 (week of May 5): 1.

Welch, Sharon
    1999   *Sweet Dreams in America: Making Ethics and Spirituality Work.* New York: Routledge.

Wilbanks, Dana
    1996   *Recreating America: The Ethics of U.S. Immigration and Refugee Policy in a Christian Perspective.* Nashville: Abingdon.

Williams, Dolores
   1993   *Sisters in the Wilderness: The Challenge of Womanist God-Talk.* Maryknoll, N.Y.: Orbis.

Yamato, Gloria
   2001   "Something about the Subject Makes It Hard to Name." Pp. 90–94 in *Race, Class, and Gender: An Anthology.* Ed. Margaret Andersen and Patricia Hill Collins. Belmont: Wadsworth.

RESIDENT ALIENS OF THE DIASPORA: 1 PETER AND CHINESE PROTESTANTS IN SAN FRANCISCO

Russell G. Moy
Church Divinity School of the Pacific

ABSTRACT

The book of 1 Peter was written to resident aliens in Asia Minor whose social location and experiences of marginalization were shared by Chinese Protestants in San Francisco in the nineteenth century. Like the Jews in 1 Peter's community, the Chinese were part of a diaspora who lived as minorities in their adopted countries. Yet the Chinese faced additional barriers because of their face and race. Despite their small numbers, the Chinese became political pawns in a national political issue that culminated in the 1882 Chinese Exclusion Act. Also like the resident aliens in 1 Peter, the Chinese were converted to a new religion. Missionaries from Protestant denominations used English classes to attract potential converts to form small Chinese churches. To form their own self-governing mutual-support society, the Chinese developed the *Zhengdaohui*, an independent Chinese organization within the white mission structure to provide training and support to survive a hostile world. Not only might this association give us a picture of the challenges that were faced by the Jewish resident aliens in 1 Peter; it also established the communal identity and solidarity envisioned in 1 Peter.

> *the stories in the Bible were more like Chinese than American stories.... If you had not told me what you have about it, I should say that it was composed by the Chinese.*
>
> (Sui Sin Far: 134)

In his recent work on 1 Peter, John H. Elliott states that, "It is not surprising that the letter has held a particular significance for 'Diaspora Christian communities' of all ages" (2000:152). Written to the *paroikoi* ("resident aliens"), 1 Peter can be applied to Chinese Protestants in San Francisco in the nineteenth century. Although separated by almost two millennia, these two diaspora communities were both marginalized and ostracized by their "foreignness." Oppressed by mainstream society, each group hoped to find a home within the Christian community. Yet instead of lessening the social dissonance, it resulted in more discrimination and hostility.

Elliott imagines 1 Peter's community asking the following questions, all of which could have been asked by Chinese Protestants in San Francisco in the nineteenth century:

> Has our conversion to this peculiar religious movement and its "new" vision of salvation brought about any actual improvement of our circumstances? How and where are we experiencing this transformation in our everyday life? Are we not the same isolated and inferior aliens which people claimed us to be prior to our conversion? Are we not as homeless and rootless as ever before? Where is the fraternity and community for which we have yearned? (1981:105)

These questions reveal the marginal conditions faced by these first-generation Christians of the first and nineteenth centuries. While the sociohistorical reasons for their marginality differed, both communities strived to create a beachhead from which the church could expand in succeeding generations.

In a hostile anti-Chinese environment, it is remarkable that a small Chinese Protestant church emerged in San Francisco. Not only did a Chinese Protestant church develop in San Francisco's Chinatown; it is more remarkable that these Chinese Protestants formed a unique self-governing organization that gave them autonomy from paternalistic denominational control. Providing leadership, discipleship, and service opportunities, the *Youxue Zhengdaohui,* or the "Young Men's Christian Association" (not to be confused with the other, more well-known organization by the same name) demonstrated the discipline of Chinese Protestants in developing identity and solidarity in the face of racial discrimination and persecution. Despite the additional barriers of racial ideology and politics, these Chinese Protestants established the communal identity and solidarity envisioned by 1 Peter.

Visible and Invisible Minority

The Paroikos *of 1 Peter*

According to 1 Pet 1:1 and 2:11, the letter was written to the *paroikoi* ("resident aliens") and *parepidēmoi diasporas* ("visiting strangers"). The literary *inclusio* of the *diaspora* (1:1) and "Babylon" (5:13) was used "to identify both the author and his Christian community as sharing with the readers such exile status" (Paul J. Achtemeier: 354). First Peter was written to a diaspora community in Asia Minor, where commercial, economic, and educational opportunities attracted immigrants, both Jews and Greeks (the latter usually arrived first). Asia Minor's diverse population was related to:

the attraction of educational opportunities (such as the university at Tarsus) and health spas (at the renowned Asclepian spring shrines) and athletic and dramatic festivals, religious pilgrimages, mass movements of deported groups, the banishment of individuals, and the peregrinations of assorted itinerant philosophers and religious missionaries. (Elliott, 1981:67)

With an estimated population of 250,000 Jews by the middle of the first century B.C.E. and large Jewish communities in places like Sardis and Ephesus (Thomas A. Robinson: 115), Asia Minor was a popular destination for Jewish immigrants.

Addressed as *paroikoi*, 1 Peter's community was composed of foreigners and immigrants who formed a separate class of people with limited legal rights and were distinct from the native population. All the provinces listed in 1:1, other than Asia, were rural so that the *paroikoi* were most likely in agricultural trades (as agriculture was the chief industry in Asia Minor). If so, they comprised the working-class segment of Roman society along with slaves and serfs. As noncitizens, they were unable to vote, to hold public office, and to own land.

> Excluded from voting and landholding privileges as well as from the chief civic offices and honors, they enjoyed only limited legal protection, were restricted in regard to intermarriage, commerce, transmission of property, and land tenure, could be pressed into military service, and were susceptible to severer forms of civil and criminal punishment. While allowed limited participation in local cultic rites, they were excluded from priestly offices, but still shared full responsibility with the citizenry for all financial burdens, such as tribute, taxes, and production quotas. (Elliott, 2000:94)

In times of turmoil and unrest, resident aliens were often singled out as scapegoats and were subjected to suspicion, hostility, and even violence even though "in everyday life, there was little apparent difference between the *paroikoi* and the full citizens" (Elliott, 1981:68–69). Even though they may have lived in Asia Minor for many generations, resident aliens were subjected to discrimination because of their noncitizen status. For 1 Peter's community, this discrimination was exacerbated by their conversion to a new religious sect.

As a new and small religious movement, Christians in Asia Minor were viewed to be a strange and exclusive sect with questionable origins. These perceptions led to suspicion, contempt, and persecution. The conversion of resident aliens in 1 Peter's community only exacerbated their marginal status, because their exclusive allegiance to a new exotic sect created misunderstanding. Being labeled "Christians" (4:14) reinforced their marginality and resulted in further suffering and ostracism despite their hope for social acceptance and economic improvement.

To counteract this marginality, 1 Peter's strategy was to develop group cohesiveness for mutual support and solidarity in a hostile world (Elliott,

1981:133, 148). First Peter does so with language of a "household" (2:5, 17; 4:17; 5:9), an "elect race" or a gathering of God (2:9, 25; 5:2). Times of social upheaval or dislocation in a new and alien environment made the promise of a new community, a new Christian *oikos* or "home" attractive to the resident aliens of Asia Minor. They were looking for a place to belong, a home, one that was denied them as resident aliens and visiting strangers in the wider society.

Textual evidence for the ethnic makeup of the *paroikoi* of 1 Peter has been used to support either Jewish or Gentile readers. Eusebius and the Greek fathers believed that they were Jewish-Christians, while contemporary scholarship views the community as a mixture of both, with the Gentiles outnumbering the Jews.[1]

According to contemporary biblical scholarship, the Jewish resident aliens would be an ethnic minority in 1 Peter's community in addition to being a religious minority within their own Jewish community. As a double minority, ethnically and religiously, they found themselves living in between Roman and Jewish worlds in Asia Minor, and in between the Jewish/Gentile Christian community of 1 Peter. In these multiple intersections, Jewish Christians in Asia Minor found themselves simultaneously living in overlapping minority worlds, and it is this group that forms the closest parallel to Chinese Protestants in San Francisco in the nineteenth century. Like the Jewish resident aliens in 1 Peter's community, Chinese Protestants were also a diaspora people who found their marginality and discrimination intensified rather than relieved with their adoption of a new religion.

Chinese As Paroikoi

Like many emigrant groups, Chinese initially came to California to look for gold. Because they were not of European ancestry, Chinese were visibly different in their facial features, language, and clothing. These differences caused them additional difficulties because of the way their physical appearances were compounded by Western racial ideologies. Unlike the Chinese in San Francisco, there were no visible physical markers that set 1 Peter's resident aliens apart (with the exception of circumcision for Jewish males). Without any visible differences, the Jewish Christians of 1 Peter could hide their ethnicity and opt to assimilate into the general society. This

---

[1] For an extensive discussion of the ethnic makeup of 1 Peter's community, and the related issue of whether their status as "resident aliens" was mainly ethnosocial or metaphorical, see Achtemeier: 174–75; Elliott, 1981:65–67; Elliott, 2000:94–97; Martin: 141–61, 188–200; and Campbell: 22, 26–30, 100.

"passing" was particularly easy since Jews dressed like their Gentile neighbors, and many took on similar names and occupations. As Shaye J. D. Cohen notes, "diaspora Jews of antiquity were not easily recognizable—if, indeed, they were recognizable at all" (67). It was not even certain that a person who associated with Jews and performed Jewish rituals was a Jew, as some Gentiles intermingled with Jews and observed their practices.

Since Chinese customs, dress, and facial features clearly set them apart as "resident aliens," European Americans signified these physical differences into a "qualitative difference" that resulted in institutionalized injustice and violence. Even before they first set foot on American soil, Chinese had an unfavorable image through the writings of traders, diplomats, and missionaries. Most traders who visited China before 1840 observed the Chinese as

> ridiculously clad, superstition ridden, dishonest, crafty, cruel, and marginal members of the human race who lacked the courage, intelligence, skill, and will to do anything about the oppressive despotism under which they lived or the stagnating social conditions that surrounded them. (Stuart Creighton Miller: 36)

Although more educated and less negative than the traders, diplomats viewed the Chinese as enslaved by their government, which made them shameless, cowardly, and untrustworthy. With their access to public opinion through the pulpits and publications, it was the missionaries who were actually most influential in (mis)educating the public. They deserve much of the blame for creating negative stereotypes of the Chinese, since their obsession with Chinese "paganism" led them to believe that idolatry was at the root of all Chinese problems, which included "lechery, dishonesty, xenophobia, cruelty, despotism, filth, and intellectual inferiority" (Miller: 77). Infanticide and treatments of women (with bound feet) were other Chinese vices that the missionaries emphasized. Because Chinese were generally not responsive to their gospel message, Chinese were seen as subjects of Satan. Since the dragon was used for Satan in Rev 12:9 and was also the symbol of the Chinese emperor, missionaries could easily interpret that China was the "Kingdom of Darkness" under the rule of "that ancient serpent." All these negative stereotypes were widely disseminated through the sensationalist penny newspapers that gave lurid "eyewitness accounts."

Thus when a growing number of Chinese arrived in California to find gold in the nineteenth century, they were already stereotyped as slaves and coolies who brought filth and contagious diseases. Chinese, as a result, became intricately involved with America's discourse on race. When people from the east coast came to California and saw the unique appearance and customs of the Chinese, "their responses were largely shaped by previous responses to Indians, to immigrants, and especially to Negroes and Negro slaves" (Alexander Saxton: 19). The assumed "racial inferiority" of African Americans was then transferred to the Chinese and, in turn, these anti-Chinese attitudes and laws were used against later Asian immigrants such as the Japanese and Koreans. As early as 1854, the California Supreme Court in *People v Hall* gave this opinion of the Chinese:

> [They are] a race of people whom nature has marked as inferior, and who are incapable of progress or intellectual development beyond a certain point, as their history has shown, differing in language, customs, color, and physical conformation; *between whom and ourselves nature has placed an impassable difference.* (Cited in Winant: 42; emphasis added)

In this case involving the murder of a Chinese individual by George W. Hall and two others, it was ruled that the Chinese could not testify in court against whites, even when the whites perpetrated a crime against them. Anti-Chinese sentiments were thus solidified into legal and political disenfranchisement, which in turn prevented Chinese from shedding their "foreigner" status in the U.S.

Tolerance and Intolerance

Despite their limited rights as resident aliens, 1 Peter's Jewish *paroikoi* enjoyed protection under the Roman government's policy of toleration. This policy gave them the right to practice their religion as a minority group. Because of Jewish military support in his civil war with Pompey in 49 B.C.E., Julius Caesar granted them the freedom to practice their religion. This "formalized and legalized what had apparently been an unwritten convention that the Jews in the empire should have religious liberty and replaced *ad hoc* enactments by a permanent, universal legislation" (E. Mary Smallwood: 135–36).

This freedom of religion permitted the Diaspora Jews to practice their law, and Caesar's successor, Augustus, continued this policy. They could build synagogues, collect funds, and send their temple tax to Jerusalem, and this communal property was protected against confiscation. Jews were also exempted from military service because of their Sabbath observance and their kosher diet.

This imperial policy did not, of course, completely shield the Jews in Asia Minor from persecution by the local population. Jews in Asia Minor repeatedly complained that Greek city authorities were attempting to steal the temple tax and pleaded with the Romans to reassert this right of the Jews. No nominal protection was, however, available to the Chinese of nineteenth-century San Francisco. They were easy targets of discrimination and became victims of many discriminatory state laws and taxes. As early as 1852, the Foreign Miner's Tax was almost solely collected against Chinese gold miners, because they could be easily identified. This tax "accounted for more than half of the tax revenues collected in California until its repeal in 1870" (Judy Yung: 21). Chinese were also barred from naturalized citizenship in 1878 until the Walter-McCarran Act of 1952.

This anti-Chinese sentiment reached into the highest offices. In his Inaugural Address in 1862, the governor of California, Leland Stanford, declared:

> To my mind it is clear the settlement among us of an inferior race is to be discouraged by every legitimate means. Asia, with her numberless missions, sends to our shores the dregs of her population.... There can be no doubt but that the presence of numbers among us of a degraded and distinct people must exercise a deleterious influence upon the superior race, and, to a certain extent, repel desirable immigration. (Cited in Cheng-Tsu Wu: 109)

One of the reasons for these anti-Chinese laws was an unfounded fear that a "yellow peril" would overwhelm the white population. Yet Chinese immigrants "never exceeded 4.4 percent of the total immigration population between 1871–1880, they dwindled to 1.2 percent between 1881–1890, and down to a tiny 0.4 percent between 1891–1900" (Mary Roberts Coolidge: 504). The largest number of Chinese admitted was just under forty thousand in 1882. Despite these small numbers, the Chinese became a large political issue in California when politicians learned that an anti-Chinese position could gain the labor vote. The Workingmen's Party was a major political force in the 1870s, led by the Irish immigrant Denis Kearny, whose every speech began and ended with his famous motto, "The Chinese must go."

As time progressed, the Chinese became more than a California issue. They became a national issue in the presidential election of 1880. The Chinese became convenient scapegoats in the huge political battle for working-class votes by deflecting attention away from the structural problems of massive unemployment and poverty that were leading the nation toward depression. Why did a California "problem" become magnified and distorted into a national "problem"?

> Chinese immigrants became the indispensable enemy not to workers but to politicians, who, in a period of converging political consensus, needed a safe, nonideological cause to trumpet. Politicians—not California, not workers, and not national racist imagery—ultimately supplied the agency for Chinese exclusion. (Andrew Gyory: 15)

Both Democratic and Republican parties put anti-Chinese planks in their platforms in order to gain the white working-class vote in a hotly contested race. Politicians of both parties catapulted the Chinese, who numbered just over 105,465 in the 1880 census, into a national issue. Again, in the words of Gyory:

> By spewing, amplifying, and propagating racist stereotypes of the Chinese and linking the well-being of workers to the exclusion of Chinese immigrants, politicians manipulated the two most volatile issues in American society—race and class—and combined them to produce the first race-based immigration act in American history.... Politicians and national party leaders were the glue welding the active anti-Chinese racism of westerners with the nascent anti-Chinese racism of other Americans. In all senses of the term, Chinese exclusion was a *political* act. (257; emphasis original)

Politicians used the powerless and voteless Chinese immigrants as pawns. In 1874, President Ulysses S. Grant pleaded before Congress to exclude Chinese emigrants:

> Hardly a perceptible percentage of them perform any honorable labor, but they are brought for shameful purposes, to the great demoralization of the youth of these localities. If this evil practice can be legislated against, it will be my pleasure as well as my duty to enforce any regulation to secure so desirable an end. (Cited in Miller: 154)

Hundreds of city and state laws were enacted against them, culminating in Congress passing the Chinese Exclusion Act in 1882, and thus fulfilling President Grant's wish. With this act, the Chinese became the only ethnic group in U.S. history to be specifically proscribed from immigrating on the sole basis of their country of origin. Its impact was dramatic as the number of Chinese admitted in 1883 was only 8,031, as compared to 39,579 in 1882 (Yung: 294).

Evangelizing (and Americanizing) the Chinese

Within this hostile climate against the Chinese, Protestant missionaries were one of their few "allies." In their efforts to convert them, these missionaries spoke out against anti-Chinese legislation. Protestant missionary outreach began to reach out to these early Chinese immigrants. In San Francisco, the Presbyterians under Rev. William Speer were the first to open a Chinese mission in 1853. He opened a chapel and erected a mission building in Chinatown the following year. Reverend Otis Gibson opened a Methodist Episcopal mission in 1868, while a Congregational and a Baptist mission were opened two years later.

They hoped that through conversion, the Chinese could be evangelists to their own people when they returned to China. As Wesley Woo points out, "missionary work in China and the conversion of the Chinese in America were viewed as two sides of the same coin" (1991:214). Evangelizing China, one of the oldest and largest nations, was key to bringing in a "Christian world order." It was thus seen as providential that God brought the Chinese to American shores to help fulfill her "spiritual" manifest destiny to

Christianize the world and to be a light to the nations. To accomplish this mission, the U.S. had to protect her institutions from pollution and corruption by immigrants such as the Chinese. Evangelizing the Chinese was synonymous with Americanizing them, as America's destiny was to convert these "heathen Chinese" and assimilate them to its civilized ways.

Teaching English As Evangelism

In equating (and confusing) America and Christianity, missionaries believed that the Chinese needed to be taught American ways. A prime example of this was teaching English—which the Chinese were eager to learn—as a way to become Christians. Thus evangelism and assimilation were intertwined in the minds of these Protestant missionaries to the Chinese.

> [T]he study of English in the Sunday school, as well as contact with Christian people and with our civilization, has brought still more into a new world, and made them into new men [sic]. It has even improved their personal appearance, and has put a new light into their countenances.... When a Chinaman [sic] once learns English he can never be the same man that he was before. (Ira M. Condit: 107)

Learning English was not a service offered by other Chinese community organizations. In response to this vacuum, many churches established Chinese Sunday schools in which English and other subjects were taught. Teaching English was one of the most important evangelistic tools in introducing Christianity to the Chinese.

> Sitting down by the side of the Chinaman [sic], and teaching him simple words was as really teaching him Christianity as in the case of the missionary who preached to him the Gospel in his own tongue. They were deeply impressed by the unselfish, self-sacrificing, loving spirit of these teachers; and their humble ministry brought forth rich fruit in many a Chinese soul. (Condit: 104)

An evening school at Speer's Presbyterian mission was soon established because of the desire of the younger Chinese males to learn English. In 1870, "an average of 71 attended.... Half an hour each evening is devoted to oral lessons, embracing the subject needful for business education, and designed also to communicate various facts in geography, history, astronomy, and other sciences; together with the important topics of current events" (Yong Chen: 134). Chinese classics were also taught using Chinese instructors.

> In 1885 the Presbyterian mission in San Francisco ran a tuition-free evening school for young men, with an average attendance of eighty. The curriculum included arithmetic, grammar, geography, history, essay writing, and Bible. The last twenty-five minutes of each session were spent in religious

instruction. Also, Chinese church members regularly held Bible study after the evening school adjourned. (Woo, 1983:42)

These Chinese Sunday schools were continued by the Methodists, who, under Rev. Otis Gibson, started a statewide system in 1869 to introduce the Chinese "to our best citizens, of acquainting them with the spirit and genius of our institutions, and leading them gradually to adopt our higher form of civilization and our purer faith" (Gibson: 176). The main school was in San Francisco, and it "began with an average attendance of twenty-five students [in 1869]. By 1876, the average was eighty students, aged eight to thirty-five. This was the only mission school to charge tuition—one dollar a month, although payment was optional" (Woo, 1983:56). As soon as they learned enough English by using the New Testament as a reader, the California Methodist Annual Conference felt that the Chinese should be included into the regular Sunday school classes.

Using English for evangelism was effective. The Chinese were so willing to learn English that they took the risk of becoming converted. Huie Kin (who later became a minister) went to three evening schools on Sunday and confessed that

> our motive, at least the conscious one, was not religion, but language. However, we were coached to recite Scriptural passages, and sometimes entire chapters, much to the spiritual edification of our teachers. For us it was a good memory test in a strange language.... we did not have sufficient mastery of the language to appreciate what we read. (31–32)

However, progress was slow since the Chinese were only taught a few hours of English a week. Even when there was progress, Gibson admitted, "Just as fast as these boys and young men acquire a sufficient knowledge of our language to make themselves readily understood in common conversation, they are at once removed from school and placed in business" (192).

Despite all these efforts and the potential benefits from church membership, Chinese converts in San Francisco were few. The Presbyterians, who had the largest mission, reported

> "with regret" its failure to produce any converts. In 1876 it had 69 members, and by then it had received about a hundred people since its establishment. By the close of the century that number had grown to 360. The second largest mission was the Methodist Episcopal mission.... In 1876 the mission had about 45 members, and the total number of Chinese converts at the four major missions in San Francisco was 147. (Chen: 133)

The total number of Chinese converts in one estimate was about "6,500 (between 1850 and 1910, approximately 326,000 Chinese immigrated to the United States)" (Woo, 1991:217). This figure of about 2 percent roughly corresponded to the percentage of Christian conversions in China.

The Cost of Christian Conversion

In suffering from racial injustice, it was no wonder that the Chinese were very suspicious of missionary attempts to evangelize them. These Chinese immigrants "cherished strong feelings of enmity against the people who had in many ways inflicted deep wrongs upon them. They had no desire to learn the religion of those who had treated them so unjustly and cruelly" (Condit: 102).

In their conversion, Chinese Protestants became a minority within their own ethnic group as their new religious identity set them apart. This religious conversion caused intragroup conflict and hostility that resulted in their persecution and ostracism by the Chinese community in San Francisco. Not only were they viewed with suspicion from the wider society; they now faced alienation from within their own ethnic group. The risk of losing the support from their family and friends was a high price to pay, because it was precisely these people upon whom the convert depended to emigrate in the first place. This dilemma was one reason why there were so few Chinese converts. For example, when Lem Chung became a Christian, his father wrote:

> What are you doing out there? Are you going to believe Jesus and leave all your countrymen [sic], and your ancestors, and idols, and Confucius unserved? ... No other way better than Confucius; so many of your countrymen [sic] do not believe Christ. You must leave off and come back to *our own way* [sic]. (Cited in Woo, 1983:204; emphasis original)

To dissuade Chin Toy (a future Congregational minister) from getting baptized, his cousin tried to lock Chin in a room. Chin observed that converts are "very much hated by our relatives, they say that the Christians are a people of no use—ungrateful, and full of infidelity, because we do not worship ancestors and believe as they do" (cited in Woo, 1983:205). Even after conversion, there was pressure to forsake Christianity. After returning to China, Fong Won had over twenty acquaintances trying to get him to smoke and gamble in order to abandon the ways of the "foreigners." These examples show the deep tension between Western Christianity and the Chinese heritage. Many viewed the two to be incompatible, thus resulting in a common Chinese saying, "One more Christian, one less Chinese."

Even converting to the dominant religion of their newly adopted country did not alleviate the suffering of Chinese Protestants. This is yet another difference between the minority religious community of 1 Peter and that of the Chinese Protestants in San Francisco. While 1 Peter's *paroikoi* were further marginalized by joining a new and small religious sect, Chinese Christians were ostracized by a Western racial ideology that mitigated their conversion to a dominant Protestantism. For example, becoming Christians sometimes made the Chinese even more of a target of Irish Catholics. Perhaps because they were themselves objects of Protestant discrimination, Irish Catholics of nineteenth-century San Francisco, in turn, attacked the Chinese as a more "foreign" group of immigrants. Their many articles against the Chinese demonstrated this anti-Chinese sentiment. Three thousand people paid one dollar apiece to hear John Chrysostom Bouchard give a lecture ("Chinaman or White Man, Which?") filled with "familiar anti-Chinese themes—such as, they paid no taxes, competed unfairly with white labor, caused health and sanitation problems, were not capable of religious conversion, and were an inferior race" (Woo, 1983:134). Being a Christian was no protection against anti-Chinese forces both within and without the Christian church. As a result, Chinese Protestants turned to each other for support and solidarity in such a hostile environment.

A Unique Chinese Christian Organization

Even within their own churches, the Chinese were under the control of white denominations and mission agencies. Whether they were serving as teachers, assistants, helpers, or colporteurs, they remained subordinate to white supervision. This was also true for Chinese pastors, since they were hired and paid by a mission board. What was needed was a Chinese Christian organization independent of white supervision. The impetus for this was provided by William Pond, a Congregationalist minister to the Chinese in San Francisco, who in 1871

> felt the need to band together potential converts for mutual fellowship and instruction, rather than allowing them to be baptized and received into church membership too soon. Therefore, he organized a Chinese Christian Class, which held prayer meetings and Bible studies and maintained fraternal watch over its members. The Chinese were screened, and only after a six-month probation period could they be recommended for baptism. (Woo, 1991:226–27)

This idea spread, and Chinese Christians in other denominations formed similar mutual support groups. The name *Youxue Zhengdaohui* was adopted. This support group was initially an ecumenical association, but later denominations began setting up their own branches across the U.S. as part of their separate Chinese missions. Each denomination (Presbyterians, Congregationalists, Methodists, Baptists, and possibly Episcopalians) had its parallel *Zhengdaohui* headquarters in San Francisco. There was rapid growth. For instance, there were over six hundred members in the Congregational *Zhengdaohui* in 1890, while the Presbyterian *Zhengdaohui* had "thirty branch societies in all [twelve states], with several hundred members. More than a thousand members have belonged to this Association since its beginning" (Condit: 116–17).

Functions of the Zhengdaohui

The religious functions of the *Zhengdaohui* were many, and they overlapped many church activities. In fact, they conducted their own worship services with members taking turns to preach (although they did not perform the sacraments). They also met for Bible study. The Methodist *Zhengdaohui*, for example, met nightly for Bible study during the 1880s. They were also responsible for screening potential church members and prepared them for baptism. "Almost all converts joined their respective *Zhengdaohui* before joining the church ... potential candidates for baptism first had to serve a six-month probationary period in the *Zhengdaohui* and then be recommended by that society" (Woo, 1983:231). Thus the *Zhengdaohui* performed a catechetical and disciplinary function in instructing fellow Chinese Protestants with strict membership rules. Potential members must be recommended by a member, have their conduct investigated, and then be approved by a two-thirds vote. There was a two-dollar initiation fee, and the new member was given a Bible and the society's constitution. According to the Preamble, the purpose of the *Zhengdaohui* was

> that we might inform each other about the true doctrine, establish ourselves to act according to the truth and not fall in crooked ways; but be loyal to our superiors, dutiful to our parents, and walk in the right path. Though it is not easy to do this, yet, as young men, we ought to learn. For mutual aid, we ought to be joined together as loving friends, so as to exhort each other more earnestly, and polish each other continually by contact. This is what we deeply expect by this Association. (Cited in Condit: 120)

Among its thirty-three rules were to study English, the Decalogue, the Lord's Prayer, the Apostles' Creed, and most importantly, to study the Bible daily. Discipline was strict:

> If any member does wrong, or breaks the rules of the Association, the officers shall warn him three times, and if he does not repent, he is suspended, and his name is hung up on the bulletin board. If he truly repents and acknowledges his fault, he can become a member again. But his name will have to be hung up for three months; thus informing the society of his desire to return. If the brethren are convinced that he is really sincere, then he will be acknowledged again as a brother. But if suspended a second time, he never can become a member again. (Condit: 123)

In addition to fulfilling these religious functions, the *Zhengdaohui* also provided important social roles for its members, since converts often risked losing friends and family. The quarters of the *Zhengdaohui* were used for socializing, reading, and even temporary lodging. Arrangements such as transportation and exit permits were provided for members who returned to China. If a member died, assistance was provided for funeral arrangements and costs. Thus the *Zhengdaohui* functioned like clan and district associations as well as secret societies.

Christian Persecution

The fact that the *Zhengdaohui* provided services found in other non-Christian organizations might have contributed to some missionaries resisting it. In 1877, John Kerr, who supervised the Presbyterian *Zhengdaohui*, felt that "non-church members dominated this organization and that the few church members were not mature Christians.... members showed an un-Christian spirit towards his authority and acted as if the church were under their control" (Woo, 1983:236). Kerr also suspected that it was mismanaged (including its finances). H. Y. Noyes, who worked with Kerr, called the *Zhengdaohui* a "hypocritical and idolatrous guild in which men too ignorant to read their own language intelligently were explaining Scripture" (Woo, 1983:237). As a result of Kerr's and Noyes's efforts, the Presbyterians supposedly severed their denominational relationship with the *Zhengdaohui* in 1878.

Some Chinese Christians apparently agreed with Kerr and wrote a letter to the Board of Foreign Missions that "those who worship idols and their ancestors have seized authority in the Association and this has given rise to disorder" (Woo, 1983:238). Unfortunately, there are no records from the Chinese who disagreed with Kerr's position. Kerr saw the *Zhengdaohui* as a challenge to his authority and viewed the Chinese as incapable of managing the *Zhengdaohui*. Obviously Kerr was unwilling to give the Chinese the autonomy to run the *Zhengdaohui* in their own way. He certainly did not see the Chinese Protestants as his equal partners.

Whether the *Zhengdaohui* was formed to circumvent control of denominational Chinese missions or not, it did allow Chinese Protestants to have more responsibility, leadership, initiative, authority, and decision making without white supervision. Thus *Zhengdaohui* could be viewed as an alternate organization for Chinese Christians, and it "became a Chinese church within the white mission structure" (Woo, 1983:279). As more and more Chinese were able to move into major and official church leadership positions in the 1920s and 1930s, the *Zhengdaohui* had served its transitional function and gradually disappeared.

Conclusion

Both 1 Peter's community in Asia Minor and Chinese Protestants in nineteenth-century San Francisco were *paroikoi*. While both groups were resident aliens, Chinese immigrants faced additional barriers of race and legal disenfranchisement. Marginalized by their distinctive facial features, dress, and hairstyle, the Chinese became an alien race, while the U.S. government enacted discriminatory city, state, and national laws against them. Like others trying to survive in such a hostile environment, the early Chinese Protestants hoped to improve their condition in a new religion. As conversion brought on more opposition from church, society, and even their own ethnic community, they organized a Christian mutual support society, the *Zhengdaohui*, for additional support and training. While other Chinese associations were based on one's family clan or village, membership in the *Zhengdaohui* was based on Christian discipleship rather than biological kinship. Yet, like these family associations, the *Zhengdaohui* were autonomous from denominational Chinese churches and missions that were under the control of whites. Its growth was a testament to the discipline of its members, who proved that they indeed were not "rice Christians." Not only might their race- and religion-related marginalization help us understand the community that 1 Peter was addressing; the solidarity and communal identity that the Chinese Protestants in nineteenth-century San Francisco achieved was a fulfillment of 1 Peter's vision. Through the efforts of the *Zhengdaohui*, the Chinese Protestant church developed into a small but growing presence in San Francisco's Chinatown that continues into the new millennium.

WORKS CONSULTED

Achtemeier, Paul J.
    1996   *1 Peter: A Commentary on First Peter*. Minneapolis: Fortress.

Balch, David L.
    1986   "Hellenization/Acculturation in 1 Peter." Pp. 79–101 in *Perspectives on First Peter*. Ed. Charles H. Talbert. Macon, Ga.: Mercer University Press.

Campbell, Barth L.
    1998   *Honor, Shame and the Rhetoric of 1 Peter*. Atlanta: Scholars Press.

Chan, Sucheng
    1991   *Asian Americans: An Interpretive History*. Boston: Twayne.

Chen, Yong
    2000   *Chinese San Francisco: A Trans-Pacific Community*. Stanford, Calif.: Stanford University Press.

Cohen, Shaye J. D.
    2000   *The Beginnings of Jewishness: Boundaries, Varieties, Uncertainties*. Berkeley and Los Angeles: University of California Press.

Collins, Adela Yarbro
    1985   "Insiders and Outsiders in the Book of Revelation and Its Social Context." Pp. 187–218 in *"To See Ourselves As Others See Us": Christians, Jews, "Others" in Late Antiquity*. Ed. Jacob Neusner and Ernest S. Frerichs. Chico, Calif.: Scholars Press.

Condit, Ira M.
    1900   *The Chinaman As We See Him and Fifty Years Work for Him*. New York: Holt.

Coolidge, Mary Roberts
    1909   *Chinese Immigration*. New York: Holt.

Elliott, John H.
    1981   *A Home for the Homeless: A Sociological Exegesis of 1 Peter: Its Situation and Strategy*. Philadelphia: Fortress.

    1986   "1 Peter, Its Situation and Strategy: A Discussion with David Balch." Pp. 61–78 in *Perspectives on First Peter*. Ed. Charles H. Talbert. Macon, Ga.: Mercer University Press.

    2000   *1 Peter: A New Translation with Introduction and Commentary*. New York: Doubleday.

Gibson, Otis
    1877   *The Chinese in America*. Cincinnati: Hitchcock & Walden.

Gyory, Andrew
    1998   *Closing the Gate: Race, Politics, and the Chinese Exclusion Act*. Chapel Hill: University of North Carolina Press.

Huie Kin
    1932   *Reminiscences*. Peiping: San Yu.

Martin, Troy W.
    1992   *Metaphor and Composition in 1 Peter*. Atlanta: Scholars Press.

McClain, Charles J.
    1994   *In Search of Equality: The Chinese Struggle against Discrimination in Nineteenth-Century America*. Berkeley and Los Angeles: University of California Press.

Miller, Stuart Creighton
    1969   *The Unwelcome Immigrant: The American Image of the Chinese, 1785–1882*. Berkeley and Los Angeles: University of California Press.

Robinson, Thomas A.
    1988   *The Bauer Thesis Examined: The Geography of Heresy in the Early Christian Church*. Lewiston, N.Y.: Mellen.

Saxton, Alexander
    1971   *The Indispensable Enemy: Labor and the Anti-Chinese Movement in California*. Berkeley and Los Angeles: University of California Press.

Smallwood, E. Mary
    1976   *The Jews under Roman Rule: From Pompey to Diocletian.* Leiden: Brill.

Sui Sin Far
    1991   "Her Chinese Husband." Pp. 133–38 in *The Big Aiiieeeee! An Anthology of Chinese American and Japanese American Literature.* Ed. Jeffery Paul Chan, Frank Chin, Fusao Inada, and Shawn Wong. New York: Meridian.

Whittaker, Molly
    1984   *Jews and Christians: Graeco-Roman Views.* Cambridge: Cambridge University Press.

Winant, Howard
    1994   *Racial Conditions: Politics, Theory, Comparisons.* Minneapolis: University of Minnesota Press.

Woo, Wesley
    1983   "Protestant Work among the Chinese in the San Francisco Bay Area, 1850–1920." Ph.D. diss., Graduate Theological Union.

    1991   "Chinese Protestants in the San Francisco Bay Area." Pp. 213–45 in *Entry Denied: Exclusion and the Chinese Community in America, 1882–1943.* Ed. Sucheng Chan. Philadelphia: Temple University Press.

Wu, Cheng-Tsu, ed.
    1971   *Chink: A Documentary History of Anti-Chinese Prejudice in America.* New York: Meridian.

Yung, Judy
    1995   *Unbound Feet: A Social History of Chinese Women in San Francisco.* Berkeley and Los Angeles: University of California Press.

URIAH THE HITTITE:
A (CON)TEXT OF STRUGGLE FOR IDENTITY

Uriah (Yong-Hwan) Kim
Pacific School of Religion

ABSTRACT

Uriah the Hittite is not the first person one remembers when one thinks about the story of 2 Samuel 11, popularly known as the story of "David and Bathsheba." However, if the readers, especially from minority groups, pay closer attention to Uriah the Hittite, his story reveals the struggle for identity among the peoples of Israel and echoes a similar struggle among the Asian Americans and other minority groups living in the U.S. Uriah was an officer of the Israelite army, a native of Jerusalem, and a faithful Yahwist, yet he is branded as a non-Israelite, as a Hittite. His hybrid identity forced the "author" of the text to give Bathsheba a double identity, "daughter of Eliam, the wife of Uriah the Hittite," in order to clearly identify her as an Israelite. His fellow Israelites, especially David, abandoned and betrayed him violently because he was not one of them. Uriah's story is a (con)text of struggle for identity that is too familiar for Asian Americans who are involved in the ongoing struggle for identity in the U.S. and are familiar with the tragic story of Vincent Chin.

INTRODUCTION

The story in 2 Samuel 11 is one of the most well-known stories in the Bible. If we mention "David and Bathsheba," "David's Adultery with Bathsheba," "the Bathsheba Affair," or simply "David's Sin," many people will not hesitate to identify such titles with this story. Although it is remembered in the Bible as "the matter of Uriah the Hittite" (1 Kgs 15:5), I wonder how many people would identify it as the story of "Uriah the Hittite." If the titles by which a story is remembered are any indication of what the readers think the story is about, then Uriah the Hittite has not been well remembered.

The story has been popular among biblical scholars and sages in the past and is still popular among scholars today. The rabbis of the distant past made excuses for David; they exonerated David by concluding that Bathsheba was given a bill of divorce and found Uriah to be a rebel deserving of death (McCarter: 288). The early Christian fathers formulated David into a theological paradigm, connecting the story of David's passion with

David's repentance and pardon by God (Petit). Then the historical-critical scholars have been busy analyzing the story as part of objective history; the story has been analyzed as part of the Succession Narrative or the Court History of David (e.g., Whybray: 11–19). In more recent years, some scholars have begun to see the story as literature and applied narrative techniques to interpret the story; they have been busy filling the narrative "gaps" in the story (e.g., Sternberg: 186–229). There are others, especially woman scholars, who are trying valiantly to rescue Bathsheba from the patriarchal text and its interpreters (e.g., Exum, 1993:170–201). However, Uriah the Hittite, the man and his story, has not received enough attention by scholars and sages.

Why am I so concerned with Uriah the Hittite anyway? It sounds a bit personal—well, it is. I am an interested reader, like everyone else, embedded in my sociocultural context. Moreover, my name also happens to be Uriah. I was a teenager when I changed my name to Uriah in order to mark the occasion of becoming a U.S. citizen and a Christian. I chose the name, somewhat innocently, because I simply wanted to be as loyal to my God and country as I thought Uriah was in the story. Obviously I became concerned with Uriah whenever I read and remembered the story. Over the years I began to see more and more similarities between Uriah the Hittite and myself. I believe that my (con)text as a member of a marginalized or diasporic community is analogous to and helpful in understanding Uriah the Hittite in his (con)text. Thus, this paper is an inter(con)textual reading between Uriah the Hittite's (con)text and my own personal (con)text.[1]

Uriah in (Con)Text

Uriah Kim in (Con)Text

A member of a diasporic community. When I received my citizenship, I was naïve enough to believe that I became an American. Too quickly did I learn that I was still viewed and treated as a foreigner—an outsider. I realized that it takes more than a certificate to become a member of the "us" group in the U.S.; it takes more than a U.S. passport to cross the group boundaries formed by "Americans." Theoretically, anyone can become an American, and many people still believe and experience the so-called "straight-line theory" of assimilation. Immigrants experience marginality at first, but, eventually, they become members of the dominant group through the

---

[1] See Liew, ch. 2, for a good discussion on "inter(con)textual" reading.

assimilation process. The notion of marginality as a transition from one world or group to another is understood as a temporary condition that will eventually end when structural assimilation occurs. But, according to Sang Hyun Lee, there is a catch to this model. The straight-line assimilation model was based on the experience of European immigrants. Therefore, Lee concludes that the situation of marginality for some groups, mostly non-Europeans, may be permanent.

The reason for this permanent marginality has to do with the boundaries or identity markers of the dominant group. Jurij Lotman's study found that "the basic group boundary is one that distinguishes ourselves from others: the us vs. not-us boundary.... This is a fundamental distinction from which others grow" (Schreiter: 63). In the U.S., the basic boundary is the color of one's skin. Ronald Takaki explains that throughout American history, many classics in the field of American history have defined "American" as "white" (1993:2).

Although the situation of permanent marginality is helpful in articulating some aspects of my situation, it is inadequate and too simplistic to explain the complexity of my situation. It sets up a binary opposition between the communities at the margin and the dominant group; the boundaries seem too definite and stable without any sense of mobility or fluidity. James Clifford defines diasporic people as those who lost the sense of rootedness or belongingness and cautions against overdrawing the distinction between European immigrant and non-European diasporic experiences. Clifford argues that it is not possible to identify borders that can sharply define diasporic in opposition to native cultures (310) and that "diaspora experiences and discourses are entangled, never clear of commodification" (313).

The borders that separate marginalized peoples from the dominant group, or diasporic peoples from the native people, are not fixed and stable. There are movements between members of diaspora and native communities; in fact, diasporic communities often recover links to homeland and diasporic populations regularly "lose" members to the dominant culture (Clifford: 328). Thus the borders between diasporic communities and the dominant group do shift over time and are blurred at times. Even within a diasporic community, disidentification (a strategy used to distinguish one group from another) and solidarity (a formation of coalition among distinctive groups within diasporic population) are drawn and redrawn constantly.

Identity struggle. As a member of a diasporic community, the struggle for identity is a prominent issue. Who am I? What is my cultural identity? Am I an American who happens to be of a Korean descent? Am I a Korean living in the U.S. separated from my homeland? Or, am I a Korean-American, a hyphenated being, who belongs to both worlds and, at the same time, who does not belong to either? Should I identify myself as an Asian American in solidarity with other Asian diasporas in the U.S., or should I disidentify myself from other Asian Americans?

Lisa Lowe describes a web in which Asian Americans struggle for their identity in this way:

> what is referred to as "Asian American" is clearly a heterogeneous entity. From the perspective of the majority culture, Asian Americans may very well be constructed as different from, and other than, Euro-Americans. But from the perspectives of Asian Americans, we are perhaps even more different, more diverse among ourselves.... As with other diasporas in the United States, the Asian immigrant collectivity is unstable and changeable, with its cohesion complicated by inter-generationality, by various degrees of identification and relation to a "homeland," and by different extents of assimilation to and distinction from "majority culture" in the United States. (27)

Two terms are helpful in understanding this complex web in which Asian Americans find themselves: (1) hybridity, which describes multiculturalism or multi-identities of members of diasporas; and (2) liminality, which describes the state of "in-betweenness" caused by hybridity.

Stuart Hall describes two interrelated yet different ways of thinking about "cultural identity": (1) one view is to think of cultural identity as something (essence, culture, past, origin) that is stable, unchanging, and continuous beneath the shifting divisions and vicissitudes of actual history; and (2) another view thinks of cultural identity as belonging to the future as well as to the past, as a matter of "becoming" as well as of "being"; it sees the ruptures and discontinuities as constituting one's identity. Such conversations on cultural identity add even more "lines" to the web of identity struggle.

I see myself entangled in such a web. I see myself as a text, a site of struggle for identity as a member of a diasporic community. My identity is characterized not only by hybridity and liminality, but is also dependent on the stability and instability, the continuity and rupturing of cultural identity in the U.S. It is not only the diasporic population that should be struggling for identity; the "native" people are also entangled in this complex web of identity struggle whether they recognize it or not.

Uriah the Hittite in (con)text. Was Uriah the Hittite also in a similar (con)text as mine? Was he also a site/text of a struggle for identity in Israel? But first, who was Uriah the Hittite anyway?

1. An officer of the Israelite army. Uriah was, of course, the husband of Bathsheba and a victim of David's machinations. But he was also an officer of Israel's army who was killed while fighting for Israel. He is named in the

list of the Thirty (2 Sam 23:24–39), which may have been David's elite corps of officers that was formed during David's flight from Saul (Mazar). Mazar argues that the last seven names, which includes Uriah, should be distinguished from the rest because they were of a different sort: "They are all either from distant regions or from the indigenous population" (318–19). Although Na'aman questions the existence of the institution of the Thirty, nevertheless, he regards the list as reflecting the organization of the professional army after David made Jerusalem his capital (77). Uriah was named in what seems to be an important official list of an elite group of officers in the Israelite army.

Uriah was a non-Israelite serving in the Israelite army. This shows the "positive" aspect of hybridity, namely, the ability to move about freely in two or more communities. It also shows the "positive" side of liminality; as long as Uriah was "wanted" by or "useful" to Israel, he was accepted by Israel as its own. It also shows the complexity of the army makeup of Israel in that Israelites were not the only ones who served the army.

2. A native of Jerusalem. Uriah's house was in Jerusalem. This may be a hint that he was a native of Jerusalem. "Uriah slept at the entrance of the king's house with all the servants of his lord, and did not go down to his house" (2 Sam 11:9 NRSV). The fact that Uriah has a house while the "servants" stayed at David's house may indicate that Uriah had his house before David built one for himself (2 Sam 5:11). According to Rosenberg, the fact that Uriah's house was so near "the king's house" may indicate that he was from a prominent member of the royal-military circles, a member of the entrenched aristocracy that antedated David's conquest of Jerusalem (108–9).

If this was so, then Uriah was a member of the community that had been displaced by the Israelites. It was David who conquered Jerusalem (which formerly belonged to the Jebusites) and made it into his capital (2 Sam 5:6–10). How did Uriah become an Israelite officer when there is no mention of a Jebusite among the list of officers in 2 Samuel 23? Is it possible that the Hittites practiced ethnic "disidentification"? This is in fact a strategy used frequently by Asian Americans in this country before the 1960s—"the act of distancing one's group from another group so as not to be mistaken and suffer the blame for the presumed misdeeds of that group" (Espiritu: 20). It is a strategy of survival for "colonized" and diasporic people.

3. A faithful Yahwist. Uriah is a good Yahwistic name. Uriah means "Yahweh is my light/fire." There are four other Uriahs in the Old Testament, and all of them are either a prophet or a priest of YHWH (2 Kgs 16:10–16; Jer 26:20–23; Neh 3:21; 8:4). How did a foreigner end up with a Yahwistic name? Did he change his original Hittite name to a Yahwistic name "as a tactfully patriotic concession to the winds of change" after

David conquered Jerusalem (Rosenberg: 108)? Or was he born in Israel (Anderson: 153)?

How important was it to have the "right" name in Israel? There is a hint in the story that it was in fact important to have the "right" name. In 2 Sam 11:21, Abimelech is mentioned as the son of *Yerubbesheth*. But we know that Abimelech's father's name was *Yerubbaal* (Judg 9:1). There are several *Baal*-names that have been "ashamed" (*bosheth*). Of course, it was not Jerubbaal who changed his own name; it was the scribes (or whoever produced the text) who changed his name. Why were the scribes compelled to change Jerubbaal's name? Were they trying to establish a group boundary? Was anti-Baalism a boundary used to draw Israel's identity? Then, was the faith in and loyalty to YHWH the basic group boundary of ancient Israelites?

Uriah, in contrast to David, is the one who abides by the Torah in the story; it is Uriah who is faithful to Yahweh's ways. In commenting on Uriah's response to David's question as to why he did not go down to his house in 2 Sam 11:11, Brueggemann puts it this way: "Uriah the Hittite, a foreigner, is not even a child of the torah. But he is faithful. It is a stunning moment of disclosure and contrast" (1990:273). Rosenberg also remarks that Uriah's response shows that:

> in the heart of the imperial phalanges we find an orthodox Israelite, quietly observing the wartime soldier's ban against conjugal relations.... it attests to the vitality of the confederate faith that it could take root amid the ranks of those structurally the most independent from the confederate polity. (111)

But Sternberg and others have pointed out that one of the ambiguities of the text is whether to understand Uriah's statement (11:11) at face value or to hear it as a sarcastic indictment against David's action (201–9; see also Garsiel, 1993: 256–58). This is not a surprising observation, since Uriah is in fact ambiguous; he is a hybrid. Would they have questioned Uriah's sincerity if Uriah were an Israelite?

Moreover, the scribes did not remove this ambiguity by dropping "the Hittite" signification from Uriah. Why not? Why did the scribes not claim Uriah as their own, as an Israelite, who was so faithful to YHWH? We would not have known that Uriah was a non-Israelite if not for the marker "Hittite" that was attached to his name. They replaced the *Baal* particle. Why did they not just drop "the Hittite"? Is this a sign of the fact that this is a site, a text of struggle for Israel's identity? They wanted to identify Israelites as anti-Baalists, but they accepted Jerubbaal as their own. On the other hand, Uriah, a loyal Yahwist, was left outside of Israel's boundaries. They claimed David, who broke the law as their own, yet they would not embrace Uriah, who was faithful to the law.

4. A Hittite. "Where are you from, Uriah?" Jerusalem. "No, no, where are you really from?" Hatti. "Where are you from?" is not a simple question to those situated outside of the dominant group. "I'm from New York" is hardly ever sufficient to those who are asking the question. What they really want to hear is where I "really" came from, that is, the place of origin, the homeland. They are not satisfied until they can place me outside their boundaries. It is one way of "othering" those whom the dominant group see as others.

Who were the Hittites, and from where did they come? The Hittites were a group of people whose capital was in central Anatolia; they established a considerable empire in the second millennium B.C.E. that eventually collapsed at the end of the Late Bronze Age (see Hoffner). Hoffner asks, "Was it the intention of the biblical writers to indicate that persons bearing the name *Hittite* or *sons of Heth* belonged to that foreign people from the north?" (152). Hoffner's opinion is that "passages referring to Hittites during the Israelite monarchy almost certainly refer to the Syrian kingdoms earlier controlled by the Hittite Empire during the fourteenth and thirteenth centuries" (152). F. F. Bruce says that the Hittites are presented clearly in the Bible in two ways: "First, as one of the ingredients in the population of Canaan, and secondly, as inhabitants of a territory to the north of Palestine" (6). John Van Seters thinks that the use of the terms "Hittite" along with "Amorite" in the Old Testament were rhetorical rather than historical; that is, they were used to mark non-Israelites. Van Seters, referring specifically to Uriah and Ahimelech, says that "[p]ossibly by 'Hittite' the author wishes merely to assert that they were non-Israelite" (80).

I agree with Van Seters that the term "Hittite" was used to designate people who were not Israelite. I think the Israelites were confused as to who the Hittites were and from where they came. They had a vague notion, but not much more. In our story, the "Hittite" is used to refer neither to a specific kingdom (which had long passed) nor a specific place, but a region outside of Israel, "somewhere" in the north. Thus the people placed in this place were non-Israelites even though they may have been living in Palestine longer than the Israelites (who also came from "somewhere" outside of Palestine according to the Pentateuch). I think it functions the way the term "Asia" is used in the U.S. No specific place is meant by "Asia." It refers to an enormous region outside of the U.S., "somewhere" in the east. Anyone who looks like a person from that region, regardless of his or her national or ethnic origin, is called an Asian. Hundreds of different groups of peoples are lumped together as "Asians," as distinct from "Americans" (who also happen to come from "somewhere" outside of America).

5. A (con)text of struggle for identity. Regina Schwartz, after contrasting the metanarrative of biblical scholarship that tried to stabilize the

"development" of monarchy, of dynasty, or of Israel's identity with the narratives of the Bible (narratives that nevertheless seem to be full of "ruptures" and "discontinuities"), sees the David-Bathsheba narrative as a site of struggle for Israel's identity. After noting that the story is surrounded by accounts of war with the Ammonites, she comments, "This is no accident: Israel's war with the sons of Ammon is a war of definition, the sexual violations are tests of definition, for in both, Israel's borders—who constitutes Israel and who does not—are at stake" (45). She continues that David is the one who acts as a *nabal* ("fool"), an outsider who violates sexual fidelity, which is analogous to being unfaithful to God; meanwhile, Uriah, non-Israelite, an "other," is the one who is faithful to God when he keeps sexual fidelity (46–50). Schwartz concludes:

> Both sexual fidelity and divine fidelity are preoccupations of a narrative that tends to construct identity as someone or some people *set apart*, with boundaries that could be mapped, ownership that could be titled. But if, as I have been arguing, the parameters of Israel's identity are very much at issue—which God is allowed and which is not, and which woman is allowed and which is not—then the identity of the nation and the people is not mapped, but in the process of being anxiously drawn and redrawn. (50)

In such a context, Uriah himself is a text of struggle for Israel's identity. The text struggles with Uriah's hybridity. Uriah is marked as an "other," but he is serving in Israel's army. He may have been a member of a ruling family in Jerusalem when the Jebusites controlled the city, but he managed to differentiate himself from the Jebusites. He is a faithful Yahwist with a Yahwistic name, but he is not claimed by the Israelites. Instead, he is labeled as "the Hittite," as a non-Israelite. When Uriah was "wanted," the Israelites claimed him as their own by placing him in their army and by differentiating him from the Jebusites. But when Uriah was "unwanted," they abandoned him with other non-Israelites and branded him as "the Hittite." Then, who was an Israelite? An Israelite was a Yahwist, but David was unfaithful to YHWH's laws. An Israelite was an anti-Baalist, but Jerubbaal (an Israelite "hero") had a Baalistic name. Thus, Uriah the Hittite is a (con)text of struggle for Israel's identity.

Uriah the Hittite Ruptures the Story

Bathsheba's Double Identity

Not Eliam, but Uriah. Bathsheba's identity disrupts the story. She is identified in the story in terms of two different relationships, "the daughter of Eliam, the wife of Uriah the Hittite" (1 Sam 11:3b).² McCarter comments that "it is unusual for a woman's patronymic to be given, especially when she is identified by her husband's Name.... This suggest that the identity of Bathsheba's father was significant" (285). Randall Bailey agrees that the patronymic relationship, which comes first, is more significant than the marital relationship (87). They seem to be saying that if there is anything significant with her double identity, then it has to do with her patronymic.

Bailey thinks that there is a very good reason for Bathsheba's double identity (85–90). He suggests that the significance of her patronymic is that it links her to the important family of Ahithophel (85–90). This is important for Bailey's understanding of the David and Bathsheba narrative because he argues that the affair happened after Absalom's revolt (90). He thinks that David's affair with Bathsheba was a premeditated scheme conceived by both in order to advance their interests through their marriage: Bathsheba wanted to improve her status after her grandfather dragged her family down by defecting to Absalom, and David wanted to reconcile his relationship with those who were associated with Ahithophel (87–90). Bailey's argument is important in that the unusual identification of Bathsheba is taken seriously into account in his reading of the story.

I disagree with Bailey's opinion, however, that Bathsheba's patronymic was significant because her father or grandfather was important. Instead, I believe that it was her husband who caused this "eruption" in her identity. As I suggested above, Uriah was marked as a non-Israelite. If the scribes had written his name without the term "Hittite," then Bathsheba would likely have been identified simply as "the wife of Uriah" without her patronymic, since her identity as an Israelite woman would have been unambiguous. But, as "the wife of Uriah the Hittite" without her patronymic, her identity would have been ambiguous: Was she an Israelite or a foreigner like her husband?³ The scribes removed the ambiguity when they added "the daughter of Eliam," who could have been a well-known Israelite without being a son of Ahithophel. Her double identity might have meant something like this: Bathsheba was an Israelite (see, her father was an Israelite) who happened to be married to a Hittite (a non-Israelite).

The right wife and the right mother. Why was it so important (and for whom) to have Bathsheba identified as an Israelite woman? Bathsheba was the daughter of Eliam and the wife of Uriah, but, more importantly,

---

2 Randall Bailey thinks that this aspect of identifying information is almost universally ignored (171n19).

3 Bathsheba's situation as a "native" married to a "foreigner" needs to be looked into. However, this is beyond the scope of this paper.

she would become a wife of David and the mother of Solomon. Exum talks about the importance of having the "right" wife and the "right" mother for Israel's identity (1993:94–147). Exum suggests that although it was through the father that the male line of descent was supposedly determined, it was the mother who not only affirmed the child's Israelite identity but also competed with the father in determining the line of descent in Israel (1993:110–11). She continues that mothers had an intrinsic advantage over fathers because motherhood was verifiable; therefore, it was just as important to have the "right" mother as the "right" father in determining Israel's identity.

Calum Carmichal in his discussion of three proverbial-type laws in Deuteronomy,[4] suggests that these laws reflect Judah's historical struggle to perpetuate his line (181–205). Moreover, these laws are interested in the establishment of David's house and are concerned with the future of the house in Solomon's time (181–82). It was crucial for David, the founder of the dynasty, to have the "right wife," an Israelite woman, in order to secure and perpetuate his dynasty. David's lineage was of a great interest to and was closely monitored in the biblical texts. The book of Kings lists the names of the mothers of all Judean kings except for Jehoram and Ahaz, but only Jeroboam I's mother is named among the northern kings (1 Kgs 11:26). This fact might be an example of the interest in David's lineage and also the importance of having the "right" mothers for the kings of Judah.

Among the mothers named in the book of Kings, only Rehoboam's mother, Naamah the Ammonite (1 Kgs 14:21), was not the "right" mother. According to Carmichal, the negative attitude toward union with foreigners was clearly expressed in the law forbidding mixed seed. Moreover, in 1 Kgs 11:1–13, Solomon's marriages to foreign women are blamed for his apostasy and for YHWH's judgment to divide his kingdom. Carmichal, in speaking of Rehoboam, comments that "it is a truly remarkable fact that this half-Israelite, half-Ammonite product is the only son attributed to Solomon" (182). Thus, Solomon was accused of threatening David's house because he had planted a mixed seed on the throne. Rehoboam lost all but one tribe (Judah) because he was the product of the "wrong" mother. It was Naamah, the "wrong" wife to Solomon and the "wrong" mother to Rehoboam, who threatened the very foundation of David's dynasty.

Bathsheba was the "right" wife to David and the "right" mother to Solomon who helped to legitimatize David's dynasty and Solomon's succes-

---

[4] The three proverbial-type laws are prohibition against sowing mixed seed in a vineyard (Deut 22:9), plowing with an ox and an ass (Deut 22:10), and wearing wool and linen (Deut 22:11).

sion. If the story left Bathsheba's identity as "the wife of Uriah the Hittite" without her patronymic, then her "Israelite-ness" would have been ambiguous. But, by adding "the daughter of Eliam," the story assured the readers that she was in fact an Israelite woman. Therefore, Bathsheba's unusual double identity was a result of Uriah being a non-Israelite.

David Did Not Pause

Reasons for not pausing. Schwartz, using Lévi-Strauss's work, argues that adultery and other sexual taboos are designed to maintain and protect the cooperation between men over the exchange of women (46–47). When David steals Bathsheba from Uriah, he is not only disrupting this cooperation between men, thereby causing fear and hostility, but he is also threatening the identity of Israel. Schwartz points out that "vigorous laws on adultery are invoked to police Israel's borders because adultery clearly threatens the identity of Israel" (48). There are serious consequences to those who break this cooperation.

In light of such an understanding, it is striking that David does not hesitate at all, after finding out who Bathsheba is, to commit adultery with her. Brueggemann puts it this way: "Now David knows who she is—and whose she is. David does not pause, however, because he is the king. The mention of Uriah might have given David pause, but it does not" (1990:273). Brueggemann, in another article, blames David's promptness to the abuse of command that is pervasive within military culture (1997:22–25). Sternberg explains the lack of hesitation in 2 Sam 11:2–5 as an example of biblical narrative techniques:

> The note or pose of "there is nothing much to tell" mainly arises from the paratactic series of verbs, which make up the bulk of the passage and laconically unroll a rapid sequence of external actions in almost assembly-line fashion.... The clash between matter and manner in the discourse greatly sharpens the irony.... This again shows how the Bible exploits the fact that literature is a time-art, in which the temporal continuum is apprehended in a temporal continuum and things unfold sequentially rather than simultaneously. (197–98)

Bailey thinks that there is "a lack of attention to sexual details and descriptions" precisely because David was not interested in sex, but in Bathsheba's political connectedness (87–88). Or we can attribute David's quick response to a sexual lust, blind love, "mid-life crisis," or other factors that weaken David's usual self-control (Yee).

David did not fear Uriah. There are other ways to explain David's lack of hesitation, but the fact that Uriah was a non-Israelite needs to be considered in trying to understand David's behavior. The question is whether David would have paused if Uriah had been an Israelite.

There was another king who killed a man in order to steal his property. King Ahab stole a property (vineyard) from a man named Naboth by first killing him (1 Kings 21). There are many similarities between David (2 Samuel 11–12) and Ahab (1 Kings 21).[5] When Naboth refused to sell his vineyard, Ahab returned home resentful and sullen (1 Kgs 21:3–4). But Ahab did not try to take Naboth's vineyard; it was only after Jezebel engineered Naboth's death that he took possession of the vineyard (1 Kgs 21:5–16). Even Ahab, one of the most faithless kings in Israel, hesitated before taking Naboth's vineyard because he respected Naboth's property right. The cooperation between men in the protection of property is maintained before a woman (Jezebel in this case) disrupts this cooperation.

David was also faithful (or made faithful) in observing this cooperation between men in the protection of property (which included women) throughout his life. For example, in 1 Samuel 25, David was "saved" from taking Abigail unlawfully when her husband (Nabal) conveniently died before David came to take his life (and Abigail's body). Then he took Michal from Paltiel the son of Laish because he owned her first and still had the property right over her: "Give me my wife Michal, to whom I became engaged at the price of one hundred foreskins of the Philistines" (2 Sam 3:14 NRSV). The biblical texts are very careful to portray David as someone who did not take things unlawfully; that is, David faithfully observed this cooperation with fellow Israelite men.

In the case with Bathsheba, this cooperation was not observed because her husband Uriah was not an Israelite. David did not hesitate because he saw Uriah as a Hittite who fell outside of this circle of cooperation. Moreover, David did not fear the consequences (fear and hostility) that can rise from breaking this cooperation because there was no *goel* (redeemer) for Uriah to avenge his blood. There was no community that could have retaliated on his behalf. David had nothing to fear from Uriah.

Bathsheba's double identity and David's lack of hesitation can be explained by Uriah's otherness. Bathsheba's "Israelite-ness" had to be unambiguous since she had to be the "right" wife of David and the "right" mother of Solomon. David did not hesitate in stealing Bathsheba because the cooperation among Israelite men did not extend to the outsiders; moreover, he did not have to fear any retaliation from Uriah's community. It is Uriah who ruptured Bathsheba's identity and discontinued David's loyalty to the cooperation among men in the exchange of women (property).

---

5 Jacob Chinitz lists nineteen elements that are similar between the two stories; see Chinitz.

Final Remarks

David is one of the most beloved personalities in the Biblical narratives. Although Uriah is not depicted in the Bible as an evil person (in fact, he was a good man), in order to save David's face and to ameliorate his crime, some readers tend to give Uriah bad press. I already mentioned that the rabbis branded Uriah as a rebel. More recently, Herbert Rand characterized Uriah this way:

> [A] career soldier in David's armed forces then engaged in an ongoing war with Ammon.... He lived close to the palace with his lovely wife, Bathsheba. Intensely loyal to David and to his comrades-in-arms, he put duty first and was *insensitive to the needs of his wife* who had to cope with the life of an army wife with *an absentee husband*. (91, italics mine)

This is remarkably similar to the sketch of Uriah's character in the 1951 film, *David and Bathsheba* (starring Gregory Peck and Susan Hayward). Exum observes that Uriah is depicted in the film as "a heartless follower of the letter of the law, and would invoke the law to have his wife stoned if he had reason to suspect her of adultery" (1996:48). In one telling scene, David becomes exasperated when he finds Uriah sleeping in the guards' room instead of sleeping with Bathsheba, and after hearing Uriah's loyalty-to-duty speech for the hundredth time (slight exaggeration), spits these words at Uriah: "You stupid, blind fool." That is exactly how Uriah is portrayed in the film. In the 1985 film, *King David* (starring Richard Gere), Bathsheba describes him as a wife beater/abuser. One scholar calls him "poor, dumb Uriah" (Willimon). Then he makes another uncalled-for remark: "In David's story, the king is the recipient of the greatest narrative interest, while *little nobodies* like Uriah are barely sketched" (224, italics mine).

This is a disturbing and dangerous reading strategy. Once a reader identifies himself or herself with David, then Uriah is easily seen as the "other." There are many ramifications that come with such a practice. Our identity is formed not only by "who we are" but also by "who we are not." And we see the "others" as "who we are not." But we differentiate ourselves from "them" with a dangerous twist. According to Schreiter, those who are inside the group boundaries (namely, "ourselves") are "the people," the civilized, but those who are outside of "us" are the nonpeople, barbarians (63). This makes it easier to make negative stereotypes and to demonize the others. But we have seen in the story that Uriah was not a "barbarian"; instead, it was David who was "barbaric." It was Uriah, not David, who behaved as an Israelite. Uriah was a Yahwist who served in the Israelite army, but he was called a "Hittite" because for some reason he did not "look" like an Israelite and he was killed as a "Hittite."

Uriah's story is familiar to Asian Americans struggling for identity in the U.S. and echoes the tragic story of Vincent Chin. Vincent was a young Chinese American whose mother's great-grandfather was an immigrant railroad laborer in the nineteenth century in the U.S. His father came to the U.S. in 1922 and served in the U.S. army during World War II. But he was killed as a "Jap" because two white auto workers thought that he was a Japanese and blamed him for the loss of their jobs. Incredibly, they did not serve a single day in jail for their crime. It could have easily been Uriah Kim, a Korean American, killed instead of Vincent Chin, a Chinese American, because I would have looked like a Japanese male to the perpetrators as much as Vincent or any other Asian male. After all, we all look alike—Japanese, Chinese, Korean, Vietnamese, Filipino, pick your choice, oh Asian, the "others," non-"Americans."

Works Consulted

Anderson, Arnold A.
    1989   *2 Samuel*. WBC. Dallas: Word.

Bach, Alice
    1993   "Signs of the Flesh: Observations on Characterization in the Bible." *Semeia* 63:61–79.

Bailey, Randall C.
    1990   *David in Love and War: The Pursuit of Power in 2 Samuel 10–12*. JSOTSup 75. Sheffield: JSOT Press.

Berlin, Adele
    1982   "Characterization in Biblical Narrative: David's Wives." *JSOT* 23:69–85.

Bruce, Frederick F.
    1947   *The Hittites and the Old Testament*. London: Tyndale.

Brueggemann, Walter
    1990   *First and Second Samuel*. Interpretation. Louisville: John Knox.

    1997   "Abuse of Command: Exploiting Power for Sexual Gratification." *Sojourners* 26:22–25.

Carmichal, Calum M.
    1985   *Law and Narrative in the Bible*. Ithaca, N.Y.: Cornell University Press.

Chinitz, Jacob
    1997   "Two Sinners." *JBQ* 25:108–13.

Clifford, James
    1994   "Diasporas." *Cultural Anthropology* 9:302–38.

Coggins, Richard J.
　1987　"The Old Testament and the Poor." *ExpTim* 99:11–14.

Espiritu, Yen Le
　1992　*Asian American Panethnicity: Bridging Institutions Identities*. Philadelphia: Temple University Press.

Exum, J. Cheryl
　1993　*Fragmented Women: Feminist (Sub)Versions of Biblical Narrative*. Valley Forge, Pa.: Trinity Press International.

　1996　*Plotted, Shot, and Painted: Cultural Representations of Biblical Women*. Sheffield: Sheffield Academic Press.

Fischer, Alexander Von
　1989　"David und Batseba: ein literarkritischer und motivgeschichtlicher Beitrag zu II Sam 11." *ZAW* 101:50–59.

Fung, Richard
　1995　"Seeing Yellow: Asian Identities in Film and Video." *Amerasia Journal* 21:161–71.

Garsiel, Moshe
　1973　"A Review of Recent Interpretations of the Story of David and Bathsheba, II Samuel 11." *Imm* 2:18–20.

　1993　"The Story of David and Bathsheba: A Different Approach." *CBQ* 55:244–62.

Geertz, Clifford
　1973　*The Interpretation of Cultures: Selected Essays by Clifford Geertz*. New York: Basic Books.

　1983　*Local Knowledge: Further Essays in Interpretive Anthropology*. New York: Basic Books.

Hall, Stuart
　1994　"Cultural Identity and Diaspora." Pp. 392–403 in *Colonial Discourse and Post-Colonial Theory*. Ed. Patrick Williams and Laura Chrisman. New York: Columbia University Press.

Hoffner, Harry A., Jr.
　1994　"Hittites." Pp. 127–55 in *Peoples of the Old Testament World*. Ed. Alfred J. Hoerth, Gerald L. Mattingly, and Edwin M. Yamauchi. Cambridge: Baker.

Hongo, Garrett
　1994　"Asian American Literature: Questions of Identity." *Amerasia Journal* 20:1–8.

Kitano, Harry H. L., and Roger Daniels
　1995　*Asian Americans: Emerging Minorities*. 2d ed. Englewood Cliffs, N.J.: Prentice Hall.

Kuan, Jeffrey
　　2000　　"Diasporic Readings of a Diasporic Text: Identity Politics and Race Relations and the Book of Esther." Pp. 161–73 in *Interpreting beyond Borders*. Ed. Fernando F. Segovia. Sheffield: Sheffield Academic Press.

Lee, Sang Hyun
　　1995　　"Pilgrimage and Home in the Wilderness of Marginality: Symbols and Context in Asian American Theology." *PSB* 16:49–64.

Liew, Tat-siong Benny
　　1999　　*Politics of Parousia: Reading Mark Inter(con)textually*. Biblical Interpretation 42. Boston: Brill.

Lowe, Lisa
　　1991　　"Heterogeneity, Hybridity, Multiplicity: Marking Asian American Differences." *Diaspora* 1:24–44.

Mazar, Benjamin
　　1963　　"The Military Elite of King David." *VT* 13:310–20.

McCarter, P. Kyle, Jr.
　　1984　　*II Samuel*. AB. Garden City, N.Y.: Doubleday.

Mullen, E. Theodore
　　1993　　*Narrative History and Ethnic Boundaries: The Deuteronomistic Historian and the Creation of Israelite National Identity*. Atlanta: Scholars Press.

Na'aman, Nadav
　　1988　　"The List of David's Officers." *VT* 38:71–79.

Nicol, George G.
　　1997　　"The Alleged Rape of Bathsheba: Some Observations on Ambiguity in Biblical Narrative." *JSOT* 73:43–54.

Omi, Michael
　　1989　　"In Living Color: Race and American Culture." Pp. 111–22 in *Cultural Politics in Contemporary America*. Ed. Ian Angus and Sut Jhally. New York: Routledge.

　　1992　　"Elegant Chaos: Postmodern Asian American Identity." Pp. 143–54 in *Asian Americans: Collages of Identities*. Ed. L. C. Lee. Ithaca, N.Y.: Cornell University Press.

Petit, Madeleine
　　1995　　"La rencontre de David et Bersabee (II Sam. 11,2–5,26–27): les interpretations des peres des premiers siecles." Pp. 473–81 in *Selon les Septante*. Ed. Gilles Dorival and Olivier Munnich. Paris: Cerf.

Radhakrishnan, R.
　　1993　　"Postcoloniality and the Boundaries of Identity." *Callaloo* 16:750–71.

Rand, Herbert
　　1996　　"David and Ahab: A Study of Crime and Punishment." *JBQ* 24:90–97.

Rosenberg, Joel
    1989   "The Institutional Matrix of Treachery in 2 Samuel 11." *Semeia* 46:103–16.

Schreiter, Robert J.
    1985   *Constructing Local Theologies.* Maryknoll, N.Y.: Orbis.

Schwartz, Regina M.
    1991   "Adultery in the House of David: The Metanarrative of Biblical Scholarship and the Narrative of the Bible." *Semeia* 54:35–55.

Sternberg, Meir
    1985   *The Poetics of Biblical Narrative: Ideological Literature and the Drama of Reading.* Bloomington: Indiana University Press.

Stoebe, Hans Joachim
    1986   "David und Uria: Uberlegungen zur Uberlieferung von 2 Sam 11." *Biblica* 67:388–96.

Stone, Ken
    1996   *Sex, Honor, and Power in the Deuteronomistic History.* Sheffield: Sheffield Academic Press.

Takaki, Ronald
    1989   *Strangers from a Different Shore: A History of Asian American.* New York: Penguin.

    1993   *A Different Mirror: A History of Multicultural America.* New York: Little, Brown & Co.

Van Seters, John
    1972   "The Terms 'Amorite' and 'Hittite' in the Old Testament." *VT* 22:64–81.

Weir, J. Emmette
    1988   "The Poor and Powerless: A Response to R. J. Coggins." *ExpTim* 100:13–15.

Whybray, Roger N.
    1968   *The Succession Narrative: A Study of II Samuel 9–20; 1 Kings 1 and 2.* Naperville, Ill.: SCM.

Willimon, William H.
    1993   "A Peculiarly Christian Account of Sin: David and Bathsheba and Sin As Conflict of Narratives." *Theology Today* 50:220–28.

Wright, David P.
    1995   "David autem remansit in Hierusalem." Pp. 215–30 in *Pomegranates and Golden Bells.* Ed. David P. Wright, David Noel Freedman, and Avi Hurvitz. Winona Lake, Ind.: Eisenbrauns.

Yee, Gale A.
    1988   "Fraught with Background: Literary Ambiguity in 2 Samuel 11." *Int* 42:240–253.

HOME AS MEMORY, METAPHOR, AND PROMISE IN ASIAN/PACIFIC AMERICAN RELIGIOUS EXPERIENCE

Rachel A. R. Bundang
Union Theological Seminary, New York

ABSTRACT

Whether forced or voluntary, exile is an uprooting, a displacement that is physical, metaphorical, or sometimes even both. Especially key to the preservation and reconstruction of our identity, culture, and community as Asian/Pacific Americans of various ethnicities is the issue of how faith is transmitted from generation to generation. We ask how we can sing our songs in a strange land and whether God still speaks to us here. We struggle to reconcile tradition and memory with new experience and revelation, to negotiate between old and new beliefs and faith practices. We wonder what we are creating, whether this new life is still true to the spirit of "home" and is a thing of integrity.

Contemporary experiences of exile can be informed by a nuanced reading of biblical understandings of exile, and vice versa. Using the text of Jeremiah's letter to the exiles in Babylon (29:4–23), this paper explores the notion of exile as a dialectical site where cultural products such as tradition, memory, and identity are preserved, contested, reconstructed, and sometimes discarded—where a sense of the sacred and of connection with God in unfamiliar territory (whether literal or figurative) is renegotiated. Reading Jeremiah's text in dialogue with a hermeneutic drawn from contemporary Asian American cultural criticism will help address the root question: At what point does exile become diaspora for us? How do displaced communities, be they Jeremiah's exiles or our own among us, maintain a sense of coherence and continuity in our moral agency without forgetting the lessons of rupture?

After stumbling and scratching in miserable frustration for weeks, trying to write this piece and tempted to cut and paste more than seemed fair, I ran across an essay by André Aciman in a recent issue of the *New Yorker*, and it was my saving grace. Aciman himself is, at root, an Egyptian Jew, expelled to Italy as a child, along with his family. Prompted by a reading of Wordsworth's poem "Tintern Abbey" early in his graduate career at Harvard, he embarks on a Proustian journey of his own. His transporting madeleine, though, is not one physical thing or sensation, but rather a memory—and an elusive one at that. In that essay, "Arbitrage," he travels back through times and places that mirror each other in kaleidoscopic infinity: New York, Cambridge, Rome, Alexandria. His memories and experiences—and even dreams and imaginings—knit together delicately, beautifully, inextricably in a seemingly endless web of self-reference. The act of remembering captures him at an eternal yet unfixed point of being everywhere and nowhere, "everywhen" and "nowhen," all at once. Thought it may not be apparent, remembering—and living with the fullness of memory—is to live ever at the cusp of the *déjà vu* because it is *déjà vécu*. As one in exile, Aciman is drawn into the hall of mirrors that memory, history, and tradition construct as labyrinths, and he draws the reader right along with him.

In Asian/Pacific American Christianity, what are our madeleines? What are our keys to understanding what home and memory mean for us if we assume an identity as peoples in exile or diaspora? How valid are these categories for us? How does the Bible speak—or not—to our life-making in the geographically, culturally, and often spiritually alien territories we wander?

As further reflective preparation for this essay, I read and reread the writings of other contemporary exiles and tried to channel Jeremiah through them. If Jeremiah were writing to the exiles today, what would he say? What would become of his directives and promises, his prophecies and calls to remembrance? The sadness, nostalgia, and sense of elusive, ever-fading memory would outweigh the anger, I suspect. I chose to focus here on Jeremiah's letter to the exiles (Jer 29:4–23) not because it has any special significance to Asian American Christian communities—this is not something I know or even have a sure way of knowing—but rather because in those lines I sense historical, emotional, and spiritual resonances with Asian/Pacific American experiences of uprooting and building new homes both physical and spiritual as depicted in our histories, arts, and literatures. Much A/P/A theological reflection thus far has taken the autobiographical or narrative route, often engaging themes of marginality and liminality, of dissonance and interstitiality—of being ever-foreign in, excluded from, in-between, in-both, and in-beyond the multiple worlds they inhabit (Phan: viii; Brock, 1998:183–96). These themes are also reflected in the preaching and other liturgical arts on the one hand, and illustrated in social-scientific studies of congregations or parallel groups on the other; granted, these categories assume a Christian base and may not encompass the breadth of A/P/A religious expression. In any case, the storytelling (or, in some cases, the history telling) provides the opportunity to resurrect and remember, reconstruct and reinterpret. The task of rebuilding, however temporary or permanent, is informed by memories of homes we left behind, dreams of homes we have only heard about in ancestors' and travelers' stories, and experiences of home-making and settlement in an often indefinite present.

Before we embark on an exploration and interpretation of Jeremiah, it is perhaps best to issue my disclaimers. First of all, I write this essay as an ethicist and moral theologian reading the Bible; while I do have some background in Scripture, it is not my primary discipline. The training in ethics, I hope, infuses the piece with careful attention to descriptive and normative tasks alike. Toward these ends, for example, I am aware of the multiple and specific meanings attached to exile and diaspora in reference to the Israel Jeremiah addresses (and its descendants) and will try to respect those particularities (Golan, Mudimbe et al.: 95–116). In reference to Asian/Pacific American communities, though, it is perhaps more appropriate to speak of them as being geographically and culturally in diaspora while being in some species of metaphysical exile, and in most cases I will use "diaspora" and "exile" interchangeably for them. Secondly, I write this as a contemporary Roman Catholic woman steeped in traditions and practices both from the Philippines of my birth and the United States of my upbringing. What this means is that, generally speaking, the Bible does not function in the lives of Catholic communities in ways that I suspect it does in other Christian denominations, nor has it done so historically. Apostolic tradition carries as much weight as does Scripture. In addition, there are multiple theological, liturgical, disciplinary, and devotional traditions that shape and color the landscape of a community's religious life. In other ministerial and recent written work, I have considered, for example, Filipino Catholic devotional practices and observances that made their way to the United States and survive in parishes and small faith communities around the country (Bundang, 1996). Lastly, my own training in Asian/Pacific American history, literature, and cultural criticism has been a labor of love and longing to make peace with family spirits. These are interstitial yet vital bodies of knowledge acquired not in any systematic fashion, as through ethnic studies courses, but rather through independent study and reading. The search for these hidden knowledges continues to be a multilayered exercise in excavation, decoding, and reinterpretation of histories we thought we had learned and understood, of experiences we thought we had had and put behind us.

I

In order to sketch the broad comparisons of the ancient and contemporary exilic communities, we should first consider how each group of hearers of Jeremiah's exhortations understand themselves as a community, as well as their relationship with God. For both groups, there are some important preexile and/or prediaspora marks of religious identity that get changed in the process of *déracination.*

Prior to the Babylonian exile, the nation that David and Solomon had forged together in succession had already been split into two separate monarchies for two hundred years: the ten tribes of Israel to the north,

Judah, along with Benjamin, to the south. In Judah lay Jerusalem, the former capital of all twelve and, consequently, the temple, which housed the ark of the covenant. In an attempt to assert some religious and political primacy of his own, Jeroboam meanwhile converted existing ancient sanctuaries at Dan in the northern end and Bethel at the southern into temples for Israel. There was no longer just one nation, one capital, one political institution, one temple—all in the hand of one God.

For Jeremiah's community—presumably those Judeans in the Deuteronomist camp, the "faithful remnant" eventually exiled in Babylon—centrality, unity, and singularity were of the utmost importance, especially in observance of the covenant in obedience to God. After the division, Israel underwent two hundred years of great political unrest, fueled by bloody intrigue both internal or civil and external, in dalliances with outside powers such as Assyria, Egypt, and Babylon. Among other things, according to Deuteronomist traditions, the northern kings generally danced a little too closely to idolatry and syncretism, drawing religious practices and imagery such as the infamous golden bull from surrounding nations of the ancient Near East who neither recognized nor heeded Yahweh. One suspects, though, that these practices were never too far from the surface anyway. The devolution or degeneration of the ideal of right relation between God and the people Israel discussed in books such as 1 and 2 Kings and 1 and 2 Chronicles provided the fodder for the warnings, pleadings, and counsels of prophets such as Amos and Hosea. Around 720 B.C.E., Assyria eventually moved in and captured Israel for its own. Most of the conquered peoples were relocated. The few who remained behind were assimilated into other groups in the area and into the empire at large.

In Judah, at least, there was still a unity of cult that in turn reflected and promoted social and political unity. Again, according to Deuteronomist traditions, Judah could have succeeded where Israel had failed—but if only they had heeded the prophets' warnings. Their collective self-identity, their self-understanding as a nation and as a people, depended upon "doing right" by God through faithful observance of the covenant, Yahweh's moral will revealed and offered to Israel at Sinai after the Exodus from Egypt. In Judah's last (relative) glory days, Josiah's zealous reforms of ensuring centralized worship and condemning idolatry (which was lapping at the edges and creeping in bit by bit) were intended to renew the people's flagging, tested commitment to the covenant. Besides those connections to God and the covenant, their identity as a people depended on the presence of the ark in the temple in Jerusalem. The safekeeping of the ark sustained Israel through the whole Exodus experience and the establishment of the monarchy. It was the focus of its worship right up until Jerusalem's destruction at the hands of Babylon. David himself had brought the ark to Jerusalem, and Solomon laid it in the sanctuary upon completing the building of the temple. Because the ark was considered both God's divine presence and a place for keeping the law (as written, i.e., the Decalogue), thus the temple—and Jerusalem in particular—were regarded as the sole legitimate locus of worship. Presumably the "substitute" temples in the northern kingdom had nothing at all like the ark.

With Josiah's inauspicious death in battle, the reform movements he initiated dissolved quickly afterward. Judah's subsequent rulers entered into intrigues of their own, trying to preserve the small nation's autonomy by playing Egypt and Babylon off each other. Babylon showed its displeasure in 597 B.C.E., initiating the first deportation from Jerusalem; the royalty and elites, including Josiah's family, were carried away. Zedekiah, the last king and, by most accounts, a puppet ruler, was ultimately ineffective. By siding with Egypt, he brought Nebuchadnezzar's wrath upon himself. Babylon destroyed Jerusalem and herded most of the rest of Judah in the second deportation in 587 B.C.E. The message that the Deuteronomist editors insist on through Jeremiah's story is that Israel's and Judah's persistent infidelity and stubborn disobedience in relation to God, as manifested through their rejection or flouting of the terms of the covenant, are the reasons for the nation's collapse, Jerusalem's destruction, and the people's exile. In other words, they invoked God's wrath and brought the punishment of displacement upon themselves.

At this point, most of Judah—certainly the elites and the elders—were exiled either in Babylon or dispersed to Egypt. It is argued that those who left for Egypt are not considered faithful because they essentially reversed the Exodus, fleeing back into the arms of their former oppressors. The people who remained in the emptiness of Judah were also dismissed, in Jeremiah's mind, because of their insistence on political machinations and collusion with those who did not have the nation's interest at heart—as manifest through faithful observance of the covenant, for example. Now, though, without Jerusalem or the temple to bind the people and a sense of moral/cosmic order together, they were challenged to transform the ways in which they related with God. In other words, how would they find God, and how would God find them? How could they continue to profess their faith? Would their myths and beliefs continue to make sense?

Despite the undoubted trauma that these Jews suffered in being uprooted and displaced to Babylon, they proved creative in marshalling their spiritual and cultural resources to be able to sing their songs in a strange land, enduring for decades. At the very least they were not enslaved as they had been in Egypt generations before. They eventually took Jeremiah's advice to settle down and make the best of things in this meantime. Deprived of land, ark, Jerusalem, and temple—all the elements they thought were essential to their faith and cultic practice—they discovered new ways of forging that sense of moral and cosmic order again. Through religious practices beyond the scope of the temple—such as circumcision and observance of the Sabbath—they rediscovered a sense of unity and found new ways to understand and define themselves as a distinct people again. God was no longer a prisoner of the temple, but rather set free, to be active and present among God's people. In addition, it was during this period that Israel started in earnest to collect its traditions in writing, from the Torah, Deuteronomic History, and prophets, to what had been practiced in the Jerusalem temple, and other things besides. They made a commitment to God through memory, particularly of the covenant. Religious unity would yield an ethnic unity, and eventually a political unity as well. According to Jeremiah, the exile would certainly be long; those seventy years, whether understood metaphorically or factually, had to be endured. But God had promised a new exodus and a restoration of Israel's glory and power, and God would deliver, making *ḥesed* manifest.

Eventually another king took over Babylon. A proponent of religious tolerance, he ultimately allowed the exiles—or, more properly, their descendants—to return "home" to Palestine. Thus came at least the symbolic, if not the definitive, end of the exile. Some left earlier, others left *en masse* as if in a new exodus; some trickled back later, and others never bothered to "return" to the work of rebuilding at least Jerusalem, the temple, and the *political* institutions of the nation. As a people, they had survived the exile remarkably intact, but with great effort, of course.

(It is worth nothing that Robert Carroll [1981; 1986; 1997] and other strict historical critics take great issue time and again with the whole notion of exile, saying that it is an ideologically loaded theological point on the part of the Deuteronomist redactors and that we have used it uncritically and indiscriminately through the ages. Carroll thinks it better to choose more neutral language, such as "deportation" instead of "exile," "migration" instead of "diaspora," "return" instead of "restoration." After all, one would be at pains to justify a restoration without an exile to "avenge.")

In this way, the exile event gave birth to the life of diaspora. And with a marked shift acknowledging the private as well as the public aspects of the religion, these diasporic/exilic sensibilities have come, through the centuries, to shape Judaism as we understand it today.

II

To make the shift and address Asian/Pacific Islander (A/PI) communities for the purposes of this question, one must first acknowledge the inadequacy of using the umbrella term "A/PI," for it obscures the multiplicity and diversity of cultures, peoples, histories, traditions, religions, and locations (social and otherwise) inhabiting and now originating from that vast sweep of land and sea. Though some were more insular and isolated than others, even prior to nationhood in the Western sense, A/PI peoples have had their own histories of conquest, encounter, and intermingling among themselves. For example, there are the Chinese who established a mercantile class in the Philippines only slightly prior to the arrival of Magellan and his crew and to this day have still managed to preserve their distinctness from the general Filipino population. There are the Malays who propagated Islam throughout the islands skirting from the Indian Ocean up into the Pacific. And there is still the complicated relationship of thwarted empire between Japan and many other nations of the continent; China, the two Koreas, and the Philippines come to mind most immediately. One is hard-pressed to limit the scope of the discussion to one single group. At the risk of spreading the comparisons between Judah and Asian America too thinly, I shall choose examples from among those groups who have settled in significant numbers here in the United States primarily during the nineteenth and twentieth centuries. Nonetheless, out of necessity, I will still have to paint in broad swaths to cover great stretches of culture, practice, and time. Not all groups I shall mention have significant Christian populations, for Christianity is not the dominant religion of Asia, except in a very few pockets. But transformations and shifts do take place over time, starting from the moment departure is even considered—and they are inevitable, if a tradition is to be living and authentic, vital and dynamic, not rendered moribund, empty, or sterile, perhaps by a stranglehold of sentiment or unduly rigid attention to form.

Even before significant A/PI diaspora to the West, there was a variety of cultural practices that fit under the broad rubric of religion, philosophy, and spirituality—but not neatly in any single one of those. What we consider Asian religions parallel traditional Native American religions in viewing life holistically, not setting religion apart from life-ways, politics, land, family, and material culture (Brock, 1996:183). In places like East Asia and Indochina, for example, there were melds and overlays of competing and complementary systems: Confucian, Taoist, Buddhist, and shamanistic or other indigenous traditions. Sometimes the practices and observances overlapped or even seemed to conflict, at least on the surface. Ancestor worship or veneration figured greatly for many; for others, love of and respect for nature was important. And there was likewise a variety of models for relationships between men and women and between the human and the divine (as such), especially if one includes the great diversity of practices, Hindu or not, in the Indian subcontinent and Islam scattered throughout nations and peoples. For example, the codified patriarchy of Confucian cultures could not be more different from the practical equality between the sexes—and even matriarchy and matrilineality for some—among many tribes of the Philippines prior to the Spanish conquest. Cultic practices and self-understandings on this vast continent, as in

Israel, were hardly static; at the very least, they could not be entirely uniform or monolithic.

The multiple A/PI diasporas of the past two centuries owe much of their complex existence, directly and indirectly, to imperial economic and/or politically interventionist policies of Western nations. There have long been legal and illegal contract workers—a lure for some, a dire necessity for others—such as Chinese railroaders of the American west; Filipinos in the U.S. military, medical establishment, and domestic work corps; Koreans and most other groups on the Hawaiian plantations; and, more recently, South Asians in high-tech industries. In the early years of these influxes, exclusionary practices that discouraged movements of entire households often led to gender imbalances in the immigrant population, with generally more men than women coming for work. This, of course, would have an impact on what cultural practices were continued, transmitted, and transformed—and how. More recently too, there are also the economic and political refugees who fled Vietnam, Laos, and Cambodia in the wake of the war; the Philippines during the Marcos dictatorship; and the various crackdowns in China. Regardless of the reason for the displacement, it probably makes more sense to consider oneself in exile, especially in the seed and first generation. Only in later generations, perhaps, can the term "diaspora" be used accurately and legitimately. "Exile" implies that there was an element of force or coercion—and hence limited agency—in the displacement. Even when considered in the metaphoric sense, the rootedness and looking backward at home are still very palpable and present. A person's primary identity is located in that (usually) singular experience of home. "Diaspora," on the other hand, has more latitude and distance, both in terms of time and sentiment. It makes itself felt in multiple ways within what is ostensibly a single homogeneous community. It implies that one has a choice of staying or going and allows for the possibility that one may or may not have loyalties to the ultimate place of origin. Certainly someone in diaspora may feel rooted and at home right where she is, embodying a transnational identity (manifest, for example, in maintaining dual citizenship), a *métissage identitaire et culturel* (Mudimbe and Engel: 4–5), a dual consciousness. As the experience of "homeland" fades into the stuff of imagination and history, ties to that ancestral home often become more abstract and tenuous. Besides all this, diaspora raises nagging questions of authenticity and (that dreaded word!) otherness in ways that do not prove as problematic for those "merely" in exile. Richard Roberts notes aptly, "The central question is the extent to which the culture of the communities in dispersal simply reflects that of their homeland, real or imagined, or produces culture and knowledge distinct from that of their homeland" (182). A tangled web of continuities and discontinuities it is indeed.

Despite these hardships and variables, A/PI communities in diaspora have managed to hold on to cultural (religious) practices from one generation to the next, as the construction of collective and self-identities have changed over time. Oddly enough, sometimes those in diaspora will cling more tightly to a practice or generally be more observant than will someone "at home" because it serves as a marker of authenticity. That person "at home" does not need to feel the added security of keeping things the same in transition because she is not challenged that way. A practice may remain the same, but the meaning will change because the context and the needs of the community are different. Drawing upon the experience of the twice-colonized (by Spain and the United States), still-colonized experience of the Philippines as an example (and for this reason, it may be a special case), I shall point out a few things that marked religious and self-identity "at home" and how they translate in a diasporic situation.

In *Contracting Colonialism*, Vicente Rafael writes that Spain colonized the Philippines by literally reordering the natives' world. From the division of land and the establishment of the town square with the church in the center, right down to language instruction that would change one's relationship to the body by recasting understandings of sex and pleasure, the Tridentine Christian worldview thus cultivated was turned inward and reinscribed. It was what an anthropologist called the practice of "deterritorialization." The natives learned well what the friars taught, almost to the point of losing their own traditions. Despite the conquest, memories and practices of indigenous religions still resurface at times and get incorporated both as autochthonous/indigenous expressions of lived faith and as "new" religious traditions forged in colonized society.

Five hundred years later, as Filipino immigrants head east to the United States and elsewhere in the world, perhaps the most striking thing is how, among the many who still remain Catholic (they either stay or drop out entirely, for conversion to another denomination is rare), so little in attitude and practice has changed. In some respects, it is as if Vatican II had never happened. Devotions to Mary, Jesus, and a host of saints remain popular; she intercedes for the lowly, he suffers with the suffering, and the rest are, broadly speaking, travel companions for the journey. The Eucharist is not as important as showing persistent faith and devotion. The body is a temptation waiting to happen. Obedience and humility before God and the hierarchy are required at all times.

Granted, these are broad strokes. But they show that, as remarked earlier, the seed generation tends to cling tightly to received values, traditions, and ways of being as markers of authenticity. In the case of the Filipino Catholic community in the United States, it takes the shape, for example, of seeking space for Our Lady of Antipolo (also known as Our Lady of Peace and Good Voyage) amidst Guadalupe and all the other "national-ethnic

Marys" in the National Shrine of the Immaculate Conception in Washington, D.C.; or hosting the Santo Niño of Cebu (Infant Jesus of Prague) for a week of devotion in one's home; or reconfiguring the *Simbang Gabi* (early morning Masses in the octave before Christmas) for suburban automobile culture. It takes the work of succeeding generations—as they make more of a home in diaspora while still keeping an eye turned toward the original ancestral home—to come to terms with the magnitude of change demanded by the worlds in conflict and to see the transformation to fruition. As they become more exposed to Western individualism, it becomes more important for them to discern their beliefs and faith journeys for themselves. The faith *per se* may not go away, but the shape it takes probably will.

III

Jeremiah's letter to the exiles gives commandments, promises, and warnings, all within a larger discussion of what constitutes true and false prophecy. In applying this text to Asian American communities, the warnings and prophecy are not as important as the commandments and promises. In being told as a people how to survive and even thrive in the state of exile, heeding those commandments demonstrates fidelity to God through a covenant relationship and committed faith in God's promises of favor, of restoration, of a long-awaited homecoming at last.

Upon first reading of the passage, especially the opening section 29:4–7, it would indeed seem that Jeremiah is prescribing assimilation as Israel's hope for survival in exile. On one level, it is as if he tells them to live in denial of their uprooted and disordered state, their exile, their being away from all that they have ever known. How could one possibly be carted away from home, presumably unwillingly, and be expected to live "normally," building houses, planting gardens, and raising families as if nothing had changed? Were they not to feel anger or grieve their loss, even in some small ways? Moreover, what sense does it make to promote pointedly the welfare of one's captors—except, perhaps, in self-interest?

Yet on another level, though, this exile is not to be a passive waiting for deliverance; after all, they may be waiting a while, with those metaphorical seventy years. Israel's experience of separation from God is hardly empty or pointless. Like a trial separation or détente in any difficult relationship, it is instead an invitation—only for a finite period of time—to contrition, reflection, and rediscovery by revisiting the small gestures and rituals that give shape to life.

This episode must be seen against the backdrop of conflicting traditions and powers being contested within Israel/Judah before and during the exile. As mentioned earlier in this essay, those exiled in Babylon considered themselves the true and faithful remnant, compared to those who were eventually dispersed to Egypt or certainly those who stayed put in Palestine. Brueggemann writes, "In his pro-Babylonian posture, Jeremiah concludes that the ones exiled are the bearers of Judah's hope for the future and the special object of God's attentive love and concern.... It is to [them] that the letter is addressed, the ones who count for the future" (1998:256). In addition, this was the point during Judah's decline following the first deportation when so-called false prophets and leaders among the exiles (whose stories are told more fully in surrounding chapters and verses) were advocating rebellion in order to escape Babylon and return home immediately. As the true prophet, however, Jeremiah recognized the religious and political instability of the period and the situation (with Israel's and Judah's takeovers practically inevitable), and perhaps he spoke out of a desire to keep the exiles safe and surviving just as much as out of righteous anger and judgment on God's behalf. Perhaps he wanted to be sure that something fresh yet still true to the spirit and the demands of the covenant would rise from the community's ashes left behind in Judah, and this was his way of sowing those seeds. Naturally he also predicted the violent death and utter destruction of those false prophets and any who followed them (vv.15–23).

The forms of resistance and negotiation that Jeremiah advised the exiles to take up hardly amounted to grand public acts of armed rebellion; in fact, those are precisely the things he sought to discourage. Instead, they lay in wholehearted prayer and, interestingly enough, in the small, private, domestic, sometimes guarded acts of caring for home and family. This was not out of a commitment to or desire for nonviolence *per se*, for Jeremiah knew all too well that he lived in a perilous time, and he could envision all too clearly the impending destruction and displacement. As a small, vulnerable, and ever-foreign community, they lived in the heart of another empire and could not withdraw entirely. God still expected them to contribute to Babylon's welfare while they were there. Yet in the hopeful acts of planting roots and growing where they were; in remembering their beliefs, practices, and God's faithfulness in past promises; in committing anew to the covenant through day-to-day living—in all these things the exiles would find more than enough resources for resisting despair. On the surface, these acts might look like passive denial of one's very real alienation, perhaps even like submission to or acceptance of it. However, they reveal a making the *de facto* choice to live and persist, and the people would negotiate the challenge to survive based on those strengths. In effect, by setting themselves apart within their larger society and not conforming with the ways of Babylon, by quietly keeping their own traditions, by accommodating without assimilating, they asserted their identity. They reinscribed and reconstructed their own sphere of agency and preserved a measure of independence. God assured the people of God's continuing presence in a land and situation distinctly unlike home in Jerusalem. In this way, God's grace and strength would find and sustain the people precisely in those intimate settings. And at the appointed time, they really would be able to go home.

The "assimilation" that Jeremiah proposes for the exiles at the beginning of this passage is not a call to them for an outright surrender or denial of their history, practices, or any part of their way of life in a potentially hostile and life-threatening situation. Rather, it is made a point of assertion and insistence: that they are to be as they were, to live as they had been—or as much as possible, given the circumstances—and exceed that, even to the point of seeking Babylon's good. Brueggemann (1998:259), for example, explores the layered and interlaced meanings of *shalom* as both task and gift for the people in exile, charged with setting themselves aright before God. The mandate to multiply and not decrease echoes God's initial covenant with Abraham and the later multiplication of the Israelites in Egypt prior to the Exodus. Likewise the promise of favor and deliverance echoes elements of the Exodus story: God would hear the cries of God's people and eventually lead them out, home to the promised land. From the quiet humility of tending their own gardens and building solid lives of faith rooted in the covenant while being held captive by an outside power (although not enslaved), they would rise again, emerge even stronger, and be able to go home.

Judah's resistance and negotiation of challenges to survival in exile is to be rooted firmly in their identity as people of the covenant—as God's people. They need only rediscover for themselves what that means and how to be observant in this different, less public, more intimate way. True, they were sent into exile, but they were not forgotten. Earlier, in the broad historical sketch, I discussed in a little more detail how this experience gave forth to a flowering of religious activity among the exiles. It was this embracing of and wrestling with their traditions that gave them purpose and gave them life. The reorientation demanded by being away from home, whether in exile or diaspora, physically and metaphorically, afforded them both a freedom *from* the forms and ideas to which they were so attached and a freedom *to* imagine and create anew. There are multiple lessons to draw from Jeremiah's letter to the exiles, but three are most important in relation to the question of assimilation versus resistance and negotiation:

1. God is always present and certainly free to live and act beyond any confines we can set, even one so honorable as the temple.

2. One can survive a situation, no matter how bad or intolerable, if God wills it; God's promises are real and to be trusted. If God is willing and capable of one Exodus, another one surely must be possible.

3. Faithfulness to the covenant brings life.

For any community—and especially a community undergoing as great a stress as exile— tradition may serve as an anchor to identity and autonomy. But traditions undoubtedly change over time, sometimes in outward form, sometimes in inner substance and meaning. Whether for Judah in Babylon or A/PI communities in North America, Christian or not, living out memories of home and adhering to practices of home, even with adjustments and reorientations that are sometimes necessary, are ultimately acts not only of faith but of sustaining, creative hope. The exile we first view as judgment may yet turn out to be a gift, revealing yet another face of the sacred that was never gone in the first place. In the heart of our pain, alienation, wandering, and loss, God remembers the promises made to us, speaks to us, and cherishes us still.

IV

With this reading of Jeremiah in mind, there are lessons I would draw for the transformation of present-day Asian American communities—immigrant or not—in relation to God, one another, and the world beyond their enclaves. For this portion, I shall rely on some critical reflections by Jane Naomi Iwamura on Asian American religious identity. Iwamura's particular contribution to that project is her revisiting Asian religious, philosophical, and spiritual traditions—specifically, ancestor worship, in her case—from an interdisciplinary Asian American viewpoint committed to community engagement. She describes the tasks as not sequential, but rather simultaneous and threefold: *retrieval, reexamination, and reconstruction*. In a sense, this triple task is what the episode of exile and the ongoing experience of diaspora have compelled Israel to do in order to address—and perhaps even heal somewhat—the multiple ruptures engendered by those experiences: moral, cosmic, social, and so forth. More than a hermeneutic or even a description of a method (for articulating an ethic and for living life critically yet mindfully, among other things), I would argue that these lessons apply as well to contemporary immigrant communities—A/PI and otherwise—faced with the challenge of traversing the sometimes vast psychic, spiritual, and cultural distance between "home" and "where we are now"—of transforming their relationships and self-understandings in exile or diaspora. It presents a choice between life or death—or at least, survival or death, with this "death" to be understood both metaphorically and literally. The experience of transformation may be disorienting and hard work, but it need not be ultimately destructive.

Before launching into an explanation of Iwamura's three-part prescription, let us remind ourselves, even if only briefly, of other factors that bear upon the realities that present-day immigrant communities face. First of all, we must be clear whether the terms "exile" and "diaspora," if they are used at all, are being used as religious or philosophical metaphors or in a sociological sense. Regardless of how they are used, these are contestable terms, and it makes a difference whether they are self-appropriated or imposed from outside. (For example, it is entirely possible that an Asian American evangelical Christian would not think of herself as exiled or diasporic at all in the racial/ethnic sense but instead in terms of standing for life choices not necessarily in tune with the currents of mainstream culture. Walter Brueggemann has spoken of Western white Protestants considering themselves cultural exiles in almost exactly this way!) Secondly, if the individual or community is confronted with having to refashion or come to a new understanding of what identity and community mean (whether individually or collectively), the challenge is to negotiate the loss of one way of life—a culture—without becoming "de-cultured" or painfully over-assimilated, without sacrificing religious and ethnic identity in the process, assuming that those are goods to be kept and cultivated. Regarding A/PI communities in the United States specifically, another point one must keep in mind is the inherent religious plurality of A/PI America and its alternative, that is, not always Christian, religious sensibilities. To add yet another layer of complexity, many among the various ethnic groups—especially those who have entered since the Immigration Act of 1965—hold transcultural, transnational identities, particularly in the first few generations. Maintaining some kind of relationship with the mother tongue—and consequently the mother land—still matters, both literally and figuratively.

Retrieval starts with the simple (and sometimes dangerous) act of remembering something of value—or at least, not forgetting—a fact or an idea, a ritual or a recipe, a teaching or a text, for instance. But it is more than the rote memory of practices ingrained in our bones, and it is certainly more than official or institutional teachings handed down and regurgitated for their own sake. In the hunger for more substance, for more of a taste of home—indeed for the full sensuality of what home is, was, and can be—we find ourselves paying more attention to the heart and subtexts of everyday things, of the little acts passed from generation to generation. Jung Ha Kim explains in brief the power of retrieval:

> To a person or community in need of recovering a sense of subjectivity due mainly to historical erasure, invisibility, and constant misrepresentation, self-reflections and autobiographies are viable means of reclaiming wholeness, rather than producing privacy. To a people or culture that resists drawing clear boundaries between the dead and the living, the past and the present, self-reflections and biographies reveal stories of people, rather than of an autonomous self. (111)

In exile and diaspora, Israel and Asian America both travel the same terrain. Israel, for example, finds comfort in its rich traditions—as embodied in rituals, texts, and food, among other things. They are concrete, grounding moments in which God's goodness can easily be recognized. They bring back a sense of the familiar. They are a soul food of hope, pointing toward an ideal, pointing homeward. And as markers of "home," they can be sweeter and richer (or sometimes even more bittersweet) than in their original setting. Likewise, the contemporary diasporas of A/PI and Latino communities in the United States, for example, have kept their own rituals—again, not only the official, institutional stuff, but also popular, domestic, "diffused" religion—in the veneration of ancestors through Day of the Dead festivities in cemeteries or through the building of home altars ornate and primitive, peppered with *santos* as well as gifts and petitions to them; in according proper deference to elders; in making pilgrimages to sites important to the life of a community; in re-enacting *pasyons* (the Philippine Holy Week procession depicting Jesus *en route* to the cross, complete with eerily masked and cloaked, self-flagellating *penitentes* calling for repentance) and *posadas* (the Mexican Christmas tradition of caroling with Joseph and Mary from house to house, looking for a place to stop, rest, and give birth). In thousands of acts like these are the ways in which we recognize, maintain contact, and surround ourselves with sacred presence every day.

But remembrance, retrieval, is not enough. Another vital component of transformation is *reexamination*. Simply put, it is making use of that critical gaze. For the well-being of the community (and the individual), it is necessary to make an honest assessment—as far as is possible—of what the situation is, how we got here, what is the same or different, what do we need, what do we keep or discard, what still makes sense or no longer does, and so forth. How, for instance, should one reconcile new values that conflict with what we know, what we have learned, how we have always done things? Should everything be "translated," or would that profane the original language somehow? Is there something in what we have retrieved that perhaps oppresses and imprisons on one level yet sustains on another, or oppresses one part of the community and not another? For example, how does a Chinese American daughter meet the expectation of caring for an aging parent while still struggling with her own financial demands on limited resources? Or how can so many Filipino Americans indulge in and justify to themselves the guilty pleasure of beauty pageants? Or what do these older generations of Filipinos get out of participating in prayer groups whose language and attitude seem not to acknowledge that Vatican II reforms ever even happened? In the case of *penitentes* in the Philippines, what does that say about the attitudes we learned regarding victimization and suffering as being necessary, inevitable, even endearing to God? How do we balance the pull of community from the home culture with the siren of individual self-interest from this one? Can we imagine doing what matters most to us in another way that still makes sense and holds dignity and integrity, yet without inflicting (as much) pain or baggage? The trick lies in treating both the cultural store of the past and the cultural promise of the present and future with due care and respect, all the while acknowledging honestly and unflinchingly where each has shortcomings and where each can afford compromise and transformation.

The result of this gathering and critical evaluation comes together in *reconstruction,* which is the union of imagination and memory being made concrete. It is a *bricolage,* a work of building according to that new vision and making something new out of all those broken pieces and fragments. One calls to mind Gadamer's notion of the fusion of horizons that ideally should take place between the reader and the text, each mutually transforming the other. That is the work to be done here; but in this case the reader may be an individual or community, and the text is a cultural/religious practice, belief, or tradition being questioned. So what will it take to get there? Therein lies the strategy for survival, and it becomes clarified in the process of working through the question or problem. These are things that immigrant communities—and communities in transition, in general—have been doing all along, even up to the present, although some with more difficulty than others. In the triple task of retrieval, reexamination, and reconstruction, there is a temptation on either side: that one clings too tightly to what is known and chokes what little may be left; or that one cast the past aside too readily. A critically constructive viewpoint is necessary in order to negotiate successfully the temptation to reject as well as accept changes uncritically.

Religion is not just a cognitive activity (beliefs) or a verbal commodity (confessions and creeds) articulated and systematized as "faith." It also lives in the everyday practices of people, whether immigrant or not. The embeddedness of the sacred, side by side with the profane, can make the process of transformation messy and often prone to unintentional offenses as well as hard choices. What would round out Iwamura's paradigm for an immigrant community, especially one faced with the challenge of transformation (whether they would claim to be in exile, diaspora, or neither), is a further lesson from Jeremiah: that prudent discernment with God at the forefront of the concern is vital in determining what course of action would be most sustaining and life-giving for them in relation to God, each other, and the world beyond themselves.

Works Consulted

Aciman, André
    1998   "Arbitrage." *The New Yorker,* July 10, 2000: 34–39.

Brock, Rita Nakashima
    1996   "Response: Clearing the Tangled Vines." *Amerasia Journal* 22:181–86.

1998   "Interstitial Integrity: Reflections toward an Asian American Woman's Theology." Pp. 183–96 in *Introduction to Christian Theology: Contemporary North American Perspectives.* Ed. Roger A. Badham. Louisville: Westminster/John Knox.

Brueggemann, Walter
1986   *Hopeful Imagination: Prophetic Voices in Exile.* Minneapolis: Fortress.

1997   *Cadences of Home: Preaching among Exiles.* Louisville: Westminster/John Knox.

1998   *A Commentary on Jeremiah: Exile and Homecoming.* Grand Rapids, Mich.: Eerdmans.

Bundang, Rachel A. R.
1996   "This Is Not Your Mother's Catholic Church: When Filipino Catholicism Meets American Culture." in *The Brown Papers* 3:1.

1997   "Sojourners, Women Warriors, Exiles: Faith, Memory, and Survival among Filipina Immigrants to the United States." Thesis, M.Div. Harvard Divinity School. Presented at the Third Annual Filipino Studies Conference, University of California, Los Angeles. (Revised and expanded for panels on Asian American Catholics at the annual meetings of the American Catholic Historical Association/American Historical Association [ACHA/AHA, January 1998] and the Association for Asian American Studies [AAAS, June 1998].)

1998a   "'May You Storm Heaven with Your Prayers': Devotions to Mary and Jesus in Filipino American Catholic Life." Unpublished paper presented at the Asian North American Religion, Culture, and Society Group, AAR/SBL Annual Meeting. (Revised and presented at the Asian Pacific American Religions Initiative [APARI] annual meeting, June 2000.)

1998b   Panel, "Religious Structures and Community Building." Fourth Annual Asians in America Conference, New York University.

Carroll, Robert P.
1981   *From Chaos to Covenant: Prophecy in the Book of Jeremiah.* New York: Crossroad.

1986   *Jeremiah: A Commentary.* Philadelphia: Westminster.

1997   "Raised Temple and Shattered Vessels: Continuities and Discontinuities in the Discourses of Exile in the Hebrew Bible." *JSOT* 75:93–106.

Golan, Daphna, V. Y. Mudimbe, et al.
1999   "The Jewish Diaspora, Israel, and Jewish Identities: A Dialogue." *South Atlantic Quarterly* 98:95–116.

Iwamura, Jane Naomi
1996   "Homage to Ancestors: Exploring the Horizons of Asian American Religious Identity." *Amerasia Journal* 22:162–67.

Kim, Jung Ha
1999 "'But Who Do You Say That I Am?' (Matt 16:15): A Churched Korean American Woman's Autobiographical Inquiry." Pp. 103–12 in *Journeys at the Margin: Toward an Autobiographical Theology in American-Asian Perspective*. Ed. Peter C. Phan and Jung Young Lee. Collegeville: Order of St. Benedict.

Mudimbe, V. Y., and Sabine Engel
1999 "Introduction." *South Atlantic Quarterly* 98:1–8.

Phan, Peter C.
1999 "Preface." Pp. vii–ix in *Journeys at the Margin: Toward an Autobiographical Theology in American-Asian Perspective*. Ed. Peter C. Phan and Jung Young Lee. Collegeville: Order of St. Benedict.

Rafael, Vicente L.
1994 *Contracting Colonialism: Translation and Christian Conversion in Tagalog Society under Early Spanish Rule*. Durham, N.C.: Duke University Press.

Roberts, Richard
1999 "Construction of Cultures in Diaspora: African and African New World Experiences." *South Atlantic Quarterly* 98:177–90.

Shifts in Reading the Bible: Hermeneutical Moves among Asian Americans

Roy I. Sano
Pacific School of Religion

ABSTRACT

Asian American Protestant Christians changed their reading of the Bible as they became aware of changes in their contexts. The article focuses on changes in race relations covering the last half of the twentieth century. Involvements in racial movements made them aware of the cognitive dissonance between a portion of the Bible they had used and their situation. They proceeded with the opening created by two critical methods to bring their use of the Bible more in synch with their context. First, this opening is created by redaction criticism and its variations, which focused more sharply on the structures and styles of literature in the biblical text as we have it. Thus Asian Americans listened to the witnesses in the Bible. However, they recognized that no individual or faith community could process the full range of the Bible at all times and all places. They therefore depended on an opening created by a second critical method, namely, canonical criticism. While canonical criticism acknowledged the authority of the "orthodox canon," Asian Americans sought to uncover the "canon within the canon," that is, their *"operating* canon" that caused the dissonance. They explored the Bible for situations analogous to theirs and consulted the witnesses to who God is and what God says and does in those kinds of situations. When they found clues, those portions became a "functional canon" within the canon to shape faith and practice in that context. The essay concludes with a theological explanation why the particularity of method and focus are both inevitable and necessary.

Introduction

"Where you sit determines where you stand." This line attributed to the late Senator Hubert H. Humphrey applies to reading the Bible as it does to politics. Where we "sit," or are situated, shapes what as well as how we read in the Bible. This essay tracks shifts in reading the Bible among Asian American Protestants as we became aware of changes in our context. I readily acknowledge my debt to companions on the way as new readings of the

Bible emerged among us in the last half of the previous century. I assume, however, my responsibility for the slants I take on the changes selected for this essay, and especially for the questions raised in this abbreviated account.¹ After describing the shifts I will address the questions raised in these changes.

From the Personal to the Social

I begin with a shift from a personal to a social focus. A change in the Bible I used will illustrate a change in the use of the Bible. When I was in college in the early 1950s, I purchased a KJV Bible. I had difficulty separating the "onion skin" pages in my Oxford edition, bound in black Moroccan leather. With use, however, some of the pages turned into something like well-worn fabric easily separated when locating a single verse. As an evangelical, vintage late 1940s and early 1950s, I confirmed my personal faith by studying the Pauline Epistles. To grow in my faith, I prayed the Psalms because Martin Luther said they were his "prayer book." Since the Pauline Letters and the Psalms helped me engage God in concrete and tangible ways, these sections were understandably well worn. They had become my "canon within the canon."

Changes in reading the Bible occurred because of new analyses of the situations we faced. Teachers at Union Theological Seminary (New York City) from 1954 to 1957 described the issues we faced in the broader world beyond our individual struggles and what we could do in those developments. They drew heavily from the prophets who witnessed to God's action in the public arena during their time of nation building. We also turned to the Synoptic Gospels because they spoke of transformations that took place outside the sacrosanct walls of the church. The RSV Bible I started to use in seminary became well worn in those sections. While a pastor in the late 1950s, I noticed the difference between the two Bibles. I became aware that changes in situations had led me from the canon operating in my evangelical days to a new, more "functional canon" within the canon.

---

¹ I am using the first-person plural here to acknowledge other people's input and to counteract the autonomous individualism that is so prevalent in the U.S. While I may have originated most of the hermeneutical moves, I have been in constant conversation with many other Asian American groups that have affirmed my perspective. That is not to say, of course, that every single Asian American will agree with what I write here.

This essay offers illustrations of the hermeneutical moves outlined in Sano, forthcoming. In a book under preparation, I am addressing a wider range of issues beyond racism in a theology of mission. It will elaborate the "spiral" in the methodology with citations of works consulted for contextual analysis, hermeneutical shifts, and implications drawn for theology and ethics.

From Universality to Particularity

In the 1950s and 1960s, most Asian Americans sought integration in the U.S. We wanted to enter the dominant patterns in residence and education, employment and income. We also wanted to be remembered for our contributions to the larger society. In sum, we assumed that if we became like them, whites would like us.

By the mid-1960s the dream of the "melting pot" turned sour. Even after we made gains in becoming more like whites, we still remained different. Periodically we heard the clear message that we were outsiders. We saw that we paid too high a price. We put aside our distinct ethnic identity as we moved into desirable neighborhoods, attended better schools, found better jobs, and raised our income.

By the late 1960s, the ethnic studies movements on college and university campuses signaled a dramatic shift. Racial ethnic minorities wanted classes and faculty, programs and departments, to nurture their unique identities, to recognize their place in history, and to celebrate the enormous contributions their people made.

Asian American Christians who joined these struggles came to see how their faith was out of line with the new energies and drives stirring in them. They recognized they had tried to relive the story about Ruth. Although she was a Moabite, a people much despised by Israelites, Ruth still wanted to move to Israel. Her aspirations summarized Asian American drive for integration. Ruth wanted to "make their God her God" (1:16), a graphic summary of acculturation into the fundamental values of the host culture. Ruth also wanted to "make their people her people" (1:16), a vivid sign of assimilation. The most important point in her life is Ruth's contribution to Israel. She became the great-grandmother of the priestly king, David (4:13–22), a model for ancient Jewish identity. Ruth symbolized the divine presence and support for immigrants who sought integration.

Asian Americans participating in the strikes for ethnic studies and in denominational ethnic minority caucuses required a more functional story. They found an alternative in Esther's story. She lived in an alien land, among an oppressed and exploited minority. And yet, she succeeded in making "their people her people." Esther did so by concealing her Jewish identity. In quick succession, she won a "beauty contest," became a queen, and moved into the royal palace (2:5–18). When she discovered a plot to exterminate her people, Esther reclaimed her Jewish identity. She risked her life by breaking protocol, tantamount to a law, and barged into the royal court without an invitation. Esther demanded the king remove the decree against her people. He did so and Esther saved her people.

The story of Esther reminded us that we may make advance in the power structures by denying our identity and looking attractive, but we still faced a daunting task. Implicit and explicit "decrees" continue to threaten our people and often require risky actions that break decorum, if not laws.

We learned from the literature associated with Esther that other constructive efforts were necessary. Although 1 and 2 Chronicles, Ezra, and Nehemiah did not appeal to most Christians in the U.S., they bore witness to God participating in the recovery of a distinct ethnic identity. Like the writers of 1 and 2 Chronicles, we rewrote our history, dramatized it in stylized re-enactments through music and dances, plays and movies. We also restated our values and ethical ideals in our version of "laws," based on our religious and cultural heritage. Like the returning exiles, we built walls around our holy city or hallowed spaces, and also restored our temples. We therefore resisted domestic and foreign investors who planned to demolish historic ethnic neighborhoods for urban "renewal" projects. Protesters, for example, virtually built a protective wall around the International Hotel in San Francisco in 1968. While it was a hovel by tourist standards, it still operated as the only available living arrangement for elderly Filipino men. They never married and had no families to care for them, since U.S. immigration laws excluded Filipina (women) and antimiscegenation laws prohibited them from marrying outside their race. They found community in the International Hotel.[2]

We must, however, address the ethnocentrism and ethnic cleansing in the stories we reclaimed. We can only say in this setting that many witnesses in the scriptures overstate or overextend what is valid and thus misrepresent God's intentions. Again, as in the case of other witnesses in the scriptures, we try to see behind the distortions who God is and what God is saying and doing of value in a given setting.

From the Prophetic to an Apocalyptic Vision

In addition to ethnicity, our ethnic theology focused on liberation. When we turned to this aspect of our efforts, we discovered inadequacies in the way we read the prophets and the Gospels. While progressive theologians and ethicists called for improvements *in* the existing structures, liberation theologians called for changes *of* the structures themselves.

Behind the difference in our calling was a different reading of our situation. Our mentors operated with a "postrevolutionary" bourgeois consciousness. In the language of the French Revolution, the bourgeois succeeded in liberating

---

[2] Accounts of the events surrounding the I-Hotel can be found in David Palumbo-Liu: 274–75; and William Wei: 23–24.

themselves from the domination of royalty, nobility, and the church. By overturning these "three estates" in the revolution, they took charge of governing themselves. No principalities or powers would operate over them.

By contrast, ethnic movements for liberation recognized the emergence of a new set of principalities and powers through individuals, institutions, and ideologies. Even if we had risen above the poverty line, we still lived under a power line. If these structures manipulated us, they managed white progressive supporters in the struggles. If these centers of power over us oppressed and exploited us, they outwitted and outmaneuvered white middle-class progressive friends. Despite denials, white middle-class progressives had becama a "kept people." Failure to recognize these realities of the power arrangements induced a false consciousness among our activist friends.

Our earlier shifts to the prophets of nationhood and the Gospels therefore caused a cognitive dissonance with our reading of the emerging context. As indicated earlier, from the late 1960s, we turned quite intentionally to Jewish witnesses in the exilic and postexilic period, because we felt we were in a comparable situation. That is why we turned to the priestly literature. As times changed, we began experimenting with the apocalyptic witnesses when Israel lived under alien powers, either in the diaspora or in their own land. Two features of the apocalyptic witness spoke for our situation. First, the apocalyptic writers acknowledged principalities and powers effectively operating over them with little regard for their welfare. We could therefore not buy into the demythologizing enterprise prominent in the 1960s and 1970s. While we did not operate with the three-storied universe writers of the Gospels supposedly lived in, we had our version of another three-storied universe. If we are on earth and God is in the heavens, intermediaries between ourselves and God controlled us more directly and immediately.

Second, the apocalyptic perspective saw very different stages in history moving in on us. The periodization of history, which was associated with the dispensational reading of the apocalyptic books and turned off many biblical scholars and theologians, was the very feature that appealed to us. We were not interested in improving the existing structures but yearned for a drastic change, a different era in human history.

We therefore turned to Daniel and Revelation to bring our efforts with God in synch with the divine mission in those situations. When I participated on a United Church of Christ panel in 1972 and mentioned this shift, I thought two highly respected theological voices in the mid-third of the last century were going to fall out of their chairs. They were scandalized by the move. (I treasure the memory of these two figures too much to mention them by name.) Quite by contrast, when uses of Esther, Daniel, and Revelation were mentioned a year or two later at a gathering of Asian American United

Methodists, Korean Americans were amazed by an ironic coincidence. A Japanese American was proposing use of these very books that Japanese colonial officials had prohibited Korean preachers to use. Quite by accident, or by an element of God's guidance, a Japanese American was led to the same sections of the Bible for an analogous situation in the U.S., albeit not as horrendous as the Japanese occupation of Korea (1895–1945). Even if we were out of step with much-admired teachers, we picked up the wisdom of Korean Christians who went right ahead and used the apocalyptic writers, because they clarified who God is and what God is saying and doing in those situations.

From Covenant to Exodus before Covenant

The promise of a very different era in the apocalyptic writers naturally led to other stories of God's liberation in human history. We appreciated the renewed attention to the exodus among biblical scholars and the restoration of liberation in theology by such figures as James Cone.

Attention to liberation highlighted the preoccupation with reconciliation in Euro-American theology. Selected theologians in the early church and the Reformation included redemption or liberation in the work of Christ for salvation. And yet, the focus in many major contemporary theologians on reconciliation, or at-one-ment, in the work of Christ effectively eliminates references to redemption or liberation from concrete expressions of evil forces beyond our control.

What was most important is that exodus, or redemption, precedes the covenant or reconciliation among the people, and between them and their God. Even if the two events originally belonged to two distinct tradition histories, we listened to the wisdom of a later faith community that said they belong together and in the sequence of moving from exodus to the covenant. This sequence had weighty consequences for ethics and its theological foundations.

As for the issue in ethics, preoccupation with reconciliation left out the conditions for integrity in the reconciliation. Reconciliation without redemption turns into appeasement and does not address the injustices of domination and exploitation in racial segregation. The measure of redemption—deliverance, emancipation, and liberation—affects the quality of reconciliation. Promoting liberation for racial harmony therefore became an ethical priority.

We recognized a major doctrinal reconstruction was required for this ethical perspective. An illustration is our proposal to reverse the sequence in that towering landmark in the history of Protestant theology, namely, Karl Barth's *Church Dogmatics* (1956–1969). Barth decided to move from the doctrine of reconciliation in volume 4 of his *Dogmatics* to the doctrine of redemption in volume 5. The fact that Barth never exhausted all he had to say about reconciliation, and therefore never turned to redemption before he died, offers a telling symbol of Euro-American preoccupation with reconciliation.[3] The preoccupation with reconciliation still leads theologians to neglect deliverance and liberation, which should be more appropriately described in a separate doctrine of redemption before reconciliation.

Opponents virtually said that evil spirits led us into ethnic liberation movements at home against racism, as well as liberation struggles abroad against classical European colonialism and the neocolonialism of the Cold War. Our focus on exodus and liberation led us to say that Yahweh, the sovereign and saving God, was acting through these liberation movements, even if their manifestation in specific efforts may fall prey to human frailty and gross failures.

From Exodus From to Exodus For

Attention to redemption in the exodus can become as addictive as the fetish made of reconciliation. The point became clear as events unfolded in the last half of the twentieth century. Internationally, liberation movements launched immediately after World War II ended the awesome classical European colonialism that had evolved from the 1500s. By the 1970s, many of the movements went off track. Maneuvers by the East and the West in Cold War neocolonialism upstaged nation building. Domestically, we saw gains in racial struggles either stalled or undergoing reversals in the early 1970s. Martin Luther King Jr. stated it succinctly: "When we drop bombs in Vietnam, they explode in the US." While new nations and racial ethnic minorities named these forces that sent promising trajectories of liberation movements in the wrong direction, we contributed to the setbacks by serious oversights.

Further examination of the biblical stories offered constructive correctives. In sum, we were reminded that preoccupation with liberation *from* oppression and exploitation could lead us to neglect what we were liberated *for*. The biblical stories suggested at least two correctives. One had to do with the destination; the second had to do with the long haul *en route*.

Various versions of the history of salvation in the Bible urged us to push ahead in the full sweep of God's mission. Ezekiel provided a succinct version that clustered key elements in three events. When the Israelites were captives in Babylonia, Ezekiel announced that God would restage a course of events reminiscent of (1) the exodus from Egypt; (2) uniting of the people before their God at Sinai; and (3) building livable space, including land and a

---

[3] In the English translation, Barth's Doctrine of Reconciliation covered more than 2,850 pages. It required four full-sized books and a slighter one described as Fragment.

nation, a capital city and the temple. Three words in the English translation succinctly summarize the three stages in the story: *"take," "gather,"* and *"bring."* The three words appear together seven times with only slight variations, and therefore sound something like a credal formula, a mnemonic, or a slogan that abbreviates a course of events in the history of salvation (Ezek 20:34–35, 40–42; 34:13, 22–25; 36:24; 37:21; 39:27–28). Even the most erudite commentaries that we consulted had not called attention to the phenomenon.

Salvation did not end with the exodus. "Gathering" and "bringing" were still necessary. They included many tasks, all of them quite difficult. In the gathering, Ezekiel heard a noisy rattling from the remnants of the dismembered people as they came together from the lands where they were scattered. Bone was fitted to bone and ordered under one head so that the "body politic" could function (37:1–8). Indeed, care in assigning the tribes to their allotted land indicated the sensitivities and difficulties involved in connecting them into a coherent whole (34:20–23; 47:13–48:35). The skeletal arrangements still required flesh to move. They needed to restore the ravaged lands and clean the polluted springs. Showers of blessing would rebuild the forests, and trees would bear fruit. Life-giving streams would flow freely. Furthermore, the body needed skin for protection. And so in a covenant of peace, God banished the wild beasts from the land, so they might live in the wild and sheep graze securely in the woods (34:25). Finally, the body came alive as it breathed in the four winds of the Spirit (37:9–10). Surely, four winds indicated that they brought something distinct from the four corners or from all directions. The salvation history in Ezekiel clearly reminded us that beyond liberation *from* enslavement, we were liberated *for* a wide range of difficult tasks if we were to reach the destination God had in mind.

Furthermore, the Israelites had a long haul ahead of them. The most familiar is the story of forty years of wilderness wandering. Similarly, the seer in Revelation has visions of a long haul in several rounds of seven. The rounds recall the seven days of creating the heavens and earth (Genesis 1), and the rounds read like a spiral in which God makes several runs for a new creation. While progress appears in the rounds, the "runs" do not produce a new creation.

In the first cycle of sevens (Rev 6:1–8:1), the opening of the fourth seal brings a pale green horse that is given authority over a fourth of the earth (6:7). In the next round of seven trumpets (8:2–11:19), the blowing of the fourth trumpet darkens a third of the sun, moon, and stars (8:12). The blowing of the sixth trumpet first releases four angels who execute God's judgment on a third of humankind (9:13–21), but those who remain do not repent of their idolatries and sins (9:15, 18, 20–21). In the final episode that follows the sixth trumpet (11:1–19), two prophets are raised from their martyrdom. An earthquake follows, and one-tenth of the city dies. Unlike the earlier remnants, the nine-tenths who survive glorify God, even if it is in terror (11:13). As if in a Sabbath rest, the blowing of the seventh trumpet (11:15–19) comes with twenty-four elders around the throne saying that God has only "begun to reign" (11:17). The cycles did not bring the fullness of God's reign and realm.

In addition to partial gains, we read of a decisive victory that does not complete God's mission (Revelation 12–13). We note the paradoxical quality of the beasts repeated three times, lest we miss the point. Although the beasts are mortally wounded, their mortal wounds are healed (13:3, 12, 14). A "mortal wound that is healed" is an oxymoron on the verbal level. And yet, the phrase is existentially sound for those who experienced the flailing of the mortally wounded beasts that still wreak havoc in the ensuing prolonged struggles against evil.

The beasts are only underlings of the dragon. We still have to do battle against the embodiment of the devil and Satan. An angel binds the dragon in chains and throws it into a bottomless pit, covers the pit and seals it. After a thousand years, however, the dragon emerges and, with the forces of Gog and Magog, surrounds the camp of the saints and the beloved city for battle. Amidst this siege, fire descends on them and throws them into a lake of fire, just as Pharaoh's legions that pursued the Hebrews were drowned in the sea (Rev 20:1–10). Only then do we see the creation of a new heaven and earth, and a new holy city in the fullness of God's reign and realm (Revelation 21–22).

In this excruciatingly long haul, we can understand why the saints cry out, "How long, O Lord, how long?" It explained why we cried out in our struggles as well. God may be with us in our efforts, but that does not ensure a quick fix. We may gain ground and even achieve a decisive victory, but the end is not yet. We may bury evil, but it can reemerge after a thousand years. Even if we are liberated *from* evil, we are liberated *for* a long, long haul in the struggles, setbacks, and suffering *en route* to the fulfillment of God's reign and realm. We cannot sustain our efforts without yielding ourselves again and again to the God working resolutely in the grand drama of salvation we found in selected strands of the scriptures.

From Exodus for to Exodus with

Further critical reflections on our experiences led us to pay more attention to personal transformation. Too many liberators were quickly co-opted and corrupted. They turned into the oppressors and exploiters they toppled. The tragic comedy of a liberator becoming a pig in George Orwell's *Animal Farm* was occurring with debilitating regularity. Nelson Mandela represents an all too rare model of integrating personal transformation during twenty-seven years in prison into the longer story of liberation, union of blacks and whites, and building a new nation.

We sought a biblical witness that paid attention to what Reinhold Niebuhr called *The Self and the Dramas of History*. We wanted to move beyond the *either/or* option (either personal or social salvation) that was dividing our denominations. We sought a *both/and*, that is, biographies of God transforming individuals included in God's drama of salvation history. We found a witness in a further rereading of the priestly prophet, Ezekiel. He paid attention to the salvation of individuals but incorporated it within the larger framework of salvation history. According to Ezekiel, within the larger sweep of salvation transforming society and recovering the environment in the "taking," gathering," and "bringing" (36:24), the conversion of individuals will occur (1) through justification, or forgiveness of sin, as a cleansing of their guilt (36:25); (2) through sanctification as a new heart of flesh in place of a heart of stone (36:26); and (3) thereby through perfection that fulfills God's commands (36:27).

In addition, one further surprising corrective came to our attention. Ezekiel said, when God stages the history of salvation with the *via salutis* "through" the people of God, the Gentiles, the outsiders, "shall know that I am Yahweh," or Sovereign Savior (Ezek 36:23b). To "know" indicates that they will also experience Yahweh as Sovereign and Savior. According to the language of the early church, Jesus Christ is Yahweh, the Lord. If we interpreted Ezekiel's witness in the light of this confession, Yahweh promises that other people will enter into an experiential knowledge of Jesus as Sovereign and Savior, or Lord and Savior. There will be an evangelistic outcome when outsiders see the history of salvation along *with* the *via salutis*.

Those of us who promoted liberation and overlooked the evangelistic consequences of liberation, as well as those who opposed liberation movements because they distracted from God's call to evangelism, have grieved the Holy Spirit. Given the shift in reading the Bible, time has come to work for conciliation between these warring factions in too many denominations.

From Old Particularity to New Particularity

Just as we were led to pay attention to God's transformation of individuals in the 1980s, developments in our communities challenged us to relook at what ethnic identity included. By the closing decade of the twentieth century, marriages by Asian Americans beyond their national ancestry and race had become so common that we had to deal honestly and fairly with children with mixed ancestry. Among Japanese Americans, for example, out-marriage rate approached 75 percent.

How do we explain parents and siblings finding delight in the children of these mixed marriages? In the broader society, the public celebrates the blended identities along with the athletic achievements of prominent national and global figures. Tiger Woods's ancestry includes

African Americans, Native Americans, and Anglo Americans on his father's side and an Asian from Thailand on his mother's side. Phil Jackson, the coach of National Basketball Association championship teams, comes from mid-America. But he draws on the spirituality of Native American neighbors, nurtures the recovery of his Pentecostal Christian heritage, and practices and teaches Zen Buddhism. The appreciation for these figures represents more than a fad. We are breaking the taboo against mixed marriage and religious syncretism.

While we used Ruth as a sign of God's company and guidance in our quest for integration into the host society and culture, we did not make it sufficiently clear that her great-grandson, David, carried a mixed ancestry. We have in Ruth a very different kind of creation story than the one we had grown accustomed to use. In Genesis 1, God "separates" one creature and another so that we see clear lines of distinction between one creature from another. Emphasis is placed on a single, pure identity. In line with this, the "Table of Nations" in Genesis 10 reports more and more lines of distinction that separate one people from another. Most of us read this to indicate that divine presence and guidance were operating in the proliferating identities among different people. The same perspective operates in Leviticus. Commands and prohibitions are based on the goodness in the differences of what God created. Mixing them or crossing the boundaries represents a transgression and a desecration of the goodness of God's intentions and actions. Thus we are prohibited from planting different seeds in the same field or crossbreeding livestock. Hybridization, animal husbandry, and other acts of mixing violate the goodness in the boundaries set by God. This perspective lies behind the postexilic ethnocentrism that prohibited intermarriage and ethnic cleansing that commanded Jews to divorce Gentiles they had married. The same story of creation lies behind the prohibition of men acting as women, which is generally interpreted to be referring to the prohibition of homosexual acts. We have in all of these instances wisdom overextended, and thus leading us to over-zealous and misguided ethical imperatives and prohibitions.

We can speak of over-zealous and misguided ethics because there is another story of creation that corrects the excesses. God mixes previously distinct creatures and produces something else that is good and an agent of divine action. The point in the story of Ruth is that God participated in the marriage of a Moabite with a Jew to produce that towering figure with blended Jewish identity in the history of the children of Israel.

The story of Ruth within the longer genealogy of Jesus in the Gospel according to Matthew became important (Matt 1:1–17). The genealogy includes not only Ruth, who introduced Moabite ancestry, but also Tamar, a Gentile, and Rahab, a harlot in Jericho. If marriage to the Gentile Uriah made her by Jewish custom a Gentile, Bathsheba was a Gentile when

David married her. Other than Mary, the four women mentioned in the genealogy gave Jesus a blended identity. To the extent that the genealogy recounts the creative acts in the providential care of God, we have in these stories of mixing ancestries another creation story generally overlooked in our preoccupation with the story in Genesis 1. Might this be connected with Jesus' outreach to Samaritans, symbolically a people with mixture of cultures and religion (Luke 10:25–37; 17:11–19; John 4)? In any case, a new reading of Ruth led us to see God's action in blending, which creates distinct identities we can celebrate.

Naming Issues, Offering Responses

Readers deserve an explanation for the repeated appeal to particularity. Clarity about the critical methods followed, their contributions to the shifts in reading the Bible, and a theological foundation for them may offer an explanation, if not a defense.

On one level, the approach followed here might be called reader responses. We sought in our responses to join God at work in our changing contexts. The responses, however, relied first on the development of redaction criticism. Other critical methods, such as form criticism and literary-historical criticism, uncover the earlier oral and documentary stages of the biblical traditions. While earlier witnesses are supposedly closer to the events, redaction criticism surmises the meanings later communities of faith saw in those events with the benefit of the intervening complementary witnesses and correctives. Redaction criticism and its variations that pay attention to structures and styles focus on the Bible as we have it. The text as we have it is the most accessible and widely used, and therefore an immediate avenue for engaging faith communities. These considerations apply, regardless of the audio or visual media, in personal and group Bible study, preaching and teaching.

No individual or community of faith can fully grasp the totality of the Bible. And, even if God is the same yesterday, today, and forever, we find different utterances and actions of God in the changing scenes of life and history. We therefore applied a version, or more accurately a variation, of canonical criticism to surmise what portion of the Bible offers us clues to join God in particular situations, however narrowly or broadly defined.

We recognized the authority of the *"orthodox* canon" that our spiritual forebears set aside as peculiarly normative. Because the redactors did not completely erase signs of the complementary and contrasting, contending and contradictory witnesses, faith communities gravitate to one strand or another. This variation of canonical or canon criticism uncovers the *"operating* canon" that, at a given time, has become particularly authoritative. When that canon causes a cognitive dissonance in a particular situation, we look for comparable situations and the witnesses of our ancestors to who God is and what God says and does in those settings. We choose portions of the Bible as our *"functional* canon" that more appropriately and adequately shapes faith and action in an emerging context. This approach does not suggest that the rest of the orthodox canon is false, but only less appropriate for particular settings.

An analogy will offer theological reasons why it is inevitable and necessary we work with particular methods of study and propose particular functional canons.

The sun radiates a vast range of energies, which we are still discovering. When it comes to light rays, we can only expose ourselves momentarily. Otherwise, we go blind with a prolonged gaze and develop skin cancer by sunbathing too long. Even if we tried, we cannot see the sun rays themselves moving through space. We only see distinct ranges as they are reflected off objects. Even in the case of rainbows, we see from different angles a spectrum of reflections in droplets of water.

The same applies to God's self and to God's revelations. Creatures can neither absorb nor reflect the fullness that God radiates. We can only receive and reflect momentarily particular aspects of God's self and a particular range of God's revelation. What is reflected is refracted through the limitations of finite media, inevitably fragile and fractured. Because certain media reflect more effectively than others, we ascribe special status to particular aspects of God, as classics or canonical, in particular kinds of situations. Such are the scriptures, by formal adoption and confirmations in the experiences of an ever-expanding variety of people in countless settings, through millennia of human history.

Certain reflections therefore guide us, with greater integrity than others, to God for a given situation. We watch for witnesses to the God who is love and experienced in loving actions, or in divine grace. When something in creation goes awry, we see the loving God responding as the Holy One. Despite being long-suffering, the Holy One is offended, or more accurately, outraged by sin, evil, and death in creation. This God therefore goes on the offensive to rectify what has gone wrong by restoring goodness and sanctity in that setting. We experience adumbrations of the Holy One when offense, outrage, and offensive actions stir within us amidst what is happening in the ongoing changes in contexts. With clues from our biblical forebears in comparable situations, we seek to clarify and bear witness to who God is and what God is saying and doing in that setting. Testing the spirits requires risky choices in faith and therefore calls for humility as we seek to join God and others in the divine mission underway. Dear God, help us. Amen.

Works Cited

Barth, Karl
    1956–1969 *Church Dogmatics.* Trans. G. W. Bromiley. Edinburgh: T. & T. Clark.

Cone, James
    1970   *A Black Theology of Liberation.* Philadelphia: Lippincott.

Niebuhr, Reinhold
    1955   *The Self and the Dramas of History.* New York: Scribner's Sons.

Orwell, George (Eric Blair)
    1945   *Animal Farm.* New York: Signet Classics.

Palumbo-Liu, David
    1999   *Asian/American: Historical Crossings of a Racial Frontier.* Stanford, Calif.: Stanford University Press.

Sano, Roy I.
    Forthcoming   "Spiral of Contextualizing Faith and Practice." In *Realizing the America of Our Hearts: Theological Voices of Asian Americans.* Ed. Eleazer Fernandez and Fumitake Matsuoka. St. Louis: Chalice.

Wei, William
    1993   *The Asian American Movement.* Philadelphia: Temple University Press.

MULTIPLICITY AND JUDGES 19: CONSTRUCTING A QUEER ASIAN PACIFIC AMERICAN BIBLICAL HERMENEUTIC

Patrick S. Cheng
Union Theological Seminary, New York

ABSTRACT

This essay suggests that the theme of "multiplicity" can be used in constructing a queer Asian Pacific American biblical hermeneutic. In particular, it focuses upon the narrative of the unnamed concubine in Judges 19, who, like the queer Asian Pacific American, is a radical sexual and geographical outsider. The essay explores four ways in which multiplicity is reflected in the experiences of the unnamed concubine and queer Asian Pacific Americans: (1) multiple naming; (2) multiple silencing; (3) multiple oppression; and (4) multiple fragmentation. The essay concludes with a number of ways in which a queer Asian Pacific American biblical hermeneutic could be applied to other scriptural texts. Paradoxically, a focus on multiplicity results in the preservation of the wholeness and integrity of both the reader and the text.

INTRODUCTION

The narrative of the unnamed concubine who is gang-raped and dismembered in Judges 19 has been the focus of a great deal of biblical scholarship during the last two decades. Scholars have written about this story from multiple perspectives, including feminist perspectives (Trible: 64–91; Bal, 1988:80–93; Bal, 1993; Exum: 170–201) and womanist perspectives (Jones-Warsaw). Other scholars have written about Judges 19 through the interpretive lens of politics (Brettler; Amit), war (Keefe), hospitality (Lasine; Matthews), homosexuality (Stone), sodomy (Niditch), and intertextuality (Penchansky). Still others have focused on close readings of the Hebrew text (Schneider).

Despite the richness of the existing body of critical scholarship on Judges 19, however, little attention has been paid to the unnamed concubine's status as a radical outsider *both* in terms of her sexuality and of her geography in the narrative. Like the unnamed concubine, those of us who are queer (that is, lesbian, gay, bisexual, transgender, transsexual, intersexed, or questioning) Asian Pacific Americans are also radical outsiders in terms of our sexualities as well as our geographies. Accordingly, this essay proposes that Judges 19 can be viewed as a foundational text for understanding the experiences of queer Asian Pacific Americans in the United States today.

Specifically, this essay examines the various ways in which the theme of "multiplicity" is reflected in the experiences of the unnamed concubine and queer Asian Pacific Americans. Four dimensions of this theme are explored: (1) multiple naming; (2) multiple silencing; (3) multiple oppression; and (4) multiple fragmentation. This essay concludes with a number of ways in which a queer Asian Pacific American hermeneutic could be applied to other biblical narratives. Paradoxically, a focus on multiplicity results in the preservation of the wholeness and integrity of both the reader and the text.

The Narrative

The narrative of the unnamed concubine who is "[c]aptured, betrayed, raped, tortured, murdered, dismembered, and scattered" (Trible: 65) in Judges 19 has been described as "one of the most distressing stories in the entire Bible" (Schneider: 245). In those days when Israel had no king, a Levite from the hill country of Ephraim took a concubine from Bethlehem in Judah. One day, the concubine "deserted" the Levite—literally, she "played the harlot"—and left him for her father's house in Bethlehem (19:2, NJPS). After four months, the Levite went to Bethlehem to "woo her and to win her back" (v. 3). The concubine "admitted" the Levite into her father's house (v. 3), and the Levite ate, drank, and lodged there for three days. On the morning of the fourth day, the Levite started to leave, but he was persuaded by the concubine's father to stay another night. On the fifth day, after more eating and "dawdling" (v. 8), the Levite refused to stay any longer, even though the day was already "waning toward evening" (v. 9).

The Levite, his attendant, and the concubine left Bethlehem and traveled to Jebus (that is, Jerusalem). As the day was already "very far spent" (v. 11), the attendant suggested that they spend the night there. The Levite refused, because he did not want to "turn aside to a town of aliens who are not of Israel" (v. 12). As a result, they continued toward Gibeah, a city of the tribe of Benjamin. When they arrived in Gibeah, the sun had already set, and they sat in the town square because "nobody took them indoors" (v. 15). Eventually, an old man who also "hailed from the hill country of Ephraim" (v. 16) passed by and, after asking the Levite where he was from and where he was going to, the old man took them into his house, warning them not to spend the night in the square "on any account" (v. 20).

While the old man's guests were eating and drinking inside, the "depraved" men of Gibeah pounded on the door and instructed the old man to bring out the Levite so they could be "intimate" with him (v. 22). The old man offered his virgin daughter as well as the Levite's concubine to the men of Gibeah, so that they would not "perpetrate this outrage" (v. 23), but the men of Gibeah would not listen to him. As a result, the Levite "seized his concubine and pushed her out to them" (v. 25). The men of Gibeah "raped her and abused her all night long until morning" and let her go only "when dawn broke" (v. 25).

When it was "growing light" outside (v. 26), the concubine came back and collapsed at the entrance to the old man's house. When the Levite got up in the morning, he opened the doors of the house and found his concubine "lying at the entrance of the house, with her hands on the threshold" (v. 27). He ordered her to get up so that they could go, but there was no answer. So the Levite put the concubine on his donkey and went home. When he arrived home, he "picked up a knife" and "cut her up limb by limb into twelve parts" and sent the parts throughout Israel (v. 29). And everyone who saw "it" (v. 30) exclaimed that there had been nothing like this since the day of the Exodus.

Sexual and Geographical Outsiders

Many scholars have acknowledged the outsider status of the unnamed concubine. Phyllis Trible has argued, for example, that the unnamed concubine is the "least" of "all the characters in scripture," because she is "alone in a world of men" and is without "name, speech, or power" (80). Koala Jones-Warsaw has compared the unnamed concubine to African American women, who "often find [themselves] near the bottom of the social ladder" (183). Despite this acknowledgment of the unnamed concubine's outsider status, however, little attention has been paid to the fact that she is a radical outsider *both* in terms of her sexuality as well as her geography. It is to this issue of multiple outsider status that we now turn.

The unnamed concubine is an outsider with respect to her sexuality. She transgresses the norms of her society by deserting, or "playing the harlot" against, the Levite (v. 2). The Hebrew root used to describe her action is *znh*, and commentators have spent much energy debating whether the unnamed concubine prostituted herself outside of marriage (Schneider: 249–50). Whether or not she actually engaged in physical fornication in this context, however, is "almost irrelevant" (251) to her outsider status. The real issue is that she dared to assert ownership over her body and to assert control over her own sexuality. Because the act of leaving the Levite was an "offense against the social order" and "the patriarchal system itself," the unnamed concubine receives "narrative punishment for claiming sexual autonomy" (Exum: 179, 200). Specifically, she is "gang-raped" and "her sexuality is mutilated" (200).

The unnamed concubine is also an outsider with respect to her geography. Throughout the narrative, there is constant geographical tension between the unnamed concubine, on the one hand, and her father and the Levite, on the other. From the outset, the unnamed concubine tries to move in a *southerly* direction. She is originally from the south (that is, Bethlehem in Judah), and she asserts her autonomy by returning to the south at the beginning of the narrative (v. 2). By contrast, the unnamed concubine's father and the Levite try to move her in a *northerly* direction. Her father initially sends her to the north to live with the Levite in the hill country of Ephraim. Later, her father sends her to the north again, after the Levite comes to "woo her and to win her back" (v. 3). The Levite takes her back north, refusing to stop even at Jebus (that is, Jerusalem), until they reach Gibeah. At Gibeah, they stay at the home of the old man, who is also from the north, and it is there that she collapses after being gang-raped all night. This geographical tension between south and north is analogous to the tension that people from Africa, Asia, and Latin America experience when they immigrate to the United States and they face marginalization on the basis of their countries of origin. Indeed, Koala Jones-Warsaw makes this analogy explicit by comparing the experience of the unnamed concubine to that of African American women (183), who have been exiled from their ancestors' geographical homes for nearly four centuries.

Like the unnamed concubine, queer Asian Pacific Americans are radical outsiders in terms of both our sexualities and our geographies. We remain outsiders, particularly in the theological academy, despite the fact that several important anthologies of queer Asian Pacific American writings have been published in recent years (Bao and Yanagihara; Eng and Hom; R. Leong, 1996; Lim-Hing; C. Tsang), as well as a number of works relating to queer Asian Pacific American spirituality (Cheng; R. Leong, 1998; Lim; Liu, 1992, 1995, 1998; Realuyo, 1993a, 1993b). With respect to our identities as *sexual* outsiders, we face seminaries, divinity schools, and departments of religion that have a "disdain for gay/lesbian related scholarship," which is "clearly seen as 'not real scholarship'" (Clark: 73). Along those lines, we also face barriers in the homophobic hiring and publishing practices of many churches and church-affiliated institutions (Clark: 71–72). With respect to our identities as *geographical* outsiders, we remain on the margins in terms of the small number of Asian Pacific American theologians, biblical scholars, and church historians in the academy (Phan and Lee: xii). Despite the fact that our ancestors have been present in the United States since the mid-1700s (R. Lee: ix), Asian Pacific Americans are still "not fully acknowledged as American" (Matsuoka: 1), and thus we remain as people in diaspora.

In sum, the unnamed concubine and queer Asian Pacific Americans are radical and multiple outsiders, in terms of *both* sexuality and geography. We now turn to a more detailed examination of how "multiplicity" is present in the experiences of the unnamed concubine and queer Asian Pacific Americans. In particular, four dimensions of this theme are explored: (1) multiple naming; (2) multiple silencing; (3) multiple oppression; and (4) multiple fragmentation.

Multiple Naming

The first way in which the unnamed concubine and queer Asian Pacific Americans experience multiplicity is through *multiple naming*. In the space of a single chapter, the unnamed concubine is described by four different Hebrew nouns: (1) *pîlegeš*, or "concubine" (vv. 1–2, 9–10, 24–25, 27, 29); (2) *na͜ʿărâ*, or "girl" (vv. 5–6, 8–9); (3) *ʾāmâ*, or "maidservant" (v. 19); and (4) *ʾiššâ*, or "woman" (vv. 26–27). This multiplicity is compounded by the fact that biblical scholars have used a variety of English names to refer to the unnamed concubine. Many, like Phyllis Trible, simply call her the "concubine" (66). However, others have invented names for her. For example, Mieke Bal calls her "Beth" by playing on the Hebrew words for "house," "daughter," and "Bethlehem" (1988:89–90). J. Cheryl Exum calls her "Bath-sheber" or "daughter of breaking," which is what the men of Gibeah and her husband do to her (176). Tammi J. Schneider calls her the *pîlegeš*, or the Hebrew word for "concubine" (247). As a result of this multiplicity, the unnamed concubine is rendered powerless. The absence of a uniform signifier encourages the reader "not to view her as a person in her own right" (Exum: 176). That is, multiple naming can be viewed as a "textual strategy for distancing the reader from the character" (ibid.).

We queer Asian Pacific Americans also experience multiple naming in our lives. With respect to our sexual identities, there has been much internal debate over when to use the terms "homosexual," "gay," or "queer" to describe ourselves (not to mention "lesbian," "bisexual," "transgender," "transsexual," "intersexed," and "questioning"). With respect to our geographical identities, there has also been much debate over when to use the terms "oriental," "Asian," "Asian American," "Asian Pacific Islander," or "Asian Pacific American" to describe ourselves (not to mention "South Asian," "Southeast Asian," "East Asian," and "Pacific Islander"). As a result of this multiplicity, there is no consensus as to what to call us. We have been called gay Asian Pacific Islanders (GAPIs), queer Asian Pacific Islanders (QAPIs), gay Asian Americans (GAAs), queer Asian Americans (QAAs), gay Asian Pacific Americans (GAPAs), Asian Pacific Islander lesbians and bisexuals (APILBs), and queer Asian Pacific Americans (QAPAs). To further complicate matters, there are many other non-English words that have been used to describe our queer siblings in Asia: *tongzhi* and *nü tongzhi* (China); *gei* and *mem-bah* (Hong Kong); *bo-li quan* (Taiwan); *sakhiyani* (India); and *doseiai* (Japan) (Chou: 1, 79–80, 82, 146; Thadani: 66; Summerhawk, McMahill, and McDonald: 6). As in the case of the unnamed concubine, this multiple naming and lack of a uniform signifier renders queer Asian Pacific Americans powerless within the dominant culture.

Multiple Silencing

The second way in which the unnamed concubine and queer Asian Pacific Americans experience multiplicity is through *multiple silencing*. In Judges 19, the unnamed concubine never speaks for herself. Instead, her own voice is repeatedly silenced by the voices of the various men who surround her. For example, we never hear the unnamed concubine's response to the Levite's attempt to "woo her and to win her back" (v. 3). She is silenced by her father, who allows her to leave with the Levite on the fifth day. Similarly, we never hear the unnamed concubine's response to the attendant's suggestion of spending the night in Jebus on the way back to Ephraim. She is silenced by the Levite, who insists that they travel further to Gibeah, where she is brutally gang-raped. We never hear what must have been the unnamed concubine's horrified response to the old man's offer to turn her over to the men of Gibeah for their "pleasure" (v. 24). Again, she is silenced by the Levite, who seizes her and pushes her out of the house to the men. Finally, after being raped all night long, the unnamed concubine collapses on the threshold of the old man's house, unable to answer the Levite's command to "get up" (v. 28). At this point, she is silenced forever.

In addition to the various ways in which the unnamed concubine is silenced by the men who surround her, there are also multiple silences *within* the narrative of Judges 19 itself. Why exactly did the unnamed concubine leave the Levite? Why did the Levite need to "woo" and "win" her back (v. 3)? Why was he subsequently "admitted" to her father's house (v. 3)? Did the unnamed concubine actually prostitute herself (Schneider: 249–51)? Or was she simply acting in accordance with the customs of patrilocal marriage (Bal, 1988:83–89)? Was the unnamed concubine dead when she collapsed on the threshold? Or did the Levite ultimately murder her (Trible: 80)? What exactly was "it" that so shocked the tribes of Israel (Trible: 81)? The rape? The dismemberment? The unnamed concubine herself? The text is provocatively silent on these and other questions.

Multiple silencing is also experienced by those of us who are queer Asian Pacific Americans. Like the unnamed concubine, our voices are repeatedly silenced by the communities that surround us. Again, this silencing is particularly acute in the theological academy, despite the fact that in recent years queer Asian Pacific Americans of faith have begun to find our own theological voices. We have done so by organizing queer Asian Pacific American Christian fellowship groups (for example, GRACE-PACTS at the Graduate Theological Union); by forming queer Asian Pacific American Christian denominational caucuses (for example, the Queer Asian Fellowship of the Universal Fellowship of Metropolitan Community Churches); and by creating queer Asian Pacific American Christian online discussion groups (for example, QueerAsianFellowship and QAPAX on Yahoo! Groups).

Despite the emergence of our voices as queer Asian Pacific Americans of faith, however, we continue to be silenced by Asian and Asian Pacific American theologians. For example, an informal survey of the indices of books by prominent theologians such as Kosuke Koyama, Jung Young Lee, Fumitaka Matsuoka, and C. S. Song reveal no mention of "homosexuality" or "sexual orientation." (Notable exceptions include books by Asian and Asian Pacific American feminist theologians such as Kwok Pui-lan [120–22], Chung Hyun Kyung [46], and Rita Nakashima Brock [Brock and Thistlethwaite: 177], but these works refer largely to queer *Asians* and not queer Asian Pacific Americans.) Similarly, our voices are silenced by queer theologians. An informal survey of the indices of books by prominent theologians such as J. Michael Clark, Gary Comstock, and John McNeill reveal no mention of "Asians" or "Asian Pacific Americans." (Notable exceptions include writings on comparative religion by Robert Goss [passim] and Carter Heyward [38], as well as works by queer theologians of color such as eliyahou farajajé [formerly elias farajajé-jones; see farajajé-jones: 330] and Renée Hill [147], but these works refer largely to *Asians in the Two-Thirds World,* and not queer Asian Pacific Americans.) In sum, we queer Asian Pacific Americans are largely invisible, even within the Asian Pacific American community and the queer community. Although these larger "communities" purport to speak on behalf of us, our voices are ultimately silenced.

Multiple Oppression

The third way in which the unnamed concubine and queer Asian Pacific Americans experience multiplicity is through *multiple oppression*. As Trible has written, the unnamed concubine is the woman "most sinned against" (81). The graphic image of the concubine "lying at the entrance of the house, with her hands on the threshold" (v. 27) represents her social location in the midst of the various forces of oppression that surround her. On one side of the door are the men of Gibeah, who gang-rape her and abuse her all night long. On the other side of the door is the old man, who initially offers her to the men of Gibeah for their "pleasure" (v. 24), as well as the Levite, who ultimately pushes her outside of the house. The unnamed concubine is caught between sexual objectification by geographical strangers, on the one hand, and rejection by her "family," on the other. Indeed, as Bal has noted, the bodily position of the unnamed concubine at the threshold of the old man's house is symbolic of her status as a "liminal figure" or an "embodiment of transition" (1993:221). This experience of liminality is reinforced by the repeated use of Hebrew words like *delet,* "door" (v. 27), *sap,* "threshold" (v. 27), and *petaḥ,* "entrance" (vv. 26–27) in the narrative, which are used elsewhere in the Hebrew Bible to separate one space from another, particularly with respect to the tent of meeting (Num 3:25) and the temple (1 Kgs 6:31–34; 2 Chr 3:7; Ezek 41:23–25).

Similarly, queer Asian Pacific Americans experience multiple oppression from the various communities that surround us. On one side of the metaphorical door is the racism of the predominantly white queer community. We are simultaneously erased and sexually objectified by this community, in the same way that the unnamed concubine is erased and sexually objectified by the men of Gibeah. With respect to *erasure*, queer Asian Pacific Americans remain largely invisible in mainstream queer magazines, newspapers, bookstores, videos, and other media, despite the fact that we have been a part of the queer liberation movement for over three decades (Cornell; C. Tsang). With respect to *sexual objectification*, we are often faced with "rice queens" within the white queer community who "fetishize Asian men" and engage in the "predatory consumption" of queer Asians as "boy toys" (Cho: 1–3). Similarly, we are objectified as the exotic "other" by the predominantly white queer community whenever it is convenient for purposes of fundraising and entertainment. For example, in 1991, a major queer institution—the Lambda Legal Defense and Education Fund (LLDEF)—held its annual fundraiser at the Broadway musical *Miss Saigon*, despite the angry protests of the queer Asian Pacific American community in New York City, which saw the musical as "perpetuating a damaging fantasy of submissive 'Orientals,' self-erasing women, and asexual, contemptible men" (Yoshikawa). LLDEF refused to cancel the fundraiser. Nearly ten years later, in 2000, another major queer institution—the Hotlanta River Expo—held a gay male circuit party called the "Year of the Dragon" that used stereotypical and highly offensive images such as "Fried Rice" and "China Doll" for the themes of its events. When faced with angry protests by queer Asian Pacific Americans in Atlanta and across the nation, the president and board of directors of Hotlanta River Expo agreed to take certain remedial steps, including apologizing for their actions, but later "violated every tenet" of a negotiated agreement, according to local queer Asian Pacific American activists (A. Leong).

The oppression experienced by queer Asian Pacific Americans is not limited to racism within the predominantly white queer community, however. On the other side of the metaphorical door is the homophobia of the predominantly straight Asian Pacific American community. We are betrayed and rejected by our very own families, in the same way that the unnamed concubine is betrayed and pushed out of the door by the old man and the Levite. For example, in 1999, thousands of members of evangelical Asian Pacific American churches in Southern California were mobilized by their pastors to sign petitions that would have prohibited any public entity from "endorsing, educating, recognizing or promoting homosexuality as acceptable, moral behavior" (C. Lee: 61). Asian Pacific American pastors began their sermons by condemning homosexuality as a "sin" and a "crime" to the choruses of "Amen" from their large congregations (ibid.). The real sin and crime, however, is the tremendous suffering inflicted upon numerous young queer Asian Pacific Americans by their very own families and pastors, which can lead to suicidal thoughts, wishes, and acts (Lim: 328–31). For many Asian Pacific Americans, "being Asian and being gay are mutually exclusive.... 'it' is a white disease" (Wat: 76). Sadly, these families and pastors are blinded from the truth that homosexuality has always existed within their communities and that many of their own children and family members are queer. In sum, we queer Asian Pacific Americans—like the unnamed concubine—are trapped between forces of oppression from both sides of the metaphorical door. We are "run over at the intersection of racism and homophobia . . . [and] forever left in the middle of the road, unacceptable to those at either side of the street" (Wat: 79).

Multiple Fragmentation

The fourth way in which the unnamed concubine and queer Asian Pacific Americans experience multiplicity is through *multiple fragmentation*. The narrative of the unnamed concubine ends with the Levite cutting the concubine "limb by limb into twelve parts" (v. 29) and scattering her body throughout the territory of Israel. Many commentators have focused upon this gruesome imagery in their readings of Judges 19. Trible, invoking a traditional christological image, has noted that the unnamed concubine's body was "broken and given to many" (64, 81). Exum has written that the multiple fragmentation serves to "desexualize Bath-sheber [that is, the unnamed concubine] by violently opening up the mystery of woman and diffusing her threat by scattering the parts" (191). Jones-Warsaw has noted that the multiple fragmentation symbolizes the many ways in which the Black woman is scattered in "every field and dumping ground," and how she must "gather together all the pieces of herself . . . and stand before God and humanity—as a whole black woman" (185). Indeed, the theme of multiple fragmentation is central to many contemporary readings of Judges 19.

Multiple fragmentation is also experienced by queer Asian Pacific Americans. We are constantly forced to choose as to which "part" of ourselves is operative in a given context. Are we queer? Are we lesbian, gay male, bisexual, transgender, transsexual, intersexed, or questioning? Are we Asian Pacific American? Are we South Asian American, Southeast Asian American, East Asian American, or Pacific Islander American? Or are we simply American? The answer always varies, depending upon whether we are with queer families, Asian Pacific American families, churches, friends, co-workers, or acquaintances from Asia and other parts of the world.

It is no surprise, therefore, that images of multiple fragmentation can be found in queer Asian Pacific American writings. For example, Cambodian

American lesbian poet Peou Lakhana draws a connection between her queer Asian Pacific American identity and the "butchering" of one-third of the Cambodian population. In reflecting upon her fragmented identity, Lakhana writes that "the next time you look into a mirror / the person you will see / contains pieces of me" (41). Queer Chinese American poet Timothy Liu also uses images of multiple fragmentation in his work. In one poem, he writes about "resting my chin / on a stump where the head has been. / Limbs severed / above the elbows the hips, its mutilated sex, testicles / hanging in a stone sack" (1992:45). Finally, queer Chinese American writer Eric Wat documents the brutal queer bashing of Vietnamese American immigrant Truong Loc Minh in 1993 on a Southern California beach. Early one morning, Minh was "beat[en] ... to a pulp" by three young white men, and his fragmented face "was so disfigured that they could hardly determine his race" (77–78).

In a thought-provoking article, Santa Clara University law professor Peter Kwan has written about the connections between queer Asian Pacific American identity and the murder of fourteen-year-old Konerak Sinthasomphone by serial killer Jeffrey Dahmer. Konerak, an Asian Pacific American immigrant from Laos, had been abducted by Dahmer, who tried to make him a "zombie" by drilling a hole in his head. Somehow, Konerak managed to escape—naked, bleeding, and disoriented—into the street. When questioned by the two police officers who found Konerak, Dahmer told them that Konerak was his nineteen-year-old lover who had drunk too much and had wandered into the street. The police officers believed Dahmer, and they returned Konerak to him. Shortly thereafter, Konerak was strangled to death by Dahmer. In his law review article, Kwan argues that Dahmer's imposition of a queer Asian Pacific American identity upon Konerak created "a fantasy scenario that posited [Dahmer] firmly as the dominant party ... [that was] so powerful as to foreclose a recognition" by the police officers of Konerak's plight (Kwan: 1290), and it literally resulted in Konerak's multiple fragmentation. The connections between this tragic real-life story and the "betrayal, rape, torture, murder, and dismemberment" (Trible: 65) of the unnamed concubine in Judges 19 are chilling. In sum, the multiple fragmentation and scattering of queer Asian Pacific American identities—in both literary and literal terms—diffuse the threat of our radical outsider status. The challenge for queer Asian Pacific Americans, therefore, is to attain wholeness and integrity in terms of our queer Asian Pacific American lives.

Applications to Other Scriptural Texts

Of course, a queer Asian Pacific American biblical hermeneutic of multiplicity would not be limited to the narrative of the unnamed concubine in Judges 19. Such a hermeneutic could also be applied to a number of different scriptural texts. These might include texts that involve the multiple naming of characters and places such as God/Lord/El Shaddai/Ehyeh-Asher-Ehyeh, Abram/Abraham, Sarai/Sarah, Jacob/Israel, Jethro/Reuel/Hobab, Mount Sinai/Mount Horeb, and Saul/Paul. Other texts might include narratives of multiple silencing, such as the mysterious Nephilim in the book of Genesis who never speak and who are wiped out by the Lord (Gen 6:1–7), and the naked young man in the Gospel according to Mark who is without either a history or a voice (Mark 14:51–52). Still other texts might include narratives of multiple oppression, such as Jesus' simultaneous oppression by both the political and religious authorities (Luke 23:13–25), and the Letter to Philemon, in which Onesimus is oppressed by both Paul and Philemon (Phlm 11–15). Finally, these texts might include narratives of multiple fragmentation, such as the shattering of Sisera's skull by Jael (Judg 4:21; 5:26–27), the trampling of Jezebel's body by horses (2 Kgs 9:33), and Ezekiel in the valley of dry bones (Ezek 37:1–14).

A queer Asian Pacific American hermeneutic of multiplicity would also look to theological sources *outside* of the Bible for connections to ultimate reality that reflect our queer Asian Pacific American identities. Some examples of these sources might include Kuan Yin (the transgender Chinese *bodhisattva* of compassion), Qu Yuan (the queer Chinese shaman-poet), Ardhanarishvara (the transgender Hindu deity that is linked with androgyny and homoeroticism), and Amaterasu Omi Kami (the cross-dressing sun goddess of the Japanese religion of Shinto) (Conner, Sparks, and Sparks: 52, 67, 208, 275–76). By juxtaposing the Bible with these cross-cultural images of the divine, queer Asian Pacific American readers could develop creative new biblical readings that would reflect our experiences as radical outsiders both in terms of our sexualities and our geographies.

CONCLUSION

In sum, a queer Asian Pacific American biblical hermeneutic is committed to preserving the complexity and multidimensionality of scriptural texts. It resists the tendency of readers to reduce such narratives into one-dimensional stories or lessons. In particular, such an approach is committed to uncovering the various ways in which "multiplicity" is present in the Bible. Like the unnamed concubine who is gang-raped and dismembered in Judges 19, queer Asian Pacific Americans are radical sexual and geographical outsiders who experience multiplicity in a number of ways, including multiple naming, multiple silencing, multiple oppression, and multiple fragmentation. Paradoxically, a focus on multiplicity in reading the Bible results in the preservation of the wholeness and integrity of both the reader and the text. It is time that we queer Asian Pacific Americans acknowledge our experiences of multiplicity. In the words of Lani Ka'ahumanu, who is a bisexual, biracial, Hawaiian-American feminist writer, poet, organizer, and activist: "It is time to nurture the organic radical integration process. / Differences recognized and appreciated give a sense of the whole.... / Assimilation is a lie. / It is spiritual erasure" (452).

WORKS CONSULTED

Amit, Yairah
    1994   "Literature in the Service of Politics: Studies in Judges 19–21." Pp. 28–40 in *Politics and Theopolitics in the Bible and Postbiblical Literature*. Ed. Henning Graf Reventlow, Yair Hoffman, and Benjamin Uffenheimer. JSOTSup 171. Sheffield: Sheffield Academic Press.

Bal, Mieke
    1988   *Death and Dissymmetry: The Politics of Coherence in the Book of Judges*. Chicago: University of Chicago Press.

    1993   "A Body of Writing: Judges 19." Pp. 208–30 in *A Feminist Companion to Judges*. Ed. Athalya Brenner. Sheffield: Sheffield Academic Press.

Bao, Quang, and Hanya Yanagihara, eds.
    2000   *Take Out: Queer Writing from Asian Pacific America*. New York: Asian American Writers' Workshop.

Brettler, Marc
    1989   "The Book of Judges: Literature As Politics." *JBL* 108:395–418.

Brock, Rita Nakashima, and Susan Brooks Thistlethwaite
    1996   *Casting Stones: Prostitution and Liberation in Asia and the United States*. Minneapolis: Fortress.

Cheng, Patrick
    2000   "God Loves Sex Too (Getting Down with the Spirit)." *DRAGÜN* 4:18–20.

Cho, Song, ed.
    1998   *Rice: Explorations into Gay Asian Culture + Politics*. Toronto: Queer.

Chou Wah-shan, ed.
    2000   *Tongzhi: Politics of Same-Sex Eroticism in Chinese Societies*. Binghamton: Haworth.

Chung, Hyun Kyung
    1990   *Struggle to Be the Sun Again*. Maryknoll, N.Y.: Orbis.

Clark, J. Michael
    1991   *Theologizing Gay*. Oak Cliff: Minuteman.

Conner, Randy P., David Hatfield Sparks, and Mariya Sparks
    1997   *Cassell's Encyclopedia of Queer Myth, Symbol and Spirit*. London: Cassell.

Cornell, Michiyo
    1996   "Living in Asian America: An Asian American Lesbian's Address before the Washington Monument (1979)." Pp. 83–84 in R. Leong, 1996.

Eng, David L., and Alice Y. Hom, eds.
    1998   *Q&A: Queer in Asian America.* Philadelphia: Temple University Press.

Exum, J. Cheryl
    1993   *Fragmented Women: Feminist (Sub)Versions of Biblical Narratives.* Valley Forge, Pa.: Trinity Press International.

farajajé-jones, elias
    2000   "Holy Fuck." Pp. 327–35 in *Male Lust: Pleasure, Power, and Transformation.* Ed. Kerwin Kay, Jill Nagle, and Baruch Gould. Binghamton: Harrington Park.

Goss, Robert
    2000   Syllabus, "The Problem of Evil." Webster University, Spring 2000.

Heyward, Carter
    1999   *Saving Jesus from Those Who Are Right: Rethinking What It Means to Be Christian.* Minneapolis: Fortress.

Hill, Renée Leslie
    1999   "Disrupted/Disruptive Movements: Black Theology and Black Power 1969/1999." Pp. 138–49 in *Black Faith and Public Talk: Critical Essays on James H. Cone's Black Theology and Black Power.* Ed. Dwight N. Hopkins. Maryknoll, N.Y.: Orbis.

Jones-Warsaw, Koala
    1993   "Toward a Womanist Hermeneutic: A Reading of Judges 19–21." Pp. 172–86 in *A Feminist Companion to Judges.* Ed. Athalya Brenner. Sheffield: Sheffield Academic Press.

Ka'ahumanu, Lani
    1994   "Hapa Haole Wahine." Pp. 432–53 in Lim-Hing.

Keefe, Alice A.
    1993   "Rapes of Women/Wars of Men." *Semeia* 61:79–97.

Kwan, Peter
    1997   "Jeffrey Dahmer and the Cosynthesis of Categories." *Hastings Law Journal* 48:1257–92.

Kwok Pui-lan
    2000   *Introducing Asian Feminist Theology.* Cleveland: Pilgrim.

Lakhana, Peou
    1994   "Who Am I?" Pp. 40–41 in Lim-Hing.

Lasine, Stuart
    1984   "Guest and Host in Judges 19: Lot's Hospitality in an Inverted World." *JSOT* 29:37–59.

Lee, Chisun
    2000   "Moral Minority." *A Magazine* April/May:60–65, 85.

Lee, Robert
    1999   *Orientals: Asian Americans in Popular Culture.* Philadelphia: Temple University Press.

Leong, Asha
    2000   Press Release, Ad Hoc Committee for Racial Justice (August 21).

Leong, Russell
    1998   "Litany." Pp. 213–21 in Eng and Hom.

Leong, Russell, ed.
    1996   *Asian American Sexualities: Dimensions of the Gay and Lesbian Experience.* New York: Routledge.

Lim, You-Leng Leroy
    1998   "Webs of Betrayal, Webs of Blessings." Pp. 323–34 in Eng and Hom.

Lim-Hing, Sharon, ed.
    1994   *The Very Inside: An Anthology of Writing by Asian and Pacific Islander Lesbian and Bisexual Women.* Toronto: Sister Vision.

Liu, Timothy
    1992   *Vox Angelica.* Farmington: Alice James.

    1995   *Burnt Offerings.* Port Townsend: Copper Canyon.

    1998   *Say Goodnight.* Port Townsend: Copper Canyon.

Matsuoka, Fumitaka
    1995   *Out of Silence: Emerging Themes in Asian American Churches.* Cleveland: United Church.

Matthews, Victor H.
    1992   "Hospitality and Hostility in Genesis 19 and Judges 19." *BTB* 22:3–11.

Niditch, Susan
    1982   "The 'Sodomite' Theme in Judges 19–20: Family, Community, and Social Disintegration." *CBQ* 44:365–78.

Penchansky, David
    1992   "Staying the Night: Intertextuality in Genesis and Judges." Pp. 77–88 in *Reading between Texts: Intertextuality and the Hebrew Bible.* Ed. Danna Nolan Fewell. Louisville: Westminster/John Knox.

Phan, Peter C., and Jung Young Lee, eds.
    1999   *Journeys at the Margin: Toward an Autobiographical Theology in American-Asian Perspective.* Collegeville, Minn.: Liturgical Press.

Realuyo, Bino Almonte
    1993a   "Epiphany." Pp. 37–38 in C. Tsang.

    1993b   "Gethsemane." Pp. 38–39 in C. Tsang.

Schneider, Tammi J.
   2000   *Judges*. Collegeville, Minn.: Liturgical Press.

Stone, Ken
   1995   "Gender and Homosexuality in Judges 19: Subject-Honor, Object-Shame?" *JSOT* 67:87–107.

Summerhawk, Barbara, Cheiron McMahill, and Darren McDonald, trans. and eds.
   1998   *Queer Japan: Personal Stories of Japanese Lesbians, Gays, Bisexuals and Transsexuals*. Norwich: New Victoria.

Thadani, Giti
   1996   *Sakhiyani: Lesbian Desire in Ancient and Modern India*. London: Cassell.

Trible, Phyllis
   1984   *Texts of Terror: Literary-Feminist Readings of Biblical Narratives*. Philadelphia: Fortress.

Tsang, Chi, ed.
   1993   "Witness Aloud: Lesbian, Gay and Bisexual Asian/Pacific American Writings." *The APA Journal*. New York: Asian American Writers' Workshop.

Tsang, Daniel C.
   2000   "Asians in North America." Pp. 76–78 in *Gay Histories and Cultures*. Ed. George E. Haggerty. New York: Garland.

Wat, Eric
   1996   "Preserving the Paradox: Stories from a Gay-Loh." Pp. 71–80 in R. Leong, 1996.

Yoshikawa, Yoko
   1998   "The Heat Is on Miss Saigon Coalition: Organizing across Race and Sexuality." Pp. 41–56 in Eng and Hom.

THE ACCIDENTS OF BEING AND THE POLITICS OF IDENTITY: BIBLICAL IMAGES OF ADOPTION AND ASIAN ADOPTEES IN AMERICA

Mary F. Foskett
Wake Forest University

ABSTRACT

In his well-known 1998 memoir, Eric Liu reflects upon his identity as an "accidental Asian." Among the many issues of identity that Asian Americans negotiate, particular concerns emerge within and around the rapidly growing population of Asian American adoptees, children born to Asian mothers in Asia and adopted by families in the United States. How can adopted Asians, especially those whose adoptive families are neither Asian nor Asian American, understand themselves as Asian Americans, and what do adopted persons bring to the self-understanding and identity of Asian and non-Asian America? In this consideration of the politics of identity, two biblical traditions are explored as resources for examining the issues that Asian American adoptees, their families, and America encounter amidst the phenomenon of inter-cultural adoption. Exodus 2:1–22 and Romans 8:12–17, 9:1–5 offer not competing, but complementary, paradigms that can inform critical reflection upon these issues.

Amid the many issues related to ethos, ethnicity, and identity that emerge when one considers the Bible in Asian America lies the challenge of determining to whom the appellation, Asian American, applies. Beyond the familiar questions and problems that stem from current constructions of a pan-Asian America lies the often overlooked phenomenon of a growing, multigenerational population of Pacific Asian–born Americans who, having been adopted in Asia as infants or children, have been or are being raised in the United States. According to figures issued by the U.S. State Department, in 1999 over sixteen thousand immigrant visas were issued to orphans entering the United States. Of these, more than seven thousand were extended to children coming to the U.S. from Pacific Asia. With every new year, such children comprise a larger and larger segment of the American population. Reflecting in some ways the experience of first-generation Asian Americans and, in others, that of their American-born sons and daughters, adoptees represent a distinct subculture within Asian America.

Recent publicity concerning the twenty-fifth anniversary of Operation Babylift and conferences for adult Korean adoptees remind us that Americans, especially Caucasian Americans, have adopted children from Pacific Asia for decades. The Korean American Adoptee Adoptive Family Network (KAAN) estimates that 100,000 Korean children have been adopted into the United States. Given this history of Asian adoption, any serious effort to account for the Asian American experience ought to include consideration of Asian adoptees and whatever insights into identity politics can be culled from their experience. Several adoptee networks, including KAAN, Mam Non (an organization that is committed to educating the adoption community about Vietnamese culture), and Families with Children from China, are dedicated, in part, to encouraging critical reflection on the construction of Pacific Asian, Asian American, and American identities. KAAN is particularly attentive to forging connections between the Korean American community and Korean adoptees and their families.

Whereas American social agencies, many adoptive families, and adoption networks in general have made great strides in recognizing the issues of identity and ethnicity that adoptees negotiate, little attention has been given to the ideology and images that inform American constructions of adoption. This essay aims to contribute to such an effort by exploring two notions of adoption that are rooted in biblical tradition, in particular. In so doing, I hope to open a door to further consideration of both adoptees and the Bible in Asian America.

In his recent memoir, *The Accidental Asian*, Eric Liu underscores both the experience and inexperience that distinguish Asian adoptees in America as he ponders questions that countless adoptees have asked:

> And you—what obligation do you incur? To live not only the life you have—the school bus, the birthday party, the instant memory of the camcorder—but also the life you never had? To link yourself to a chain of greater meaning? What duty have you to reconnect the cord—and if not a duty, then what desire? (195–96)

That this kind of sympathetic interrogation can be put to Asian adoptees as a whole underscores the degree to which race and ethnicity figure in both the adoptive and the Asian American experience. Remarking that "[t]hese are the questions I would ask an Asian child raised by a Caucasian family," Liu quickly adds, "[t]hey are the very questions I sometimes ask myself" (196). While noting issues of identity that are shared, in large measure, by all Asian Americans, Liu nevertheless raises specific challenges that adoptees regularly encounter. Underneath many adoptees' questions about racial/ethnic identity and lost familial bonds lie concerns and conflicts that depend not only on how Americans talk about race/ethnicity, but on how adoption itself is constructed and represented. In contrast to most other Asian Americans, adoptees' questions about race/ethnicity and familial obligation are predicated upon the dual realities of relinquishment and chosenness, of lost origins and initiation into new familial histories. The severed cord to which Liu alludes, one that the adoptee neither chose nor initiated, is an accident of being that generates a multitude of images and elicits a range of responses. Biblical images of adoption resonate with and reinforce aspects of the adoptive experience.

Moses and the Return to Origins

As previous interpreters have demonstrated, adoption imagery is found throughout the biblical tradition. Two images of adoption are especially relevant for the present discussion. The first is drawn from the biblical representation of Moses in Exodus 1–2 and the second (to which I give less attention here) is derived from chapters 8– 9 in Paul's Letter to the Romans.

In detailing the birth and early life of Moses, Exod 1:8–2:10 focuses on the activity of five females who not only thwart the will of Pharaoh but secure the life of the one who will liberate the Hebrew people from oppression in Egypt. Together three of these characters, Moses' mother, Pharaoh's daughter, and Moses' sister, form a network of support for the as-yet-unnamed infant. Having hidden Moses for as long as she could to save him from Pharaoh's program of genocide, Moses' mother places her son in a papyrus ark among reeds along Nile's edge. When Pharaoh's daughter comes to the river to bathe, she sees the child, and having compassion for the crying infant, she declares, "This is one of the Hebrews' children" (2:6). At once, Moses' sister, who has been keeping watch from a distance, offers to retrieve a wet nurse, namely, Moses' mother, from among the Hebrew women to nurse the child for Pharaoh's daughter: "Shall I go and call for you a nurse from the Hebrews to nurse the child for you?" (2:7). Thus Pharoah's daughter, who gives the baby an Egyptian name, takes custody of the child once he has been nursed and weaned by his mother.

J. Cheryl Exum (1983; 1994), Brevard S. Childs, Meir Malul, and others have observed both the absence of any formal or legal designation for Moses' relationship to the daughter of Pharaoh and the resemblance of their relationship to that of adoption. Malul notes the similarity between details in the Moses saga and the ancient Near Eastern practice of giving an adopted infant to its birth-mother for wet-nursing. Childs even suggests that the practice may have been a way of asserting one's newly acquired parental rights over that of the birth mother. As Exum writes, "In what appears to be some form of adoption, the child 'became a son' to the princess. Thus secured from any further attempts of Pharaoh to deal with the Hebrew population, the future liberator grows up in the house of the oppressor" (1983:78). Whether formally adopted or not, Moses is clearly raised not by his birth-mother but by Pharaoh's daughter. So immersed is he in his new context, the adult Moses is later identified by strangers, without qualification, as "an Egyptian" (2:19).

In recounting the story of Moses' birth, adoption, and youth, Exodus displays not only a decidedly androcentric bias (Exum, 1983; 1994) but what Renita Weems identifies as well as an ideology of difference that reinscribes and exploits presuppositions concerning class, gender, and ethnicity:

> Exodus 1 does not challenge the notions of differences between people, be they male or female, or Egyptian and Hebrew.... The notion of difference between people is not challenged, but is simply inverted and coopted for his or her own purposes and for his or her own ideological interests. The narrator does not challenge the fundamental premise that Hebrews are different from Egyptians; the narrator simply exploits difference by insisting that the Hebrews are not the ones who are inferior, but are in fact superior to the Egyptians. (32)

While Weems rightly observes that the narrator's aim is to establish religious rather than ethnic superiority, it remains quite clear that ethnic identity serves as a means of contesting religious claims. Serving as the very faultline along which Moses' identity is negotiated, the difference between Hebrew and Egyptian plays a critical role in the biblical representation of Moses.

The young Moses of Exodus 1–2 is a figure caught between two distinct identities. As Weems notes, both the Egyptian dread of the Hebrews that explains the actions Pharaoh takes against them and the Hebrew midwives' claim that "the Hebrew women are not like the Egyptian women" (1:19) are predicated upon the Egyptian assumption that the Hebrew people are essentially different from themselves. That the narrator also assumes such a difference between the two peoples is illustrated by the text's multiple and oppositional allusions to them. Over the course of Exodus 1–2, the narrator establishes a sequence of references that sets the Egyptians and Hebrews in opposition to one another (all quotations from NRSV):

> 1:1a These are the names of the *sons of Israel* who came to Egypt with Jacob....

> 1:5b–7 *Joseph* was already in Egypt. Then *Joseph* died, *and all his brothers, and that whole generation.* But the *Israelites* were fruitful and prolific; they multiplied and grew exceedingly strong, so that the land was filled with them.

> 1:8–9 Now a new king arose over Egypt, who did not know *Joseph*. He said to his people, "Look, the *Israelite people* are more numerous and more powerful than we...."

> 1:12 But the more *they* were oppressed, the more *they* multiplied and spread, so that the Egyptians came to dread the *Israelites*. The Egyptians became ruthless in imposing tasks on the *Israelites*....

1:15 The <u>king of Egypt</u> said to the *Hebrew midwives*....

1:19 The *midwives* said to <u>Pharaoh</u>, "Because the *Hebrew women* are not like the <u>Egyptian women</u>; for *they* are vigorous and give birth before the midwife comes to them."

2:6–7 When <u>she</u> opened it, <u>she</u> saw the *child*. *He* was crying, and <u>she</u> took pity on *him*, "This must be one of the *Hebrews' children*," <u>she</u> said. Then *his sister* said to <u>Pharaoh's daughter</u>, "Shall I go and get you a nurse *from the Hebrew women* to nurse the *child* for <u>you</u>?"

2:11–15b One day, after *Moses* had grown up, *he* went out to *his people* and saw *their* forced labor. He saw an <u>Egyptian</u> beating a *Hebrew, one of his kinsfolk. He* looked this way and that, and seeing no one *he* killed the <u>Egyptian</u> and hid <u>him</u> in the sand. When *he* went out the next day, *he* saw two *Hebrews* fighting; and *he* said to the *one* who was in the wrong, "Why do you strike your fellow *Hebrew?*" *He* answered, "Who made *you* a ruler and judge over *us?* Do *you* mean to kill *me* as *you* killed the <u>Egyptian?</u>" Then *Moses* was afraid and thought, "Surely the thing is known." When <u>Pharaoh</u> heard of it, he sought to kill *Moses*. But *Moses* fled from <u>Pharaoh</u>.

2:19 They said, "An <u>Egyptian</u> helped us against the shepherds...."

Given the text's concentration on Egyptian/Hebrew identity and its consistent emphasis on Hebrew-Egyptian opposition, it comes as little surprise that Moses' Egyptian upbringing remains completely unnarrated. All that the text records of Moses' youth is that he did mature (2:11, "after Moses had grown up..."). For the narrator, Moses' adoption into the household of Pharaoh serves not so much to add detailed nuance to the hero's portrayal as to explain both the boy's survival and the acquisition of his Egyptian name.

That the text is interested in distancing Moses from his Egyptian relations is made especially clear in Exod 2:11–15b. Revealing more about the narrator's perspective than that of Moses, 2:11–15b opens with the following: "One day, after Moses had grown up, he went out to *his people* and looked on their forced labor; and he saw an Egyptian beating *a Hebrew, one of his people*." As the text goes on to narrate Moses' murder of the Egyptian, it refrains from indicating whether Moses is motivated by ethnic solidarity with the Hebrew slave, protest against Egyptian injustice, or both. Although the omnipotent narrator is clearly aware of Moses' ethnic identity, it is unclear whether Moses himself is even aware of his Hebrew origins. What cements Moses' distance from his Egyptian relations is his flight from Pharaoh. When Pharaoh, who presumably does know Moses' ethnic identity, hears of the murder, he seeks the life of his daughter's son. Thus Moses flees from Egypt to take refuge in Midian.

As interpreters have noted, as ambiguous as the text is about Moses' self-awareness, it is very clear about how he is perceived by strangers.

When the priest of Midian asks his daughters how they were able to water their flock in such a timely manner, they respond by recounting how Moses assisted them: "An Egyptian helped us against the shepherds..." (2:19). Since the text provides no explanation for the women's identification of Moses as an Egyptian, no specific evidence appears necessary. Moses is easily recognizable as an Egyptian and not as a Hebrew. Finally, over the space of just two verses, Moses not only meets the priest of Midian but also receives the priest's daughter, Zipporah, as his wife and names their firstborn son Gershom, " for he said, 'I have been an alien [*ger*] residing in a foreign land'" (2:22b). Thus the narration of Moses' early life and maturation end with the protagonist giving voice to his sense of displacement. The poignancy of the statement is not lost on readers who recognize the dual displacement of a Hebrew-born Egyptian who has had to take refuge in Midian.

Having succinctly portrayed his ethnic and social dislocation at the close of Exodus 2, the text quickly moves to establish Moses' reconnection with his people. Moses is soon revealed as one who will not only reidentify himself with his people, but who will serve as their very liberator. Following his divine commissioning by the God of Israel, Moses shows explicit recognition of his Hebrew identity. The word of God reveals that together with the elders, Moses will refer to "The LORD, the God of the Hebrews" as "the LORD *our* God" (3:18). Having aligned himself with his people and their God, he is never again identified as an Egyptian. Thus when Moses later announces that he is leaving Midian to return to his "kindred in Egypt," the reader knows that the Israelite hero is referring to his Hebrew kin (4:18).

The shifting identity of the Israelite hero is not lost on interpreters. Identifying Exod 2:1–10 as a late addition to the final form of the narrative, Randall Bailey sees in the present birth-adoption account the de-Africanization of Moses. He argues that "as one looks at the materials in the later units, the clear message is that Moses is Egyptian.... many aspects of the narrative in Exod 2:1–10 are intentionally geared to counteract these impressions" (26). Whether or not one is persuaded by Bailey's thesis regarding the redaction of Exodus 2, his observations underscore the tension that characterizes the canonical text. In a narrative that stresses the polarization and difference that distinguishes the Egyptians from the Hebrews, Moses cannot be portrayed as one whose identity is hybrid. The birth-adoption account functions both to explain Moses' Egyptian name and to delimit the significance of his Egyptian upbringing and identity. Thus whenever Moses' Egyptian ties are underscored by the narrative, the text quickly falls silent thereafter, accounting for neither the details of Moses' early life nor the characteristics that lead others to identify him as Egyptian.

Reading with the ideological grain of the narrative, Ernest Neufeld sees in Moses "the transformation of an all but assimilated Hebrew into an uncompromising champion and defender of his and God's chosen people" (58). Neufeld perceives the ambiguity of Moses' Hebrew consciousness in Exodus 1–2 and sees in the larger story evidence that "[w]hatever ember of his Hebrew self existed in his subconscious had to be stirred" (53). Reifying the ideology of difference that permeates the narrative, he contends that just as Pharaoh could not have considered Moses a "true Egyptian," Moses eventually became "seized with cognition of his true identity. He was an Israelite! He was not an Egyptian!" (56).

These interpretations of the Moses saga remind us that readers choose to read either with or against the ideological presuppositions that drive Exodus's representation of its protagonist. Although it is surely the triumph of Israel's God and the liberation of the Hebrew people, not adoption imagery, that serve as the central interests of the narrative, the ideology of difference that permeates the story of Moses gives rise nonetheless to a particular construction of adoption. By rendering mute any positive valuation of Moses' upbringing and establishing the championing of his people and the defeat of the Egyptians as proof positive of his ethnic self-identification, the text reinforces the notion that intercultural adoption signifies, at worst, a betrayal of one's origins, and at best, a dislocation that can only be corrected by a return to one's "true identity."

While the political and genocidal circumstances surrounding Moses' adoption by Pharaoh's daughter and his later reidentification with the Hebrew people aptly serve to bolster the ideology of liberation with which Exodus is chiefly concerned, the text's insistence on the exclusivity of Moses' self-identification perpetuates the double bind in which adoptees often find themselves. The demand to identify with one people over and against another, even and perhaps especially in the case of oppression or conflict, can itself be oppressive. This has proven to be true for some Korean and Vietnamese orphans of war who were subsequently adopted and raised in the U.S. The notion of a purer, or truer, identity, cleansed of the complexity that adoption invites, is one that adoptees regularly encounter and are confronted with by other Americans and Asians. The Exodus account reinforces the ideology of difference and exclusivity with which Americans, as a people, struggle and sometimes counter. For Asian American adoptees who yearn to claim both their American lives and identities as well as gain at least some access to their families of origin and heritage in Asia, the identity issues it raises are particularly pertinent and potentially painful.

Adoption As *Telos*

In chapters 8 and 9 of his Letter to the Romans, Paul makes repeated reference to the spiritual adoption (*huiothesia*) and inheritance that believers are to experience fully in the future and, in part, even in the present. Referring to the ancient practice whereby adopted males inherited property from their adoptive fathers, he writes, "For all who are led by the Spirit of God are children of God.... When we cry, 'Abba! Father!' it is the Spirit itself bearing witness with our spirit that we are children of God, and if children, then heirs, heirs of God and fellow heirs with Christ" (Rom 8:14–17). For Paul, believers who experience the life-giving and life-animating gift of the Spirit have not only been manumitted from slavery (Rom 6:16); they have been ushered into an adoptive relationship with the deity modeled upon that shared between Christ and God. In Rom 9:25–26, Paul reinforces this notion by citing Hos 2:1 to argue how divine election calls both Jews and Gentiles to be children of the living God. Thus in each of these instances, Paul draws upon the image of adoption to describe the present and future eschatological identity of believers. The metaphor of adoption is used to describe the transformation that believers claim and a particular *telos* at which they have partially arrived and to which they are still moving. In contrast to the images of adoption that emerge in Exodus 1–2, adoption is here a means of emphasizing not origins lost but newly found identity. The metaphor works for Paul precisely because it underscores not what believers have been, but what they have become and are becoming.

Yet neither is Paul completely unconcerned with history and the accidents of being. His identification with Israel is no less significant than that of Moses. For in addressing what he perceives as the problem of Jewish non-participation (and the potential for Gentile arrogance), Paul argues strenuously that to Israel, his people and "kindred according to the flesh" (Rom 9:3), belong "the adoption, the glory, the covenants, the giving of the law, the worship, and the promises" (Rom 9:4). If God's promises are faithful and reliable, then Israel's identity and covenant relationship with the deity are yet relevant. Thus Paul's use of adoption imagery erases neither ethnicity nor race nor other sources of identity. Keeping to the central theme of Romans ("For I am not ashamed of the gospel; it is the power of God for salvation to everyone who has faith, to the Jew first and also to the Greek," Rom 1:16), Paul's allusions to adoption support his notion that identity is a source of distinction but not of redemption or exclusive privilege.

Reflections

In bringing forth these two biblical traditions, I intend to present them not so much as competing notions upon which to reflect but as complementary images of adoption that resonate with the identity issues that loom large for Asian American adoptees. For many adoptees, adults as well as adolescents and children, the longing for the recovery of lost origins and the sense of having reached a certain *telos* form a dual reality. In keeping with the biblical traditions in Exodus and Romans, each of these realities is met by certain challenges from within and without. The desire to reconnect with one's unknown beginnings must at some point grapple with the myth of pure origins as well as the problems that stem from contemporary ideologies of difference and exclusivity. The sense of having arrived at a *telos* through the journey from relinquishment to adoption can ring hollow if it does not examine and engage the continuing relevance of all the accidents of one's being. The biblical images that we have considered here bring to light all of these aspects of the adoptive experience.

Finally, as Liu hints, the phenomenon of Asian adoption and the experience of Asian American adoptees raise essential questions about race, ethnicity, and the politics of identity that are relevant to the Asian American community as a whole. In his reflections on Asian America, Liu too asks about purity and hybridity and writes that "the choice, in fact, is not between real and fake. It is not between the pure and the despoiled. It is about ... what sort of synthesis we will bring into being" (201). Interestingly enough, he concludes by invoking biblical language to cite an excerpt from a wedding poem:

> It ends, as all things begin, with a covenant: "We release you. Our own fairy tale compels us,/ We will not ask you to realize our ambitions,/ To exact our revenges, to redeem our mistakes./ Our hands are open. We give you our blessing./ Go. Make up your own story." (203)

As a particular population of Asian Americans, adoptees are faced with the challenge and opportunity to discover and create a host of new stories, even while seeking the elements, known and unknown, lost and recovered, with which to tell them.

Works Consulted

Bailey, Randall C.
    1995   "'Is That Any Name for a Nice Hebrew Boy?' Exodus 2:1–10: The De-Africanization of an Israelite Hero." Pp. 25–36 in *The Recovery of Black Presence: An Interdisciplinary Exploration*. Ed. Randall C. Bailey and Jacquelyn Grant. Nashville: Abingdon.

Childs, Brevard S.
    1974   *The Book of Exodus: A Critical, Theological Commentary*. Philadelphia: Westminster.

Dunn, James D. G.
    1998   *Romans 1–8*. WBC 38. Dallas: Word.

Exum, J. Cheryl
    1983   "'You Shall Let Every Daughter Live': A Study of Exodus 1:8–2:10." *Semeia* 28:63–82.

1994 "Secondary Thoughts about Secondary Characters: Women in Exodus 1.8–2.10." Pp. 75–87 in *A Feminist Companion to Exodus to Deuteronomy.* Ed. Athalya Brenner. Sheffield: Sheffield Academic Press.

Johnson, Luke Timothy
1997 *Reading Romans: A Literary and Theological Commentary.* New York: Crossroad.

Liu, Eric
1998 *The Accidental Asian: Notes of a Native Speaker.* New York: Random House.

Malul, Meir
1990 "Adoption of Foundlings in the Bible and Mesopotamian Documents: A Study of Some Legal Metaphors in Ezekiel 16:1–7." *JSOT* 46:97–126.

Melnyk, Janet L. R.
1993 "When Israel Was a Child: Ancient Near Eastern Adoption Formulas and the Relationship between God and Israel." Pp. 245–59 in *History and Interpretation: Essays in Honor of John H. Hayes.* Ed. M. Patrick Graham, William P. Brown, and Jeffrey K. Kuan. Sheffield: JSOT Press.

Neufeld, Ernest
1993 "The Redemption of Moses." *Judaism* 42:50–58.

Scott, James M.
1992 *Adoption As Sons of God: An Exegetical Investigation into the Background of YIOTHESIA in the Pauline Corpus.* WUNT 2/48. Tübingen: Mohr.

Weems, Renita J.
1992 "The Hebrew Women Are Not Like the Egyptian Women: The Ideology of Race, Gender and Sexual Reproduction in Exodus 1." *Semeia* 59:25–34.

MY FATHER HAS NO CHILDREN: REFLECTIONS ON A *HAPA* IDENTITY TOWARD A HERMENEUTIC OF PARTICULARITY

Henry W. Rietz
Grinnell College

ABSTRACT

I do not have the privilege of speaking from a generally recognized social location. My mixed, or *hapa*, heritage precludes me from claiming any one identity with integrity. I am both Asian American and Euro-American, and yet I am neither. I am an "other" to the Other. The first part of this essay consists of an autobiographical narrative that tells some of the particularities of my story. For most of my life, I had been a secret to my father's Japanese American family. My *hapa* identity, my very existence, threatened the honor of my father's family. So, for them, my father had no children.

The second part of the essay reflects upon my *hapa* identity and how it may contribute to discussions of identity constructions and hermeneutics. I will suggest that my *hapa* identity reveals some of the limitations of identity constructions that use categories such as Americans of Japanese ancestry or even Asian American. Such categories are based on the commonalities of its members and their difference from a larger group. While recognizing the political expediency of such categories, constructing identity in this manner tends to homogenize members of the group while also exoticizing and ostracizing them from others. Instead, drawing on my own experience, I will propose a model of identity construction that emphasizes particularity as the basis for community and communication. Finally, I will close with a brief example of how a hermeneutic of particularity affects the way that I read the Dead Sea Scrolls.

I do not have the privilege of speaking from a generally recognized social location. My mixed, or what we call in Hawai'i *hapa*, heritage precludes me from claiming any one identity with integrity. I am both Asian American and Euro-American, and yet I am neither. I am an "other" to the Other.[1]

My family situation has always seemed normal to me. My mother was born in Germany and emigrated to the United States, eventually settling in

---

[1] I am indebted to James H. Charlesworth, Don Juel, Inn Sook Lee, and Dennis T. Olson for reading portions of earlier versions of this paper. I would also like to thank Tat-siong Benny Liew for inviting me to contribute this piece and for going above and beyond the call of an editor.

Hawai'i. My father was born in Hawai'i to parents who had immigrated from Japan. I was just like many *hapa-haole*[2]—that is, half-white—boys growing up in Hawai'i in the 1970s and early '80s. I have often wondered, however, if anyone else shared a similar story. What is different about my story is that while my father is Japanese,[3] I have my mother's *haole* last name.

Among Japanese people, a family's name is one of its most prized possessions. The family's name is the vessel that conveys honor or shame across the generations. Honor is ascribed to people on the basis of the actions of their ancestors through the family name. People's actions, however, can also bring shame to their ancestors, and thus dishonor the family's name. Protection and preservation of the family name is important to an honorable Japanese family.

So was the case of my father's family. My father's mother had an honorable family name. There were, however, no sons to carry on the name. Therefore, as the oldest of three sisters, it was my grandmother's obligation to marry a man who was willing to accept her family name, what is called in Japanese, a *yoshi*. Her marriage to my grandfather was *shimpai*, "arranged." After they were married, it was expected that the couple would take her family name, but my grandfather's father would not permit it; he wanted his own family's honorable name to be preserved. When my father was twenty-one years old, both of his parents passed away. As the eldest son, he assumed the duties and responsibilities of running the family's soap factory and of raising his younger brother and sister. Soon after his parents' deaths, his maternal grandmother approached him urging him to abandon his father's family name and to assume his mother's. But my father refused.

The problem of preserving my grandmother's family name was seemingly resolved when my great-grandmother arranged a marriage for her youngest daughter. Finally a *yoshi* was found. But as fate would have it, they had no children. So great-grandmother arranged to have one of the *yoshi*'s nephews adopted by the couple. A male progeny with the family name was ensured, despite the fact that he did not have the family's "blood." When the adopted son reached adulthood in the '70s, my father's nieces were pressured to marry the man who bears the family name in order to restore the family's blood to the name. All refused. Such is the extent to which an honorable Japanese family will go to preserve the family's name.

---

2 *Haole* is Hawaiian for "foreigner" and is popularly used in Hawai'i for people of European descent. *Hapa* is Hawaiian for "half." A person who is *hapa-haole* is "half-*haole*."

3 People of Japanese ancestry in Hawai'i usually identify themselves as simply "Japanese," rather than use a term such as Americans of Japanese Ancestry, as is more common on the mainland United States. *Japanese* is not being used here to identify people born and raised in Japan.

Being a (My)story

In 1966, my mother became pregnant with me. This situation posed a dilemma for my parents. For my father to marry a *haole* woman—a white woman—would bring shame and dishonor to his Japanese family. But my father, being an honorable man, proposed to my mother, offering to sell his property and move with her to the mainland. My mother, however, refused. She would not allow him to abandon his family. My mother, who grew up in Germany during World War II, was orphaned as child and later lost her only brother. Most of her extended family were killed either by the hands of the Nazis (they were Hungarian "gypsies" and French Jews) or in the senseless Allied bombing of Dresden. She, who had no family, understood the importance of family. She, a *haole,* knew to sacrifice her own feelings for her family.

For most of my life, my father's family did not know about my birth. My father's family did not know anything about me; they did not even know that I existed. To them, my father had no children.

I grew up in a four-unit apartment building on the island of O'ahu, about a fifteen-minute walk from Waikiki Beach. On our street, which was only one block in length, there lived people from various ethnic and cultural heritages: Japanese, Chinese, Filipino, Portuguese, *haole,* Korean, and Samoan. It was a typical neighborhood in Hawai'i. Our landlord and her family, which spanned three generations, lived in two of the apartments. They were Portuguese and *haole.* My mother and I lived in the third apartment.

Growing up, I received many culturally mixed messages. Some of the cultural messages originated on the mainland and were imported into Hawai'i through various media such as television, movies, and magazines. These images of the dominant *haole* culture of the United States were reinforced by our landlord and her family. They were members of the American Legion. The American flag flew in front of our apartment building during every holiday. Their ideal was John Wayne. He was the tough, brave, strong, white American man. In comparison to John Wayne, I, as a Japanese boy, seemed to be small, weak, and timid.

Elsewhere the messages were different. Whenever I went to the beach or other places where other local kids congregated, I often felt a sense of fear. "Eh, *haole* boy. Wat cha' you lookin' at?" "Eh bra', you get one problem or wat?" "Heh, *haole* boy, I talkin' to you. You like beef or what?" Because I looked white, I was often harassed, and I feared being hurt.

At school many of my friends were of Asian ancestry, especially Japanese. Most of the girls that I was attracted to were Japanese. I often wished my brown hair were black and straight. I felt odd when roll was taken in class, and I was one of only a few students with a *haole* last name. I wished I had a Japanese middle name like so many of my friends. After school, many of them went to Japanese Language School. I always wanted to go to Japanese Language School. Every year, Japanese families celebrate Boy's Day by flying over their house a flag of a carp for each son in the family. I always wanted to have a carp fly over our house.

My parents did not marry. A few years after I was born they had a falling-out, and their relationship became strained. They, however, maintained a friendship for my sake. Throughout my entire childhood, I saw my father virtually every day. He came by every afternoon. He ate dinner with us and spent the evening with us. Each night, before we went to sleep he would drive home. Growing up, I never felt insecure because of my birth. My friends *eventually* heard my story. I did not keep it as a secret from them. I was never ashamed of my situation.

Although I was never ashamed, I did find it difficult growing up "without" relatives. I had no family heritage that I could claim. Or maybe, more accurately, there was no heritage that would claim me. The community of Hawai'i is small. Somehow, in some way, everyone's paths cross. When people meet for the first time, the conversation often turns to their extended families, and they discover how they are connected by their extended families. One's identity derives from one's family name.

The most difficult thing about my family situation was not knowing what to do in the event of an emergency. For example, I often wondered what I should do if my father would become sick and hospitalized. Should I visit him in the hospital and risk exposing the secret of my existence, risk bringing shame upon my father? What would happen if he should pass away? Should I attend his funeral? I eventually resolved that I would not visit the hospital, and I would not attend his funeral. I would honor my father's life by not attending the services for his death.

Growing up, I longed to meet my relatives. I wished I could get to know them. I wished they could get to know me. Since the island is so small, my father would occasionally run into one of his relatives when we were out together. Although my father never told me to, I knew even as a young child to quietly walk away. I had met some of my relatives. None had ever met me. For all they knew, my father had no children.

When I was a junior in high school, I began to date a girl of Chinese ancestry. She was the second of three daughters. She came from a family with a very honorable Chinese name. Since the family had only daughters, there was no male heir, no one to carry on the family name. Her parents were from an aristocratic family in northeast China, and they had witnessed the brutality of the Japanese invasion of China during World War II. They had fled from the communists in 1949 and eventually emigrated to the United States in the 1960s. Although they were "strong" Christians, they were very Chinese in their thinking. They believed that their Christianity reinforced their Confucian heritage. Her parents opposed our relationship, and they cited various reasons for their opposition. I did not come from a "Christian" home. My grades were poor. I wasn't "doctoral material" (her father was a professor, and they wanted all of their daughters to go to medical school, or at least earn a Ph.D.). The actual source of their opposition, however, was racial. They did not like the fact that I was not Chinese. And, to make matters worse, I was not only *haole* but also Japanese.

Throughout most of our relationship, which lasted through college, I was a secret. We had to be discrete when we went out, "lest one of her parents' friends sees us." I never attended any of her family's parties, though they would often fix me a plate of food to eat in my car. At these parties, her parents would introduce her to "desirable" young Chinese men. Over time they slowly began to make concessions to our relationship. They allowed me to work for them, doing the yard work, painting their house, and repairing a second house they rented out. All the while they kept my relationship with their daughter a secret from their relatives and friends.

The rejection of my girlfriend's family was painful to me. I longed to be accepted into an extended family. I longed to be connected with a heritage. I resolved to meet all of their criticisms. My grades improved, and I started going to church. My girlfriend even made known to her parents that if we were to get married, I would be willing to take their family name. I was willing to become a *yoshi*.

In the end our relationship did not last, and we broke up soon after graduating from college. Eventually, I married a *haole* woman from the mainland. For most of my life, I had experienced alienation from my Japanese heritage. In an Asian American context, I was always conscious of how *haole* I was. I had struggled to be accepted by and connected to an Asian heritage, a struggle I had always lost. Now, living on the mainland and being in a relationship with a *haole* woman, I began to discover different aspects of my identity. In order to succeed in a *haole* context, I found myself adopting *haole* strategies of relating and *haole* expressions of identity. While I was able to function in a *haole* context, I did not feel comfortable. I did not "feel at home." Living in a *haole* context, I began to recognize how really Japanese I was. I began to face the challenge of forming a *hapa* identity, to integrate both heritages rather than to assimilate one into the other, or to accept one at the expense of the other.

The challenges of constructing a *hapa* identity became even more complicated as I moved from forming my own identity to participating in the formation of my children's identity. In the spring of 1995, my then wife was expecting our first child. It was then that I became convinced that the secrecy pervading my family must end. I could not bring a child into a world in which she did not exist. *Kodomo no tame ni* is a Japanese phrase that epitomized the ethics I had learned from my father and that he, in his own way, modeled honorably for me his entire life. *Kodomo no tame ni*. "For the sake of the children." I was now becoming a father. It was now my responsibility to give my daughter a heritage, an identity. So I asked my father on behalf of my daughter for something that I could never ask for myself. I asked my father that he make our existence known to his family. Over the years I had known that my father wanted to introduce me to his family. Though we had never spoken about it before, I had sensed the pain he felt because he could not acknowledge me publicly. He was as much a victim of the situation as I. Over the years, we each silently had endured. And now my father bravely did what I am sure he had always longed to do, but could not do, not for himself. He told his family about us, about me. *Kodomo no tame ni.*

A month after Maile, my daughter, was born, my father brought us to the family columbarium at the Soto mission, to the ashes of my grandparents. We brought flowers and offered incense. There, my father introduced us to his parents. The next month my parents were married. The wedding service was performed in the same Shinto shrine as my grandparents'. A friend of my mother's and I were the only witnesses.

My father's family was surprised by the news that my father had a son, and now a grandchild. Despite how small the island is, they never knew that my father had a son. My cousins and other extended family received me warmly and welcomed me into the family. Even my father's matriarchal aunts seemed to accept me. Now, to everyone we meet, my father proudly introduces me as his son and Maile as his *"haole* granddaughter."

The only person who could not recognize my existence, who could not accept me, was my aunt, my father's sister. The news that my father has a son devastated her and their relationship. The image of her brother, the one who had taken care of her and honorably looked out for her all these years, shattered. The man who had accepted all the responsibilities as the oldest son of a Japanese family, who tended the family altar, who represented the family at the funerals of the relatives of all the people who came to his parents' funerals, who provided wise counsel and leadership, the man who modeled what it really means to be Japanese to the family, the man who brought honor to the family, that man now, in her eyes, had dishonored the family. To her, my existence brings shame on the family name. She cannot see that my father is indeed an honorable Japanese man.

I am saddened by my aunt's reaction, but the hurt I feel cannot approach the pain my father experiences from the rejection of his sister. While I am hurt by my aunt's rejection and while I am angered by the pain it causes my father, I cannot self-righteously condemn her reaction. As a *hapa-haole,* my existence is a greater danger than merely bringing shame on her family name. I embody a loss of the Japanese culture, a threat to Japanese heritage. The process of forming my own *hapa* identity involves integrating seemingly contradictory elements from both of my heritages. As a *hapa-haole* living on the mainland for over a decade, I too feel the threat to my Asian identity. Being part *haole* living in a predominantly *haole* context, I struggle with the temptation to assimilate rather than transculturate or integrate. It is too easy for me to "pass" as another *haole,* if not in appearance, at least in demeanor. So I combat that temptation, at times with the determination to preserve my Asian identity at all costs.

My desire to protect my Japanese identity even affects who I am as a father. A part of me feels a sense of loss that my daughter Maile, who is only one-quarter Japanese, has blue eyes and blond hair and does not have many Asian features. I am saddened that she doesn't have a strong *hapa* appearance, that she doesn't look like me. Despite all that I have experienced, I still harbor some fears that some day she will marry a *haole* man from the mainland. Although I am sure that I will fully accept him into our family and love him, part of me probably will mourn the increasing loss of our Japanese heritage and culture, a loss that becomes greater with each successive generation. Will my children know what it means to be part Japanese? Will they preserve some of our Japanese customs and take pride in their Japanese heritage? Will they remember their ancestors? Will they bring honor to their family name?

Identity of Interpretation, and Interpretation of Identity

I wonder about my inclusion in a project dedicated to Asian American interpretations, to discussions of Asian American identity. What is my place? Where do *hapa* fit in? Do we have a contribution to make, or are we merely a threat that "dilutes" Asian American identity? And what about my daughters, who are one-quarter Japanese, and eventually their children? What will be their place?

So how may the story of my *hapa* identity contribute to this project? I would suggest that my *hapa* identity reveals some of the limitations of categories such as Americans of Japanese ancestry, and especially Asian Pacific American. Simplistically speaking, such categories tend to construct identity by emphasizing differences from a majority group while emphasizing commonalities among its minority members. While recognizing the political expediency of such strategies, especially to prevent assimilation, there are also dangers. By emphasizing differences from others, such constructions at best may result in exotification, and at worst alienation and self-marginalization from others. By emphasizing commonalities among its members, identity construction in this manner tends to homogenize its members, eliding the tremendous differences that do exist among us. Whose identity is being privileged by the category of Asian American?

Hapa complicates the situation even further, since there are no clear distinctions between categories, between Asian Americans and others, or even amongst ourselves. What specific cultures and heritages have those of us who are *hapa* integrated into our individual identities? Have we been accepted and integrated into our Asian cultures, or were we adopted into a white family, raised without even knowing another person with Asian ancestry? How do *others* see and treat us, as Asian Americans, as whites, blacks, or hispanic? Even as *hapa,* our stories are so different.

My experience leads me to propose a mode of identity construction that emphasizes particularity as the basis for community and communication. In my search to find someone in a similar situation, I have yet to find another *hapa* person with the same story as mine. But despite the differences, and even because of the differences, I have learned from listening to the stories of others. There is power in hearing and in sharing our particular stories, by maintaining both the similarities as well as the differences. When we maintain the particularities, we communicate; we are in relationship, not as stereotyped caricatures or abstractions, but as two distinct individuals, each with a rich nexus of relationships and experiences. This perspective influences my reading of ancient literature and the ways that I conceptualize early Jewish and Christian communities.

The Dead Sea Scrolls: Toward a Hermeneutic of Particularity

My study of the Dead Sea Scrolls began while I was a divinity student at Princeton Theological Seminary. Eventually, I decided to do my dissertation there on the Qumran community. Inspired by Rudolf Bultmann's identification of the eschatology and apocalyptic worldview of the Christian scriptures as being unbelievable to "modern man [sic]" (2–6), I turned to the Dead Sea Scrolls to give me a background so I could better understand and perhaps meaningfully reinterpret the eschatology of the early Christians for a modern Western context. However, as I became more immersed in the Scrolls and even more secondary literature (I was writing a dissertation, after all!), my hermeneutic of particularity—a hermeneutic that discerns differences as well as similarities—pushed me beyond the familiar category of eschatological beliefs.[4] Coming from a nonliturgical Protestant Christian background, one that emphasized "faith not works" and did not at all emphasize a distinction between "sacred" and "profane" time, halakic concerns and liturgy were some of the major ways that I discerned the Qumran community as different from my personal experience of religion. My hermeneutic of particularity, however, did not allow me to

---

[4] See the discussion by Donald S. Lopez Jr., who convincingly challenges the notion that "belief" is the basic category for investigating religions.

disregard or otherwise bracket those differences. Rather, I felt compelled to seek to integrate them in my understanding. Thus, as my research progressed, I moved away from investigating the so-called "eschatology" of the Qumran community to using the broader category of "time" to encompass, not only the community's understanding of history and cosmology, but how that understanding is related to the community's practices, that is, to halakot and ritual.[5]

It has long been recognized that the historian is not merely an "objective" observer who describes a subject in a detached fashion. Rather, the historian's interests and perspectives in some measure affect and determine interpretations and descriptions. This influence is especially the case when the subjects of study are religions, or the writings left by religious persons. Thus, it is no surprise that the modern academic descriptions of the Qumran community that produced the sectarian Dead Sea Scrolls fall into groups that reflect contemporary religious positions. Broadly speaking, historical descriptions of the Qumran community tend to fall into two categories. On the one hand, there are studies that tend to use theological categories to emphasize its "mystical," "apocalyptic," and "devotional" aspects. These descriptions are usually produced by scholars who come from Christian (see, e.g., James H. Charlesworth; John J. Collins; Jerome Murphy-O'Connor; Helmer Ringgren; Krister Stendahl; and James C. VanderKam, 1994) or liberal Jewish traditions (see, e.g., Geza Vermes). On the other hand, there are studies that tend to emphasize "halakic" regulations and liturgical instructions. These descriptions often are produced by scholars who emerge from Jewish traditions that tend to be more orthodox (see, e.g., Joseph M. Baumgarten; Lawrence Schiffman, 1975; and Schiffman, 1994 [but see his part 5 and Schiffman, 1989]). The problem is not that these scholars have allowed their "subjective" perspectives to influence their supposedly "objective" historical descriptions. Indeed, I contend that much of the value of their descriptions comes from the unique empathies that each brings from his or her own perspective. The difficulty is that while these two types of descriptions are not necessarily mutually exclusive, it is often difficult to imagine how they describe the same community. How are we to understand the members of a community who, on the one hand, were obsessively concerned about such seemingly mundane matters as what constitutes work on the Sabbath and, on the other hand, believed themselves to be living in the "latter days" awaiting the imminent arrival of the "Messiahs of Aaron and Israel"?

In my study of the Qumran community through the particulars of previous scholarship (both by those who emphasize the apocalyptic theology

---

[5] My full treatment of the subject can be found in Rietz, 2000.

and those who emphasize the rituals and halakot of the Qumran community), I found that the category "time" could bring together the community members' understanding of history and the community's halakot (or interpretations of Jewish law). I found that the Qumran community's adherence to a sectarian 364-day calendar is rooted in their halakic concern to keep the Torah commandments to worship God and honor the Sabbath.[6] The community inherited traditions asserting that God commanded this specific calendar (see, e.g., *Jub.* 6:32–35). The use of this calendar enabled the community members to keep the Torah commandments to observe the various festivals while at the same time honoring the commandments concerning the Sabbath (CD MS A XI, 17–18; see also Schiffman, 1975). For instance, the *Rule of the Community* states that members "shall not stray from any one of all God's orders concerning their appointed times; they shall not advance their appointed times nor shall they retard any one of their feasts" (1QS I, 13–15). Similarly, the *Damascus Document* stipulates that members are "to keep the Sabbath day according to the exact interpretation, and the festivals and the day of fasting, according to what they had discovered, those who entered the new covenant in the land of Damascus" (CD MS A VI, 18–19).

Their halakic concern is, in turn, rooted in their cosmic belief that the liturgical and Sabbath commandments are observed in the heavens as well as on earth. The Qumran community shared the cosmology common in early Judaism, namely, that the cosmos consists of the heavens above and the earth below. Despite the bifurcation of the two realms, the structures and inhabitants of each realm are conceived as paralleling the other. Humans on earth are paralleled by divine angelic beings in the heavens (see, e.g., the *War Scroll* and the *Songs of the Sabbath Sacrifice*). The Jerusalem Temple corresponds to a celestial sanctuary. Members of the Qumran community believed that the commandments regarding the Sabbath and the festivals had been given not only to Israel but also to the celestial beings and the angels (see, e.g., *Jubilees* 2 and the *Songs of the Sabbath Sacrifice*). In other words, the Sabbath and the festivals are to be celebrated in the heavens as well as on earth (see again the *Songs of the Sabbath Sacrifice*). Thus, the liturgy of the two sanctuaries is to be coordinated not only in actions, but also in timing. That is to say, worship in the Jerusalem Temple is to be synchronized with the heavenly worship. In this way, a connection, even an experience of community, is established between the celestial and the terrestrial beings. The 364-day calendar was then understood not only as an expression of God's will, but also as God's ordering of the cosmos.

---

[6] For a helpful survey of scholarship on the Qumran calendar(s), see VanderKam, 1998:52–70.

Therefore, if the commandments are not observed at the appropriate time by following the correct calendar, the continuity between the heavens and earth is severed, and thus the earth becomes estranged from the divine presence. The Qumran community believed that indeed the continuity had been broken, because the Jerusalem Temple was governed by the wrong calendar, the 354-day lunar-based calendar. Thus God revealed to the community "hidden matters in which Israel had gone astray: God's holy Sabbath and God's glorious feasts, God's just stipulations and God's truthful path" (CD MS A III, 13–15). From their perspective, God has not only ordered the cosmos according to the annual cycles of the 364-day calendar, but God has also ordered the course of history. "From the God of knowledge (comes) all that is and (all) that shall be" (1QS III, 15; see also *Sabbath Song* 5). Specifically, members of the community believed that God has arranged history into "periods" and that God has predetermined the character, duration, and events of each of these periods (CD MS A XVI, 2–4; 4Q180 1, 1–2a). Within this understanding of history, the regnant priests' failure to observe in the Jerusalem Temple the community's halakot—especially the calendar—indicated to the members of the community that they were living in "the latter days" of an "evil period" in history.

For members of the community, human praxis had cosmic implications; failure to observe the community's halakot in the Temple created a cosmic disturbance. To be "out of synch" with God's ordering of the cosmos by not observing the Sabbaths and the festivals at the correct time was sin and made one liable to God's wrath. Ultimately, the Qumranites predicted that the period of evil would culminate in a full-blown war between the forces of good and evil in the heavens and on the earth (see the *War Scroll*). So the community retreated into the wilderness, "to prepare there the way of the LORD," to await the end of the present evil age and to prepare for the age when the divine presence returns to Israel (see 1QS VIII).

Because of the strong spatial dualism, references to the war often portray two parallel battles occurring, one on earth and the other in the heavens. Nevertheless, within the context of the war, there are also claims that divine beings—angels and even God—are present in the community. Significantly, the wording of some of these claims echoes affirmations of communion with the divine associated with worshiping God at the correct time; "for the holy angels [are] together with their hosts" (1QM VII, 3–6; see also 1QSa II, 3–9 and a composite of 4QD^a [4Q266] 8 I, 7–9, CD MS A XV, 15–18, and 4QD^e [4Q270] 6 II, 8–9). These echoes suggest that, as members of the community believed that terrestrial worshipers should be synchronized with the heavenly counterparts, they also conceived of their combatants on earth as needing to be synchronized with their heavenly allies.

The association of the community's worship on the Sabbath, for instance, and battle is supported by the common *Sitz im Leben*, namely, in ritual contexts. War in many cultures, including the ancient Near East and especially in early Judaism, is a religious phenomenon requiring cultic rituals and purity. This aspect of war is well attested at Qumran by the *War Scroll* and the *Rule of War*, both of which are essentially liturgies for battle. Formally, liturgy consists of music (songs, chants, as well as the playing of instruments) and ritual actions (choreographed movements and even dance). Group performance of music and ritual actions often involves a synchronization of participants. The phenomenology of music suggests that perhaps the Qumranites' experience of community, and even unity with the divine, are products of the synchronicity facilitated by their rituals and liturgies. Within a worldview in which members of the community believed they were "in time" with the heavens, the experience of unity among members of the community in liturgy would have been understood as including the divine. The experience of the divine in worship represents an in-breaking, or even a collapsing of the heavens and the earth. Thus, for the Qumranites, the proper observance of time meant a fulfillment of God's promise: "If you follow my statutes and keep my commandments and observe them faithfully ... I will place my dwelling in your midst ... and I will walk among you, and will be your God, and you shall be my people" (Lev 26:3, 11–12).

Conclusion

The hermeneutic of particularity, which I use to understand and appropriate the stories of others as I struggle to form my *hapa* identity, also informs and guides my study of the Qumran community. It pays attention to the similarities as well as the differences that I perceive between the Qumranites and myself. Since differences can coexist without necessarily canceling each other out, my hermeneutic of particularity leads to a reading of the religion of the Qumran community that emphasizes both its theological and its ritualistic dimensions.

Works Cited

Baumgarten, Joseph M.
    1977   *Studies in Qumran Law*. Leiden: Brill.

Bultmann, Rudolf
    1961   "New Testament and Mythology." Pp. 1–44 in *Kerygma and Myth: A Theological Debate*. Ed. Hans Werner Bartsch. Trans. Reginald H. Fuller. New York: Harper & Row.

Charlesworth, James H., ed.
    1994   *Jesus and the Dead Sea Scrolls*. New York: Doubleday.

Collins, John J.
　1995　　*The Scepter and the Star: The Messiahs of the Dead Sea Scrolls and Other Ancient Literature*. New York: Doubleday.

Lopez, Donald S., Jr.
　1998　　"Belief." Pp. 21–35 in *Critical Terms for Religious Studies*. Ed. Mark C. Taylor. Chicago: University of Chicago Press.

Murphy-O'Connor, Jerome
　1991　　*Paul and the Dead Sea Scrolls*. New York: Crossroad.

Rietz, Henry W.
　2000　　"Collapsing of the Heavens and the Earth: Conceptions of Time in the Sectarian Dead Sea Scrolls." Ph.D. diss., Princeton Theological Seminary.

Ringgren, Helmer
　1995　　*The Faith of Qumran: Theology of the Dead Sea Scrolls*. New York: Crossroad.

Schiffman, Lawrence
　1975　　*The Halakah at Qumran*. Leiden: Brill.

　1989　　*The Eschatological Community of the Dead Sea Scrolls: A Study of the Rule of the Congregation*. Atlanta: Scholars Press.

　1994　　*Reclaiming the Dead Sea Scrolls*. Philadelphia: Jewish Publication Society.

Stendahl, Krister, ed.
　1997　　*The Scrolls and the New Testament*. New York: Crossroad.

VanderKam, James C.
　1994　　*The Dead Sea Scrolls Today*. Grand Rapids, Mich.: Eerdmans.

　1998　　*Calendars in the Dead Sea Scrolls: Measuring Time*. New York: Routledge.

Vermes, Geza
　1994　　*The Dead Sea Scrolls: Qumran in Perspective*. Minneapolis: Fortress.

PART II

READING READINGS OF THE BIBLE IN ASIAN AMERICA

The "Hidden Manna" That Sustains: Reading Revelation 2:17 in Joy Kogawa's *Obasan*

Jane Naomi Iwamura
University of Southern California

ABSTRACT

Joy Kogawa opens her seminal work, *Obasan*, with Revelation 2:17. Despite the insightful nature of the literary criticism that has accompanied the book, these accounts have not adequately addressed this biblical reference, which, I argue, must be taken as an integral dimension of the overall work. Indeed, this brief biblical citation, along with the memorandum sent by the Co-operative Committee on Japanese Canadians to the House and the Senate of Canada in 1946 with which the book ends (248–50), function as a "rhetorical frame" in which the protagonist's personal narrative is to be viewed. By linking Naomi's story to both biblical prophecy and political document, such a frame challenges conventional secular readings of Kogawa's work as mere "literature" or "history." One must consider *Obasan* as offering spiritual witness to not only the complex faith of Asian North Americans but also the unexpected, yet significant ways God and history merge within a people's concrete struggle.

> *To him that overcometh*
> *will I give to eat*
> *of the hidden manna*
> *and will give him*
> *a white stone*
> *and in the stone*
> *a new name written....*
> The Bible

Joy Kogawa begins her seminal work, *Obasan,* with this passage from Revelation (2:17). Sparse, unobtrusive, and almost commonplace in English-language novels, the biblical epigraph first appears as a manageable convention. Although popular reviewers and literary critics, as well as everyday readers, may appreciate the author's deployment of biblical allusion and

---

* This essay is dedicated to the memory of Amy Ling.

metaphor, I surmise that they have yet to recognize the political gesture it represents or the social environment that makes biblical citation, in this instance, a revolutionary act.

Obasan first appeared in Canada in 1981. Since its initial publication, the book has gone on to garner a host of impressive literary awards and has seen republication in the U.S., England, and Japan. The positive reception that *Obasan* received has conferred upon the work "the seal of authority and authenticity to its narration of Japanese Canadian internment" (Miki: 135) and, by appropriated extension, Japanese American internment as well. As a result, *Obasan* is often taken as a representative text of the Japanese North American internment experience and is read widely in high school and college classrooms throughout the continent.[1]

A fictional narrative that melds historical document with poetic vision, *Obasan* offers unique insight into the plight of Japanese North Americans during the Second World War—the racist mistreatment suffered in the name of national defense and the legacy of this oppression. The nonlinear narrative recounts the narrator Naomi Nakane's coming to terms with the disappearance of her mother, whom, she discovers at the novel's end, had fallen victim in the nuclear bombing of Nagasaki. Through the personal revelation that accompanies her discovery, Naomi is able to recognize the unconditional love underlying the apparent abandonment by her mother. The protagonist-narrator's tale is interspersed with her own experience of the Japanese Canadian internment and dispersal, which parallels the repressed trauma of her mother's disappearance. The novel also gives witness to Naomi's own struggle to negotiate between two distinct ways of coping with these events as exemplified by her two aunts: Aunt Emily, who engages in political action and harnesses the written word to fight racial oppression, and Aya Obasan, who suffers in silence. Through a perspective that draws from, yet transcends both these ethical responses, Naomi begins a journey of healing necessitated by the traumatic events that have so profoundly shaped her life.[2]

Obasan has inspired a multitude of secondary articles, a testament to its literary accomplishments. Many of these articles discuss the religious dimensions of the text, especially explicating the Buddhist and Christian frameworks that help shape Kogawa's humanistic vision (Davidson; Gottlieb;

---

[1] For a summary of *Obasan* that includes a discussion of the novel's background and context, as well as the pertinent issues it raises, see Lo.

[2] A picture of Naomi's journey of self-discovery and healing is incomplete without reading Kogawa's second novel and continuation of the protagonist's story, *Itsuka*. Whereas *Obasan* perhaps emphasizes the psychological and spiritual implications of the internment experience, *Itsuka* more readily demonstrates how political action is an integral dimension of healing as it recounts Naomi's involvement in the Japanese Canadian struggle for redress.

Kruk; Ueki). However, these perspectives—mainly from Anglo critics—often privilege the Buddhist elements (Davidson; Gottlieb; Ueki). For these critics, the Christian symbolism and iconography operating in the novel are "superimposed" or grafted onto a worldview fundamentally shaped by Buddhism and Japanese folk religion (Kruk: 90). As such, they mainly express the commentator's own vision of the syncretic religiosity as practiced by Japanese North American Christians that informs the sensibility of the text.

Asian American and Asian Canadian literary critics take another tack. For these commentators, Christianity is viewed as part and parcel of the Canadian nationalist project. As Roy Miki comments:

> Within a conventional literary treatment of reference, the [biblical] epigraph can be read—and has been read—as a premonition that the narrative conflict of *Obasan* will be resolved. The implication is that the protagonist, Naomi Kato, will emerge with a new identity after she has made her descent into her repressed history and memory. When read as a reaction to racialization, the same biblical frame reverses into a doubled discourse of white supremacy and reveals itself as a mechanism (as Christianity was used in colonization) of an enforced assimilation. The "othered" racial "object" undergoes translation into whites; her former subject identity, already under erasure by the racism of the past, is abandoned for a new name written on "white stone." (139)

For critics such as Miki, to identify as Christian becomes analogous to identifying as Canadian, and henceforth, "white." Although Christian discourse is prominent in the text, *Obasan* is recuperated by Asian North American commentators who posit Kogawa's stance toward biblical reference as essentially ironic. Shirley Geok-lin Lim and Cheng Lok Chua note, respectively:

> *Obasan* carries a bitter critique of Christian discourse. The images offered in the use of biblical language are contextually "ironized" and depleted of their significance. (Lim: 305)

> These [Christian] symbols [Kogawa] has "displaced" into an ironic narrative mode and this technique in turn puts an ironic question to the Christian ethic professed by Canada's majority culture. (Chua: 101)

Within these interpretive frames, the professed faith of the Japanese Canadian Christian community—its belief in an ethic of unconditional love and forgiveness—is undercut by the historical events that Naomi's narrative bears witness. Similar to this interpretive strategy, commentators also point out the ways the alignment of Christianity with the nation is intimately tied to patriarchy and the silencing of the feminine voice (Lim; Kruk; Potter) and how *Obasan* offers an alternative discourse that counters such suppression.

Although these perspectives offer insight into the unique faith of Japanese North Americans or critical commentary on the role of religion in the construction of national identity, they seem to elide the author's own religious commitments that invariably inform the text. Kogawa was born and raised in Canada—the daughter of an Anglican minister. (Her father would serve as inspiration for the character of Nakayama-sensei in the book.) In published interviews, such as her conversation with Magdalene Redekop, Kogawa claims Christianity as her faith and the religious metaphors and tales it provides as the "language" with which she works:

> MR: Does Christianity come out in the language of *Obasan* because that's what you grew up with?
> JK: Well, yes, it's my window, it is a window. It's the only window I've got to eternity. (laughter) (16)

Although literary interpretation oftentimes extends the vision the author holds for a text, in the case of *Obasan* it has thus far missed a key reading of the religious references that is perhaps more in line with the author's original intention. For Kogawa, I would argue, biblical reference does not simply serve a literary function—to illuminate the story at hand or act as ironic target—but emplots Japanese North Americans within an ongoing realization of (biblical) history as the "unfolding Word."

In the case of *Obasan,* Kogawa's implied assertion of a Christian identity is indeed a revolutionary act. Within a conventional anticolonial frame, such an assertion may not appear subversive, since it seems expressive of an assimilationist mentality that seeks acceptance by the dominant culture. But read from within an informed understanding of Asian North American Christianity and the particular burdens Asian North American Christians have had to bear, this reclamation is a potent one. As David K. Yoo articulates:

> For Asian American Christians, a shared faith with the dominant religious tradition of the nation has not been enough to bridge the gap created by race. Although the prevailing assumption is that Asian American Christians are more assimilated than their non-Christian counterparts, the fact remains that individuals and communities have consciously forged religious identities in opposition to the discrimination they have encountered despite shared faith with the majority of their fellow Americans. At the same time, the long-standing presence of independent racial-ethnic denominations attests to how Asian American Christians have created institutions that reflect their concerns and cater to their own needs. Separate racial-ethnic churches, programs, and governing bodies within majority Euro-American religious institutions, moreover, suggest the complex and contested nature of Asian American Christianity. In Christ there may be no East or West, but for Asian Americans the observation made by

the Reverend Doctor Martin Luther King Jr. still rings true: Sunday morning worship is the most segregated hour in America. The privileging and power of the Euro-American Christian tradition have meant that all others, even coreligionists, have been relegated to second-class status. (7–8)

Asian North American Christians are viewed as "second-class citizens" in the sense that their religious practice and faith are often considered *derivative* from those of their white progenitors. Framed as essentially Buddhist, Hindu, Taoist, or Confucian, their identity as Christians is often taken as newly adopted and "impure," that is, noninfluential. In these insidious ways, Asian North Americans are seen as bearing no legitimate claim as interpreters or innovators of the Christian tradition; they are literally written out of the history of Christianity.

Given this representational dilemma, *Obasan* makes a noteworthy intervention. In the reading that follows, we will see how Kogawa harnesses the authority of one dominant tradition (Christianity) to undermine that of another (nation). As a result, the Christian Word operates not as an oppressive structure, but as a source of liberation and hope. Furthermore, Kogawa, through her recontextualization of biblical verse, leads the reader to draw specific connections between the Japanese Canadian history and the biblical past. The Bible, in this way, not only informs a contemporary text, but the contemporary text revivifies the tradition and demonstrates how its truth and meaning are expressed even today in the concrete struggles of a particular community. Through this two-way dynamic, *the Word is made flesh*.

Revelation in *Obasan*

To understand this dynamic, one must first consider how the biblical text offers added significance to *Obasan* as postbiblical narrative. Kogawa deploys a wide range of biblical metaphors and stories, but it is Rev 2:17 that she chooses to frame the novel. Literary critics have loosely discussed the elements of the verse—"manna," "new name," and "white stone"—and how these elements evoke the biblical topoi of exile and resurrection. But they have not examined the passage within its original context. Hence, it seems necessary to elaborate on this context before one proceeds to draw the metaphorical links between biblical citation and Kogawa's narrative.

The book of Revelation has been popularly attributed to the prophet John and begins with warnings and praises to seven churches in Asia Minor (modern-day Turkey). Although the exact date of its composition is not known, it can roughly be traced to the first century, when Asia Minor was part of the Roman Empire and the imperial cult was popularly maintained. The social context is an inherent dimension of the book and is especially evident in chapters 1–3, the "seven letters" addressed to particular communities. The author seems especially concerned with the compromises toward Roman civil religion these communities make in order to maintain their social and economic place in Roman society.

For the church in Pergamum, to which the words in Rev 2:17 are directed,[3] a legacy of resistance, as well as the fear of execution for one's commitment to Christ, is an integral part of the community's memory. By citing the martyr Antipas (Rev 2:13), the author acknowledges the sacrifices that Pergamum Christians have already made. But the contemporary environment in which the church now exists makes the need for such sacrifices and acts of resistance less evident. As long as Christians "did not provoke their neighbors by active witness and by nonparticipation in the ordinary social and patriotic decencies, then they would come to no harm" (Sweet: 653). Here, the pressure to participate in rituals of the state is more indirect and insidious. The external compromises that Christians in Asia Minor are now compelled to make, in comparison with past abuses, seem mild and harmless. For these believers, such concessions have become well worth the social reward of acceptance.

In response to this situation, the author not only admonishes the church for its complacency but also exhorts its members to resist the compromises that will inevitably lead to their assimilation into Roman life. Devotion to the state and an embrace of its economic and social values erode Christian identity and, more importantly, the ethic of love, mutual recognition, and aid, on which that identity is based. As Elisabeth Schüssler Fiorenza points out in her interpretation of the book's rhetorical context:

> The exhortations of the seven-message section aim primarily at prophetic interpretation and critical evaluation. The strength of the Christian community in Asia Minor consists: in mutual love, in service to others, in fidelity and steadfastness, in the keeping of God's word and the rejecting of false teachers, in the confession of its faith even during persecution, and in consistent resistance. The author emphasizes the works, or the *praxis,* of the Asian churches. However, not all the churches are still doing "the works of their first love." (1991:53)

The call for such critical evaluation is not the only dimension of the letters; they also include encouragement as well. This encouragement comes in the form of an eschatological promise, and in the case of the letter addressed to

---

[3] Biblical scholars point out that although each of the seven letters bears an address to an individual church, the number "seven" symbolically carries a universal nature along with its use. Therefore, the author's message should be read as a general one to all the churches of Asia Minor.

the church in Pergamum, Rev 2:17 represents that promise. The "hidden manna" as well as "the white stone " with "a new name written" are the rewards and consolations that the faithful can look forward to.

Having sketched a broader view of the social context that informs the biblical verse, one can now draw relevant parallels between Christians in Pergamum and the Japanese Canadians in Kogawa's novel. As we have seen, the author of Revelation takes into account the community's past history of suffering and sacrifice, but his words address that community in its contemporary situation.[4] Similarly, *Obasan* contains within its narrative the suffering of those of Japanese ancestry in the name of Canada's national defense. Like the Christians in Pergamum, at a specific moment in history, Japanese Canadians were seen as a *direct* threat to the government. And through the process of authorized internment and sanctioned dispersal, their identity as ethnic citizens is unduly sacrificed. However, Naomi's words do not simply narrate the past, but also reveal the state of Japanese Canadians in the present. Naomi and Stephen especially bear the burden of their family's repeated compromise: "Do not tell..." (1984:242). The consensual decision to endure the traumatic events of the past and its lingering consequences in silence ("Kodomo no tame—for the sake of the children—gaman shi masho—let us endure" [245]) leaves what is left of the community confused, fragmented, and numb. Kogawa makes this compromise understandable, and it is framed as one that is originally forged in love and the need for psychic survival. But continued repression transforms the condition of silence into one that is ultimately damaging—damaging in its refusal to bear witness and to reveal injustice. Through silence, one ultimately becomes complicit with the forces of injustice.

The book of Revelation also becomes linked to Kogawa's novel, in the sense that both authors address the issue of identity and assimilation within the framework of empire and nation-building. Both texts first account for a time when the state took drastic measures to punish those who would not pledge their unconditional allegiance. More accurately, this historical moment

---

[4] Martyrdom is similarly mentioned in *Obasan* and specifically linked to Naomi's childhood. She remembers a time when Aunt Emily read to her a story from "a wine colored encyclopedia" entitled *The Book of Knowledge:*

> "Look, Nomi," she says, pointing to the picture of a little girl carrying a candle and walking in the dark to get a secret message to her father in a dungeon. It's a story in part of the encyclopedia called "The Book of Golden Deeds", which is filled with tales of martyrs and brave children and people going through torment and terror. Could I, I wonder, ever do the things they do? Could I hide in a wagon of hay and not cry out if I were stabbed by a bayonet? (Kogawa, 1984:72)

Here Kogawa deploys the trope of martyrdom to foreshadow the suffering of the internees, as well as allow Naomi to call into question her own fortitude.

represents a time when both Rome and Canada could only view the identity of the marginal community as essentially divided and opposed (Roman versus Christian, Canadian versus Japanese). As mentioned previously, the book of Revelation is most likely written in a more relaxed time, when Christians are able to maintain their identity somewhat as long as they show proper respect to the state. Post-war Japanese Canadians found themselves in a similar situation. Again, such compromises probably seemed like a small price to pay, making the internal assimilation of both communities all the more easy.

Revelation's author—as well as Kogawa, I would argue—implore their readers to resist this path and hold steadfastly onto a vision of their unique identity. In Revelation, this is written into the eschatological promise outlined in 2:17. By citing the verse, Kogawa likewise harnesses the power of this promise for Japanese Canadians. The key to its full relevance resides in the different metaphorical elements of the verse that I will now examine.

Manna

Biblical citation in *Obasan* actually depends on a chain of meaning in which Kogawa invokes New Testament scripture that in turn references Old Testament events. Revelation 2:17, with its allusion to manna, links the situation of the Christians in Pergamum to that of the Israelites and their exodus from Egypt. By citational extension, Kogawa links the story of Japanese Canadians to these spiritual struggles. Although *Obasan*'s commentators bypass the significance of the New Testament moment, they often are able to discern the Old Testament connection:

> Stone and manna, when combined, provide the reader a clue with which to translate the meaning of silence kept in unison by Uncle, Obasan and Aunt Emily. The quoted passage regarding "the hidden manna" is based on a Biblical legend that Jeremiah concealed "a golden jar of the manna" in an unknown place before the fall of Jerusalem in 587 BC (2 Maccabees 2:5); however, a more pertinent image comes from Exodus, chapter sixteen, which talks of the heavenly bread of manna given to the wandering Israelites as proof of the existence of God's love in the midst of their despair in the wilderness. As mentioned earlier, the fate of the Japanese-Canadians banished into the Canadian wasteland is comparable to that of the Israelites. (Ueki: 15)

Here it is interesting to note an aspect of the Exodus narrative that commentators often overlook: the impetus for God's dispensation. Manna rains down from the heavens in response to the Israelites' "grumblings." As their hunger erodes their faith in God's plan, the Israelites begin to criticize harshly Moses' and Aaron's decision to lead them out of resource-rich Egypt into the desolate wilderness: "Would that we had died by the Lord's hand in the land of Egypt, when we sat by the pots of meat, when we ate bread to the full" (Exod 16:3). This discontent and suspicion is similarly written into *Obasan*. For the narrator, pre-internment symbolizes a time of comfort and well-being: "When I am hungry, and before I can ask, there is food. If I am weary, every place is a bed" (57). However, this seemingly Edenic period is soon disrupted by the onset of war. And as Japanese Canadians are dispersed throughout Canada, the narrator's dissatisfaction is evident. When forced relocation further disbands the community, Nakayama-sensei, as well as the adults, reconfirm their faith in God through a communal prayer. However, the solemnity of the moment is broken as Naomi's brother, Stephen, fidgets and breaks from his kneeling position, reflecting an uneasiness with the pronouncement. This uneasiness is reinforced by the following scene, in which Kogawa figures Christian faith as the nameless missionaries who bid Naomi, Stephen, and the other internees farewell on the train platform:

> The missionaries are moving through the crowd, saying good-byes. One of them bends down saying, "Good-bye, Naomi. Good-bye, Stephen."
> "Good-bye."
> "Will you miss us?"
> "Nope," I say with a toss of my head.
> "You won't miss us even a little bit?"
> "Nope." I am uncomfortable with all this talking.
> She puts her arms out to hug me and I stiffen and draw back bumping into Kenji's big brother, Mas. (180)

The fact that Naomi and Stephen as children embody disillusionment with religious authority acknowledges the response as genuine and understandable. But it also suggests the possibility of an alternative perspective as the historical narrative is allowed to progress.

Passionate dismay is most poignantly set out in the passages in which the young Naomi seeks word from her father (208) and inquires about the whereabouts of her mother (26). The adult Naomi finally receives her answer through the letters recounting her mother's disappearance and the spiritual revelation they initiate:

> I am thinking that for a child there is no presence without flesh. But perhaps it is because I am no longer a child I can know your presence though you are not here. The letters tonight are skeletons. Bones only. But the earth still stirs with dormant blooms. Love flows through the roots of the trees by our graves. (243)

"Love" becomes the alternative response to injustice and tragedy—that is evident from the beginning, but its significance is only fully comprehended by the protagonist at the story's end. Like the manna that miraculously dusts the harsh landscape, it is the love often incomprehensible in times of trial that ultimately sustains.

Although manna refers specifically to the food given to the Israelites in the wilderness by God, it more generally alludes to aid that is given unexpectedly in a time of anxiety and isolation. In addition to love, manna suggests something intangible and "unearthly" that is given to those in times of trial and persecution—the will to live and survive. Like the Israelites, it is this intangible spirit that has allowed both the Christians in Pergamum and Japanese Canadians to endure the trials they have already undergone and is all the more necessary for their continued survival.

White Stone

The "white stone" is probably the *tessera* of ancient times. It was used variously as a voting ballot or a ticket to public functions. It was also used when drawing lots in a criminal case; the white stone signified a favorable verdict or right to life for the accused. Each of these meanings points to the political nature of Rev 2:17 that is significant to both the situation in Pergamum and the one in Canada. Both marginalized communities struggle with their public identity, as well as their access to national life. This trial establishes an irreconcilable dichotomy between the government and a particular community that the authors each highlight. The white stone symbolizes that it is the community that is judged favorably and government that is condemned. Also read as the entrance into public life and acceptance, "stone" renders the permanence of this condition, and "white" suggests victory and joy.

The parallel between the community of Pergamum and that of Japanese Canadians is striking. Seen only as the enemy in the eyes of the nation, Japanese Canadians endured a trial of their loyalty and commitment. In the biblical context, the Pergamites' identity as Christians is taken as an offense to the government and unduly challenged; in the North American context, the Japanese are similarly persecuted. Even when such outright oppression ends, those in Pergamum and in Canada still suffer as a result of this legacy. Each author points up the ways these defining events make their communities susceptible to compromises that are inevitably destructive. The metaphor of the "white stone" within this situational context is meant to remind these communities of a higher authority to which they are ultimately responsible, as well as hold forth the promise of a favorable verdict by this authority.

There is a notable difference between the situation in Asia Minor and the one in Canada, and it is important to take this difference into account. In the New Testament setting, the conflict with the state is posed in terms of religious loyalty and practice. Revelation's words are meant as a form of exhortation and encouragement to the Pergamum Christians as they confront the dominant religion of the Roman Empire. In the New Testament realm, Christian identity and national identity are oppositionally drawn. The situation with the characters in Kogawa's book is more complicated. These Japanese Canadians practice the same religion as that embraced by the state and the majority of its citizens. It is their racial-ethnic identity that poses a threat to the nation.

However, despite this difference, the Roman empire and Christianized Canada both represent *institutionalized* forms of religious belief in which the state views itself as a reflective embodiment of the religious tradition. Within the context of Kogawa's novel, one must therefore further distinguish between Christianity as it is appropriated by the racialized state ("white Christian nation") and Christianity as it stands as a spiritual truth and ideal that is meant to continually challenge such worldly expressions. In relation to the former, the critical perspective of Miki and other Asian North American commentators becomes more salient. Kogawa does employ irony to call into question the actions of the Canadian government, given its rhetorical espousal of Christian beliefs. Through Nakayama-sensei's desperate prayer of hope, the nation's hypocrisy is implicitly exposed:

> We humbly beseech Thee most mercifully to receive these our prayers which we offer unto Thy divine Majesty; beseeching Thee to inspire continually the universal church with the spirit of truth, unity and concord. And grant, that all they that do confess Thy holy Name may agree in the truth of Thy holy word, and live in unity and godly love. We beseech Thee also to save and defend all Christian Kings, Princes and governors; and specially Thy servant George, our King: that under him we may be godly and quietly governed. (Kogawa, 1984:176)

In this scenario, the state is clearly the target of Kogawa's ironic gesture. Hence, Christianity is implicated only so far *as it is identified with the state,* and the author clearly makes room for Christian faith beyond this limited expression. The "white stone" therefore should not be associated with the rewards of assimilation (as in Miki), but rather with a complex vindication of the persecuted community.

New Name

To Hebrews and the ancient world at large, the name of an object or person was no mere label, but an essential expression of its personality and being. A change of name was often given in the case of serious illness. If the patient survived, the new name bore a reference to life or to some Old Testament saint whose life was especially long. It was also intrinsically connected with a name of God. In addition, the word "new" in Rev 2:17 is derived from the Greek word *kainos,* which is an expression of salvation and perfection.

Within the story that Kogawa weaves and as one that is expressive of the larger narrative of Japanese North Americans, the "name" with which the community is initially branded is a racial name ("Japanese" or "Jap"). And as the history of internment and dispersal has demonstrated, it is both false and destructive. Naomi elaborates:

> None of us escaped the naming. We were defined and identified by the way we were seen. A newspaper in B.C. headlined, "they are a stench in the nostrils of the people of Canada." We were therefore relegated to the cesspools. (118)

The way Japanese Canadians were so readily identified and defined made them susceptible to violent treatment by the larger society. The disease of racism that ravaged the lives of Japanese North Americans and their subsequent survival from this social ill make them eligible for a "new name" that bears witness to the community's endurance, as well as the promise of a new identity.

As in Revelation, this "new name" never explicitly appears in *Obasan*. One may notice that Kogawa's citation ends in an ellipsis that accurately suggests that the verse is not fully referenced. Indeed, the ending that is left out of the epigraph reads: "a new name written on white stone *that no one knows but the one who receives it.*" Again, this promise is eschatologically posed, that is, one whose ultimate fulfillment is yet to come. Similarly, Kogawa's text suggests the open-ended nature of Japanese Canadian identity that is in the process of naming itself. *Obasan* documents this process, not simply through the words of the characters, but also through their actions and the allegiances they form within the community and without.

One could suitably argue that this "new name" is an ethnic identity that not only transcends given categories (the old name) but is crafted through an embodied realization of the atrocities that could be undertaken by the state and forges links between similarly oppressed groups. Aunt Emily is one representation of this, as she battles injustice in its many forms ("the Japanese-Canadian issue or women's rights or poverty" [34]). But perhaps more revealing is the poignant moment shared between Rough Lock Bill and the protagonist, where the First Nations survivor discloses to Naomi the paradoxical nature of the "new name" she will eventually receive:

> "Birds could all talk once. Bird language. Now all they can say is their own names. That's all. Can't say any more than their names. Just like some people. Specially in the city eh? Me, me, me." He jabs his chest with his thumb and grunts. "But smart people don't talk too much. Redskins know that. The King bird warned them a long time ago." (146–47)

Rough Lock Bill's simple tale demonstrates amazing foresight. His words are prescient for a multicultural national identity that Canada would adopt during Naomi's lifetime—an identity that seeks to recognize racial-ethnic diversity as a defining feature of the country.[5] Such a change is something that individuals like Aunt Emily (who has lived her entire life "in the city") have worked hard to accomplish. However, within this seemingly progressive environment, communities become divided one from the other, until each of these groups "can't say any more than their [racial-ethnic] names." Through Rough Lock Bill's economical statement, Kogawa cautions the reader that political recognition is simply not enough. Rather, the "new name" or new identity that is forged in hardship carries with it not only a deeper sense of oneself but also an ethic of sympathy and love that goes beyond mere words. This self-understanding and ethic—something *that no one knows but the one who receives it*—undergirds genuine projects of liberation (political, social, and spiritual).[6] The ineffable reality of this sense constitutes a secret knowledge that the author of Revelation passes on to the churches of Asia Minor, and that Kogawa similarly transmits to her reader. In this way, *Obasan* draws an inextricable link between objective political action and subjective spiritual state.

As a visionary promise, Rev 2:17 offers the spiritual impetus that propels the novel forward. Kogawa uses the religious myth of the dominant culture, linking it with the contemporary painful reality of "the other" in order to affirm the marginalized community and pass critical judgment upon the dominant culture. Embedded in the citation is the call for Japanese Canadians to critically assess their present identity, as well as the silent, yet dangerous compromises that are understandably made out of fear in the name of survival. However, the verse is not simply lodged as a form of critique and examination, but also serves as a resource for courage and hope.

Obasan As Revelation

In addition to the metaphorical significance of the biblical reference, one must also consider the author's citational method in order to understand fully *Obasan* as a religiously subversive text. Kogawa engages the biblical

---

[5] The Canadian government officially adopted a policy of multiculturalism in 1971. "The policy not only recognized the reality of pluralism in Canada, but seemed to reverse the earlier attempt to assimilate immigrants. It challenged all Canadians to accept cultural pluralism, while encouraging them to participate fully and equally in Canadian society." See the "Canadian Multiculturalism Act," http://www.pch.gc.ca/multi/html/act.html.

[6] I speculate that Kogawa chose not to include this phrase as part of her citation because of the way in which it focuses the reader on the believer's subjectivity; the "new name" can easily be misconstrued as simply an interior state that makes no impression on the outside world.

text beyond insightful allusion. By drawing careful and inextricable parallels in theme and content, she stakes a claim for Japanese Canadians and their lived experience within Christian history.

Obasan is especially unique in its typological biblicizing of the World War II experience of Asian Canadians. Biblical typology, formally defined, is "the practice in the New Testament and the early church whereby a person or series of events occurring in the Old Testament is interpreted as a type or foreshadowing of some person (almost invariably Christ) or feature in the Christian dispensation" (Hanson: 784). This discursive mechanism intimately weds biblical history and the contemporary text. As Anthony Tyrrell Hanson notes:

> The very possibility of such typology depends on the Christian assumption that the Bible recounts the course of salvation history. By this is meant the Bible as a record of the long development by which God, with redemptive purpose always in mind ... establish[es] a people of God whose membership is open to all.... Clear examples of typology occur in 1 Corinthians 10.1–11, where the events of the crossing of the Red Sea, the giving of the manna, and the water issuing miraculously from the rock are taken as types of baptism and of the bread and wine in the Eucharist. What is more, the presence of the preexistent Christ with Israel in the wilderness is implied. (784)

Here the newly adopted practices of baptism and the Eucharist recorded by New Testament authors are not only brought into alignment with Old Testament history, but also gain their authority as rituals that significantly redefine the tradition. Biblical history receives a newly defined meaning, as contemporary claims are "read back" into that history and distinct moments in time are inextricably linked.

As Sacvan Bercovitch notes in *Typology and Early American Literature*, such typology has been used by postbiblical writers as well. This literary mechanism "provided a means whereby life in the [early American] colonies became the literal realization of scriptural metaphor" (Jeffrey: 455). Like other North American writers who rely on typological biblicizing,[7] Kogawa works from the assumption that the words of biblical writers "might bear a deeper or fuller sense than they were aware of" (Hanson: 784). This fits squarely into the author's theological view, which confidently

---

[7] David Lyle Jeffrey notes that this use of typology is more a feature of the literary tradition of the U.S. than it is of Canada. However, whereas the U.S. was often figured as "a recovered Eden, a new Canaan, or Promised Land in the here and now" by American writers, Kogawa's use of typology emphasizes events of suffering such as the fall and exile. Canada, as promised land, is always forestalled, yet is sustained in the hopes and actions of the Japanese Canadian citizenry. See Jeffrey: 454–60.

sees God's love through historical events and human acts that are continually unfolding. Of this connection between Christianity's well-defined past and rearticulated present, Kogawa carefully speaks:

> Naomi's experience of the abandonment of her mother was to me an analogy for people's experience of the abandonment of God: that love, once a reality, had disappeared. But Naomi's experience of the constancy of that love was not a powerful love but a powerless love, a helpless love; but it was still powerful in its reality of love which has the capacity to heal. As she says, "Love flows through the roots of the trees by our graves."
>
> There is a way in which, as Rosemary Ruether puts it, the key to divine abandonment is that God has abandoned divine power completely and utterly into the human condition that we might not abandon one another. That's her sense of it. So what Naomi is experiencing is a capacity to elicit from the universe—from the world, from the earth, from the graves, from all the signs that are—that love is still there. And when she gets it through her dreams, when it comes to her out of the unknown, there she knows that love is not dead. When she hears at the age of thirty-six, that her mother could not have helped her, but loved her, then she is empowered; she is healed by that realization. I guess the faith that I have (or the hope that I have) is that if *all that energy* we once upon a time had in our past faiths that there was a transcendent God, if that same belief can be transposed into some confidence that that same power continues to exist in our human interactions, that it is accessible and available and we can genuinely apprehend it, then that is *wonderful, incredible*—that's more powerful than any atomic bomb we can imagine. *If* we have the capacity to apprehend it.
>
> What I think Naomi does is to be able to get out of her dreams and her mother's letters sufficient evidence to give her the next stage of life, the next momentum for it, and that's enough. It's manna. It's like finding a new name within the stone. And today it's a matter of being alert to and ready for those tiny, invisible, infinitesimal, incomprehensible miracles that exist, and see them in ourselves when we are transformed somehow. When we suddenly become poetry. At least I see that when it happens to me, it feels like a tremendous miracle. (Ackerman: 220–21)

As the author more readily states in an earlier interview: "I don't see that as being only a humanist statement, but as a statement of continuing faith in a terrifying Love that teaches us and does not abandon us" (Garrod: 142). It is important to note how Kogawa not only qualifies her use of biblical metaphor (as "analogy"), but also adopts language ("Love") that speaks to an audience who, unlike her, may not be Christian. Such accommodations allow her to expand a theologically informed sensibility beyond the confines of both the Christian community and the biblical text on which that community is founded. Still, there resides the hope "that that same power [gained in the past belief of a transcendent God] continues to exist in our human interactions, that [this power] is accessible and available and we can genuinely apprehend it." For Kogawa, then, the imperative of God's love figures the Bible not as a closed text, but rather as something that is continually being revealed and rewritten.

If biblical typologizing is fully at work in *Obasan*, one must ask what new events and rituals are at stake for the author. As Davina Te-Min Chen points out, Kogawa's religious view as it is expressed in *Obasan* shares an unbeknownst affinity with that of liberation theologian Gustavo Gutierrez. For both spiritual visionaries, "liberation has 'three levels of meaning: political liberation, human liberation throughout history, [and] liberation from sin and admission to communion with God'" (Chen: 102). According to this schema, issues of spiritual salvation are deeply tied to ones of political advocacy and worth. As Chen further draws out the significance of the biblical metaphor:

> With [manna's] connection to bread, another set of images piles on top of the stone, the most significant allusion being, of course, to the Eucharist. The sacrament of communion is celebrated in the novel on the eve of the Nakane family's second forcible dispersal, and early in the novel, Naomi refers to Emily's documents as "wafers" (41). Later, this comparison becomes explicit: "In Aunt Emily's package, the papers are piled as neatly as the thin white wafers in Sensei's silver box—symbols of communion, the materials of communication, white paper bread for the mind's meal" (182). This image provides further symbolic significance to Naomi's process of learning to hear the silence of the stone. Emily tells her, "Don't deny the past. Remember everything.... Denial is gangrene" (50). As she begins to ingest and digest the contents of the documents, she begins to come to terms with her history, and to heal psychologically and spiritually. (Chen: 111, referring to pages in Kagawa, 1984)

The salvific documents that are handed down to Naomi include "letters from the government ... copies of telegrams and the copy of the memorandum for the House of Commons and Senate prepared by the Co-operative Committee on Japanese Canadians" (Kogawa, 1984:182), as well as "newspaper clippings" (193). They attest not only to the political representation and exchange surrounding the traumatic events of internment, but also to the political interventions made on behalf of the Japanese Canadians. The memorandum sent by the Co-operative Committee on Japanese Canadians to the House and the Senate of Canada in 1946, included in Aunt Emily's package, is especially significant, for it is an excerpt from this document that ends the novel. This official statement strongly protests the "Orders in Council" that initially sanctioned the internment and dispersal of the Japanese Canadian population.

Hence, biblical verse and political document provide the rhetorical frame for Naomi's personal narrative. The internment of Japanese Canadians becomes the historical event that is highlighted within the parameters of the frame and given spiritual significance by the biblical citation. And through the memorandum and other documents that are figured as "white paper bread for the mind's meal"—Kogawa links Naomi's eventual salvation to the fight for political justice. This ongoing work on behalf of the oppressed becomes the new ritual proposed. Both events of internment and the ritual of political advocacy are given spiritual weight through citation of the biblical text. But beyond this metaphorical authorization, Kogawa, through her strategic use of typologizing, offers both contemporary event and ritual as a redefinition of the biblical text. The plight of the Pergamites, as well as that of the Israelites, in light of the experience of Kogawa's Japanese Canadians, becomes a struggle for political self-determination, recognition, and freedom.

In *Obasan*'s sequel, *Itsuka*, Rev 2:17 once again serves as the epigraph that opens the work.[8] However, in place of the "Memorandum," *Itsuka* ends with the "Acknowledgement" or formal apology of the Canadian government for its unfair treatment of Japanese Canadians. The repetition of Rev 2:17 demonstrates the unrealized hope of "heaven on earth" and the constant need to bring this hope into reality. Although both *Obasan* and *Itsuka* can be read teleologically as they trace a community's journey from silent repression to political voice, they present history—God's history—as that which is constantly unfolding and never fully realized. "God in history," through the author's intepretive lens, becomes intimately linked with human responsibility, action, and love, and even more specifically with those qualities as they are uniquely expressed in the Japanese Canadian community. As such, Joy Kagawa as the quiet revolutionary crafts a realm where Asian North Americans and other marginalized peoples are no longer politically and spiritually "second-class citizens" and can envision a reality otherwise.

---

[8] The epigraph only appears in the first edition of *Itsuka*. The novel underwent substantial revision for the second edition, and whether by Kogawa's choice or the editor's, Rev 2:17 is no longer part of the book. See Chen for a discussion of the impact that the verse's dismissal has on the overall work.

WORKS CONSULTED

Ackerman, Harold
    1993   "Sources of Love and Hate: An Interview with Joy Kogawa." *American Review of Canadian Studies* 23.2:217–29.

Bercovitch, Sacvan, comp.
    1972   *Typology and Early American Literature.* Amherst: University of Massachusetts Press.

Brock, Rita Nakashima
:   1992   "Dusting the Bible on the Floor: The Loss of Innocence and the Power of Wisdom in Asian American Women's Writing." In *God's Image* 11.3:3–10.

Chen, Davina Te-Min
:   1994   "Naomi's Liberation." *Hitting Critial Mass: A Journal of Asian American Cultural Criticism* 2.1:99–128.

Cheung, King-Kok
:   1993   *Articulate Silences: Hisaye Yamamoto, Maxine Hong Kingston, Joy Kogawa.* Ithaca, N.Y.: Cornell University Press.

Chua, Cheng Lok
:   1992   "Witnessing the Japanese Canadian Experience in World War II: Processual Structure, Symbolism, and Irony in Joy Kogawa's *Obasan.*" Pp. 97–108 in *Reading the Literatures of Asian American.* Ed. Shirley Geoklin Lim and Amy Ling. Philadelphia: Temple University Press.

Davey, Frank
:   1993   *Post-National Arguments: The Politics of the Anglophone-Canadian Novel since 1967.* Toronto: University of Toronto Press.

Davidson, Arnold
:   1993   *Writing against the Silence: Joy Kogawa's Obasan.* Toronto: ECW Press.

Garrod, Andrew
:   1986   "Joy Kogawa." Pp. 139–53 in *Speaking for Myself: Canadian Writers in Interview.* St. Johns: Breakwater Books.

Goellnicht, Donald C.
:   1989   "Minority History As Metafiction: Joy Kogawa's *Obasan.*" *Tulsa Studies in Women's Literature* 8:287–306.

Gottlieb, Erika
:   1986   "The Riddle of Concentric Worlds in *Obasan.*" *Canadian Literature* 109:34–53.

Hanson, Anthony Tyrrell
:   1993   "Typology." Pp. 783–84 in *The Oxford Companion to the Bible.* Ed. Bruce M. Metzger and Michael D. Coogan. New York: Oxford University Press.

Harris, King-Kok
:   1990   "Broken Generations in *Obasan:* Inner Conflict and the Destruction of Community." *Canadian Literature* 127:41–57.

Hsu, Ruth Y.
:   1996   "A Conversation with Joy Kogawa." *Amerasia Journal* 22.1:199–216.

Jeffrey, David Lyle
:   1993   "Literature and the Bible." Pp. 438–60 in *The Oxford Companion to the Bible.* Ed. Bruce M. Metzger and Michael D. Coogan. New York: Oxford University Press.

Kanefsky, Rachelle
1996   "Debunking a Postmodern Conception of History: A Defense of Humanist Values in the Novels of Joy Kogawa." *Canadian Literature* 148:11–36.

Kogawa, Joy
1984   *Obasan*. Boston: Godine.

1992   *Itsuka*. New York: Viking.

Kruk, Laurie
1999   "Voices of Stone: The Power of Poetry in Joy Kogawa's *Obasan*." *ARIEL: A Review of International English Literature* 30.4:75–94.

Lim, Shirley Geok-lin
1990   "Japanese American Women's Life Stories: Maternality in Monica Sone's *Nisei Daughter* and Joy Kogawa's *Obasan*." *Feminist Studies* 16.2:289–312.

Lo, Marie
2001   "*Obasan* by Joy Kogawa." Pp. 97–107 in *A Resource Guide to Asian American Literature*. Ed. Sau-ling C. Wong and Stephen H. Sumida. New York: MLA.

Miki, Roy
1998   *Broken Entries: Race, Subjectivity, Writing*. Toronto: Mercury.

Potter, Robin
1990   "Moral—In Whose Sense? Joy Kogawa's *Obasan* and Julia Kristeva's *Powers of Horror*." *Studies in Canadian Literature* 15.1:117–39.

Redekop, Magdelene
1989   "The Literary Politics of the Victim." *Canadian Forum* 68.783:14–17.

Schüssler Fiorenza, Elisabeth
1985   *The Book of Revelation: Justice and Judgment*. Philadelphia: Fortress.

1991   *Revelation: Vision of a Just World*. Minneapolis: Fortress.

1993   *Bread Not Stone: The Challenge of Feminist Biblical Interpretation*. Boston: Beacon.

Sweet, John
1993   "The Book of Revelation." Pp. 651–55 in *The Oxford Companion to the Bible*. Ed. Bruce M. Metzger and Michael D. Coogan. New York: Oxford University Press.

Ueki, Teruyo
1993   "*Obasan:* Revelations in a Paradoxical Scheme." *MELUS* 18:5–20.

Yoo, David K.
1999   "Introduction: Reframing the U.S. Religious Landscape." Pp. 1–18 in *New Spiritual Homes: Religion and Asian Americans*. Ed. David K. Yoo. Honolulu: University of Hawai'i Press.

AMERICA SEEN THROUGH A DIFFERENT LENS: THE BIBLE IN THE WORKS OF YOSHIKO UCHIDA

Fumitaka Matsuoka
Pacific School of Religion

ABSTRACT

In the literary works of Yoshiko Uchida, the Bible plays an illustrative but not necessarily a normative role in shaping the distinct cosmology for the Japanese American *nisei* (the second-generation) Christian community. This article examines how the Bible is treated in the literary works of a representative Japanese American writer and explores the ways the identity of Christian faith community is shaped when the foundationally normative authority of the Bible is not assumed.

INTRODUCTION: AMERICA'S INVISIBLE LITERATURE

Mary climbed into the back seat of their car and looked back at the somber gathering. The chill of winter was already in the air, and the men and women looked cold in their thin black coats, like a cluster of drab birds in a field that offered no nourishment or joy. Mary did not relate their being here to either life or death. It just seemed another function of the church, as though these few had come to sing hymns and read the Bible to old friends who could no longer come to church on Sundays. (Uchida, 1987:125)

The scene at the cemetery on the Sunday before Armistice Day was distressing to Mary in Yoshiko Uchida's novel *Picture Bride*. The memorial service was unbearably long and boring for the precocious and fun-loving child. "Mary knew about Reverend Okada's 'short' services" (123). For Mary the service was for the church folks to "sing hymns and read the Bible to old friends who could no longer come to church on Sundays." Uchida's depiction of this seemingly ordinary event is illustrative of the way the Bible serves within the context of a Japanese American Christian community. The Bible for them is literature that helps enrich both the joy and the sorrow of an everyday life. It reminds them of the web of relationships that goes beyond the realm of the living to include their communion with the deceased family members, friends, and ancestors. At the same time, it is also a reminder of the "drab" religious rituals the children are forced to endure on Sundays. The Bible is significant to the extent that it enhances the ritualistic understanding and practice of Christian faith for the Japanese American Christian community. Its claim to authority is somewhat foreign, if not irrelevant, in such a setting.

Asian American Literature: Translocal Reading of America

Werner Sollors of Afro-American Studies at Harvard asks this question about the outlines of American literature: "Is there something in the transnational character of the works [of non-English language literature] that may make their authors bolder than those situated firmly in culture and language?" (B5). There has been a relative neglect of the intersection between ethnicity and language among scholars of American studies and comparative literature in the past twenty years. Those scholars who have come to pay attention to race, gender, and ethnicity in American literary works have tended to ignore language as a defining part of American culture. Works by American writers who introduce non-English linguistic traditions have the potential to challenge the predominance of Anglocentric English, its underlying worldviews, and their undeclared assumptions about American society within which the literature is often studied.

Yoshiko Uchida introduces into the American literary scene Japanese language, the cultural traits of Americans of Japanese descent, and their corresponding cosmological worldviews even though she writes in the medium of English language. Uchida's English is not the English that predominates in mainstream American literature. It is an unconventional English. It bears simplicity, subtlety, and the flavor of the Japanese language spoken at her home. Along with this linguistic difference, the readers are introduced to a world that is culturally hybrid and fluid with its own distinct perspective of life and values. This distinctness of Uchida's writings frames our discussion on the role the Bible plays in her writings.

Yoshiko Uchida's prolific writings encompass autobiographical memoirs, numerous children's books, and novels, totaling some thirty volumes. She was born to Christian parents who were both graduates of Doshisha University, a Christian school, in Kyoto, Japan. Uchida grew up in the Japanese American community in Berkeley, California, in the 1920s and '30s and attended Independent Congregational Church in Oakland (currently Sycamore Congregational Church, United Church of Christ). Her parents assumed leadership roles in the church. Her home was frequented by many visitors, mostly from Japan, some of them ministers and students studying at the Pacific School of Religion in Berkeley, California. Uchida and her sister nicknamed some of them "gray-blob mushroom" for their sometimes balding and gray looks and their usual silence like a mushroom.

The outbreak of World War II and the subsequent internment of Japanese nationals and Japanese American citizens into the internment camps scattered around the country subjected Uchida and her family to the painful and humiliating experiences of this nation's historical injury inflicted upon them. This phase in her life, too, became a fertile ground for her prolific writings, particularly in her *Desert Exile* and *Journey to Topaz*.

LITERATURE AND ASIAN AMERICAN FAITH COMMUNITIES: NARRATIVE EXPRESSION OF LIFE

The examination of the role biblical rhetoric plays in Uchida's literary writings begins with the narrative character of the unfolding Japanese American history, identity, and community as reflected in her works. For the Japanese American community as represented in Uchida's writings, human consciousness is inherently organic in its relationship to time and memory. Time works differently in a narrative sense than in a scientific sense, as pointed out by H. Richard Niebuhr in *The Meaning of Revelation*. In a narrative, history is "internal," a subjective perspective of living selves with their resolutions and commitments, their hopes, and fears (Niebuhr: 46). Memory, too, functions distinctly. The individual in a community literally adopts memories to become part of the narrative community, and events are remembered or forgotten according to the value to the community. Uchida's community is not, furthermore, merely a collection of individuals, but individuals are only a derivative of a community that comes before them. So are their identities. They are formed through the stories of the community, which consists of *isseis* (immigrants) and their American-born offspring. They *are* the stories they hear about themselves and their cultural heritage. The stories are based on historical injuries, and they are enacted both communally and individually. Uchida's narratives connect the past and the future into a coherent whole so that we may become conscious of history and beings fashioned toward a future that is informed by the past. In narratives, the past, present, and future are reunited into an organic whole as in the case of the Buddhist cosmology. Either way, both the past and the future are connected, but this connection is also fluid: we can work toward new goals and read our past differently because of our interactions with other and different narratives in light of our own narrative past.

Furthermore, Uchida's deceptively simple stories, whether religious, cultural, or traditional, reflect basic Japanese American worldviews and faith. As with Robert Scholes and Robert Kellogg, narratives for Japanese Americans are the basic form from which all genres, including lyric and drama, are derived. The various stories that we live out—such as family stories, the Christian story, stories handed down from other faith traditions, and even well-known fictional stories—are brought into dialogue with each other to determine what needs to be reinterpreted in each to make a coherent notion of life for the individual and community. Doctrines and systematic treatments of the Bible and theology are only reminders of the narrative character of life in faith. Doctrines, even in their confessional forms such as a credo, do not have an authoritative role on their own and do not take the place of these narratives.

Spiritual life is thus pursued by modeling the common life story of our community after paradigmatic stories of various faith traditions embodied in our families and communities. These stories can be in scripture, the history of our churches, inherited Buddhist, Confucian, and other faith traditions of Japan, folk tales, or from within our own communal and individual lives. These are much more central to living faith than doctrines and principles extracted from narrative. The biblical narratives are thus interwoven with other significant narratives that constitute the Japanese American Christian communities and their members. The Bible thus functions within this wider context of "traditioning" that is going on within the Japanese American Christian community.

Morality, too, is understood as an expression of ongoing narratives of those who came to the shores of North America and of the subsequent generations. We are born into a narrative structure of life, which we become part of by modeling ourselves after certain paradigmatic characters and through "practice" as, for example, defined by Alasdair MacIntyre. Since morality takes place within communal narratives, moral absolutes that apply to all narratives do not exist. Right and wrong actions are only to be judged within our narratives. The only option in moral argument is to work from commonly held beliefs in each competing narrative or by converting the other narratives into one's own narrative. This is certainly the case for Uchida's writings. Moral action does not arise from individually rationalized decisions but from the character one is developing through the narratives that have been shaped within the particular community.

Thus narratives of Japanese American community precede that of the individual in Japanese American Christian communities. Their experience of relocation and internment during World War II no doubt shaped the character of their communal narratives. It is also the case for our Christian communities. Contrary to the Enlightenment worldview, which valued the powers of individual reason and tended to portray historical communities such as the church as authorities that went against reason, the community is the basic human unit for Japanese Americans. The individual is dependent upon community in the sense that it is necessary for individuals to draw life from community. Even in the current fluid, hybrid, and multiple state of the Japanese American identity, community and their memories of the past still play a significant and determinative role for those who identify themselves as Japanese Americans.

Therefore, it is no accident that Yoshiko Uchida's writings embody these narrative characteristics of Japanese American communities and their members. Her stories are not merely her own. They give a glimpse into the history and lives of Japanese immigrants and their subsequent generations of offspring. Her stories are part of the larger stories of those who came to North America under difficult circumstances and underwent the traumatic experience of betrayal by the very government and people who taught them "life, liberty, and the pursuit of happiness." These are the stories of those who have tenaciously proven their own worth and citizenship for the larger society in spite of their painful past. In turn, their communal narratives are at once the common narrative of the U.S. shared by us all. The biblical narratives that appear in Uchida's writings are only intelligible within this context of the wider narrative of Japanese Americans and of America itself.

POWER OF CRITIQUE IN SIMPLICITY: AN INSURGENT FUNCTION OF THE BIBLE

> The budding plum
> Holds my own joy
> At the melting ice
> And the long winter's end.
>
> The Creator's
> Blessings overflow,
> And even the single lily
> Has its soul. (Uchida, 1982:145)

These *hike* were written toward the end of her internment at Camp Topaz. The readers of Uchida's works are struck with the *hike*-like simplicity of her language. Her writing style is deceptively simple but fraught with rich meanings. They require a degree of sensitivity to the Japanese American worlds of early immigrants and their second-generation offspring in order to appreciate their richness. Coupling her allusion to the "lilies of the field" passage in the Bible (Matt 6:28–34) with the symbolic expression of her impending release from the camp imprisonment ("the melting ice"), Uchida's "single lily" suggests an insurgent utterance about the injustice done to the Americans of Japanese ancestry. Expressed in the subtlety and simplicity of Japanese *hike*, Uchida appeals to the subversive power of the Bible and communicates her own dignity and that of her people in the face of their massive betrayal by her government and the American people. Using the Bible for such an insurgent character and power is also echoed in the writing of another Japanese American writer, Monica Sone, in her *Nisei Daughter*. In the writings of both Uchida and Sone, there permeates a thread of gentle and yet powerful critique of the dominant culture and its behaviors through the use of biblical passages. Absent in their writings is an abrasive confrontational and oppositional posture toward fellow human beings even for their oppressive acts.

Given the conventional myth of the internment of the people of Japanese descent during World War II as potential spies against the U.S., what Uchida strives for is the corrective to "official" accounts that rationalize the mistreatment of her people. The importance of truth-telling becomes more apparent when one takes into account her resistance to the conventionally accepted image of Japanese and Japanese Americans at that time and her courageous facing up to what really happened to her people. It took the U.S. government almost fifty years to acknowledge the nature of their wartime actions against Japanese and Japanese American citizens. Only after considerable pressure had been brought to bear by the truth-tellers was the acknowledgment of the injustice that was brought about.

Truth-Telling from a Margin

> At last the bearded minister reached the close of his sermon and asked the worshipers to bow their heads in prayer. "Our dear Heavenly Father [sic]," he intoned, "bless these Thy children who have come from afar, leaving behind their native land to begin new lives in this land. Their hardships are many and they are not always welcome here. Help them, dear Father [sic], to face their trials with courage and Christian love." Hana lifted her head slightly to observe the minister's face. She wondered what he meant about their not being welcome. (Uchida, 1987:15)

Embedded in Uchida's description of the life of Japanese Americans is also an insightful depiction of the American society beyond the historical injury of internment inflicted upon her people. Uchida critiques the society and its dominant culture, which does not tolerate what Jean François Lyotard terms *differend,* or stories that are either inconvenient for an official version or viewed as marginal. Uchida sees America to be a curious mixture of both exclusionary currents and a naïve sense of hospitality extended to newcomers from foreign shores. Both co-mingled in its dominant culture and its people at the same time. Christian faith tempered by both insurgent and comforting biblical passages is alive in the Japanese American church community and sustains Uchida's dignity as a person in the midst of societal prejudice and condescension. It also strengthens her resolve to be a constructive member of the society even in the midst of the hardship. For Uchida, when one is willing to see the reality of life as it is experienced rather than what is imposed from the outside (as terrible and difficult as it may be), then a truly viable future is possible.

The perception gap between the dominant group's view of America and that of Uchida becomes painfully clear on a personal level. Through many layers of memories intersecting each other in Uchida's discovery of the mother-daughter bond, particularly in fictional works such as *Picture Bride*, Uchida gradually comes to acknowledge the conflation of self and race through the painful events pointing to the distance created between the Japan-born mother and the American-born daughter.

> Hana [Mother] knew very well why she and Mary [her daughter] were becoming strangers. They were gradually losing the means of communicating with one another.... Now Mary spoke as an adult, while Hana was still a child in the English language.... Hana could not utter the words of explanation Taro was waiting to hear. She simply sat down on one of the crates, took off her hat and said in a tired voice, "It's too late. Papa. It's too late." (1987:135)

The "speaking silence" of Hana bears testimony and re-creates the event that was the cause for the silenced voice. Moreover, the memory of the internment of Japanese Americans is juxtaposed with the memory of a relationship between a silent mother and a fearful but vocal child. The power of assimilation into the dominant culture is the reality and context in which truth-telling takes place as a "speaking silence."

However, Uchida's truth-telling is not merely set within the notion of recouping silenced voices. She does not place speech and silence in simply binary opposition. Uchida departs from a conventional notion that speech is inherently superior to all forms of silence. Instead, the story offers a complex interpretation of both, loosening the strict demarcation between the two and illustrating how both can be forms of communication. The value of silence as a powerful form of communication, a distinctly Asian posture toward life, is transmuted into the racial identity of Asian Americans in Uchida's work. There is a voice in silence for Uchida. This is also a common theme in another piece of internment trauma literature by Joy Kogawa, *Obasan*.

Biblical Authority in Illumination of Life

> For many months after Yamaka and her infant son died, Hana had felt only anger and resentment toward Taro's God. But she felt, too, that she deserved His [sic] wrath. Finally, one Sunday as Reverend Okada preached that theirs was a God of love and forgiveness, she realized that her salvation lay in being forgiven by this God.... "Never forget," he said, as she appeared pale and eager at his class, "Jesus Christ is always at your side." And he read to her from the book of Matthew. "Come unto me all ye that labor and are heavy laden, and I will give you rest." (Uchida, 1987:65)

Faith for Uchida is not totally dependent upon the authority of the written Bible. The Bible is authoritative to the extent that it illumines the experiences of a given community with insights that would sustain through the pain of life and provides joy in it. The difference between the biblical worldview and the lived experience of Japanese Americans is not really a decisive issue. There is a fluid permutation of the Christian view of life expressed in the Bible and Japanese spirituality that informs the life of Japanese Americans. The Bible is thus accorded no special status or sole authority, *sola scriptura*, apart from the constellation of ingredients that help enlighten the depth of life.

> Kiku confessed that she rarely went to church on Sundays because she could not sit through Reverend Okada's sermons. She had a small Buddhist shrine in her living room, however, and occasionally lit incense there to pray for her ancestors. "I guess I'm part-Buddhist, part-Christian and part nothing at all," she laughed. (1987:13)

The Bible is not the sole sustainer of one's life. It both informs and comforts. It enlivens their lives. To this extent, the Japanese spiritual and cosmological heritages are carried over to the lives of Japanese American Christians.

There is also a bold critique of Christians and their worldviews in the works of Uchida. This critique is particularly prominent in her autobiographical works such as *Desert Exile* and *The Invisible Thread*.

> Some of the Japanese ministers who visited us were humble and kind, but others were pompous and pedantic. One could sing all the books of the Bible to the tune of a folk song, while another left his dirty bath water in the tub for my mother to wash out. Most of them stayed too long, I thought, and talked too much. (1982:11)

If the Bible itself is relatively tangential for Uchida's notion of life's sustenance and enrichment, significant people in one's life (parents, spouse, friends) are role models in developing a sense of one's personhood and identity. Uchida's portrayal of her own mother and the character Hana, the picture bride, points to a new womanhood in the American society for those who are at its margin. Her mother commanded her children never to divulge their problems to anyone outside the family. Her father, at the same time, provided moral guidance for her character formation, particularly in her childhood. Uchida's view of her father is contrasted to the negative stereotypes of Asian fathers who rigidly reinforce the traditional Asian characteristics of obedience and inferiority. On the contrary, he provided an even keel for her family in the midst of the tumultuous decades of the twentieth century. The role Uchida's father played also signaled the poignant dimension of the immigrant Asian family in America who sustained a sense of dignity and pride in their cultural heritage.

The duality of Uchida's sense of independent self and respect for her parents is eventually merged into an uncomfortable and unresolvable whole. For Uchida, her cultural values forged within this conflictual merger of two different cultural heritages and religious values—as nurtured in the web of both family and church relationships—come together even with an apparent contradistinction of one from the other. The Christian faith with its foreignness and her lived experience of being Japanese American coexist in her life. Christ and culture inform each other in the formation of personhood and community identity for Uchida.

Thus in the works of Uchida, the Bible assists the Japanese American Christian faith community in finding the depth-meaning of life in (1) the development of a coherent web of relationships cultivated under a series of historical injuries inflicted upon the people; (2) the community's insurgent challenge to oppressive societal values and practices; (3) locating directionality in their life narratives as the faith community participates in creating a just and equitable society; and (4) ultimately in shaping a cosmology that expresses the vision of life for Japanese Americans.

In Uchida's work, the distinctiveness of the Christian identity based on the Protestant notion of *sola scriptura,* either in the original meaning articulated by Martin Luther or in its mutated form of the literal accuracy and authority claim of the Bible, does not assume a central significance. The primary issue for her is the way the Bible facilitates Japanese American Christians' participation in the shaping of a wider society. It is based not on a conflictual and oppositional dynamic of relationships but on reconciling efforts amidst the differences and experiences of alienation of this marginalized group with the racially, culturally, and politically dominant group. Thus, the *actus tradendi* (the church's activity of the handing on the gospel to a new generation, "traditioning") role of the Bible goes beyond the historical interpretation of "reasoned elaboration" within a faith community in the service of the scripture itself. The *actus tradendi* plans a role for transforming Christian faith community in the service of and for the well-being of a wider society. This is a new and radical notion of "tradition-making." In Yoshiko Uchida's writings, the credibility and authenticity of the Bible derive from the illuminating, facilitating, and supportive roles the Bible plays for the particular faith community to be fashioned toward this end. Furthermore, the Bible aids in developing a particular cosmology for Japanese Americans that is derived from but is also distinctive of the Asian cosmologies inherent in Mahayana Buddhism, Confucianism, and Taoism. Such a newly emerging cosmology has, in its core inclusiveness of diverse elements of life, a coherent harmony of all things, simplicity of life, and value in silence. In this sense, Christian faith is being transformed into a new vision of life rather than occupying an authoritative central role.

The Place of the Bible in the Asian American Women's Literature: The America of Their Hearts

Yoshiko Uchida is a representative voice among the few Japanese North American women who address the subject of Christian faith in their literary writings. (Joy Kogawa and Monica Sone are other representative literary figures.) Their treatments of Christian faith need to be seen within a wider context of the emerging Asian North American women's literature. Though their writings began mainly in the 1950s (such as Diana Chang's *Frontiers of Love*), it was in the '70s when their voices began to be heard as the stereotypical perception of people of Asian descent as the other, the "Oriental," weakened in both the American mainstream consciousness and the Asian North American psyche. In the '80s and '90s a broadened awareness of the positive historical collective identity of Asian North Americans continued along with a push within the community to highlight the ethnic differences within the group.

Asian North American women began to address these challenges through various mediums, such as literature, music, plays, and films. In the literary circle, they began to reflect upon their individual and communal experiences through both fiction and anthology in order to claim their own voices and to contemplate their vision of the future—their place in the wider society and the society itself through their own experiences and perceptions. The styles of their expressions differ, but a certain pattern has emerged in their storytelling, beginning with one's communal history, moving to individual story/reflection, and culminating in the larger political group identity and reflection on wider societal issues commonly shared with other groups of people, particularly women. The topics that emerged in their works are immigration, war, work, generations, gender identity, sexuality, injustice/racism, and visions of what the society can be. A thread that runs through their writing is the redefinition of language, worldview, values, and religion for the purpose of both the survival and the well-being of Asian North Americans, and a common vision of the future for the society.

Commenting on Asian American women's writing, Elaine Kim points out that although sexism has been an issue in Asian American communities, racism has usually been pinpointed as the more important barrier to social and economic equality for Asian American women (250). Asian American women in their writings generally address themselves directly to affirming both their racial and gender identities. Maxine Hong Kingston, for example, seeks to portray Asian American women as "warriors" instead of victims, thus breaking out of a stereotypical image of them as docile and submissive persons.

Christian faith is treated in this context by Asian North American women, both Christians and those of other faiths. Faith for them is often politicized rather than introspective and individualistic. As in the case of Uchida's writings, it is not treated from an exclusive confessional stance but rather interwoven with other faith and cultural traditions. Such claims as the sole and absolute truth claim of Christian faith and exclusive moral stance on various societal issues that are exercised in some Asian North American evangelical Christian circles are perhaps a reaction against the more inclusive life-orientations of their earlier generations. Such an interweaving trend may even correlate with the high rate of out-marriage that has been changing the Asian North American identity.

Family and community, furthermore, play a key role in the faith formation for Asian North American Christian women. While atomic individualism has begun to penetrate the Asian North American communities, the web of relationships still remains a significant factor for them. Christian faith as well as other faiths continue to help sustain the web. The Bible, therefore, cannot be treated as an independent entity apart from the complex web of both relationships and societal engagements for Asian American Christians. It is a thread that holds their individual and communal identities, while at the same time it weaves in an impetus for them to envision what this society can be. In the literary works of Asian North American Christian women, the Bible plays an instructive and illustrative role in building a society not on an oppositional dynamic, but on reconciling efforts amidst the differences and experiences of alienation of one group from another.

The Bible is always being handed on into new and, in varying degrees, unprecedented circumstances. Historically, its traditioning, or traditionmaking, is inescapably understood to involve "reasoning" for the sake of maintaining continuity. In the case of Yoshiko Uchida and other representative Asian North American Christian women, the real impetus for *actus tradendi* is not disembodied notion of "reason" but the whole constellation of their life experiences, their cosmological, religious, and cultural heritages born of Asia, the historically imposed injuries they have suffered, and their efforts to forge a new identity on the North American continent. The Bible serves to illuminate the life lived with these experiences of Asian American Christian women as powerfully as possible in their circumstances.

Works Consulted

Brock, Rita Nakashima
    1996   "Response: Clearing the Tangled Vines." *Amerasia Journal* 22.1:181–86.

Chang, Diana
    1994   *The Frontiers of Love*. Seattle: University of Washington Press. [Orig. 1956]

Cheung, King-kok, ed.
    1997   *An Interethnic Companion to Asian American Literature.* Cambridge: Cambridge University Press.

Hong Kingston, Maxine
    1976   *The Woman Warrior: Memoirs of a Girlhood among Ghosts.* New York: Knopf.

Kim, Elaine H.
    1982   *Asian American Literature: An Introduction to the Writings and Their Social Context.* Philadelphia: Temple University Press.

Kogawa, Joy
    1984   *Obasan.* Boston: Godine.

Lee, Rachel C.
    1999   *The Americas of Asian American Literature: Gendered Fictions of Nations and Transnation.* Princeton, N.J.: Princeton University Press.

Lim, Shirley Geok-lin, and Amy Ling, eds.
    1992   *Reading the Literatures of Asian America.* Philadelphia: Temple University Press.

Lyotard, Jean François
    1988   *The Differend: Phrases in Dispute.* Trans. G. Van den Abbeele. Minneapolis: University of Minnesota Press.

MacIntyre, Alasdair
    1984   *After Virtue.* 2d ed. Notre Dame, Ind.: University of Notre Dame Press.

Niebuhr, H. Richard
    1941   *The Meaning of Revelation.* New York: MacMillan.

Pak, Young Mi Angela
    1996   "Anthologizing by Asian American Women: Selves-In-Community and the Politics of Recognition." *The Brown Papers* 2.10:1–15.

Scholes, Robert, and Robert Kellogg
    1966   *The Nature of Narrative.* New York: Oxford University Press.

Sollors, Werner
    1998   "The Blind Spot of Multiculturalism: America's Invisible Literature." *The Chronicle of Higher Education*, October 30:B5.

Sone, Monica
    1953   *Nisei Daughter.* Boston: Little.

Uchida, Yoshiko
    1971   *Journey to Topaz: A Story of the Japanese American Evacuation.* New York: Scribner's.

    1972   *Samurai of Gold Hill.* New York: Scribner's.

1982	*Desert Exile: The Uprooting of a Japanese American Family.* Seattle: University of Washington Press.
1987	*Picture Bride.* Flagstaff, Ariz.: Northland.
1991	*The Invisible Thread.* New York: Messner.

Wong, Sau-ling Cynthia
    1993   *Reading Asian American Literature: From Necessity to Extravagance.* Princeton, N.J.: Princeton University Press.

WRITING NEW AND JOYFUL SONGS: CON-VERSING WITH JOY KOGAWA

Tat-siong Benny Liew
Chicago Theological Seminary

ABSTRACT

Joy Kogawa is the author of the critically acclaimed novel, *Obasan*, and thus a "canonical" figure within Asian American literature. In this interview, Kogawa talks about how she understands, reads, and uses the Bible. After responding to several questions about Asian American literature, she also shares a portion of her recent writing that has not been published previously.

Persons familiar with the "ethnic canon" (David Palumbo-Liu) of Asian America will no doubt recognize the name of Joy Kogawa. Her first novel, *Obasan*, is a tragic story about what World War II and a racist internment policy did to the Japanese Canadian community in general and Naomi Nakane's family in particular. The book has won many awards and has been translated into several different languages. Twenty years after its publication, it is still being studied regularly by undergraduates, Ph.D. students, and professors of Asian American literature.

As many critics have pointed out, *Obasan*'s continuing significance has to do with more than its treatment of Japanese Canadian internment (and by extension, similar internment policies for persons of Japanese descent within the U.S.). The novel also seems to reflect and revamp many (postmodern) theoretical inquiries that have become important in various branches of literary and cultural studies. Examples include the relationship between silence and speech, or that of memory, writing, and truth (Ruth Y. Hsu: 200–202; Marie Lo: 103–4).

Besides *Obasan*, Kogawa has published two other novels: *Itsuka* and *The Rain Ascends*. The former continues Naomi Nakane's story into the struggle of the Japanese Canadian community over redress; the latter concerns Millicent Shelby's relationship with her father, an effective and respected Anglican minister who is also a pedophile. Although critics have, comparatively speaking, been less attentive to the deeply religious aspect of Kogawa's novels, one can find within each of them clergypersons, religious concepts like mercy and justice, as well as numerous biblical citations and allusions.[1]

---

[1] For examples of critics who do pay attention to the religious dimension of Kogawa's novels, see Jane Naomi Iwamura's essay in this volume; Cheng Lok Chua; and Teruyo Ueki.

Kogawa is also a published poet. Her latest published poem, *A Song of Lilith*, deals with a religious legend and has been described as a "feminist *Paradise Lost*" (2000: back-cover endorsement).[2] She is a recipient of the Order of Canada and numerous honorary doctorates, including one from a seminary. In 2001, Kogawa received a Lifetime Achievement Award from the Association of Asian American Studies. In addition to writing, she devotes her time to furthering the cause of social and economic justice in the city of Toronto (currently serving as President of the Toronto Dollar Community Projects Inc.).

This conversation focuses on Kogawa's understanding and use of the Bible, her views on Asian American literature, and concludes with a portion of her recent writing (I have placed *some applicable* scriptural citations and allusions in brackets throughout for easy reference). I find Kogawa a quiet but very inquisitive person. It is important for me to point out that in the short time that we have known each other, she has asked me many deliberate and difficult questions about the Bible. Kogawa's openness is most impressive. She is honest, straightforward, unassuming, and unpretentious. I can think of no better words to describe her than the ones that she herself used below to describe an author she admires: "humility and humanity"—she is full of both.

TBL: You start your first novel, *Obasan*, with Rev 2:17, a verse from the Bible about hidden manna, white stone, and a new name. How do you see that verse functioning for your entire narrative? Why do you use that verse to begin the book?

JK: It spoke to me of endurance, of transformation, of heavenly nourishment from the unseen and invisible places, of *Obasan* symbolizing that which is not seen. I thought that the verse suggested that people who remained steadfastly committed to love would be able to find nourishment in the hidden manna—the daily bread of love in lives not normally on the public stage—and so Obasan too, through her steadfast spirituality, found nourishment in places not normally seen. And what is a white stone? It is so suggestive ... water and stone dancing. And what is the new name?

TBL: When you mentioned Obasan and her steadfast spirituality, are you referring to Aya Obasan only, or do you include in that other women characters in the book like Emily, Naomi, and Naomi's mother?

---

[2] Lilith is the legendary "first woman," or "first feminist," in some Jewish traditions. Like Adam, she was created out of the earth in Eden, but ended up leaving in protest after Adam refused to see her as an equal. Eve, being created out of Adam's rib after Lilith's withdrawal, was in such traditions a "secondary replacement." A brief account of the Lilith legend can be found in Kogawa, 2000:xvi–xxi.

JK: Aya Obasan, by her silence, by her acceptance, by her rootedness in an ancient culture that valued silence, speaks to me about a spiritual power that is below the surface of speech and sound. Emily is marching on the earth, above ground. She is doing the work of justice, which, in my estimation, is the Spirit at work. Naomi watches her two aunts. Watching and waiting are also spiritual endeavors. And Naomi's mother, absented and trapped in the insanity of war, symbolizes for me that Love which does not abandon us, but is not perceived by us.

TBL: So your use of Obasan refers to a number of women characters in the novel by the same title. I am curious to know why you decided to use the Bible? Biblical references are also used in your other novels besides *Obasan*. Do you refer to the Bible because you are familiar with it, or are there other reasons?

JK: I grew up with the notion that the book, the Bible, was the living word of God. That gave it more weight than the dictionary or Shakespeare or *Encyclopedia Britannica*. However much I mull over the old, old stories, there is more to learn. It feels like a well to me, a well of constantly wonderful water. Where it jars, the anti-Jewish sounding references, the homophobic references, I find myself willing to struggle with it rather than to dismiss it and walk away. When I understand the context of the writings, I am more able to accept that they are part of a larger story being told. And it matters to understand what the story is telling us.

TBL: What do you mean that the Bible "was the living word of God"?

JK: I guess what I mean by the Bible being a living word ... actually I've never thought about what that meant.... I guess I mean that it is still the book that tells the stories that still give direction.

There is a story in the New Testament about a time when there was a huge storm when Jesus was sleeping in the boat, and the disciples were afraid and they woke him. He woke up at that point, calmed the wind, and rebuked them for their lack of faith [Matt 8:23–27; Mark 4:35–41; Luke 8:22–25]. To me, that story is alive in my life, because life is filled with storms: our values, our controversies, many times our warfare, our sufferings. These are the storms in our lives. I feel that if we in the midst of the stormy events awaken the things of love in our lives, we go to the source of love, we go to wherever love is, then the power of that love calms the storm for us. That is the way the stories from the Bible come to speak to me; that is an example of the way the Word lives.

At the same time, you know that I am quite embarrassed about my totally unscholarly way of using the Bible. My use of the Bible is "wonky" and would be termed superstitious. I use it the way people would use tarot cards or the *I Ching*. I stab at it. I let the stories or the fragments nudge me. Anyway, my random *I Ching* or tarot type of reading is more or less my way of being. I glean messages from the walls of my skull and the veins of my heart which are as nonsensical as the twirling of gnats. I do a random reading of the Bible generally every morning. I sometimes force-fit whatever I've read into my day. Sometimes it's just the first word my eyes catch. I often wish I understood more of the context of what I am reading.

TBL: Given what you said about the anti-Jewish and homophobic references in the Bible, do you think that your way of using the Bible actually gives you some "leverage" over this "double-edged" book? I mean, with verbs like "stabbing" and "force-fitting," do you imply in a sense that you want to—knowing its history and potential for both destruction and liberation—subject the Bible to your service rather than subjecting yourself to the service of the Bible?

JK: You are suggesting, by this question, that the Bible was made for us, not us for the Bible, as in "the Sabbath was made for people, not people for the Sabbath" [Mark 2:27]? I have heard of an old Jewish saying that "where the laws of God are in conflict with the well-being of people, the well-being of people shall prevail." I think that where the use of the Bible is in conflict with the well-being of people, the well-being of people should prevail.

I know a woman who was from Japan. Her child was murdered by her husband. The minister of her church, a Japanese Canadian minister, told her that if she wanted to divorce him, she should not divorce him, because the Bible said it was wrong. He told her that if she ever did divorce him for whatever reason, then she did not have the right to remarry, since this was clearly stated by Jesus in the Bible [Matt 19:1–9; Mark 10:1–12]. He was imposing upon her unbelievable suffering, that she would have to remain with the man who had murdered her son even though the man was insane, or on the other hand, she would have to bear the consequence of never having another love relation. This minister said that his view was right, and he was basing that on his literal interpretation of the Bible. My response to that would be that these "laws" are made for love's sake, they are made for our well-being. When you slavishly insist that there are those human conditions by which these "laws" rule supreme, then you are placing an extra burden on people that is not conducive to their well-being. Didn't Jesus condemn the legalistic people of his day for doing this?

The amazing thing is that this woman herself has a scripture that she used. I don't remember exactly what passage it was because her interpretation did not make that much sense to me, but it had something to do with Elijah and the widow who fed him with a bottle and the bottle never went empty [1 Kgs 17:8–24]. She read from that story some meaning about the abundance in life and the possibility of abundance for herself, so she was able to use her interpretation of the Bible to release herself from her husband and her minister.

To me, those are two problematic interpretations of the Bible (though problematic in different ways), but I am glad that the woman was able to do what she had to do with her reading of the Bible. After all, the Bible is used in very interesting ways by all kinds of people for all kinds of reasons. I mean whether it is to applaud slavery and apartheid, or for others, it is to destroy slavery and apartheid. So there must be some other measures that we need to use. For me, one measure is whether a reading facilitates the work of love, the work of love that we are here to do.

TBL: Despite your previous emphasis on knowing the "original context" of a biblical passage, you actually seem to emphasize more, for your purpose of human "well-being," the practice of reading the Bible with an "endless decontextualization and recontextualization" (John D. Caputo: 100). Since you spent quite a few pages on the Bible Belt in your second book, *Itsuka*, would you share with me some of your personal observations about how the Bible is used and understood in that circle and within the Anglican tradition that you grew up with and currently embrace? If you have to compare and contrast their use of the Bible, what would you say?

JK: I would say that the fundamentalist Christians in the Bible Belt treated the Bible as God's literal word, which is why they argued against the theory of evolution, for example. I was ten when we went to Southern Alberta. I heard their reasoning but could not agree, and felt burdened by a faith that felt arrogant and unloving in its insistence that others who did not agree with their "truth" were forever damned. I thought they would have killed Galileo. I thought they were worshiping their understanding of the Bible and were not worshiping a God of love. But I did admire their passion, their zeal, their commitment to the person of Jesus. In fact, at the time, I felt that if I had to choose, I would rather spend time with them than with the lukewarm Anglicans who would mouth the words written by someone else in a book but could not speak from their own hearts. Today, I find fundamentalism very scary and very unloving.

TBL: In *Obasan* as well as *Itsuka*, you seem rather determined to present different viewpoints that members of the Japanese Canadian community have about the internment and redress. You seem to present all these varying viewpoints with equal ambivalence, whether they are represented by Emily and Obasan, or Nikki Kagami and Morty Mukai. You do not champion any single viewpoint as the definite answer, nor do you dismiss any single viewpoint as totally illegitimate or invalid. For me at least, this ambivalence helpfully brings out the complexity of living as Japanese Canadians. Is it fair to say that you have a similar ambivalence about the ways fundamentalists and mainline Christians use the Bible?

JK: I think in *Itsuka*, I align myself with the forces for democracy, and I would not today align myself with fundamentalist Christianity. I like the reverence that fundamentalists have for the Bible and the fact that they memorize it and know it so well. But I think their literalism too often leads them into unloving attitudes, into prideful, militant, superior, arrogant, intolerant, exclusivist ways which are not the ways of the One they follow. So I don't feel ambivalent about fundamentalists. I think they are today's heretics. And of course, they would see me as a heretic.

TBL: If I am not mistaken, I think Father Cedric only quoted the Bible once in *Itsuka* (209). In contrast, biblical verses are constantly rolling out of the tongue of Pastor Jim. I do find it interesting also that you depicted quite a few women students at Pastor Jim's fundamentalist Bible Institute in *Itsuka*, like Lydia, Annie, and Erna. I am curious about your reading and your use of the Bible as a woman. What do you do when you read something in the Bible that contradicts or offends your feminist sensibilities?

JK: I am lucky that the church I attend, The Church of the Holy Trinity in Toronto, is concerned about language and feminist sensibilities. So the jarring language that could cause me to throw up my hands and walk out are generally taken care of. With so many others taking up the banner, I find I can relax. I am grateful to them for fighting this one.

TBL: From where you are, then, what would you see to be the most urgent battle that you have to help fight regarding the Bible?

JK: In our days, we are so engulfed. I mean, each culture in each age has this box within which we live. And the color of the box of our days, I think, results in us a kind of blindness to the possibilities that are outside of the box. The perimeters of the box, the limitations of our minds may be scientific methodologies. For some people, they may be the limitations of a certain politics; they may be limitations of "correct" analysis, the limitations of "rationality." They could be anything that limits our openness to possibilities. So I would say the challenge would be something to our openness to possibilities.

When it comes to the Bible, I guess the tendency is to demystify it since the Enlightenment. The two hundred plus years of the Enlightenment must be set within the larger time frame of human civilization, and things are changing so quickly too with all the possibilities of new understandings and discoveries. I just wonder whether we, in the effort to demystify, have destroyed something that is more valuable. I have in mind the passion for attending to the suffering in the world. I think that the Bible lifts up for us, assists us and guides us in the stress of the world, that is in this world that we love, to attend to the suffering. And if something takes us away from that and dulls our hearts and our minds, and gets us lost even in the strongest controversy on "truth," then we have lost our souls. I would say that the thing that is valuable for me in the study of the Bible is whatever that keeps us attuned to suffering.

When we study the Bible, we need to ask ourselves, "Why are we doing this?" Are we doing this so we would be challenged mentally? And if that is what we are doing alone, then I think we are making an idol of that. If we are being challenged to find strength to do the work of love that needs to be done, then maybe our study of the Bible is a partner with us. If not, we are demanding to know rather than obeying the calls to love.

On the other extreme of demystifying the Bible, there is the tendency on the part of the conservatives to believe so passionately in the "truth" as they understand it that they end up limiting their passion to that rather than to the work of love. How can we read the Bible in a way that helps us to remain open to possibilities and to do the work of love? I think that is the challenge.

TBL: In addition to the Bible that you grew up with, you also grew up with, I assume, quite a few Japanese legends and stories. I am thinking, for example, of the story of Momotaro, which plays quite a repeated role in *Obasan*. I cannot recall at the moment if you refer to that story in your other writings, but what do you find meaningful and significant in Momotaro?

JK: Tenderness. I recall the tenderness between the dear old people and the baby in the peach, the tenderness for the old ones by the youth. The tenderness in my mother as she told me the story. The love that dwells in me was given to me in the closeness of her body, and the love in the story. Both my parents were born and raised in Japan and rooted in the value of intergenerational love. My father was an Anglican minister. One of his favorite stories was about his conversion and the stations of the cross. But he was Buddhist to start with, and his filial piety, his love of his mother found expression for him in the story of Jesus on the cross when he said to the beloved disciple, "Behold thy mother," and to Mary, "Woman, behold thy son" [John 19:26–27].

TBL: In light of what you said about your father's filial piety and what you said about Momotaro, may I ask you how you see the Bible vis-à-vis other cultural traditions like Buddhism? Do you see them as compatible, as mutually supplementary, or even as mutually corrective?

JK: I think the way that the Bible has been traditionally read is to make it an exclusive thing that eliminates the entire world. And I think that is antithetical to the call to love. Therefore, I think one needs to put aside those superior and triumphant attitudes in advance and come into those ways of reading which are not so arrogant and unloving. If there appears to be a contradiction with the Bible, I can either love or I can insist what I read from the Bible is "true" and therefore justify any cruelty. Traditionally it justified murder, it justified forcing people to be baptized and all these things, which we look back on with some abhorrence. I think some of us are beginning to say, "We have erred and strayed in our ways like lost sheep. We have followed too much the devices and desires of our own hearts." We have offended the most holy law that Paul speaks so much of, the most holy law of love [1 Corinthians 13; Gal 5:22–6:10]. So when we come across something that contradicts our understanding of love, I think it is better to err on the side of love than it is to err on the side of "truth."

So I would personally see the Bible as a partner of other cultural traditions like Buddhism instead of placing one on top of the other, so to speak. I would rather be accused of being in error because I love than to be in error because I am so legalistic in my understanding of "truth."

TBL: You speak very consistently of the importance of love and mercy. What about justice? Both justice and love are emphasized in the Bible, and your own books seem to deal with the tension between those two emphases rather constantly. I am thinking here of the difference between the activist Aunt Emily who keeps fighting for justice and the long-suffering but steady Aunt Obasan in *Obasan*. I am also thinking of Millicent Shelby in *The Rain Ascends*, who faces the dilemma between reporting her clergy father's molestation of children and protecting this community leader whom she adores, this aging father who has fallen ill. I love the way you present Millicent's dilemma as a reversal of the biblical narrative about Abraham hearing the call to sacrifice his son Isaac [Genesis 22]. What do you think about these two concepts and how they relate to your writings?

JK: Love, mercy, justice, freedom, and truth. They all belong together in my mind. Where is that verse? "As the hart pants for water, so pants my heart for Thee," or something like that [Ps 42:1]. My heart pants for the God of all these values.

TBL: I understand that your frequent reference to the Bible has to do with your own upbringing, but is there any sense that you are also using the

Bible as a strategy to confront a (racist) North American society that is supposedly "rooted" in biblical traditions?

JK: I am not consciously using the Bible that way. I am so steeped in the Bible that the stories are there as a grid of meaning, which helps to give direction to my life. Racism is clearly something to overcome.

TBL: By the way, the first edition of *Itsuka* also contained the epigraph from Rev 2:17 about the hidden manna, white stone, and new name, but is removed in the second edition. Is this your choice or that of the publisher? And what are the reasons behind the change?

JK: I wanted continuity so I put it in. After all, I thought, *Itsuka* was about transformation of community from silence to speech, from scattered people to regrouping. So it was a new name that was being received by those who refused to bow down to the easier path of resignation. Then the book got a scathing review in the Globe and Mail. The reviewer said it was an unprintable book with pages and pages of painfully embarrassing writing, or something like that. It knocked me out for about a year. I tried to rewrite it and took out things that I worried made it embarrassing. And I haven't been able to look at the book since that revision. The Bible quote probably came out in that flush of pain. The book was quickly out of print in the U.S., but I see that it is into another printing, and continues in Canada. Once when I was on an airplane, I saw that some group in Edmonton had chosen it for their study group as a book they found notable.

TBL: Can you tell me how *Obasan* became a part of the redress movement? How did that all come about and come together for you and others in the movement after its publication?

JK: *Obasan*'s publication got me into a public realm that I was not used to. And I was asked to speak, for example. It was a rather uncomfortable time. The book was published in 1981. In 1983, I got "yanked" into the redress movement in Toronto. There are some people who felt the book helped the redress movement, and there are some in the redress movement who feel the movement helped the book. Who knows? At any rate, when redress was announced, a section of the book was read in Parliament and another section in a press conference by, first, the head of the New Democratic Party, Ed Broadbent, and by Gerry Wiener, the Minister for Multiculturalism in Canada.

TBL: Given *Obasan*'s biblical allusions and *Obasan*'s role in the redress movement, would you say that the Bible or biblical rhetoric is very much a galvanizing force in the movement?

JK: I don't think so. I personally don't think I ever talked about redress using biblical language.

TBL: Your father was an Anglican clergyperson, do you remember what and how he used the Bible during the internment? Did he use the Bible to comfort, to provide hope, and/or to express protest? Were there passages that he consistently referred to?

JK: I don't think he expressed protest. He did the rest. He did the readings as given in the lectionary and spoke around them. And he had his favorite passages. I believe he had confidence that Jesus came to save sinners.

TBL: I remember you told me once that you corresponded with Maxine Hong Kingston once or twice many years ago. What do you think about what we call "Asian American literature" these days? Do you have any problem with the term or the concept? Do you read other Asian American writers?

JK: Back in the 1970s when I went to California to meet some Japanese American writers, I was told in a dream that I would meet no one greater than the author of *Yoneko's Earthquake*. I was very impressed with Hisae Yamamoto DeSoto—her humility and humanity. I don't really read Asian American literature. I am more interested in our struggles with our values—whoever "we" are. I care about justice and mercy and truth and all that stuff, more than our ethnicities.

TBL: You are a Canadian, do you feel that the inclusion of, say, *Obasan*, in Asian *American* literature is in any sense inappropriate?[3] Do you see that as another imperialistic appropriation on the part of the United States?

JK: I guess I should think about this question. I do love Canada and mourn its loss of sovereignty.

TBL: We both know that your latest novel, *The Rain Ascends*, is very seldom mentioned within studies of Asian American literature. Am I correct to say that you actually see *The Rain Ascends* as your most meaningful work? What do you think are the dynamics behind the very different receptions of *Obasan* and *The Rain Ascends* by Asian American communities?

---

[3] For example, Kogawa is the only "novelist" featured in the MLA's *Resource Guide to Asian American Literature* who is not based in the U.S.

JK: Well, *The Rain Ascends* doesn't have an Asian person in it, so I guess that's why it's not out there in the Asian North American literary landscape. The book has meant the most to me because it transformed me the most. *Obasan* transformed me from a private to a more public person because of the way it was received, but *The Rain Ascends* transformed me from within because of the journey of it, because I went to hell. I was driven by a hunger for mercy and truth.

TBL: I recently read an Asian American literary critic who names you rather approvingly as one Asian (North) American writer who does not "exoticize" or "commodify" Asian (North) America for mass consumption (Sheng-mei Ma: xiv). I wonder if you have any comments concerning that observation about you and other Asian American writers.

JK: How do we "commodify" people, how do we not do that? I would like to know that myself. In *Obasan*, I used a lot of Japanese Canadian material simply because the life of the people was my experience. The thing is at the time I was writing it, I thought they were the last things that people would want to read. My first published short story was about a white family called the Parkins. And the story was about a man and a boy; there was no woman in the story either. At that point (1963), I probably looked in the mirror and saw myself as white and male. Then a poet friend, George Bowering, told me to write about the Japanese Canadian experience. A revolutionary thought. *Obasan* started for me with a dream to go to the archive in Ottawa, where I came across Muriel Kitagawa's paper. After the book appeared, one Japanese Canadian told me that I had "used" the Japanese Canadian story and exploited my "Japanese Canadian-ness" for my own gain. I was quite unnerved by that. Anyhow, I think this accusation of "commodification" somewhat odd, and I don't understand it.

TBL: Yes, I remember reading that you are very attentive to dreams (Hsu: 206). *Obasan* and *Itsuka* are both very intertwined with the history and well-being of the Japanese Canadian community, and you are personally very active in doing community work, is it important for you to relate what you write to community?

JK: I don't think about whom I am writing for when I write. I guess since I do it for publication, it does matter that people read it. But I just don't give too much thought about a "targeted audience." I am too busy listening to where the story is coming from.

TBL: Do you mind sharing with me what you are working on now? Does the Bible and does the question of race/ethnicity play a role in your new project?

JK: I am thinking about this character who is probably going to be a third-generation Japanese Canadian. One thing that interests me a bit is cultural differences. For example, in *The Rain Ascends*, I have a British character called Eleanor who wants the "truth" of her father-in-law as a pedophile addressed, but people of other cultures, especially Asians, may see any publicizing of this sort as unbearably shameful and a heavy burden on the family. In the West, people are taught to be more individualistic, to stand alone and away from family and to still have dignity. But many of us who are Asian understand both group-centered and family and community values, especially if we have been raised by first-generation parents in North America. So my new project has something to do with cultural differences. That is if I actually do write. I am a slow writer. Of course, a lot depends on how things work out, but I do think there is something to explore there.

Regarding the Bible, you know my primary identity is not my ethnic identity. My primary identity is my spiritual identity, so it would be hard to keep the Bible out of whatever I am writing. The stories from the Bible will be there; I do not know yet in what ways. When I started *Itsuka*, I was going to write a story of three different ministers, and how they deal with the issue of sexual immorality. I had in mind that one of them would be like the elder brother of the prodigal-son parable [Luke 15:11–32], a self-righteous priest who did not stray but also would not love. And then the fallen one, who did stray and yet did also love. That was the story that I wanted to write and started to write, but I did not really know where it would go, and then it got sidetracked by the redress movement. So I am wondering if I still need to go back in some way to that, and that would be full of the Bible stuff. But none of this is in paper and ink, so I don't know what will actually happen. It is something that I have been thinking about, but it may or it may not happen.

TBL: One last thought. I particularly like a section of writing that you have shown me. It is not specifically about the Bible, although the Bible is again alluded to. It is about a friend of yours, and it is about the Christian calendar and the atrocities perpetuated by a Christian country against a "heathen" nation. At the beginning of our conversation, you talked about waking the sleeping face of love, and in this piece, you talk about the culture of Okinawa and suggest that it may be the face of love in our day—a culture that is said to live by forgiveness and not by vengeance. Are you implying that God's love is more evident in that culture than in the European or Middle Eastern cultures where there are cycles of horror and vengeance? Or are you suggesting that we need to look to the sources of such forgiveness?

JK: I wonder if this is all too glib since I really know nothing about Okinawa culture. I know that at least some of the martial arts started there, and

I know that they are said to be some of the longest-living people on the earth today.

TBL: May I share the section with readers of *Semeia*?

JK: Go ahead.

> As I write this in my studio in Vancouver's west end, I have just learned that Hiroko, my best friend of my childhood days in southern Alberta, has died. Hiroko's ancestry, like my ex-husband's, is half Okinawan.
>
> ***
>
> Hiroko's funeral is on a blue sky perfect Okanagan summery day. Old friends from forever are here—from Coaldale, Calgary and Edmonton, from the old Alberta prairie days. The church holds six hundred. It's full.
>
> In the morning, in the motel room, a newspaper arrives with an advertisement for a book announcing the secrets of Okinawan longevity. As I sit on the bed, the newspaper spread around me, I have an eerie sense of Hiroko's presence, prodding me to tell what little I've heard about the wonders and horrors of Okinawa, that little known "island of peace."
>
> I don't know when the west first came across that magical land, but in 1815—it was my brother who told me this—Captain Basil Hall of the British navy, steamed into Naha, Okinawa. He buried on Okinawan soil, some of the deceased members of his crew. The story goes that on his way back to England, he dropped in to the island of St. Helena and had a conversation with Napoleon.
>
> "I have been to an island of peace," the captain reported. "The island has no soldiers and no weapons."
>
> "No weapons? Oh, but there must be a few swords around," Napoleon remarked.
>
> "No. Even the swords have been embargoed by the king."
>
> Napoleon, we're told, was astonished. "No soldiers, no weapons, no swords. It must be heaven."
>
> It must surely have been a culture as close to heaven on earth as we humans have managed. And perhaps therefore a special target for the forces of hate. There was an entirely bloodless coup when Japan, that warring nation, took over the kingdom. And when Japan sought soldiers from Okinawa to help with their invasion of Korea, there were none to be sent. A disobedient people, Japan concluded. A kingdom without soldiers was clearly impossible.

The first land invasion of Japan during World War II was in 1945 in Okinawa. There is something surreal about the Christian calendar and the dates of the war atrocities. Easter day, 1945 marked the beginning of the twelve-week, eighty-four day battle of Okinawa, the worst battle that had happened on the earth up to that point. 234,000 people were killed, more than all the people who died in the two atomic bombings combined. What unholy Easter forces mocked the Prince of Peace on the "island of peace"?

Then August 6, the Day of the Transfiguration [Matt 17:1–8; Mark 9:2–8; Luke 9:28–36] on the Christian calendar, the atom bomb was dropped on Hiroshima. The Japanese word for "transfiguration" is also the word for "disfiguration." Ken yo bo. On the day when the face of Christ was transfigured and became "glistering" white (my brother used that word) a Christian country disfigured the innocent people of a nation deemed to be heathen.

Okinawa's culture of peace defies western imagination. While I was writing *The Rain Ascends*, my brother and his wife were in Okinawa participating in a breathtaking action of speech. For twelve weeks, for eighty-four days, beginning on Easter day in 1995, the fortieth anniversary of the Battle of Okinawa was being remembered by the reading of names. The pastoral candle was lit. And for two hours at noon, and two hours at night, twice a day, the names of all the people who died were read. This was not just the names of the Okinawan victims, not just the names of parents, grandparents, the infants, friends, the schoolchildren. The reading included the names of the men who had wreaked this holocaust upon the most gentle of peoples. The Japanese soldiers, the American soldiers, blindly obedient to the Gods of War were not released, as Abraham was, from the slaying act [Gen 22:1–14]. These, the killers, were equally embraced in the memorial.

Is not Okinawa the cultural face of Love in our day? And how should the guilty now atone for their crimes? Could the perpetrating countries not at least begin by trying to understand?

"It's understanding that you have to have. You have to hear all the stories."

We are still living in Abraham's time. We are still sacrificing thousands of children on the altars of the voracious gods of our day. But we don't have to do this. We can slay instead the fictions of our time. We can work to make visible the foundational values that underlie systems of destruction—such as self-interest above all. We can walk Abraham's walk of trust, knowing that the ram is waiting for us.

WORKS CONSULTED

Caputo, John D.
    2001   *On Religion*. New York: Routledge.

Chua, Cheng Lok
    1992   "Witnessing the Japanese Canadian Experience in World War II: Processual Structure, Symbolism, and Irony in Joy Kogawa's *Obasan*." Pp. 97–108 in *Reading the Literatures of Asian America*. Ed. Shirley Geok-lin Lim and Amy Ling. Philadelphia: Temple University Press.

Hsu, Ruth Y.
    1996   "A Conversation with Joy Kogawa." *Amerasia Journal* 22:199–216.

Kogawa, Joy
    1993   *Itsuka*. New York: Doubleday. [Orig. 1992]

    1994   *Obasan*. New York: Anchor-Doubleday. [Orig. 1981]

    1995   *The Rain Ascends*. Toronto: Knopf.

    2000   *A Song of Lilith*. Artwork by Lilian Broca. Vancouver: Polestar.

Lo, Marie
    2001   "*Obasan* by Joy Kogawa." Pp. 97–107 in Wong and Sumida.

Ma, Sheng-mei
    2000   *The Deathly Embrace: Orientalism and Asian American Identity*. Minneapolis: University of Minnesota Press.

Palumbo-Liu, David
    1995   *The Ethnic Canon: Histories, Institutions and Interventions*. Minneapolis: University of Minnesota Press.

Ueki, Teruyo
    1993   "*Obasan*: Revelations in a Paradoxical Scheme." *MELUS* 18:5–20.

Wong, Sau-ling Cynthia, and Stephen H. Sumida, eds.
    2001   *A Resource Guide to Asian American Literature*. New York: The Modern Language Association of America.

Evangelical and Mainline Teachings on Asian American Identity

Russell Jeung
Foothill College

ABSTRACT

Asian American pan-ethnic congregations are emergent phenomena in the San Francisco Bay area. Yet ministers do not agree on their teachings on Asian American identity. Their institutional locations, as either mainline Christian or evangelical, shape their biblical interpretations and inform these divergent teachings. In particular, the two groups employ different institutional logics that govern how they organize their churches. With these logics, ministers read Scriptures in ways that promote specific understandings of ethnic/racial identity. Organized around tolerance and justice, mainline Christians see Asian Americans as individuals who need to reclaim their ethnic identity and struggle against racial discrimination. Evangelicals, in contrast, organize around personal concerns and church growth. They view Asian Americans as individuals with similar family patterns, psychological issues, and social needs. Both groups utilize various biblical passages to support these understandings of Asian American identity.

Introduction

If you're Japanese American or Asian American, that has some particular shape to it. It shows up in lots of common ways: "Where are you from?" And you say, "San Francisco." And they say, "No, really. Where are you from?"

That's one set, the racial set. I think that's primary in terms of being the most intense, the thing that surfaces early as to character formation. The other thing has to do with a person's discovery of who they are in terms of their ancestry. Or who they are as a generation of peoples. That's a common thing I call ethnic.

—A mainline Christian minister

I'm not sure this is specifically the Asian American experience. These are the general principles: The idea of the focus on education or the idea of accomplishment. The idea of having parents that were not as affirming or

> affectionate. Dealing with the struggle of Asian friends as well as Caucasian friends. Many Asian American Christians have a very bitter, past experience with the [ethnic] church. We have had to deal with two cultures and some that come into play as well. Those may be the characteristics of what an Asian American is like.
>
> —An evangelical pastor

These ministers' definitions of Asian American, pan-ethnic group identity differ significantly.[1] The first, representative of mainline Christian ministers, understands Asian Americans as a racial minority group with a common history of cultural oppression and racism. According to these ministers, Asian Americans experience marginalization as outsiders to mainstream society, which is evidenced by the oft-asked question, "Where are you from?" Asian Americans must deal with the reclaiming of their ethnic identity and heritage because of this cultural oppression. In contrast, evangelical pastors see Asian Americans as a spiritual consumer target group made up of personal networks and lifestyle affinities. As the above quotation suggests, they view Asian Americans as a group with an emotionally distant upbringing and an ethic for academic and professional success. Why do these ministers teach such different understandings for the same group of people, Asian Americans?

I argue that the differing institutional locations of evangelicals and mainline ministers shape their interpretations of Scriptures and, subsequently, their understanding of Asian American identity. Pan-ethnic groups, as defined by David Lopez and Yen Le Espiritu, are politicocultural collectivities made up of people of previously distinct tribal, ethnic, or national origins.[2] Sociologists of race and ethnicity note that pan-ethnicity is first and foremost a political category that groups utilize to further their material interests (Padilla; Cornell; Espiritu; Omi and Winant).

Ministers, however, have ideal interests in organizing groups of Asian Americans in that they seek to make congregations grow, evangelize, or be a prophetic voice for justice to a people. These religious interests provide impetus to establish new, pan-ethnic congregations that are different from ethnic-specific congregations. In order to motivate and mobilize their congregations to form along pan-ethnic lines, ministers must develop teachings that legitimate pan-ethnic identity. The distinctive institutional

---

[1] I include in the category "Asian American" any American of Asian descent. In the 2000 U.S. Census, persons could check off as either Asian Indian, Chinese, Filipino, Japanese, Korean, Vietnamese, Native Hawaiian, Guamanian or Chamorro, or Samoan.

[2] I equate pan-ethnicity with the concept of race, which itself is a socially constructed category.

locations of evangelical and mainline Asian American ministers help them develop different notions of pan-ethnic identity. By articulating these particular traits, the ministers define the social and the symbolic boundaries of the group—the markers that create distinctions between themselves and others (Barth; Taylor and Whittier; Nagel).

This paper will first explore the *organizational fields* that divide mainline Asian American Christian ministers from evangelicals. These fields are professional circles—ministerial networks, seminaries, publishing houses, and denominational caucuses—that promote certain *logics* for congregational development. Institutional logics are organizing imperatives that shape and constrain the development and culture of an institution (Friedland and Alford). Second, I elaborate on the institutional logics of mainline Christians that encourage tolerance and social justice. The teachings of one mainline Asian American congregation reveal the linkages between these institutional logics and its teachings of the Bible. Third, I discuss the institutional logics held by evangelicals. Contrasting sharply with the views of mainline Christian ministers, these logics focus on personal relationship with Jesus and church growth. Teachings from an evangelical Asian American church demonstrate how this group applies Scriptures to the experience of contemporary Asian Americans.

Methods/Data Gathering

The idea of a group of people, Asian Americans, is still new. Ministers, as cultural entrepreneurs, thus have much say and influence over the construction of this new grouping. Their sermons, teachings, and writings make up religious discourse that establishes the categories by which their congregations view and interact with the world. Week after week, congregational members hear and process the messages about the sacred, their identity in the world, and their role in their faith community. What ministers say—and do not say—about pan-ethnicity in front of the congregation represents their articulation of racial meanings.

This study includes in-depth interviews of forty-four ministers who pastor Asian American Christian congregations in the San Francisco Bay area.[3] I interviewed the ministers about their views on topics such as the nature of racial and ethnic groups, their theology, and the role of the church

---

[3] From lists of the Northern California Japanese Christian Church Federation, the Asian American Bay Area fellowship, and James Chuck's exploratory study of Chinese Protestant congregations (1996), I compiled a random list of English-speaking congregations. I later included two ministers from pan-ethnic congregations that were originally Korean American for comparison purposes.

within the community.⁴ Thirty-one of the congregations are fundamentalist or evangelical, and thirteen are mainline Christian (see appendix).⁵

To understand how pastors' institutional affiliations affect their biblical teachings, I have conducted participant observation for a year each at a mainline pan-ethnic congregation and an evangelical pan-ethnic congregation. These congregations are exemplary in demonstrating the connection between evangelical or mainline institutional logic and pan-ethnic identity. Both of these churches, located within three miles of one another, began as Japanese American congregations but now claim to be Asian American ones. Their members are similar in generation, class background, and educational attainment. Yet their ministers' interpretations of biblical passages illustrate very different institutional locations.

Differing Institutional Locations: Mainline versus Evangelical Organizational Fields

Asian American ministers clearly divide into two camps. Not only do the ministers align as either fundamentalist/evangelical or mainline, but they also identify themselves by articulating their differences from the other camp. This process of self-categorization transforms individuals into groups (Hogg). Furthermore, ministers affiliate more with those on their side of the spectrum and network within their own separate organizational fields. An organizational field includes "groups or organizations producing similar products or services as well as their critical exchange partners, sources of funding, regulatory groups, professional or trade associations, and other sources of normative and cognitive influence" (Scott: 173). Within a religious organizational field, ministers circulate similar normative and professional expectations about the role, function, and activities of churches. They develop common worldviews about ministry, which in turn affect biblical interpretations.

The Mainline Christian Organizational Field

Mainline church leaders look to their denominations, seminaries, and nonprofit organizations within their organizational field to establish assumptions

---

[4] Of these ministers, twenty-seven were Chinese Americans, eight were Japanese Americans, five were European Americans, two Filipino/Chinese Americans, and two Korean Americans.

[5] Within the sociology of religion, the two-party thesis is that American Christians fall into two basic groups with mainline, liberal and progressive Christians on one side and conservatives, evangelicals, charismatics, and fundamentalists on the other. Depending on the scholar, the basis of this dichotomization varies from a private versus public emphasis (Marty, 1981, 1998); a nascent versus institutional faith (Warner); a conservative versus liberal cultural morality (Wuthnow; Hunter); or an internal versus external locus of authority (Roof).

about biblical interpretation and racial understandings. Mainline denominations recognized and established pan-ethnic Asian American professional caucuses and youth camps as early as 1971. Acknowledging a need for Asian American leadership development, representation on boards, and resources for Asian American ministries, these caucuses advocated official recognition within their respective denominations.[6]

Mainline seminaries promote understandings about pan-ethnicity as well. The mainline Graduate Theological Union (GTU), for example, has trained several Asian American ministers in the Bay area. As early as 1972, GTU has provided institutional space for the Asian Center for Theologies and Strategies, now called the Pacific Asian Center for Theologies and Strategies (PACTS). PACTS and other schools of GTU sponsor courses on "Asian American Religions" and employ texts such as *Out of Silence: Emerging Themes in Asian American Churches* (Matsuoka). Formal education thus establishes normative pressures to organize along pan-ethnic lines.

The community nonprofit world also furnishes ideas about ethnicity and race to the church. Mainline liberal congregations, which tend to be involved in community issues of race and social justice, work closely with these nonprofit organizations. Within the San Francisco Bay area, the Asian American nonprofit sector is especially well-established with long-standing organizations such as the Asian Law Caucus, Asian Neighborhood Design, and Asian Health Services. Because their congregations work with the same kinds of concerns and constituencies as these agencies, mainline ministers often borrow language and rhetoric from them.

Institutional structures within denominations, educational curriculum that recognizes Asian American pan-ethnicity, and nonprofit organizations mobilizing around racial issues shape how ministers think about congregational identity. As they respond and comply with institutional and professional expectations, they help make their own congregations similar in form and structure.[7] They establish pan-ethnic congregations with understandings from these institutional bases that circulate a broad definition of the group, Asian Americans.

---

[6] By 1977, the following denominations had officially recognized these national caucuses or offices to deal with Asian American ministries: Asian American Baptist Caucus, Asian Presbyterian Caucus, National Federation of Asian American United Methodists, Pacific American and Asian American Ministries of the UCC, Episcopal Asian American Strategies Task Force, Reformed Churches of America—Asian Office, North American Pacific Asian Disciples of Christ, and the Evangelical Lutheran Church of America—Asian Ministries. I have one Catholic priest in my sample, whom I have included with the mainline Protestant ministers. His views on race and ethnic ministry are similar to theirs.

[7] Normative pressures to become organizationally similar stem primarily from professionalization and standards set by the organizational field (DiMaggio and Powell).

The Evangelical Organizational Field

Evangelical ministers work together and learn from each other in an organizational field separate from mainline ministers and thus have a very different understanding of Asian Americans. Just as mainline ministers receive formal training from certain seminaries, evangelicals learn about church-growth methodology within their educational institutions. But instead of looking to denominations and the public nonprofit sector for insights on serving Asian Americans, evangelical ministers look more to leading evangelical publications and their professional networks to target and minister to this group.

Since the 1980s, campus ministries have recognized the growing presence of Asian Americans on campuses and have sought to evangelize students along these groupings (Busto). Throughout California and on elite university campuses in the United States, InterVarsity Christian Fellowship (IVCF) and the Japanese Evangelical Missionary Society (JEMS) have established evangelically oriented Asian American Christian Fellowships (AACFs). Once graduated, students seek similar fellowship and church settings.

Theological seminaries also promote and legitimate pan-ethnicity by offering courses tailored toward this grouping. The largest seminary in North America, the evangelical Fuller Seminary in Pasadena, California, offers the course, "Multiculturalism Today: Reflections and Response," and the instructors use the text, *Racial Conflict and Healing: An Asian American Theological Perspective* (Park). These courses, texts, and Asian American instructors are official, professional recognition that pan-ethnicity is a valid grouping, field of theological study, and ministerial concern.

Most importantly, evangelical pastors have professional and ministerial networks that introduce pan-ethnic models of congregational development. On-line, Chinese American pastors keep connected on a mailing list called "Chinese American Christians" (CAC). In the San Francisco Bay area, official networks include the Bay Area Asian American Youth Fellowship, the Promise Keepers, and the Asian American Bay Area Fellowship. For example, the Asian American Bay Area Fellowship is made up of about fifty Chinese, Filipino, Japanese, and Korean American evangelical pastors who meet irregularly. Since 1991, they have addressed similar issues as those posted on CAC, including the role of ethnic culture in the church and Asian American racial reconciliation between individual ethnic groups. These professional networks are the "interorganizational contexts" within which the discourse of pan-ethnicity and race become circulated, appropriated, and infused with meaning.

With limited options of strategies and rules about church growth circulating within the evangelical field, ministers often follow leaders in the field.⁸ Within the local Bay area Asian American church networks, ministers perceive pan-ethnic congregations as being successful in attracting members and nurturing them. For example, this pastor felt called to establish a ministry similar to other pan-Asian ones:

> Most of the successful churches, either in Southern California or here, they're mostly pan-Asian. They have been very successful, not only in terms of numbers but also spiritual growth. So I thought that this church ... that's why God placed me here.

Pan-ethnic churches emerge as new congregations copy other successful pan-ethnic ones.⁹

In summary, ministers interact with others within the same organizational fields that promote certain discourses and ideas. In particular, fields recommend specific institutional logics that govern how a congregation should develop. For mainline Asian American churches, these logics dictate that ministries should orient themselves towards tolerance, community, and social justice.

The Institutional Logics of Mainline Asian American Congregations

Mainline Christians have general theological orientations and tenets of faith that govern their congregational values and practices. Despite the broad range of churches in this grouping, mainline or liberal Protestantism does convey specific meanings for the ministers in this study. Two main traits of what Hoge, Johnson, and Luidens call "lay liberalism" include belief in tolerance and a prophetic morality about justice.

The Tolerance of Lay Liberalism and Embracing of Asian Cultural Traditions

The first organizing logic, the tolerance of mainline and liberal churches toward other religions and traditions, opens up space for the celebration of Asian heritage by Asian American congregations. Hoge, Johnson, and Luidens describe the theological perspective that they call "lay liberalism":

> [I]ts defining feature is a rejection of the orthodox teaching that Christianity is the only true religion. Lay liberals have a high regard for Jesus, but they

---

⁸ Mimetic isomorphism refers to the tendency of organizations to mimic other organizations perceived to be successful. Even if the innovations do not prove to be effective in increasing church growth, they are still adopted to demonstrate that the ministers are trying to effect some kind of reform and to meet the demands of what potential members expect (DiMaggio and Powell)

⁹ In particular, pastors often referred to Evergreen Baptist Church and New Song Covenant Church in Southern California as large and growing Asian American congregations.

do not affirm that He is God's only son and that salvation is available only through Him. (112–13)

Instead of assenting to a doctrinal statement of truth, this perspective espouses that the heart of religion is its ethical standards. These standards comprise a general moral code of faith and good works.

Similarly, mainline ministers in this study did not unite around common creeds or doctrinal beliefs, but they did share a rejection of orthodoxy and embraced a tolerant view of other religions and traditions. They maintained that faith in Jesus Christ was central to their beliefs and that this faith distinguished them from the secular world and other religions, but that other faith traditions also held truth. One minister explained how Christianity is true for him but other religions are not necessarily invalid:

> To me, it's the Christian gospel that motivated me, as far I'm concerned, to have a concern for community. Now it may be true that another kind of approach is found in Buddhism. And if the end product is compassion and unity and community, or if the values of equality and justice come out of a Japanese or Chinese culture, to me that's fine. I really feel we need to try to identify the richness of God's revelation in all kinds of approaches to reality, or different religions.

Their postmodern, relativistic view of truth stems from a critique of Western, missionary forms of Christianity. Along with other Asian and Asian American theologians, these ministers see Western Christianity as a colonizing mode of thought that universalizes particular Western ideals as it delegitimates the Asian as the "Other" (Loo; Ng; Sugirtharajah). Indeed, they argue that this colonization of thought accompanies the economic and political oppression of Asians both in Asia and in the United States. One minister argued that neither mainline pastors nor their members could accept White Christianity as dogmatic truth anymore:

> The problem with that is a lot of Christian tradition is bad stuff. It's twentieth century stuff and it's Western, European stuff and has passed. The trick is, the people who can give us information about the spiritual stuff are the people who are struggling with it themselves. So it's not like they can come here and I'll read the Book to them or I'll teach them the lessons.

If Western forms of Christianity are culturally biased and if other religions contain truth, then Asian perspectives and ideas could provide correctives and insights to the Christian faith. Mainline ministers look to Asian traditions as cultural resources that are rich in wisdom. As one explained,

> I think what we consider Christian identity is not very clear because it's sort of a Euro-Western perspective of what it is to be Christian. So when [an Asian American] person goes back to his [sic] roots, you realize that

within your culture and background there are a lot of realities from God—revelation that is from God and that can accentuate what we believe is the heart of Christianity.

There are so many things within the Japanese, Chinese, Asian culture that can be affirmed within Christianity if a person studies it in depth. The Euro-Western approach is to say those things are maybe pagan or heathen or primordial or primitive. Not so! There are ancient cultures which are longer than what we have in the West, and there are a lot of riches. If we find the contribution we can make towards reality or Christianity that comes out of culture, that'd be great.

An examination of one's Asian heritage, then, provides Asian American Christians with a fresh understanding of the faith that may build up the church universal.

Not only does embracing Asian traditions correct the Western biases in Christianity, but it also helps Asian American Christians integrate their faith with their culture and heritage. Mainline ministers hope to help church members accept themselves, identify with their Asian heritages, and acknowledge the goodness and truth found in their traditions. Christ and culture may complement one another as sources of wholeness. One minister expressed why he placed emphasis on Asian cultural practices, especially to his youth members. He legitimated the construction of a strong ethnic identity as part of "God's design":

By exposing them to their own culture, their own roots, we also give them the sense that God is also God of the new immigrants, of the Chinese, as well as of the young [Asian] Americans. They have their own culture to keep as well the people of their own roots—which is also a part of the design of God. That's the multicultural context which I would include in my ministry and my message to them.

A Social Justice Frame and Ethnic/Racial Issues

Another institutional logic of mainline congregations is that Christian teachings call for a commitment to service, peace, and justice. The theology and denominational influences of mainline Christianity encourage social change efforts through the public sphere. Roof asserts that mainline churches have a heritage as "bridging institutions—concerned with public well-being and the larger social order" (241). Other authors have also asserted that liberal Protestantism emphasizes a social justice platform of public responsibility (Marty, 1970, 1981; Warner; Wuthnow).

Likewise, mainline Asian American ministers believe that, more than just preaching the gospel, the church is to embody the values of the faith by living out Christ's teachings. This pastor emphasized a broader concern for the community:

> Where Scripture leads me, my focus is on service and justice issues. Some people concentrate on salvation—that's their big part of Scripture they'll concentrate and preach on. If you were to hear my sermons, mine is really on justice and what that means for us and how to act that out. I preach a lot on issues of homelessness, preach on youth and empowering people.

With this frame of social justice, ministers examine the lives of their congregational members and the injustices that they experience or their community experiences. The racial situation of Asians in America clearly becomes the issue around which these ministers mobilize. To empower Asian American population and address justice issues within it, mainline congregations organize their ministries by claiming rights as minorities in the United States.

Mainline ministers in this study often named racism, both institutional and individual, as the major cause for the social inequities and marginalization that they and their members experienced. On a broad level, racism creates barriers for Asian Americans in gaining acceptance and power within American corporations and institutions. One minister discussed how his church members felt insignificant because they were segregated in the past and lacked access to authority and resources within the United Methodist denomination. Even though Chinese and Japanese American churches joined larger denominational structures in the 1960s, they remained largely powerless. As described earlier, the creation of separate Asian/Pacific Islander caucuses within mainline denominational structures in the 1970s stemmed from a need for greater voice.

Mainline ministers express that on an individual level, racism affects members' self-esteem and interpersonal relationships. For example, a pastor discussed the lack of positive media images for Asian American youth, especially the boys. He noted,

> It's very clear to the high school students, the perception of Asian women versus Asian men in our society, particularly from the media. And the notion in the movies, it was always the white guy that got the Asian woman and the Asian guy never did. They are conscious of it. For some guys, it's a real source of anxiety. There's a fair amount of anger there.

This pastor also shared experiences of Asian American church members who attempted to join local white congregations but felt excluded:

> Others would share stories about how they would go for a couple of months and people were still coming up to them and saying, "Oh, is this your first time here?" Others would say they've been at a church for a long time and nobody ever invited them or included them in certain activities.

They felt excluded. Maybe not unconsciously or not inadvertently ... some of them felt they maybe were advertently excluded, left out.

Oriented toward mobilizing their congregations around issues of social justice, Chinese, Japanese, and Asian American mainline pastors develop a "theology of struggle."[10] This heightened consciousness of Asian Americans as racial minorities who are oppressed both individually and institutionally shapes how ministers see the role of their churches—as sanctuaries for people facing discrimination, as community institutions facilitating positive identities, and as congregations working for societal change.

These two organizational logics regarding tolerance and justice in turn shape how mainline ministers read the Bible and address matters of identity. Tolerance of Asian traditions enables ministers to embrace Asian religious beliefs and cultural practices as part of the Asian American heritage. The concern for justice promoted by mainline churches leads Asian Americans to examine their own oppression and marginalization. Teachings at Park Avenue United Methodist Church (PAUMC)[11] demonstrate how each of these logics operate to influence biblical readings.

The Teachings at PAUMC, a Mainline Asian American Church

As a pan-ethnic, mainline liberal congregation, PAUMC teaches that Asian American identity involves both pride in one's ethnic heritage and solidarity with other oppressed minorities. This church helps to construct this identity through the reinvention of ethnicity, the reclamation of one's heritage, and uniting against racial injustice. Sermons often either educate members about current issues facing the community or provide theological understandings of why the church engages in particular ministries.[12] These themes thus acknowledge the sacred nature of one's ethnic and racial background that is to be integrated with one's faith identity.

PAUMC's core belief statements in their mission statement best exemplify this understanding of Asian American identity. One of PAUMC's core

---

10 Asian American mainline theology takes as its starting point the grounded experiences of Asian Americans. This process may involve "the uncovering of painful stories," such as relating the pain of the Japanese American internment experience to one's relationship with God (Yoshii). A "theology of struggle" is Matsuoka's phrase to depict Asian American Christians' community-building efforts in the face of racism.

11 Names of institutions and individuals have been changed.

12 One year, the theme for the Lenten Season was "Environmental Justice," and the next year it was "Culture, Faith and Community Health." Periodically, speakers from outside nonprofit organizations, such as Hospice of Northern California, the National Asian Pacific American Families Against Substance Abuse, and the Asian Pacific Environmental Network, come to speak about their work in the community.

belief statements reads, "Within each person and all of creation, God can be known through many traditions." In this statement, they affirm the value and uniqueness of each individual because the spirit of God can be found in that individual. Another core belief states, "Having worked in our history as a Japanese American church, God continues to give us a unique role in the Asian American community and society." Here they recognize how God acts in history by using ethnicity and race to bless people and speak to people. These statements do not merely legitimate ethnic and racial boundaries, but they also intentionally affirm them as God's good creation.

Asian American identity first involves the reinvention of ethnicity, in which cultural traditions and values are transformed and reaffirmed. In one sermon entitled "Standing in the Shadows: Honor, Shame and New Life" (sermon notes, 2/28/99), Pastor Bill challenged the ethnic self-hate, stereotypes, and cultural bondage that some Asian Americans may hold. In relation to the topic of substance abuse, he expounded upon John 10:1–10, the parable in which sheep enter through a gate to find pasture and new life. He praised the virtue of Asian values such as honor and face but admitted that they can be roadblocks. He taught:

> the values of honor and shame are virtuous but they can become barriers to seeking help. The world has changed and there are more resources for us. We have a greater awareness of how different cultures get help and seek help.

Cultural practices, if inappropriate to the changed world we now live in, need to be shed in order to obtain new life and health. To deal with substance abuse, Asian Americans must let go of honor and face in order to admit their problems and seek help.

Pastor Bill then related this Scripture passage about being "born again" to the need to change some old patterns:

> Fundamentalists say we have to be born again to get to heaven, but there are many possibilities of what it means to be born again. We may be enclosed by culture that blocks the pathways of new life. We may need a new way of looking at things. God doesn't condemn, shame, or dishonor but offers hope and peace.

Among the "many possibilities of what it means to be born again" is becoming a new type of Asian American who does not keep quiet about one's personal or family problems, but actively seeks community in addressing them. Here, Christian transformation and new life involve the reinvention of ethnic patterns that are not suited to contemporary culture.[13]

---

[13] Similarly, PAUMC teaches that gender inequalities need to be challenged and women's leadership roles lifted up. These teachings seek to transform traditional Asian

Although PAUMC identifies certain cultural practices and values as unhealthy, the congregation still promotes a positive Asian American identity through the reclamation of heritage. In sermons and liturgies, PAUMC incorporates cultural traditions and provides strong ethnic role models. On Dr. Martin Luther King's birthday weekend (sermon notes, 1/18/98) the children's sermon followed a Scripture reading of 1 Cor 12:1–11, Paul's discussion of different kinds of spiritual gifts. Pastor Bill related this passage of individual gifting to the children and exhorted, "God made you different and special in your way. God wants you to be all you can be." He showed a picture of Dr. Martin Luther King and discussed how he used his gifts to fight for rights. Then Pastor Bill showed a news photograph of Fred Korematsu with President Bill Clinton (see Sandalow). He asked:

> Do you know what is he known for? Japanese Americans were taken away and he said he didn't think it was right and he was sent to jail. He was like Dr. Martin Luther King speaking truth that something is wrong and he fought to help others without hurting anybody.

By highlighting a hero in Japanese American community, Pastor Bill consciously provided a secular role model for the children to whom they were supposed to relate. Dr. King was a role model, but the Japanese and Asian American community has its own leaders who fought for civil rights as well. Although the school system may not teach about these community heroes, the church serves as a "community of memory" to remind the youth of their role models.

Pastor Bill further added, "We also have people with us who speak for the truth and do the right thing." He pointed out parents in the audience who were attorneys or activists who did work in the Asian American community. As noted in the discussion of mainline organizational fields, mainline Asian American ministers maintain close ties with the nonprofit community. By valorizing the efforts of these individuals and how they used their gifts and skills for the community, Pastor Bill created living ethnic symbols that the youth were to learn from and emulate. Not only are one's talents gifts from God, but one's ethnic background is also God's gift.

Besides promoting a healthy ethnic self-image, PAUMC teaches its members to join in solidarity with other people of color. Sermons decry the use of race in creating inequalities and call on the church to challenge racist injustices. In a sermon called "Covenanting with God" (sermon notes, 3/15/98), Pastor Bill taught from Acts 3:25, which states that "you are heirs

---

cultural values, not necessarily to assimilate to American ways, but so that people can fully embrace the love of God.

of the prophets and of the covenant God made with your fathers." He began by sharing the story of a woman near an oil refinery who got cancer. The people in the community recognized that industry pollution correlated to higher rates of cancer in that area and found that race is the most significant factor in determining where facilities are to be situated. Pastor Bill continued to explain that such policies constitute "environmental racism" because industries' policies disproportionately affect people of color, the groups least likely to oppose corporations. He challenged the church to be in covenant with God and to turn away from the forces of evil. Instead of spiritual complicity with racist policies, the church was to repent of them and follow Jesus' call for justice. As heirs of the prophets who spoke out against oppression and as heirs of the covenant with God, members were to stand against racism.

This reinvention of ethnicity by challenging unhealthy cultural practices, the promotion of a strong ethnic identity by reclaiming one's heritage, and the racialization of members by challenging racist environmental policies are ways that PAUMC consciously and strategically integrates faith and identity. PAUMC more readily embraces the multiple identities that people now possess. By reasserting its ethnicity and racial heritage, PAUMC provides an institutional space to support a faith-based Asian American identity that takes pride in ethnic heritage and stands in solidarity with fellow racial minorities. In contrast, Asian American evangelicals have a different understanding of the relationship between racial identity and faith.

THE INSTITUTIONAL LOGICS OF EVANGELICAL ASIAN AMERICAN CONGREGATIONS

The widely accepted definition of American contemporary evangelicalism is that it includes two tenets: a born-again experience and commitment to converting others (Hunter; Ammerman; Warner; Shibley).[14] These tenets of faith have become institutional logics for church development. In their belief that Jesus is one's personal Savior, evangelicalism now focuses on the personal, that is, an individual's concerns for self-fulfillment and therapeutic health. In their practice of sharing the faith, evangelicals have developed church-growth strategies that involve target marketing and church specialization.

A Personal Jesus and the Asian American Self

In contrast to mainline Christians, born-again evangelicals emphasize the need to accept Jesus as one's personal Savior and Lord. This process

---

[14] The other main tenet of evangelicals is their literal interpretation of the Bible, which is believed to be inerrant.

involves repentance of one's sins and spiritual rebirth through the atonement of Jesus Christ. Today, however, churches emphasize more the *personal* benefits of Christianity. Jesus still saves, but not just from the future punishment of sins. He also saves people from career and work stress, family and personal dysfunctions, addictions and relationship problems. Evangelical congregations and ministries have responded to Americans' need for individual fulfillment by promoting positive new religious experiences and becoming therapeutic. Mark Shibley, in his ethnographies of the Vineyard Christian Fellowship and Calvary Chapel, cites that "the religious culture in these congregations, mirroring the direction of change in the wider culture, is more individualistic and therapeutic than social and moralistic" (90). Given their theological orientation upon the individual within the contemporary American context, evangelical pastors tend to see members primarily as individuals with personal emotional and moral needs.

Asian American evangelicals thus tend to view Asian Americans as a people with common family dynamics and psychological issues. For example, InterVarsity Christian Fellowship, a national campus ministry, recently published a Bible study guide for Asian Americans entitled *Losing Face and Finding Grace* by Tom Lin. Its two main sections deal with "finding our identity" and "breaking free" from dysfunctions of shame and parental control. Despite the range and diversity in Asian American family experience, from low-income refugees in inner cities to fifth-generation professionals growing up in affluent suburbs (Lowe), evangelical Asian American ministers highlight certain family histories as being characteristically definitive. They note that since Asian American parents raise their children with high expectations, their offspring often must deal with issues of self-worth and perfectionism. One explained that "typical" Asian Americans share a family pressure to succeed with little emotional support:

> You look at the typical childhood experience for many of us growing up. I share this at different camps, retreats and it strikes an instant nerve. What was it like when you were a kid? You come home, you got a test and you got a score of 98 percent. Your parents shower you with positive affirmation that you did so well? Hardly ever. If anything, they might yell at you for missing the two percent!

These family pressures to succeed also shape how they grow up and interact with the broader society. Another pastor asserted:

> The third generation of Japanese Americans has utterly the identical experience of growing up as the Chinese Americans. They're peers! They went to the same schools, they were friends; they had the same difficulties, the same problems in relating to wider society as Chinese Americans. From my outside perspective, they look and behave the same way, and they're marrying each other. Their experiences in school and society were the same—they

faced the same obstacles and problems while their parents still are very much Japanese and Chinese with cultural differences.

Seeing Asian Americans as a group with specific identity, psychological, and emotional issues, evangelical ministers believe that these distinctions make Asian Americans a viable grouping to serve. Although they teach and stress spiritual development and one's relationship with God, they find that these particular markers bond Asian Americans together. One summarized:

> [God's calling us to] building an Asian American church where people of Asian American descent feel comfortable coming. We don't exclude non-Asian Americans, but there are definitely needs, concerns, family issues, relational issues that a lot of Asian Americans face that people from other ethnic cultures or races don't. We want a ministry designed for those Asian Americans.

Sharing the Faith: Targeting Asian American Professionals

Another defining characteristic of evangelicals is their commitment to converting nonbelievers. With their exclusive approach toward salvation, Asian American evangelicals must be committed to evangelism or else their friends and families are destined for hell. As one minister explained, "We think evangelism should be a theme that permeates the entire ministry of the church."

All of the evangelical ministers referred to "church growth" leaders and principles that are renowned within the broader American evangelical subculture. Often, they employ leading evangelical principles of church growth that inform the formation of new Asian American church plants.[15] Ministers build churches around personal networks of existing members. They then market programs based upon what they believe are the needs and desires of their audiences. Together, these methodologies reinforce pan-ethnic identities based on personal networks and lifestyle affinities.

Perhaps the most influential principle of church-growth strategy is "friendship evangelism." Instead of relying on large-scale events, such as a Billy Graham crusade or a revival meeting, churches seek to grow one by one as members invite their friends to church small groups and activities.

---

[15] Leading innovators in the evangelical field who are emulated include Bill Hybels of Willow Creek Community Church in Illinois, Rick Warren of Saddleback Community Church in Southern California, and Donald McGavran of Fuller Theological Seminary. Each of these individuals has built or studied large mega-churches, has written books to recount their successes, and frequently holds seminars to teach others his principles and understandings of church growth.

This way, over time, church members can introduce Christianity to their non-Christian friends in a "nonthreatening, nondogmatic" manner. When looking at who were the friends and personal networks of their church members, ministers saw that they were primarily Asian American. Asian American pan-ethnic congregations, then, developed out of a focus of growing churches around the personal networks and friendship circles of existing members. One pastor found out:

> [W]e draw more towards relationships, relationships that we build. That is what we're focusing on right now. Not trying to minister to all these strangers, but to say, "Who are our natural contacts?" You may find that for Asian Americans, a lot of our natural contacts still may be Asian. With those personal contacts, we draw them in.

Pastors surmise that if church growth comes from members inviting other friends, then those friends will also most likely be Asian American. This minister recounted:

> A lot of times, Asian Americans tend to hang around with Asian Americans. I worked at Xerox for ten years and on my team we had a Japanese, a guy who was Irish, had a black, Filipino, just the whole thing. And I found while I liked them all and we all worked together, I found for some reason I talked a little more to the guy who was Filipino and the guy who was Japanese.
>
> That's why I think, initially [in the new church plant], we'll be much more Asian just because this is the place for our members to start from. I'm expecting there'll be more of an Asian influx than anything else. Just because of networks. We're not going to deliberately eliminate anybody, but just acknowledging the way that the Asian community operates, we tend to see more Asians.

By assuming that churches grow fastest when they are homogeneous, that friends of church members most likely share the same needs and desires as the members, and that these needs tend to be individualistic in nature, Asian American evangelicals build a certain type of community. It is not only racially pan-ethnic, but also similar in class and generational composition.

Pastor and author Rick Warren states another principle of church growth: congregations need to target a market group by identifying its cultural mindset. A target group such as Asian Americans needs to be defined culturally, and as a result, many of the ministers look at Asian Americans in these particular ways. According to Warren, culture refers to "a lifestyle and mindset" and "to a people's values, interests, hurts and fears" (165). Understanding the culture of a congregation's target group is critical in ministering to them, dealing with their "felt needs" and "hang-ups," and then communicating effectively to them.

In looking at their target group, evangelical ministers have examined the lifestyle and mindset of Asian Americans and see a group of young, urban professionals. They believe that Asians' work ethic and stress on education have led Asian Americans to share common class backgrounds and class interests. Congregations are remarkably similar in their professional status, their upwardly mobile families, and spare-time activities. Lifestyle affinities thus characterize these Asian American networks.

Asian American professional lifestyle and networks begin at a young age. To start, Asian American high school and college students have enormous parental pressure to do well and succeed. A youth pastor joked:

> When I went to Berkeley, these Asian American students were like Junior Republicans! I got a sense that they were there because their parents sent them there, because they wanted to go to the best schools, and they were gonna get their MBAs, and they were going to get their engineering degrees and make six figures right off the bat.

Another found that this stress on professional and career success is a common Asian American trait:

> There is a shared experience in terms of being second *generation:* immigrant drive to success, focus on education. Again, I also understand that's also part of the Asian American ethos. What draws the Chinese American or Japanese American together oftentimes is the fact that they come out of this environment which has stressed education, which has stressed success, family and that kind of ties them together in a way that I'm not sure is in Caucasian churches.

To deal with these concerns of professionals, one congregation plans to establish a ministry center using "applied biblical principles" for non-Christians. Its pastor foresaw:

> In terms of church planting, what I see is a ministry center. I think worship services will draw the Christians, not too many non-Christians. But if we have a place where we can start up another group, could be a class or seminar or things like that from a Christian perspective—another parenting thing, financial management, could be marital counseling, whatever—people will say, "Hey, yeah, there's something good that's going on over there. Let me see what it is." And then if they like it, that's great because we're Christians and because we're doing what we're doing based on the Bible.

The felt needs that this pastor mentioned—parenting, finances, and marital counseling—are not exclusive to Asian Americans, yet those are the interests and fears that these people supposedly share.

These two organizational logics, that churches should meet the therapeutic needs of individuals and should grow by target marketing, shape how evangelical ministers read the Bible and understand Asian American identity. By focusing on psychological issues of Asian Americans, evangelical ministers see family upbringing as a significant factor in one's identity. Target marketing of Asian Americans highlights the lifestyle affinities of this professional grouping. Teachings at Grace Faith Church (GFC) exemplify how these logics affect their understandings of identity.

The Teachings at GFC, an Evangelical Asian American Church

As an evangelical church, GFC teaches that Asian American identity is relevant in that family issues affect one's personal relationship with God, and social networks become the basis of evangelism. Yet being Asian American was an assumed identity but not an issue significant enough to warrant teaching from the pulpit. According to church annual reports, none of the sermons or sermon series from 1987 to 1999 dealt directly with issues of race and ethnicity.[16] Nevertheless, to make these topics relevant, speakers often did address concerns about identity and thereby instructed church members about the "true nature" of one's identity. In their teachings, speakers alluded to how race and ethnicity might fit into these spiritual concepts and how members might want to understand their ethnic and racial backgrounds.

One's interior state is understood to be the source of one's "true" identity. A GFC-sponsored conference, "Get Real: A Seminar on Relational Health with God, Self and Others," aptly captured this view of one's identity. The promotional brochure explains how the shame-based culture of Asian Americans affects how people view and present themselves:

> Many of us have grown up with the pressure of perfection. At times we all feel insecure or struggle with shame. We push our strengths to the front, hoping others will love and accept us because we *appear* perfect. But inside, we know our weaknesses well. How often do we wander away from His love as we invent and reinvent ourselves, trying to earn the worth we have already been given by grace?

This inventing and reinventing of one's identity is an attempt to please others and gain acceptance that may have been withheld by Asian parents. Yet an Asian American identity, based on accomplishment and perfectionism, is a false front that needs to be unmasked. The conference encouraged people to "get real" and "get free":

---

16 Topics of sermon series included lessons on spiritual disciplines (Learning to Pray, Stewardship, Doctrine of Scripture, Sharing your Faith), teaching on worship and community (Worship His Majesty, Life in the Spirit, Authenticity), and doctrines of the Bible (Living a Grace-Filled Life, How Faith Grows).

In this seminar, we will look at some of the blocks to experiencing God's love and the identities that are built around them. As we begin to put aside that which is false, we trust that God in His [sic] mercy and grace will bring forward all that is true and all that is real, both in our hearts and in our relationships with each other.

The teachings of GFC thus recognize an Asian American identity as legitimate and as a valid basis for church mobilization, but also state that a more real and authentic identity can be found in knowing Jesus Christ. These two identities coincide as parallel identities. Unlike PAUMC, where Asian American identity is integrated with one's Christian identity, GFC separates one's ethnic/racial identity from one's spiritual identity. Being Asian American is a cultural background that is associated with family patterns, a lifestyle, and a social set of relationships. Being Christian is an interior and spiritual state of being that should influence how one relates and behaves in this world. At times, Christians must overcome their Asian American heritages to find their "true" selves. This process of identity construction includes renunciation, affirmation, and discernment of calling.

In a sermon entitled "The Pathway to Authentic Relationships" (sermon notes, 11/3/96), Pastor Bruce preached on Eph 4:15–16, 25, where Paul exhorted believers to "speak the truth in love." Pastor Bruce began by sharing a practical joke on the *Candid Camera* television show. An actor sitting at a lunch counter would reach over to another customer's plate and take his or her French fries. Nine out of ten victimized customers would not say anything to the thief. Pastor Bruce asked, "Does that surprise you? Not if they're Asians, huh?" And the audience laughs because Asians are known to avoid conflict and not to confront others directly. Like Pastor Bill from PAUMC, Pastor Bruce raised the Asian issue of saving face and the problems that it brings about:

> When we submerge our true feelings in order to preserve harmony, we undermine the integrity of the relationship. We preserve peace on the surface, but underneath there are hurt feelings, troubling questions, and hidden hostilities waiting to erupt. It's a costly price to pay for a cheap peace and inevitably leads to inauthentic relationships.
>
> It's human nature to prefer peacemaking over truth. We'll never experience true community and authentic relationships until we learn to speak the truth in love to one another.

Drawing concepts from M. Scott Peck's book, *The Different Drum: Community Making and Peace,* Pastor Bruce argued that groups must be willing to engage in "chaos," when "hurts are unburied, hostilities are revealed, and tough questions are asked." He supported this confrontational stage by reasoning, "The scriptures say that we should speak the truth in love. We're not going to grow up the way Christ wants us to grow up unless we learn to speak the truth in love." After identifying the scriptural and discipleship reasons to speak truth in love, he provided some practical tips on how to speak the truth:

> An issue we need to think through is communication skills. How we say things is very, very critical. It makes all the difference in the world. One of the things they tell you in counseling training is that whenever you're dealing with confrontation, whenever you have to share negative feelings, use "I" statements instead of "you" statements. The "you" is always accusing and most people will either flight or fight. If I can put it in an "I" statement, it's so much less threatening. Plus I'm sharing something about myself.

He suggested that by being humble and by applying these communication techniques, the church could go further in terms of building healthy relationships.

In this sermon, Pastor Bruce investigated an Asian American cultural pattern under the light of both Scripture and American therapeutic discourse. He made light of an Asian stereotype of being nonconfrontational, but then went further to diagnose it as possibly an inauthentic and unhealthy pattern of relating. Instead, Asian Americans were to aspire to authenticity, health, and true community in which people spoke the truth in love. In this sermon, Pastor Bruce called on people to renounce Asian cultural patterns to become more authentic in addressing one's issues.

In another sermon on "Welcoming All People," a seminary student speaker affirmed and even privileged one's spiritual identity over one's ethnic or even sexual identity (sermon notes, 2/23/97). She preached on Mark 6:34, in which Jesus saw a large crowd and had compassion on them "because they were like sheep without a shepherd." If Christians were to have the same outlook as Jesus, they would also see others as lost and needing salvation. During her talk, she related a story when she visited a Hispanic church but did not feel welcomed. She wanted to leave but explained that "as a good Asian American, that would be rude." So she stayed and sat through the service. Later, she reflected on how churches needed to be much more friendly and welcoming. She noted, "We need to see people as Jesus did—their value, their need, their potential. But we focus on differences of dress, speech, thinking." As another example, she talked about being shy at the home of a gay person, a brother of her friend. She said she overcame her hesitation "by focusing on what's behind the exterior. He was no longer a gay man nor a friend's brother, but a seeker with potential."

In this sermon, the speaker alluded to her Asian American identity as a cultural mode of behaving. As an Asian, she did not want to appear rude, lose face, or embarrass others. So she endured sitting through a service where she could not even understand the language. Although she acknowledged her background and used it as a humorous point of commonality with her audience, she urged people to look beyond the "exterior" to see people based on their needs, value, and potential. Ethnicity, race, and sexuality are not as important as one's privatized needs for a relationship with God. Instead, what is affirmed is one's identity as potential to become a child of God.

Evangelical Asian American Christians are bound together not by their common racial experience but by their common mission to evangelize others. Evangelical Asian American identity thus also involves a calling to reach out to others. In a sermon on "Being a Caring Family," Pastor Dan taught that one characteristic of a caring church is that people "support each other and let go of differences by focusing on what's common—their mission in Jesus Christ" (sermon notes, 2/9/97). Expounding on the early church, where "every day they continued to meet together" and "the Lord added to their number daily" (Acts 2:42–47 NIV), he explained how ethnic differences can be overcome when people become concerned with evangelism and the state of others' souls.

He shared that as a Chinese American, he was initially apprehensive about leading a Bible study for Japanese American elderly people. He said that he "began working with Issei and Nisei, and thought they were foods!" Months later, he saw a breakthrough moment when the Japanese American seniors talked about inviting their Chinese American senior friends to church. Previously, these elderly people had thought of their church as a Japanese American one, but now they had let go of differences and focused on a mission of introducing other people to Jesus Christ. The church identity, based on the mission to reach out to Asian Americans, was to supersede one's ethnic identity.

In GFC's understanding of identity, traditional ethnic understandings of these concepts have given way to more contemporary, American ideals of selfhood and relating. As therapeutic language and values have seeped into American evangelical discourse, so they have entered the evangelical Asian American churches. GFC teaches its Asian American members that their identities should be spiritual in nature. At times, Asian American Christians may have to renounce Asian cultural practices that are unhealthy or dysfunctional. They can then affirm their "true" identities and gain freedom as the children of God. This spiritual identity also includes a calling to evangelize others. Given this mission, Asian American Christians are to reach out to their friends and families. By establishing programs and activities for evangelism, GFC paradoxically reinforces the social and racial network of Asian Americans while encouraging a different type of identity.

Conclusion

PAUMC's mainline minister directly relates biblical terms to his members' Asian American identity. Being "born again" involves transforming outdated cultural ways. However, because mainline Christians are open to and tolerant of other faith traditions, PAUMC invites members to embrace their heritage. Their "spiritual gifts" include one's ethnic and racial background that may be used to bless others. And because mainline Christians emphasize the church's call for peace and justice, "covenanting with God" at PAUMC means working with God to challenge racial injustice.

Just a few miles away, GFC's speakers read the Bible in different ways to understand Asian American identity. Given evangelicals' orientation toward therapeutic discourse, GFC exhorts members to be true to their emotional and spiritual selves. If Asian American Christians are to relate authentically and "speak the truth in love," they must give up their ethnic desire to preserve harmony. Being "sheep without a shepherd," Asian Americans are primarily seen as lost people in need of salvation. Yet not only are Asian Americans called to be saved, but they are also called to evangelize their family and friends. Those who are Christian are "to continue to meet together," to pursue their common mission to evangelize other Asian Americans.

These two different understandings of Asian American identity stem from the division among Asian American Christians. Ministers derive their discourse and worldviews from separate organizational fields, where institutional logics become tenets of faith. With these logics, the pastors of Park Avenue United Methodist Church and Grace Faith Church are oriented to read and teach the Scriptures with different concerns and assumptions. These logics help establish the symbolic boundaries of Asian American identity, both as an emergent congregational form and as an understanding of selfhood.

APPENDIX: CLASSIFICATION OF CONGREGATIONS SURVEYED

Original Target Ethnic Background of Congregation	N	Adopters of Pan-ethnicity
Chinese American	23	8
Evangelical	16	7
Mainline	7	1
Japanese American	10	6
Evangelical	6	4
Mainline	4	2
Korean American	2	2
Evangelical	2	2
Asian American Start-Ups	7	7
Evangelical	6	6
Mainline	1	1
Multi-Ethnic Start-Ups (predominantly Asian American)	2	
Evangelical	1	
Mainline	1	
TOTALS	**44**	**23**

WORKS CONSULTED

Ammerman, Nancy
    1987   *Bible Believers: Fundamentalists in the Modern World*. New Brunswick, N.J.: Rutgers University Press.

Barth, Fredrik
    1969   *Ethnic Groups and Boundaries*. Boston: Little Brown.

Busto, Rudy V.
    1999   "The Gospel according to the Model Minority? Hazarding an Interpretation of Asian American Evangelical Students." Pp. 169–87 in *New Spiritual Homes: Religion and Asian Americans*. Ed. David Yoo. Honolulu: University of Hawaii Press.

Cornell, Stephen
    1988   *Structure, Content and Logic of Ethnic Group Formation*. Cambridge: Center for Research on Politics and Social Organization.

DiMaggio, Paul, and Walter Powell
    1983   "The Iron Cage Revisited: Institutional Isomorphism and Collective Rationality in Organizational Fields." *American Sociological Review* 48:147–60.

Espiritu, Yen Le
    1992   *Asian American Panethnicity*. Philadelphia: Temple University Press.

Friedland, Roger, and Robert Alford
    1991   "Bringing Society Back In: Symbols, Practices, and Institutional Contradictions." Pp. 232–63 in *The New Institutionalism in Organizational Analysis*. Ed. Paul DiMaggio and Walter Powell. Chicago: University of Chicago Press.

Hoge, Dean, Benton Johnson, and Donald A. Luidens
    1994   *Vanishing Boundaries: The Religion of Mainline Protestant Baby Boomers*. Louisville: Westminster/John Knox.

Hogg, Michael
    1992   *The Social Psychology of Group Cohesiveness*. New York: New York University Press.

Hunter, James
    1983   *American Evangelicalism*. New Brunswick, N.J.: Rutgers University Press.

    1991   *Culture Wars: The Struggle to Define America*. New York: Basic.

Jacobsen, Douglas, and William Vance Trollinger, Jr., eds.
    1998   *Re-forming the Center: American Protestantism, 1900 to the Present*. Grand Rapids, Mich.: Eerdmans.

James, Chuck
    1996   *An Exploratory Study of the Growth of Protestant Chinese Churches in the San Francisco Bay Area, 1950–1992*. Berkeley, Calif.: Bay Area Chinese Churches Research Project.

Lin, Tom
  1995 *Losing Face and Finding Grace.* Downer's Grove, Ill.: InterVarsity Press.

Loo, Dennis
  1974 "Why an Asian American Theology of Liberation?" *Church and Society* January-February: 49–54.

Lopez, David, and Yen Le Espiritu
  1990 "Panethnicity in the United States: A Theoretical Framework." *Ethnic and Racial Studies* 13:198–224.

Lowe, Lisa
  1991 "Heterogeneity, Hybridity, Multiplicity: Marking Asian American Differences." *Diaspora* 1:24–44.

Marty, Martin
  1970 *Righteous Empire: The Protestant Experience in America.* New York: Dial.

  1981 *The Public Church: Mainline-Evangelical-Catholic.* New York: Crossroad.

  1998 "The Shape of American Protestantism: Are There Two Parties Today?" Pp. 91–108 in Jacobsen and Trollinger.

Matsuoka, Fumitaka
  1995 *Out of Silence: Emerging Themes in Asian American Churches.* Cleveland: United Church.

Nagel, Joane
  1994 "Constructing Ethnicity: Creating and Recreating Ethnic Identity." *Social Problems* 41:152–77.

Ng, David, ed.
  1996 *People on the Way: Asian North Americans Discovering Christ, Culture and Community.* Valley Forge, Pa.: Judson.

Omi, Michael, and Howard Winant
  1994 *Racial Formation in the United States.* New York: Routledge.

Padilla, Felix
  1985 *Latino Ethnic Consciousness: The Case of Mexican Americans and Puerto Ricans in Chicago.* Notre Dame, Ind.: University of Notre Dame Press.

Park, Andrew Sung
  1996 *Racial Conflict and Healing: An Asian American Theological Perspective.* Maryknoll, N.Y.: Orbis.

Peck, M. Scott
  1987 *The Different Drum: Community Making and Peace.* New York: Simon & Schuster.

Roof, Wade Clark
  1993 *A Generation of Seekers.* New York: Harper Collins.

Sandalow, Marc
   1998   "A Defiant Stand for Freedom: Japanese American Honored Years after Arrest, Internment." *San Francisco Chronicle* Jan. 16.

Scott, Richard
   1991   "Unpacking Institutional Arguments." Pp. 164–82 in *The New Institutionalism in Organizational Analysis*. Ed. Paul DiMaggio and Walter Powell. Chicago: University of Chicago Press.

Shibley, Mark
   1996   *Resurgent Evangelicalism in the United States: Mapping Cultural Change since 1970*. Columbia: University of South Carolina Press.

Smith, Christian
   1998   *American Evangelicalism: Embattled and Thriving*. Chicago: University of Chicago Press.

Sugirtharajah, R. S.
   1999   *Asian Biblical Hermeneutics and Postcolonialism: Contesting the Interpretations*. Sheffield: Sheffield Academic Press.

Taylor, Verta, and Nancy Whittier
   1992   "Collective Identity in Social Movement Communities." Pp. 104–29 in *Frontiers in Social Movement Theory*. Ed. Aldon Morris and Carol Mueller. New Haven, Conn.: Yale University Press.

Warner, R. Stephen
   1988   *New Wine in Old Wineskins: Evangelicals and Liberals in a Small-Town Church*. Berkeley and Los Angeles: University of California Press.

Warren, Rick
   1995   *The Purpose-Driven Church*. Grand Rapids, Mich.: Zondervan.

Wuthnow, Robert
   1988   *The Restructuring of American Religion*. Princeton, N.J.: Princeton University Press.

Yoshii, M.
   1996   "The Buena Vista Church Bazaar: A Story within a Story." Pp. 43–62 in Ng.

THE SCANDAL OF THE "MODEL MINORITY" MIND? THE BIBLE AND SECOND-GENERATION ASIAN AMERICAN EVANGELICALS

Antony W. Alumkal
Iliff School of Theology

ABSTRACT

Mark Noll argues in *The Scandal of the Evangelical Mind* that the American evangelical subculture suffers from a lack of intellectual rigor, detailing evangelicals' problematic thinking concerning the Bible, science, and other areas. Given that Asian Americans have been dubbed "the model minority" and portrayed as excelling in the academic arena, one might expect many Asian American evangelicals to be immune from this intellectual "scandal." Drawing from an ethnographic study of two Asian American churches (one Chinese and one Korean), I argue that this is not the case, but that second-generation Asian American evangelicals have adopted the same problematic thinking regarding the Bible as their white counterparts. Furthermore, these individuals seemed to be unaware of the Anglo-American roots of evangelical hermeneutics, treating these beliefs as essential parts of Christianity. Finally, the fact that many of these individuals had university-level training in scientific fields did not lead them to read the Bible more critically, but rather seemed to reinforce biblical literalism by encouraging them to treat the Bible as a scientific text.

In 1994 evangelical historian Mark Noll published a sweeping critique of the anti-intellectual tendencies within his religious tradition. Titled *The Scandal of the Evangelical Mind,* this book detailed the ways in which contemporary American evangelicalism neglects the life of the mind and the historical factors producing this situation.[1] Noll had this to say about the culture of evangelicalism:

> To put it most simply, the evangelical ethos is activistic, populist, pragmatic, and utilitarian. It allows little space for broader or deeper intellectual effort because it is dominated by the urgencies of the moment.... As the Canadian scholar N. K. Clifford once aptly summarized the matter: "The

---

[1] Of course, Noll is hardly the first one to accuse American evangelicals of intellectual weakness. The book is noteworthy both because it is an assessment by an "insider" and because Noll skillfully traces the historical trajectory of evangelicalism's intellectual habits.

Evangelical Protestant mind has never relished complexity. Indeed its crusading genius, whether in religion or politics, has always tended toward an over-simplification of issues and substitution of inspiration and zeal for critical analysis and self-reflection." (12)

According to Noll, evidence that evangelicals have neglected the life of the mind can be found in the fact that while they have a vast array of institutions, evangelicals have not created "a single research university or a single periodical devoted to in-depth interaction with modern culture" (4). Equally important, contemporary evangelicals have failed to cultivate critical thinking in the areas of science, politics, and social analysis. For example, during the Gulf War evangelical writers failed to produce significant discussions of the moral, political, and economic dimensions of the war. Instead, according to Noll, "evangelicals gobbled up more than half a million copies [of] each of several self-assured, populist explanations of how the Gulf crisis was fulfilling the details of obscure biblical prophecies" (140).

Noll describes three factors that led to the intellectual weakness of contemporary evangelicalism. The first is a populist heritage emphasizing revivalism. The second is the uncritical acceptance of ideas associated with the Scottish Enlightenment, including common-sense philosophy. The third is the continuing influence of the fundamentalist movement that, in an effort to defend Christian orthodoxy, gave new impetus to anti-intellectualism.

Like most of the general literature on American evangelicalism, Noll's book makes no mention of this subculture's increasing racial and ethnic diversity, including the growing number of Asian American evangelicals who are especially noticeable on college campuses (Busto). If we accept even partially Noll's critique of evangelical anti-intellectualism, this raises questions about the possible complicity of evangelicalism's many Asian Americans in the "scandal." Asian Americans, of course, have been labeled by the popular press as "model minorities" who excel in scholarship. While the "model minority" stereotype is an obvious exaggeration that overlooks the diversity within Asian America, it is true that Asian Americans have done reasonably well in the sphere of academics. This can be traced partly to the disproportionate number of Asian immigrants with high levels of education who consequently have high expectations for their children. Additionally, the fact that many Asian immigrants experienced downward economic mobility upon coming to the United States puts additional pressure on the second generation to succeed academically and economically (Takaki). With this background in mind, one might expect Asian Americans to be immune from the evangelical intellectual scandal.

Significantly, much of evangelical theology, including the features that Noll criticizes, is rooted in Anglo-American cultural traditions. We might expect Asian Americans, as racial minorities and people with non-Western cultural influences, to have some degree of critical distance from mainstream American evangelicalism—further protection from the intellectual scandal.

Yet, based on my observations of second-generation[2] Asian Americans who are evangelicals, I would argue that they suffer from the same intellectual scandal as their European-American counterparts. To a large extent, they have accepted mainstream American evangelical theology as synonymous with "Christianity." Consequently, they have absorbed much of evangelical thinking about the Bible, science, and politics.

Field Sites

The data for this article comes from an ethnographic study of two Asian American evangelical churches in the New York metropolitan area with English worship congregations serving members of the American-born/raised second generation. Chinese Community Church (CCC)[3] is a large, nondenominational church located in a suburban area. In addition to a Mandarin and a Cantonese congregation for immigrant members, CCC has an English congregation whose worship service draws approximately two hundred adults per week. Members of the English congregation are primarily second-generation Chinese Americans, including many university students and young professionals.

Glory Korean Presbyterian Church (GKPC) is located only a few miles from CCC. It is a medium-sized church with separate Korean and English congregations. The Korean congregation draws about seventy adults each week to its worship service and has a membership primarily consisting of second-generation Korean Americans who are either university students or young professionals. While GKPC is a member of the Presbyterian Church (USA), I should point out that it is staunchly conservative, like most Korean churches in its denomination. Furthermore, members of the second generation have little or no sense of denominational connection. Instead, they follow the common evangelical practice of identifying themselves as "Christians," while using this term in an exclusive manner such that it is synonymous with "evangelicals." (For example, many members are unsure whether Roman Catholics should be considered "Christians.")

I gathered data through participant observation of worship services and fellowship meetings for second-generation members in the two churches. I

---

[2] Following standard sociological usage, I label immigrants as "first-generation" ethnics and their American-born offspring as "second-generation." I also include in the latter category those ethnics who immigrated as children and were raised in the United States.

[3] The names of the two churches and all individuals have been changed to protect their identities.

also interviewed twenty-four members in each church, including church leaders and active second-generation members. Anyone interested in more details about the churches or my methodology should consult my dissertation (Alumkal).

It is significant that more than half of the individuals in both congregations were either presently or formerly university students majoring in a field related to science or technology. Quite a few of these were studying or working in fields related to biology (e.g., pharmacy, biochemistry, premedicine/medicine) and were thus exposed to evolutionary science taught at the university level. The consequences of this educational background on biblical interpretation will be discussed below.

Finally, I would like to add a note on the generalizability of the findings from these field sites. In addition to these two churches, I have also observed second-generation Asian American evangelical ministries in the San Francisco Bay area, Illinois, and central New Jersey. In all cases I found a theological orientation that was nearly indistinguishable from that of mainstream American evangelicalism. As Gary Dorrien argues in *The Remaking of Evangelical Theology*, there is considerable diversity within evangelicalism, including a growing number of "postconservative" theologians who are willing to challenge biblical inerrancy. However, most American evangelical institutions, including campus ministry organizations such as InterVarsity Christian Fellowship and Campus Crusade for Christ, remain committed to biblical inerrancy. It is the orientation of these latter institutions that most influences Asian American evangelicals. Therefore, I do not claim that my findings apply to *all* second-generation Asian American evangelicals, but I do believe I am describing the dominant theological orientation of this population.

Affirming Biblical Inerrancy

Among the central features of contemporary American evangelicalism is a commitment to the doctrine of biblical inerrancy—the belief that the Bible contains no errors of any kind, including statements related to history, science, and geography. Many evangelical institutions, such as seminaries and campus ministry organizations, require that their workers affirm this doctrine.[4] Despite the claim by evangelicals that biblical

---

[4] Campus Crusade for Christ is explicit in its affirmation of biblical inerrancy. InterVarsity Christian Fellowship, perhaps because it is an older organization, does not use the word "inerrant" in its faith statement. However, InterVarsity leaders have long affirmed inerrancy even while not making it part of the organization's official faith statement (Hunt and Hunt).

inerrancy is an integral part of Christian (or Protestant) orthodoxy, this doctrine represents a departure from the early Reformers, such as Luther and Calvin, who only recognized the Bible as infallible in matters pertaining to salvation (Dorrien).

The last few decades have witnessed a proliferation of evangelical apologetic literature, mostly produced by individuals connected to campus ministry organizations (e.g., McDowell; Knechtle; Little). While most of this literature purports to defend "Christianity,"[5] the authors give considerable attention to defending doctrines specific to contemporary evangelicalism, including inerrancy. Also significant is that this literature is aimed at a popular lay audience. It is common for evangelical campus ministry groups to draw upon this literature when "discipling" new converts to Christianity and when preparing members for doing evangelism on their campuses. It is also common for evangelical churches to include the literature in their Sunday school curriculums.

During the course of my interviews with second-generation members of the two churches, I asked them which view of the Bible most closely matched their own belief: (a) the Bible is infallible in all matters, including history and science; (b) the Bible is infallible in theological matters but not necessarily in matters of history and science; (c) the Bible is inspired by God but contains human error of all kinds; or (d) the Bible is just a human book. All but two people I talked with chose the first response, the one consistent with the doctrine of biblical inerrancy.

Karen is a member of CCC's Young Adult Fellowship with a degree in psychology from an elite university. When asked to defend her belief in biblical inerrancy, she gave the following response:

> There are a lot of tests you can give to determine whether a document is historically reliable. And [the Bible] passes all the tests externally and internally. And also, I think it's inerrant because I believe it was divinely inspired by God. And God is perfect, so He [sic] can't make a mistake.

Given that Karen has no training in biblical scholarship, she clearly does not have the necessary expertise to evaluate the historicity of biblical texts. Rather, her statement indicates her acceptance of contemporary evangelical apologetics. Note that she used the term "inerrant" without prompting by the interviewer, suggesting further that she is familiar with contemporary evangelical discourse about the Bible.

---

[5] Many observers of evangelicalism have noted the tendency of members of this subculture to equate their own beliefs with "Christianity," implicitly or explicitly casting doubt on the authenticity of other Christian traditions.

Glenda, another member of CCC's Young Adult Fellowship with an advanced degree in computer science, also strongly affirmed biblical inerrancy and gave the following justification for her belief:

> Because I firmly believe that the Bible is inspired by God. Nothing that went into the Bible was inspired by man [sic]. And so, if it's inspired by God and the Word of God, there shouldn't be anything extra in it, and anything that should be in it should not be missing. I don't think God would allow for that.

Like several people I talked with, Glenda accepted as nearly self-evident the evangelical understanding that the biblical texts are the "Word of God," with this signifying that they are complete and flawless. She seemed to be unaware that Christians have arrived at a variety of understandings concerning both the relationship between the Bible and the "Word of God"[6] and the very meaning of "Word of God."

Members of GKPC gave similar responses when asked to explain their belief in the Bible as an inerrant text. Nancy, a premedical biology major, had this to say:

> I don't think I've met one person who can actually challenge what is in the Bible and prove to me what the Bible says is false. Because I believe it's not, first of all, and second because there hasn't been any proof that the Bible has been wrong in any way. And I believe that all scripture is God-breathed. So in any area, whether it's history or theological matters, it's true.

Once again, we can see the influence of contemporary evangelical apologetics. The statement that no part of the Bible has ever been disproven is common among evangelical apologists (e.g., Little), though it is an assertion that most critical biblical scholars would dispute. As with Karen above, Nancy's statement clearly reflects an acceptance of evangelical apologetics rather than any independent research.

Literalism and Science

In addition to inerrancy, a primary feature of contemporary American evangelical theology is a favoring of literal readings of biblical texts. To be sure, this is not an absolute tendency. Evangelicals generally do not insist that references in the Psalms to inanimate objects praising God should be

---

6 For instance, the neo-orthodox view holds that the Word of God is not equivalent to the biblical text itself but arises in the reader of the text through the action of the Holy Spirit.

taken literally. Neither are most middle-class evangelicals likely to follow literally Jesus' command to give all of their possessions to the poor. Nonetheless, the tendency to favor a "plain" or "common-sense" reading of scripture remains pervasive.

Without going into an exhaustive history of the development of evangelical hermeneutics, it is accurate to say that there are a few principal influences responsible for the development of biblical literalism. One is the long-standing tradition in the United States of religious populism that produced a distrust of elite scholars and placed the authority to interpret the Bible in the hands of common people. As Nathan Hatch argues, Luther and Calvin began the Protestant Reformation with populist rhetoric but ultimately did not trust the masses of lay people to interpret the Bible without ministerial guidance. The religious populism that has especially characterized American evangelicalism was thus a significant innovation.

A second major influence on evangelicalism responsible for encouraging biblical literalism was the philosophy of the Scottish Enlightenment. This included an emphasis on "common sense" as a source of truth. Applied to the Bible, this led American evangelicals to assume that whatever reading of a biblical passage appeared sensible to common people was most likely to be correct. The Scottish Enlightenment also included the scientific thinking of Francis Bacon. Noll describes the influence of Baconian thinking on evangelical theology:

> In divinity, rigorous empiricism became the standard for justifying belief in God, revelation, and the Trinity. In the moral sciences, it marked out the royal road to ethical certainty. It also provided a key for using physical science itself as a demonstration for religious truth. (91)

A third influence encouraging biblical literalism was the creation-science movement, whose proponents, taking the common-sense philosophy and Baconian traditions of American evangelicalism to new extremes, argued that Genesis gave a literal, scientific account of the creation of the world. Contrary to popular perception, earlier generations of evangelicals were neither firmly committed to a literal reading of Genesis nor unanimous in their disagreement with Darwinian evolution (Livingstone). Creation science thus represents a twentieth-century phenomenon rather than an integral feature of American evangelical tradition.

Noll sees the rise of biblical literalism, culminating in the rise of creation science, as a key facet of the evangelical intellectual "scandal." As he argues:

> Creationists regularly reaffirm the principles of Baconian science: no speculation without direct empirical proof, no deductions from speculative principles, no science without extensive empirical evidence. The tragedy is

that creationists preserve a misguided Baconianism for the Bible and abandon a healthy Baconianism for science.

Evangelicals make much of their ability to read the Bible in a "simple," "literal," or "natural" fashion—that is, in a Baconian way. In actual fact, evangelical hermeneutics, as illustrated by creationism, is dictated by very specific assumptions that dominated Western intellectual life from roughly 1650 to 1850 (and in North America for a few decades more). Before and after that time, many Christians and other thinkers have recognized that no observations are "simple" and no texts yield to uncritical "literal" readings. (197)

I found that the individuals in my study adopted the same literalistic approach to biblical interpretation as other evangelicals. Furthermore, their exposure to science did not lead them to question the scientifically problematic beliefs associated with contemporary evangelicalism, but rather seemed to reinforce a Baconian approach to the Bible.

I asked Glenda from CCC whether she viewed the creation story in Genesis to be a literal or a symbolic account. Her answer clearly reflects the influence of Baconianism and common-sense philosophy on the evangelical tradition:

> I'd probably say I take it literally. It says in the Bible it took God six days to create the world. I've heard other Christians say, "Well, that's a symbolic day because what is a day for us might be a split second for God." But then I think if it took thousands of years, why didn't God say it took thousands of years? God said it took him [sic] a day to create this or that, and so it was six days. So I take the Bible at face value.

Others I talked with were more explicit that the Bible was factually correct as a *scientific* document. For example, a premedical student named Ernie who attended CCC cited Isa 40:22, which refers to God sitting above "the circle of the earth," as proof that a biblical writer was aware that the earth orbited the sun, showing insight beyond the scientific knowledge of the day. (This view, of course, ignores the more likely possibility that Isaiah is referring to the earth as a flat disc.) Another member of CCC named Michael, a biochemist, revealed a similar perspective:

> I: Do you interpret Genesis literally or symbolically?
> R: I struggled with that when I first became a Christian. I would say I'm a literal six-day creationist. I used to try to make evolution fit with the Bible. Now I take a scientific approach to reading the Bible.

Taking a "scientific approach" to reading the Bible clearly meant viewing the Bible as science rather than letting science inform his reading of a biblical text.

Finally, several members of both congregations confronted evolutionary theory directly and claimed that it lacked scientific rigor, making literal creationism the more scientifically responsible choice. Nancy from GKPC, whom I mentioned above is a premedical biology major, had this to say:

> I believe in creation literally. Evolution, believe it or not, has so many "ifs"—so many! I have spoken with many non-Christians about this, and it is just as amazing to me that they believe in evolution as it is to them that I believe in creation. So, in my view, evolution is even more of a mystical process. Non-Christians take it as fact because they say, "Oh, it's scientific." But really, it's a theory because it hasn't been proven.

Jill, a molecular biologist who attends CCC, had a similar perspective:

> I believe things evolved, but I don't think you can go from a fish to a bird. Basically, it doesn't work for me. It's just too illogical. I'm a scientist, and that doesn't work for me. They can try to look at it and arrange it the best that they can, but there's no link. And God is a very logical God.... I like approaching the issue [of creation] from a biblical basis. I assume the Bible is correct.

Her insistence that "God is a very logical God," in contrast to the old maxim that "God works in mysterious ways," suggests that Baconian philosophy indeed has had a pervasive influence on her theology.

American Evangelicalism and Race

Evangelical biblical hermeneutics impact evangelicals' thinking not only about science but also about political and social issues. The recent high-profile role of evangelicals in politics is well known, but less well known is the fact that evangelical leaders have been involved in addressing the lingering problem of racism in the United States. Campus ministry groups like InterVarsity Christian Fellowship and Campus Crusade for Christ, as well as the Promise Keepers,[7] have made "racial reconciliation" one of their primary goals.

The biblical texts evangelicals most commonly cite to support their view of racial reconciliation are drawn from the Pauline epistles. Ephesians 2:14 speaks of Christ uniting Jews and Gentiles, "For he himself is our peace, who has made the two one and has destroyed the barrier, the dividing wall of hostility" (NIV).[8] Another text evangelicals commonly cite is Gal 3:28:

---

[7] One of the seven promises of the Promise Keepers' statement of purpose is, "A Promise Keeper is committed to reaching beyond any racial and denominational barriers to demonstrate the power of biblical unity" (Janssen and Weeden). Note that the issue of racial unity is tied directly to the Bible.

[8] I quote the New International Version since this is the translation most commonly read by contemporary American evangelicals.

"There is neither Jew nor Greek, slave nor free, male nor female, for you are all one in Christ" (NIV). Evangelical leaders draw several conclusions from these and other biblical texts. First, racism is fundamentally a *spiritual* problem, a sin that requires repentance. While some leaders acknowledge that government has some role to play in addressing the problem of racism, they argue that churches and other Christian organizations must take primary responsibility. Additionally, these leaders believe that the ultimate solution to racism is reconciliation through Christ. The reconciliation process does not involve casting off ethnic and racial identities, but allowing these to be transcended by a more fundamental identity "in Christ." (For examples of these arguments, see Graham; McCartney)

While this commitment to ending racism is preferable to evangelical leaders' previous silence on the issue, their analysis of racial issues, like other areas of American evangelical thought, is marred by a lack of sophistication. These leaders fail to understand that Paul was addressing specifically ethnic tensions in the Christian church, not in the larger society. Even more significantly, they fail to explain how "reconciliation in Christ" can succeed in a religiously pluralistic society. Finally, the evangelical emphasis on racism as an individual attitude overlooks the fact that racism is also a matter of social structure, especially for members of the black underclass.[9]

To what extent have the second-generation Asian Americans in the two churches I examined adopted the racial ideology of American evangelical leaders? My findings were mixed. By attending an ethnic church, members of the two congregations demonstrate that attachment to their ethnic group matters to them. These individuals affirmed this during interviews, often stating that they "felt more comfortable" or could "relate to others more easily" in an ethnic church. Yet, these same individuals echoed contemporary evangelical racial discourse by strongly insisting that ultimately it was Christian identity, not ethnic or racial identity, that really mattered. This perspective led most members of both churches to insist that their churches should not be ethnically exclusive but should seek to minister to all people, regardless of their race or ethnicity. As Tom, an undergraduate member of CCC shared with me:

> I think it is important for the church to minister to Chinese Americans, but it's also important for us to reach non-Asians, non-Chinese, because Christianity is for everyone, not just for Asians.... I think it's important for the church to be multiethnic because God doesn't see color. He [sic] sees us as his [sic] children.

---

[9] See Emerson and Smith for a detailed discussion of this last issue.

In fact, the English congregations in both CCC and GKPC have written mission statements encouraging members to minister to members of all ethnic groups.

In spite of this, there were signs that these individuals had not fully accepted contemporary evangelical thinking about race relations. No one talked about engaging in "racial reconciliation" outside of their congregation, and no one talked about the role of Christians in solving America's racial problems. Furthermore, when I asked members of GKPC to reflect on the Los Angeles riots, many said that there needed to be more understanding between the African American and the Korean American communities. However, no one suggested that "unity in Christ" was a part of bringing this understanding about. In sum, American evangelical leaders' "scandalous" thinking about race relations had only limited acceptance by these second-generation Asian Americans. Perhaps the latter's experience as racial minorities remained the primary influence on their thinking about race.

Cultural Crisis and Doctrinal Rigidity

At this point, it is worth stepping back and asking why evangelicalism has so much appeal for second-generation Asian Americans. While it is true that the Baconian logic of evangelical theology can appeal to those steeped in the fields of science or engineering, it is just as possible that such individuals could follow the traditional liberal Protestant path of demythologization, abandoning those elements of the faith judged to be unacceptable to a modernistic worldview. Yet, it is evangelicalism rather than liberal Protestantism that is attracting large numbers of second-generation Asian Americans. At least some of evangelicalism's growth can be accounted for with "supply side" explanations—evangelical organizations have been making considerable effort to market themselves to Asian Americans, especially on college campuses. On the "demand side" is the fact that Chinese and Korean Americans from Protestant backgrounds overwhelmingly grew up attending evangelically oriented churches and thus have been socialized into an evangelical ethos. Still, further explanations are needed.

Fenggang Yang in his study of a Chinese American church suggests that the turmoil that Chinese immigrants experience is one of the factors encouraging them to accept evangelicalism.

> Living in this fast-changing, pluralistic, relativistic, and chaotic world, conservative Christians are assertive in proclaiming that the sole and absolute truth can only be found in the inerrant Bible. Evangelicals assure believers of absolute love and peace in this world and eternal life after death. For new Chinese immigrants, both premigration traumas and postmigration uncertainties in modern American society fortify their desire for absoluteness and certainty. (94)

While the experiences of American-born Asian Americans are surely different from those of immigrants, they often contain traumas of their own. Rather than adjusting to a new culture, second-generation ethnics have the task of integrating cultural elements from their ethnic communities with those found in the larger American society. Furthermore, as racial minorities Asian Americans often find they lack full acceptance by members of the dominant society regardless of their level of cultural assimilation (Tuan). Finally, the "model minority" stereotype creates pressure on Asian Americans to succeed and produces resentment among other racial groups, especially on college campuses (Takaki). For individuals in these circumstances, the unambiguous theology of evangelicalism can have considerable appeal.

Much of the discourse I heard during participant observation and interviews emphasized the certainty that an evangelical-style Christian faith provided. Individuals who struggled with reconciling their Chinese or Korean identities with their American identities took comfort in the fact that their *true* identities were as Christians. This demand for certainty applied to other areas of belief, including the Bible. Danny, a member of GKPC who planned to attend seminary after college, has this to say about the Bible:

> I don't think [the belief that the Bible contains errors] is acceptable because it is called "the Word of God." It would worry me if someone thought the Word of God had flaws. Why would I want to obey the Bible if it had flaws? So it creates a sense of uncertainty if you view it as flawed.

I am not arguing that Asian Americans are alone in desiring an unambiguous religious system. Evangelicalism obviously appeals to a large segment of the population. I am only arguing that the culturally and racially "liminal" space that second-generation Asian Americans inhabit can heighten their need for certainty and encourage their acceptance of contemporary American evangelical theology, including its Baconian and common-sense elements. In these circumstances, exposure to science does not lead to a skeptical attitude toward religious doctrine but to viewing the Bible as scientific truth.

Conclusion

In *Preaching the Presence of God: A Homiletic from an Asian American Perspective,* Eunjoo Mary Kim suggests that Asian American churches can draw upon their cultural heritage to arrive at a hermeneutical approach distinct from that of European American Christianity.

> In East Asia, Confucianism and Buddhism have developed particular hermeneutical methods based on their unique histories of canonization and

views of scriptures. Although little attention has been paid to them in developing Christian hermeneutics, it seems that their perspectives are promising in arriving at a particular method of biblical interpretation for Asian American congregations. They will complement theories of Christian hermeneutics and furthermore contribute to creating a new hermeneutical perspective for Asian American preaching. (77)

However, many second-generation Asian American evangelicals do not appear to be interested in developing their own contributions to Christian theology. Instead, they remain committed to the theology of American evangelicalism with little awareness of its roots in Anglo-American culture.

Creating a distinctly Asian American evangelical theology would require Asian Americans to step out of the comfortable certainty that the contemporary evangelical subculture promotes. They would need to recognize that much of evangelical theology, including biblical theology, far from representing "old-time religion" or "orthodoxy," is of relatively recent vintage and has been shaped by particular cultural influences. Only then would Asian American evangelicals be able to escape the scandal of the evangelical mind.

WORKS CONSULTED

Alumkal, Antony
    2000   "Ethnicity, Assimilation, and Racial Formation in Asian American Evangelical Churches: A Case Study of a Chinese American and a Korean American Congregation." Ph.D. diss., Princeton University. Ann Arbor, Mich.: University Microfilms International.

Berger, Peter
    1967   *The Sacred Canopy*. New York: Anchor.

Busto, Rudy
    1996   "The Gospel According to the Model Minority? Hazarding an Interpretation of Asian American Evangelical College Students." *Amerasia Journal* 22:133–47.

Dorrien, Gary
    1998   *The Remaking of Evangelical Theology*. Louisville: Westminster/John Knox.

Emerson, Michael O., and Christian Smith
    2000   *Divided by Faith: Evangelical Religion and the Problem of Race in America*. New York: Oxford University Press.

Graham, Billy
    1993   "Racism and the Evangelical Church." *Christianity Today* 37 (Oct. 4): 27.

Hatch, Nathan O.
  1989   *The Democratization of American Christianity*. New Haven, Conn.: Yale University Press.

Hunt, Keith, and Gladys Hunt
  1991   *For Christ and the University: The Story of InterVarsity Christian Fellowship of the U.S.A./ 1940–1990*. Downers Grove, Ill.: InterVarsity Press.

Janssen, Al, and Larry K. Weeden, eds.
  1994   *Seven Promises of a Promise Keeper*. Colorado Springs: Focus on the Family.

Kim, Eunjoo Mary
  1999   *Preaching the Presence of God: A Homiletic from an Asian American Perspective*. Valley Forge, Pa.: Judson.

Knechtle, Cliff
  1986   *Give Me an Answer That Satisfies My Heart and My Mind*. Downers Grove, Ill.: InterVarsity Press.

Little, Paul E.
  1988   *How to Give Away Your Faith*. Rev. ed. Downers Grove, Ill.: InterVarsity Press.

Livingstone, David N.
  1987   *Darwin's Forgotten Defenders: The Encounter between Evangelical Theology and Evolutionary Thought*. Grand Rapids, Mich.: Eerdmans.

McCartney, Bill
  1994   "A Call to Unity." Pp. 157–67 in Janssen and Weeden.

McDowell, Josh
  1980   *Answers to Tough Questions Skeptics Ask about the Christian Faith*. San Bernardino, Calif.: Here's Life Publishers.

Noll, Mark A.
  1994   *The Scandal of the Evangelical Mind*. Grand Rapids, Mich.: Eerdmans.

Smith, Christian
  1998   *American Evangelicalism: Embattled and Thriving*. Chicago: University of Chicago Press.

Takaki, Ronald
  1989   *Strangers from a Different Shore: A History of Asian Americans*. Boston: Little, Brown, & Co.

Tuan, Mia
  1999   *Forever Foreigners or Honorary Whites? The Asian Ethnic Experience Today*. New Brunswick, N.J.: Rutgers University Press.

Yang, Fenggang
  1999   *Chinese Christians in America: Conversion, Assimilation, and Adhesive Identities*. University Park: Pennsylvania State University Press.

SECOND-GENERATION CHINESE EVANGELICAL USE OF THE BIBLE IN IDENTITY DISCOURSE IN NORTH AMERICA

Timothy Tseng
American Baptist Seminary of the West

ABSTRACT

Evangelicals dominate the landscape of Chinese Christianity in North America today. Their rapid growth parallels the influx of Chinese immigrants from Asia over the past three decades. As the children of these immigrants (who were born or raised in North America) came of age, their religious orientation and use of the Bible have developed in a manner distinct from that of their parents. How these second-generation Chinese evangelicals appropriate the Bible will be the focus of this article. I will argue that second-generation Chinese evangelical biblical interpretation has been bound by two perspectives: (1) the European immigrant experience as the model for their identity discourse; and (2) a white American "evangelical universalism" that subordinates racial identities. Consequently, there is a subtle Orientalism implicit in second-generation Chinese evangelical discourse that needs to be critically engaged and eventually excised.

INTRODUCTION

This essay has been a struggle to write because of my continued participation in the Chinese evangelical community in North America. I was raised in a close-knit Chinese evangelical community in New York City. The stubbornly separatist and narrowly fundamentalist worldviews fostered by that community limited my exposure to wider religious and sociopolitical realities. Nevertheless, the religious world of my childhood was a loving environment that inculcated a strong commitment to a passionate religious experience and insulated us from the harsh realities of a racialized American society. At times, I grieve at this community's missed opportunities to voice Asian American concerns and to make a positive sociopolitical impact upon an increasingly diverse postmodern North America. But I remain hopeful that as Chinese evangelicalism comes of age in the next several years, both American-born and overseas-born Chinese will become lively participants in ecumenical Christianity and American society.

This essay will attempt to make two points. First, current second-generation Chinese evangelical experience in North America can be best understood in light of the history of Christianity in the Chinese Diaspora and within the context of recent mainstream American evangelicalism. One must explore the world of second-generation Chinese evangelicals in North America in order to understand how they address questions of identity through their use of the Bible. "Americanized" Chinese evangelicals are much more complex than generalizations about their desire to emulate the "model minority." The contradictions between their "lived" experiences and an evangelical "pop" theology that subordinates racial/ethnic particularities under a purportedly color-blind "biblical" cultural canopy generate much conversation about identity and power. Much of this discourse takes place within the contexts of congregations dominated by overseas-born and Chinese-speaking leaders. By looking at the rich sociohistorical contexts from which second-generation Chinese American evangelicals emerge, one can better understand why they interpret and appropriate the Bible through assimilationist and Orientalist lenses. Secondly, this essay will use Acts 6:1–7 as an interpretive site through which second-generation Chinese evangelical identity discourse is generated. Understanding which characters in the passage they identify with exposes some of the limitations of contemporary Chinese American evangelical discourse that is mediated through the assimilationist and Orientalist lenses. In the end, I want to suggest that a reading of Acts 6 that identifies American society with the Hebraic Christians can help second-generation Chinese American evangelicals open up a discourse that takes their racialized experiences more seriously.

The Historical Context of Chinese Protestantism in North America

Historians of the American religious experience have differed in their definitions of Anglo-American evangelicalism. Most agree that its doctrinal roots can be traced to the Protestant Reformation, but most of its best-known characteristics were stamped by Continental Pietism, English Puritanism, and eighteenth-century Trans-Atlantic revivals. Fueled by Wesleyan and Arminian theological influences, evangelicalism became the most vibrant religious movement for social control and reform in nineteenth-century America. By the early twentieth century, however, in the face of receding cultural influence, evangelicalism fragmented amidst the fundamentalist–modernist controversies. Losers in the fight for control of the mainline denominations and alienated from mainstream American culture, fundamentalists disappeared from public view and retreated into a strongly doctrinaire and separatist ethos in the 1920s through the 1940s. What came to be known as mainstream American evangelicalism was an extraordinarily successful mid-century reform movement that sought to make fundamentalism intellectually and socially respectable. Following Billy Graham's cue, these evangelicals were more willing than their fundamentalist cousins to embrace mainstream American culture and work cooperatively with nonevangelicals. Their efforts led to the creation of impressive organizations such as InterVarsity Christian Fellowship, Fuller Theological Seminary, and the widely read magazine *Christianity Today*. Nevertheless, despite the recent reemergence of evangelicalism and its apparent popularity in American Protestant life, most North American evangelicals continue to retain much of the separatist and doctrinaire attitudes of fundamentalism (Carpenter; Marsden; Tseng and Furness).

Chinese evangelicals in North America adhere very closely to the theological and cultural assumptions of mainstream evangelicalism and share a similar history of growth. Their explosive growth to dominance among Chinese American Christians since the 1970s, however, was more a result of changing immigration patterns than winning adherents from mainline Protestants. Chinese evangelicals are riding the crest of the second wave of Chinese immigration to North America that started with a trickle when the Chinese Exclusion Acts were repealed in 1943. This second wave has grown dramatically since the 1965 Immigration Act placed Asian immigration on an equal basis with Europeans.

The contrasts between today's evangelicals and those who planted the oldest Chinese congregations are relatively sharp. With the exception of a few independent congregations, the "historic" churches (such as First Chinese Baptist and First Chinese Presbyterian churches in San Francisco) were started with the help of mainline Protestant missionaries in the late nineteenth century. Reflecting the characteristics of the initial wave of Chinese immigration, these struggling mission stations were all located in urban settings and comprised largely of migrants from impoverished and rural Kwangtung communities. The missions did not completely mirror the Chinatown "bachelor society," however. During the first half of the twentieth century, the missions were centers of Chinese nationalist activism and family formation. Thus, as an American-born generation came of age in the 1920s, Chinese women began to play prominent roles in their churches and communities. Theologically, this first wave of Chinese Christians were evangelical in orientation, but they did not exhibit the separatist or dogmatic attitudes of fundamentalism—nor did they appear to get caught up in the fundamentalist-modernist controversies in China and the United States. It's likely that living in the shadow of Chinese exclusion, where experiences of marginalization and disempowerment were daily realities, these "first-wave" Chinese Christians found civic engagement and political activism more relevant than debating religious ideology. In any case, by the 1950s and 1960s, these "mainline" congregations became better established and were led predominantly by American-born Chinese.

In contrast, Chinese evangelical leaders who immigrated after World War II were more likely to emphasize individual piety and doctrinal rigor than community service and Chinese political nationalism. Most grew up in provinces other than Kwangtung or in the Chinese Diaspora and were greatly shaped by the social dislocation caused by the Sino-Japanese conflict and the Communist victory in China. They came to North America only to find, in their view, mainline Chinese Protestant churches dominated by "old-timer" Cantonese or "Americanized" Chinese. These seemed to have lost their religious fervor and appeared to be entrenched in social and political concerns. In some churches, conflicts led to unhappy splits. Most evangelicals started independent urban Chinese congregations or campus ministries among the growing population of Chinese students. Though greatly admired for their courage and devotion, these evangelical immigrant pastors were often not well-educated or theologically trained. While they may have been uncompromising in maintaining evangelical doctrines such as biblical inerrancy, virgin birth, bodily resurrection, bodily return of Christ, or substitutionary atonement, most preferred to stress Confucian ethics and evangelical piety. Indeed, the spirituality of these pioneer evangelists was more akin to the holiness side of fundamentalism than to the Reformed or Dispensational wings. In part, this ethical and pietistic emphasis reflected their dissatisfaction with the perceived "dry rationalism" of an earlier generation of mainline Chinese Protestants, who through the 1920s to the 1940s had sought to embrace theological liberalism and link it to Chinese political nationalism. These evangelists, nevertheless, felt strongly nationalistic about Chinese culture and represented a shift away from state-oriented nationalism toward a diasporic perspective (Tseng, 1996; 1999; forthcoming).

Up to the mid-1970s, most Chinese evangelicals in North America worshiped at small urban congregations or in Chinese Bible study groups on college campuses. Though Mandarin was becoming the dominant dialect on campuses, the urban churches were still predominantly comprised of Cantonese-speaking and working-class immigrants. Over the past two decades, waves of highly educated and wealthier immigrants have made their way into Chinese congregations. A significant number of students found professional work and stayed in the United States and Canada. Some Bible study groups grew large enough to become congregations. Indeed, many Chinese congregations have completely bypassed the urban experience and started their ministries in the suburbs among affluent professionals. Para-church ministries such as Ambassadors for Christ and Chinese Christian Missions have provided a sense of common purpose among these scattered and independently minded congregations. Chinese migration patterns, however, have created such linguistic, cultural, and economic diversity among Chinese churches that efforts by the North American Congress of Chinese Evangelicals (NACOCE) in the 1970s and the Chinese Coordinating Congress for World Evangelization (CCCWE) in the 1980s to create a unified movement have largely failed.

A significant number of congregations have affiliated with evangelical denominations such as the Christian Missionary Alliance, the Southern Baptists, and the Evangelical Free Church, but few have joined mainline Protestant denominations. Many more remain staunchly independent of any denominational affiliation. Even among those who affiliate with a denomination (mainline or evangelical), Chinese congregations in North America have formed very few relationships or partnerships with non-Chinese Protestants. Though theologically conservative missionaries in pre-Communist China and post–World War II Chinese Diaspora had influenced an earlier generation of Chinese leaders, Chinese evangelicalism in North America has been largely an indigenous movement with few formal connections with white American Christians.

Because immigrant Chinese evangelicals are so proudly independent, most of their second-generation youth grew up with very little contact with Christians who are not Chinese. Their primary interactions with non-Chinese people occur at school and work. Furthermore, today's second-generation Chinese live in a time when Asian Americans are often lifted up by the media as the "model minority"; this, to a degree, insulates them from feeling racially discriminated against. Finally, most grew up with relatively greater affluence than earlier generations of Chinese. Hence, their experiences appear to differ greatly from those of second-generation mainline Chinese Protestants.

In the 1930s and 1940s, most Chinese were segregated from whites in public life. Because mainline denominations provided missionary support for their churches, second-generation Chinese Protestants of this earlier time had greater opportunities to develop relationships with non-Chinese Christians. These mainline denominations also publicly supported racial integration at a time when racial segregation was quite obvious. These second-generation Chinese were therefore more willing to engage the public arena and join the Protestant efforts to overcome racial discrimination because they were experienced with interracial relationships. They were also willing to participate in Asian caucus movements within mainline denominations in the 1970s. Today's second-generation evangelicals tend to approach the public realm with less confidence and often attribute this to their cultural upbringing. Without meaningful connections with a wider church body, there are few outlets to develop religious leadership skills beyond the English-speaking Chinese evangelical context. They share with the earlier second-generation a similar ambivalence about their Chinese identity, but they have not utilized this ambivalence to engage the wider Christian church or to critique society.

Since the 1970s, identity discourse among Chinese evangelicals in North America has focused on urging immigrant church leaders to accept their socialization into North American culture and to share power and resources more equitably. During the NACOCE conferences in 1972, 1974, and 1978, advocates for North American–born Chinese pressed for greater attention. In 1978, a small group of West Coast American-born pastors received endorsements from NACOCE to form the Fellowship of American Chinese Evangelicals (FACE). This group sought to address the perceived problem of a high "drop out" rate among American-born Chinese (ABC) in Chinese churches, cultivate ABC church leadership, advocate for ABC ministries within Chinese churches, and support ABC laity toward "responsible leadership in the church." In April 1979, they started publication of the *AboutFACE* newsletter. *AboutFACE* has—surprisingly for evangelicals—not devoted much attention to biblical interpretation or theological reflections upon ABC evangelical experience. But its goals were clear. It usually addressed one or two ABC evangelical issues, included some amateur sociological, psychological, or cultural analyses, and provided lots of practical suggestions for those involved with ministry among American-born Chinese evangelicals. Over the years, it has also served as a communication tool for ABC evangelical clergy and laity.

Interestingly, the first biblical passage to be highlighted was Acts 15 (*AboutFACE*, Aug. 1979). Wayland Wong suggested that ABCs drop out of Chinese churches because the Christian gospel was not contextualized enough for them to own the faith. Pointing to the difficulty that "Jewish Christians" had in accepting "Greek Christians," Wong argued that the Asian culture within Chinese congregations, much like the Jewish Christians, has become a stumbling block for the American-born to fully participate in the life of the church. "For many ABCs, fitting into a transplanted Chinese church from Asia appears to be too great a hurdle," Wong asserts. Thus, the solution "is not to make the children of the Chinese church culturally more Chinese in order to reach them. This is like the Jews requiring the Greeks to be more Jewish in order to become good Christians." Rather, the Chinese church must make the gospel contextually relevant to each new culture it reaches—namely, the American-born Chinese. This is equivalent to Paul and the Jerusalem Council's decision to embrace Gentiles without requiring circumcision. Wong concludes with a call for an "indigenous ministry" where "radical changes and creative innovations must take place."

A few issues later (*AboutFACE*, Nov. 1979), Hoover Wong appropriated Acts 6:1–7 and referred to the same cultural tensions between Hellenist and Hebrew-speaking Jewish Christians. Claiming that "FACE took its roots" from this passage, H. Wong drew clear parallels between the Hellenists and the American-born Chinese while identifying the Hebrews with the Chinese-speaking and overseas-born. In order to resolve the contemporary crisis, Chinese church leaders must empower the English-speaking to exercise their gifts for ministry.

AboutFACE's challenge to the Chinese church in North America stirred up much discussion and some controversy in the early 1980s. Most theologically trained immigrant Chinese (or overseas-born Chinese [OBC]) evangelicals expressed sympathy for the American-born. They agreed that Chinese cultural identity should not be viewed as a fixed reality, since it had undergone many changes over time and in different cultural contexts. Rather, one's North American Chinese identity falls along a wide continuum from the least to the most assimilated. Furthermore, they asserted that one's identity moved back and forth along this continuum, depending on the contexts and length of time spent in North America. In spite of these pleas for reconciliation and unity, the real issue for *AboutFACE* editors was to persuade the congregations dominated by Chinese-speaking and overseas-born leaders to provide resources for ministries relevant to ABCs, and to share power more equitably. While the irenic OBC scholars were content to describe cultural identity issues of the American-born to help Chinese-speaking and overseas-born evangelicals better understand their children, ABC leaders viewed identity discourse as a means to achieve their desire for greater power and recognition in church congregations (Tan; Law; Ling).

One seasoned pastor, however, defended the maintenance of Chinese culture with strong nationalist overtones. In 1983, Stephen Chan wrote "For My Kinsmen, My Flesh" for *Challenger,* newsletter of the Chinese Christian Mission. Citing Paul's passion for his fellow Jews in Rom 9:3 ("I could wish that I myself were accursed and cut off from Christ for the sake of my own people, my kindred according to the flesh" NRSV), Chan argued for an exclusive focus on evangelizing the millions of Chinese in the world. "We should love all the people in the world," he acknowledged, "but, we do not love them all the same because relationships are different." In fact, "Chinese Christians must bear a God-given responsibility in leading the Chinese people to Christ." While the apostle Paul attempted to welcome Gentiles into the church, his strategy was to go to the Jews first. Furthermore, Chan noted that Moses retained his own national heritage and that Daniel resisted Babylonian assimilation:

> In my opinion, Chinese Christians who have immigrated all over the world and obtained different nationalities should ponder and give heed to the examples set by Moses, Daniel and Paul. If the Hebrews, who are only a small portion of the world's population, are capable of withstanding the many years of persistent assimilation by foreign cultures, how can we Chinese Christians forsake our responsibility towards our Chinese brethren who make up one quarter of the world's population? (95–96)

The key for Chinese in North America was to retain the Chinese language. Drawing upon seventeen years of ministry experience in Southeast Asia, Chan observed that the "newly established small countries often tried to assimilate their Chinese residents by preventing them from learning Chinese. This blocked their means of relating to their own culture so they become indifferent to their fellow brethren." Despite this, he scoffed at "the erratic notion about the gradual demise of the Chinese-speaking churches in North America, although it was foretold 30 to 40 years ago. In fact, the Chinese churches are still flourishing today." Therefore, why "should we restrict ourselves from all the opportunities of sharing with the Chinese-speaking people and limit ourselves to a small group of English-speaking Chinese? We should equip our youth to speak the Chinese language so God can use them in evangelizing more Chinese people" (Chan: 96–99). It is likely that this perspective was the dominant view of most pioneering Chinese pastors.

Chan's vigorous apologetic for the maintenance of the Chinese language drew a sharp response from *AboutFACE*. Peter Yuen rejected the charge that drawing attention to the differences between OBCs and ABCs was divisive and presented Chan's insistence on forcing ABCs to learn Chinese as a demonstration of ignorance. "He has not been here [North America] long enough and has not had contacts with ABCs sufficiently enough to understand them adequately to pronounce a design for meeting their needs. He has not raised a generation of ABC children of his own to know the plight of children growing up here and in the context of a Chinese church" (*AboutFACE*, Feb. 1984). Yuen then argued that North American Chinese churches had room to accommodate and support all different types of ministries. Two issues later, Yuen appropriated the Acts of the Apostles to demonstrate that even the New Testament church was able to minister to two different cultural groups with parallel ministries (*AboutFACE*, Aug. 1984).

AboutFACE continued to pursue the point that the differences between OBCs and ABCs were great enough to warrant separate but equal Chinese ministries. What accounted for the differences was the seemingly inevitable movement toward assimilation of American-born Chinese into North American life. As early as 1981, Yuen had argued that "OBCs should be gradually becoming more Americanized by the influence of ABCs rather than ABCs becoming more Chinese by OBCs" (*AboutFACE*, Nov. 1981). Thus, to second-generation Chinese evangelicals the appeals for unity appeared as efforts to reverse the direction ABCs were moving. Accordingly, Sam Moy reinforced this argument about "significant differences between ABCs and OBCs" (*AboutFACE*, Nov. 1984). For Moy, Asian culture emphasized the group, duty, hierarchy, deference, restraint, and achievement, but Americanized Chinese stressed the individual, rights, equality, assertiveness, expressiveness, and personal growth. Consistently, the pages of *AboutFACE* advocated for greater attention to ministry among the American-born by employing the "different-from-OBC-but-equal" and "inevitable-assimilation-into-American-culture" themes.

By the early 1990s, impatient with the slow response of OBC ministries, some *AboutFACE* writers began to advocate the planting of specifically ABC churches as well as promoting parallel ministries with OBCs. At the same time, pan-Asian congregations or ministries began to receive a great deal of attention. In particular, the impressive growth of the multi-Asian Evergreen Baptist Church in Rosemead, California—which was at one time a declining Japanese congregation—made the term "Asian American" more appealing (Fong). Para-church campus ministries such as Asian American Christian Fellowship and InterVarsity Christian Fellowship have also popularized the term. The large number of Asian Americans in many of InterVarsity's campus chapters is also gaining some attention (Cho). InterVarsity Christian Fellowship's Asian American staff has written resource materials to address the concerns and needs of Asian American college students. But for many, the term "Asian American" still refers largely to East Asians—Chinese, Japanese, and Korean (Yep et al.; Lin).

AboutFACE editors chose not to embrace the term "Asian American" despite its growing popularity. "In order for us to continue to make an impact in the Chinese church and have a part in shaping the future of the church to be effective in reaching ABCs," noted Yuen, "we must maintain that narrow focus and use terminology that keeps us in touch with OBC leaders whom we are intending to convince" (*AboutFACE*, May 1992). As recently as 1998, W. Wong noted that "most ABC seminarians are being trained to think 'Asian American' because it is the politically correct way for the moment. Meanwhile, most Chinese churches are not ready for this, thus making it difficult for ABC seminarians to become suitable candidates for Chinese churches. These churches are still very ethnocentric and the Asian-American theme is a threat to their very existence" (*AboutFACE*, Nov. 1998). Indeed, so long as the high rate of Chinese immigration continues, few OBC leaders will be willing to reorient their ministries toward non–Chinese-speaking Asians. Though the editors of *AboutFACE* recognized the benefits that pan-Asian ministries offered to those alienated from Chinese congregations, they reaffirmed their commitment to transforming Chinese churches.

These multiple and contested discourses among Chinese American evangelicals are examples of literary critic Lisa Lowe's argument that Asian American identity should not be considered a fixed or established "given." Rather, Asian American cultural practices and its identity-producing process should be the foci of social analysis. Indeed, the latter are never complete and always constituted in relation to historical and material differences. The existence of a growing global Chinese Christian community destabilizes the Orientalist discourse that projects an East-West religious divide. Second-generation Chinese American evangelical identity discourse further destabilizes efforts at homogenizing Chinese American cultural identity. But this form of evangelical "heterogeneity, hybridity, and multiplicity" does little to advance Lowe's hopes of disrupting the "current hegemonic relationship between 'dominant' and 'minority' positions" (Lowe: 66–70). Though they may decry racism, Chinese American evangelicals do not have tools to critique the norms of society. To this problem, we now turn our attention.

The Limits of Evangelical Appropriation of the Bible

By lifting up the missiological themes in the Acts of the Apostles, the American-born editors of *AboutFACE* successfully launched a critique of the immigrant leaders who dominated Chinese evangelical congregations. Acts 6 provides an important backdrop for ABC evangelical identity discourse. The key to their interpretation of this biblical text is to identify the immigrant generation with the Hebrew Christians in the Jerusalem church, and themselves with the neglected Hellenistic widows. The strength of this interpretation lies in its apparent consistency with an evangelical commitment to Christ's "Great Commission" in Matt 28:16–20. The Great Commission mandates the crossing of cultural and national boundaries in order to invite all people to become Jesus' disciples. Many evangelical missiologists have recently rejected a cultural-imperialist usage of the Great Commission. Rather than imposing one's culture upon another, there is now a greater emphasis on making the Christian message "contextually relevant" by divesting it of the "cultural baggage" of the missionaries but embracing the recipients' cultural contexts. These missiologists point to Paul's efforts in the Acts of the Apostles as an example of how the New Testament church rejected a narrow Jewish nationalism to embrace a Greco-Roman culture. Paul's own words in 1 Cor 9:20–22 are often cited to justify contextualization:

> To the Jews I became as a Jew, in order to win Jews. To those under the law I became as one under the law (though I myself am not under the law) so that I might win those under the law. To those outside the law I became as one outside the law (though I am not free from God's law but am under Christ's law) so that I might win those outside the law. To the weak I became weak, so that I might win the weak. I have become all things to all people, that I might by all means save some. (NRSV)

Thus, to the extent that second-generation Chinese evangelicals have embraced this more recent missiological emphasis on contextualization, their frustration is a reaction to the perceived immigrant ethnocentrism akin to that of the "Judaizers" in the New Testament church. They believe that the Chinese church in North America is being unfaithful to the Great Commission by focusing exclusively on Chinese-speaking communities. ABC evangelical discourse, as we have seen, underscores their linguistic and cultural differences from the first generation. Consequently, Chinese churches are urged not only to contextualize their ministries so that English-speaking Chinese may be included but also to engage in cross-cultural missions.

But underlying this is an unspoken assumption that "assimilated" Chinese is a cultural group that also differs from white North Americans. Just as hellenized believers in Acts 6 were not Gentiles, Americanized Chinese are not fully white Americans either. Thus, the burden of responsibility for attending to the needs of American-born Chinese evangelicals falls primarily on immigrant pastors and church leaders, not white evangelicals. By identifying the first generation with the Hebraic believers in Jerusalem, the American-born have found a means to challenge the OBCs to pay closer attention to the specific needs and concerns of their "Americanized" evangelicals.

Ironically, the recent popularity of the term "Asian American" or "Asian Pacific American," when applied to American-born Chinese, inverts this Hellenist-Hebraic conflict strategy. Those who promote pan-Asian ministries can argue that ministries targeted only to American-born Chinese are just as ethnocentric and "Hebraic" as those exclusively directed toward the Chinese speaking. Why focus on English-speaking Chinese when there are so many other English-speaking Asian ethnics? Indeed, similar debates over identity and strategy can be found in Korean and Japanese congregations as well. Since "Americanized" Asian evangelicals share so much in common, these advocates urge the formation of pan-Asian American congregations and ministries regardless of the acceptance or rejection of this development on the part of first-generation immigrants.[1] Again, the belief in the inevitable assimilation of Asians in North America does not necessarily result in the dissolution of race-specific congregations. Rather, similar to *AboutFACE*'s claims about American-born Chinese, the "pan-Asian" congregation is also a new cultural formation along racial rather than ethnic lines. In many ways, "pan-Asian" ministries parallel developments noted by Yen Le Espiritu on pan-ethnicity.

Nevertheless, a similar critique about the theological legitimacy of English-speaking Chinese congregations can also be leveled at pan-Asian congregations. If the Great Commission leads to the dissolution of ethnic or racial particularities, then wouldn't the ultimate goal be the breaking down of such barriers in worship each Sunday? Shouldn't all congregations be multiracial and blind to color or cultural differences? Recent sociological studies have questioned the excesses of identity politics by noting its limitations with regards to multiracial people and asserting the fluidity of ethnic

---

[1] Ken Fong, however, has recently changed his mind and observes that stereotypes of immigrant ethnocentrism have been exaggerated, because a growing number of individuals who worship at his pan-Asian congregation are, in fact, immigrants.

and racial identities in North America (Hollinger; Spickard and Burroughs). Biblical passages such as Gal 3:26–28 or Eph 2:14–22 seem to support the dissolution of cultural particularities. These passages lead Daniel Boyarin to conclude that the essence of Paul's ministry was to dissolve particular identities within a universalizing Christian vision.[2] This is particularly salient among evangelicals who privilege religious identity at the expense of other expressions of identity. While evangelicals are beginning to address questions of racial reconciliation, they do not seem to have the theological or sociological tools to legitimize the continued existence of ethnic or racial congregations (Emerson and Smith).

Yuen's recent editorial about this matter reflects this ambivalence toward asserting racial/ethnic identities among Asian American evangelicals (*AboutFACE*, Feb. 1999). Addressing the Anglo church (he uses the term "the wider church"), Yuen gives advice about how to minister to Chinese Americans who leave Chinese churches in North America. He argues that the difficulties of establishing ministries among Chinese immigrants by white American Christians may be insurmountable, for "Americans unfamiliar with adapting to other cultures are likely to be stretched beyond their expectation." However, ABCs "would be easier to work with since there should be minimal problems with language and culture." Nevertheless, he discourages "specialized" ministries for ABCs within a congregation and urges a "gradual assimilation in a color-blind manner." Indeed, the "whole church community would be healthier if there is gradual assimilation of minorities into the wider church without separating people by ethnic or racial groups." Clearly, Yuen is encouraging the full integration of ABCs in the "wider church." He not only appeals for unity in diversity by highlighting passages in Galatians and Ephesians but also argues that the "wider church" should ensure "that the leadership, both laity and staff on the church, is chosen regardless of race or ethnicity." However, Yuen sees no place for creating a separate space for ethnic or racial groups, because when Chinese or ABCs gather themselves together in the wider church, that too is racial discrimination in reverse—something that ought not to be in the community of Christ. What has been successful in promoting healthy Christian fellowship across racial/ethnic lines is to keep from having any special racial/ethnic groups within the wider church. Gradually, over the months and years, close Christian relationships will be established without regard to race or ethnicity.

Yuen then alludes to the difficulties that colleges have in encouraging students of differing races to "mix socially," despite the successes of affirmative-

---

[2] For a partial rebuttal of Boyarin's thesis, see Volf.

action programs. He regrets that "ethnic-specific clubs are formed" even in Christian schools. "That should not be so among Christians," he writes. In the end, "balkanization" remains a great problem for Yuen, as it is for most white evangelicals.

In this editorial, Yuen does not appear to view organizing along racial/ethnic lines as an effective vehicle for "assimilation" and participation. In congregations (or any organization dominated by one group), however, mobilizing minority interests is the only way to ensure that a diversity of perspectives is reflected in staff or lay leadership. Indeed, Yuen's own efforts to advocate for ABCs would have been impossible without a distinct ABC group identity. In the end, what Yuen and many American-born Chinese evangelicals are hesitant to question openly is how white evangelical norms have shaped their own perspectives.

What is missing in Chinese American evangelical appropriation of Acts 6 is a critique of how structural racism operates in white American evangelical circles. Without tools for structural analysis, ABC evangelicals may be in danger of making "whiteness" their norm and perhaps open themselves up to criticism that they are "investing in whiteness."[3] Without an interrogation of white evangelical norms, analysis of their ministries is circumscribed by an understanding of "assimilation" that assumes European immigrant experience as the basis for their identity discourse. Furthermore, by uncritically embracing a mainstream American evangelical theological universalism, their own experiences as racialized people in church and society are dismissed. This strategy of "investing in whiteness" allows anti-Asian consciousness in the fabric of American history and contemporary society to seep into the way American-born Chinese perceive Chinese immigrants. Recently published studies provide alternative perspectives. Mia Tuan's study, *Forever Foreigners or Honorary Whites? The Asian Ethnic Experience Today*, offers a more complex and ultimately more satisfying account of the identity formation of "Americanized" Chinese and Japanese in California. In her study, she finds evidence that these Asian Americans were influenced by both assimilation and racialization processes. In other words, while it is true that second- to fifth-generation Chinese Americans are becoming acculturated into white American cultural norms, they still cannot escape the taint of "foreignness." Anti-Asian racism is distinct from other forms of racism because Asians, more than any other group, are viewed as permanent "aliens." Robert Lee describes the legacy of anti-Asian sentiment as a historically constructed American popular discourse in his important study,

---

[3] "Investing in whiteness" is a phrase utilized by recent scholars about the racial formation of "whiteness." See Lipsitz; Roediger; and Hale.

Orientals: Asian Americans in Popular Culture. The subtle but deeply rooted forms of "Orientalism" in American media and other arenas of pop culture inform how most Americans perceive Asian Americans. Indeed, efforts of earlier Asian American writers to demonstrate their "American" identity in contrast to stereotypical images of Asian American immigrants has ironically betrayed a subtle use of "Orientalism." The overwhelming tendency for both ABCs and Asian American evangelicals to confront Chinese and other immigrant Asians without offering a critique of anti-Asian racism suggests that a more structural understanding of American society is much needed. But this is difficult for mainstream evangelicals to do, since they are so closely identified with the national culture. Second-generation Chinese American evangelicals have the potential to destabilize stereotypical images of Asian Americans, but they will have to aquire the critical tools for analyzing the dominant culture and social structures.

In this regard, a new reading of the Bible can offer a constructive step. Acts 6 can be utilized as a helpful interpretive tool for ABC evangelicals if they begin to identify North American society with the "exclusivist" Hebrews. Refusing to be either ontological strangers or "integrated" Hebrew-speaking people, Hellenistic Jewish believers in Acts find their own voice and encourage the church at Jerusalem to broaden its horizons and embrace the "alien." In order to read Acts in this manner, the implicit Orientalism that renders Asian Americans as permanent foreigners or fully assimilated "model minorities" needs to be excised. Indeed, Asian American leaders in mainline denominations and a few scholars have already employed an approach to the Acts of the Apostles that identifies white American society with the Hebrew-speaking disciples in Jerusalem (Kim; see also González). This challenge to mainline Protestant denominations in particular has resulted in the creation of significant space for Asian Americans in these church bodies.

Though Chinese American evangelicals tend not to utilize Acts 6 in this manner, they are definitely dissatisfied with the perceived exclusivity of mainstream evangelicals. In my oral-history interviews with Chinese American evangelicals, the history of Asian American exclusion and the dominance of white evangelical norms are clearly recognized. For instance, Ken Fong, in response to his seminary professor's well-intentioned call for Asian Americans to join his congregation for the sake of racial reconciliation, questions why that professor didn't think about joining his pan-Asian congregation instead (interview with Ken Fong, June 1996). The growing presence of Asian Americans in evangelical settings and the universalizing ethos inscribed in evangelical identity may be the reason why second-generation Chinese American evangelicals are silent about this other reading of Acts 6. But insofar as Chinese Americans are willing to interpret their experiences and read the Bible through the lenses of racialization, the potential for a powerful second-generation Chinese American evangelical engagement in social issues without denying their Asian American history and identity remains a real possibility.

Works Consulted

Boyarin, Daniel
    1994   *A Radical Jew: Paul and the Politics of Identity.* Berkeley and Los Angeles: University of California Press.

Carpenter, Joel
    1997   *Revive Us Again: The Reawakening of American Fundamentalism.* New York: Oxford University Press.

Chan, Stephen
    1986   "For My Kinsmen, My Flesh." Pp. 95–99 in *A Winning Combination: ABC-OBC, Understanding the Cultural Tensions in Chinese Churches.* Ed. Cecilia Yau. Petaluma, Calif.: Chinese Christian Mission, 1986. [Originally published in *Challenger*, August 1983]

Cho, David
    1999   "Asian Americans Changing Face of Christianity on Campus." *The Philadelphia Inquirer*, Feb. 2:R1, R4.

Emerson, Michael O., and Christian Smith
    2000   *Divided by Faith: Evangelical Religion and the Problem of Race in America.* New York: Oxford University Press.

Espiritu, Yen Le
    1992   *Asian American Panethnicity: Bridging Institutions and Identities.* Philadelphia: Temple University Press.

Fong, Ken Uyeda
    1999   *Pursuing the Pearl: A Comprehensive Resource for Multi-Asian Ministry.* Valley Forge, Pa.: Judson.

González, Justo L.
    1995   "Reading from My Bicultural Place: Acts 6:1–7." Pp. 139–48 in *Reading from This Place*, vol. 1: *Social Location and Biblical Interpretation in the United States.* Ed. Fernando F. Segovia and Mary Ann Tolbert. Minneapolis: Augsburg Fortress.

Hale, Grace E.
    1998   *Making Whiteness: The Culture of Segregation in the South, 1890–1940.* New York: Vintage.

Hollinger, David
    1995   *Postethnic America: Beyond Multiculturalism.* San Francisco: HarperCollins.

Kim, Chan-Hie
  1995 "Reading the Cornelius Story from an Asian Immigrant Perspective." Pp. 165–74 in *Reading from This Place,* vol. 1: *Social Location and Biblical Interpretation in the United States.* Ed. Fernando F. Segovia and Mary Ann Tolbert. Minneapolis: Augsburg Fortress.

Law, Gail
  1986 "A Model for the American Ethnic Chinese Churches." Pp. 131–41 in *A Winning Combination: ABC-OBC, Understanding the Cultural Tensions in Chinese Churches.* Ed. Cecilia Yau. Petaluma, Calif.: Chinese Christian Mission.

Lee, Robert G.
  1999 *Orientals: Asian Americans in Popular Culture.* Philadelphia: Temple University Press.

Lin, Tom
  1996 *Losing Face and Finding Grace: Twelve Bible Studies for Asian-Americans.* Downers Grove, Ill.: InterVarsity Press.

Ling, Sam
  1986 "Beyond the 'Chinese' Way of Doing Things: The Continued Search for a Theology of Culture." Pp. 61–82 in *A Winning Combination: ABC-OBC, Understanding the Cultural Tensions in Chinese Churches.* Ed. Cecilia Yau. Petaluma, Calif.: Chinese Christian Mission.

Lipsitz, George
  1995 "The Possessive Investment of Whiteness: Racialized Social Democracy and the 'White' Problem in American Studies." *American Quarterly* 47:369–87.

Lowe, Lisa
  1996 *Immigrant Acts: On Asian American Cultural Politics.* Durham, N.C.: Duke University Press.

Marsden, George
  1980 *Fundamentalism in American Culture: The Shaping of Twentieth-Century Evangelicalism, 1870–1925.* New York: Oxford University Press.

Roediger, David R.
  1991 *The Wages of Whiteness: Race and the Making of the American Working Class.* New York: Verso.

Spickard, Paul, and W. Jeffrey Burroughs, eds.
  2000 *We Are a People: Narrative and Multiplicity in Constructing Ethnic Identity.* Philadelphia: Temple University Press.

Tan, Che Ben
  1986 "Chinese Church in Tension between Two Cultures." Pp. 3–15 in *A Winning Combination: ABC-OBC, Understanding the Cultural Tensions in Chinese Churches.* Ed. Cecilia Yau. Petaluma, Calif.: Chinese Christian Mission.

Tseng, Timothy
    1996   "Religious Liberalism, International Politics, and Diasporic Realities: The Chinese Students Christian Association of North America, 1909–1951." *Journal of American-East Asian Relations* 5.3–4: 305–30.

    1999   "Chinese Protestant Nationalism in the United States, 1880–1927." Pp. 19–51 in *New Spiritual Homes: Religion and Asian Americans*. Ed. David Yoo. Honolulu: University of Hawaii Press.

    forthcoming   "Unbinding Their Souls: Chinese Protestant Women in Twentieth-Century America." In *Women and Twentieth Century Protestantism*. Ed. Virginia Brereton and Elizabeth Bendroth.

Tseng, Timothy, and Furness, Janet
    forthcoming   "The Reawakening of Evangelical Social Consciousness." In *The Social Gospel Today*. Ed. Christopher Evans. Louisville: Westminster/John Knox.

Tuan, Mia
    1998   *Forever Foreigners or Honorary Whites? The Asian Ethnic Experience Today*. New Brunswick, N.J.: Rutgers University Press.

Volf, Miroslav
    1996   *Exclusion and Embrace: A Theological Exploration of Identity, Otherness, and Reconciliation*. Nashville: Abingdon.

Yep, Jeanette, et al.
    1998   *Following Jesus without Dishonoring Your Parents*. Downers Grove, Ill.: InterVarsity Press.

 Society of Biblical Literature

Other Ways of Reading
African Women and the Bible
Musa W. Dube, editor

This volume of essays highlights some of the unique ways in which African women read and interpret the Bible in their diverse historical and cultural contexts. Featured methods include storytelling, postcolonial feminist reading, womanhood/*bosadi* and womanist reading, divination, and reading from and with grassroots communities. This book, originating from the Circle of Concerned African Women Theologians, is a significant contribution to global biblical scholarship and hermeneutical reflection.

Code: 060807   264 pages   2001
Paper: $24.95   ISBN: 1-58983-009-1

The Labour of Reading
Desire, Alienation, and Biblical Interpretation
Fiona C. Black, Roland Boer, and Erin Runions, editors

How might the task of reading the Bible be regarded as labor? What happens when biblical texts are read in ways that highlight the work of interpretation? Gathered to honor the scholarship and teaching of Robert Culley, these essays seek to carry on his legacy. Covering both the Hebrew and Greek Bibles, they range through cultural and literary studies, philosophy, sociology and feminism, among other disciplines.

Code: 060636   336 pages   1999
Paper: $30.00   ISBN: 0-88414-011-3

Reading the Bible as Women
Perspectives from Africa, Asia, and Latin America: Semeia 78
Phyllis A. Bird, editor

Code: 062078   165 pages   1998
Paper: $19.95   ISSN: 0095-571-X

Postcolonialism and Scriptural Reading
Semeia 75
Laura E. Donaldson, editor

Code: 062075   240 pages   1998
Paper: $19.95   ISSN: 0095-571-X

Society of Biblical Literature • P.O. Box 2243 • Williston, VT 05495-2243
Phone: 877-725-3334 (toll-free) or 802-864-6185 • Fax: 802-864-7626
Online catalog: http://sbl-site.org/Publications/catalog
Shipping and handling extra

HERMENEUTICS AND ASIAN AMERICAN PREACHING

Eunjoo Mary Kim
Iliff School of Theology

ABSTRACT

Contemporary hermeneutical theories challenge Asian American preachers to examine, theologically as well as methodologically, the use of the Bible in their preaching. According to my analysis of recently published Korean American sermons, many Korean American preachers use the biblical text as proof text, supporting their theological perspectives rooted in an ideology of blessing. As a way of improving Korean and other Asian American preaching, I propose a hermeneutic involving a liberating theological perspective and metaphorical interpretation. The former helps a preacher approach the Bible as a source of identity formation for a community of faith by highlighting the paschal mystery. The latter makes it possible for a preacher to interpret the text beyond its literal meaning by using three strategies: (1) reading the text as a performative act; (2) utilizing interpretive methods eclectically; and (3) linking the text and the context relationally. Using a metaphorical interpretation from a liberating theological perspective to interpret Psalm 137, I will illustrate how a new meaning can be created for the Korean American community of faith.

Most Asian American churches have long regarded the Bible as the primary source of Christian life and faith. The Bible has functioned not only as the norm of Christian moral life and theology but also as the major resource for preaching. How, then, has the Bible been interpreted and preached in Asian American churches? How do the particular cultural elements and experiences of Asian American communities influence biblical interpretation for preaching? What constructive suggestions may one make for the future of Asian American preaching?

With regard to these hermeneutical issues, this essay examines the relationship between biblical hermeneutics and Asian American preaching. The development of contemporary hermeneutical theories and methods challenges Asian American preachers to reconsider their use of the Bible in preaching and to develop new hermeneutical perspectives and strategies to create new meanings out of the text that are relevant to their congregations. Thus, this essay aims to help Asian American preachers to reflect on their practice of biblical interpretation and to give some hermeneutical insights into developing their biblical interpretation for preaching.

When we deal with Asian American preaching and its hermeneutics, we have the following problems. First, it is not possible to identify Asian American preaching with a certain type of preaching because Asian American preaching is not homogeneous, just as Asian American churches are not. Asian American churches are as varied as Asian American communities, which are different in their ancestries, cultural and religious backgrounds, immigrant histories, geographical locations, and degrees of assimilation within American culture. Second, just as Asian American preaching is diverse, so are the hermeneutical approaches. Consequently, it is not possible to present a certain theory or method of biblical interpretation as *the* Asian American hermeneutics. Finally, such a broad approach to Asian American preaching and its hermeneutics is too general and superficial to help a particular ethnic group of Asian American preachers.

Given these problems, this essay will limit its attention to Korean American preaching. Before I deal specifically with Korean American preaching and its hermeneutical approaches, I will briefly explore, in the first section of this essay, the relation between contemporary hermeneutics and homiletics. The second section will focus on evaluating the use of the Bible in Korean American preaching, particularly in relation to the sociopolitical and cultural context of the Korean American community. To have a firm understanding of current Korean American preaching, I have collected and reviewed recently published sermon books written by Korean American preachers.[1] The third section will propose a hermeneutical approach in relation to specific theological perspectives and exegetical strategies. The proposal in this section is not an absolute set of hermeneutical theories but an alternative model that may point Korean American preachers to a new direction in using the Bible for their preaching. Last, I will look at Psalm 137 to illustrate how the proposed hermeneutical method may be used to interpret the Bible in Korean American preaching.

Although this essay proposes a hermeneutic for Korean American preaching based on my evaluation of its present situation, I hope that my hermeneutical proposal in this essay will not be considered exclusively for Korean American preaching *per se* but be extended to other Asian American

---

[1] I collected as many sermon books written by Korean American preachers as I could from Korean American Christian bookstores in Los Angeles, New York City, Washington, D.C., Chicago, Boston, and Fort Lee, New Jersey. The books I collected and reviewed include Chang; Choi; Council of the Korean American Church in New Jersey (includes forty pastors' sermons from various denominations preached in Korean American churches in New Jersey); Council of the Korean Presbyterian Church in the West (includes sermons preached by twenty Korean Presbyterian pastors in California); M. Kim; D. Lee; S. P. Lee; Y.-J. Lee; Yim; Yoon, 1994, 1997; and Y.-K. Lee.

and ethnic minority preaching. It will be interesting to imagine its applicability to these other diverse settings and contexts.

Hermeneutics and Preaching

Hermeneutics, in its simplest definition, is an art of understanding. It strives to study the methodological principles of interpretation to provide concrete guidelines to understand ancient texts properly. In the Protestant tradition, hermeneutics has focused on developing rules and principles observed in exegesis of biblical texts because the Reformers emphasized scripture's autonomous power of revelation with the doctrine of *sola scriptura*. Because of the development of historical-critical studies throughout the nineteenth and twentieth centuries, there has been a general tendency to identify hermeneutics with biblical exegesis, which has the primary task to discover and explain the original meaning of a text (Ferguson: 4–5).

However, hermeneutics in our time is not limited to the field of biblical studies. The term hermeneutics has also been used in a much broader sense in other fields, such as philosophy, literature, aesthetics, and theology. Friedrich Schleiermacher, Wilhelm Dilthey, Martin Heidegger, Hans-Georg Gadamer, Paul Ricoeur, and others have influenced contemporary hermeneutics to consider the act of interpretation in more complex ways. For example, according to Gadamer and Ricoeur, the task of hermeneutics is not simply to explain the original meaning of an ancient text with scientific investigation. Rather, the task of hermeneutics is to understand a text by reflecting on its truthful meaning relevant to the contemporary reader. As such, hermeneutics is concerned with bridging the gap between the world of the text and that of the contemporary reader.

In this broad sense, hermeneutics means more than techniques or skills of exegesis. It involves the reader's particular perspective in reading a text, like her ideological, psychological, sociopolitical, and methodological conceptions and assumptions. The reader's particular perspective consciously or unconsciously influences her interpretation. Thus, there is no value-free understanding of a text, because every reader already has a prejudice or preunderstanding. In Gadamer's term, this "historically effected consciousness" (360) is a product of the interaction between the self and her particular environment, which is conditioned historically, socially, culturally, and personally. Duncan Ferguson describes this preunderstanding as "colored glasses" and says, "We peer at the world through colored glasses and make sense out of what we see in reference to the particular shade of the lenses" (11). Ferguson further indicates that this preunderstanding may function as either a negative or positive influence on seeing reality. It may function positively by providing the reader with a precondition for understanding our reality, negatively by distorting the reader's perception of things in reality (14).

The notion of a reader's preunderstanding in the process of interpretation has led contemporary hermeneutics to reconsider traditional interpretive methods and to develop a new hermeneutical emphasis from a reader's perspective. In the Christian church, a two-step procedure from explication to application has traditionally been used to interpret the Bible. This two-step procedure was reinforced by the development of historical-critical methods. First, the reader-as-interpreter treats the text as an object that needs scientific investigation and analyzes the object to explicate what it meant in its original context. Second, the reader-as-interpreter turns to apply the objective knowledge of the text to one's contemporary situation to determine what it means now. However, in this polarity between explication and application, a reader's preunderstanding is not considered seriously as a major factor in the practice of biblical interpretation. Contemporary hermeneuticians question this linear order of explication to application and try to develop new approaches. For example, Ricoeur suggests a dialectical interaction as an alternative, circulating "from understanding to explaining and then ... from explanation to comprehension (74). In this model, a reader's preunderstanding is neither ignored nor reduced to an objective understanding of the text. Instead, the reader-as-interpreter creates new meaning of the text by relating her experience in reality to her scientific knowledge of the text.

Considering that one of the primary tasks of homiletics is to reflect on how an ancient biblical text has meaning for the congregation, hermeneutics is closely related to the field of homiletics. The role of the preacher-as-interpreter is to bridge the world of the text and that of the congregation and to create a new meaning contextually—one that is relevant to listeners of a biblical text that was written within a different worldview and cultural tradition. In order to make a biblical text the word of God for contemporary listeners, the preacher-as-interpreter has much to learn from contemporary hermeneutics.

Contemporary hermeneutics reminds us that all preachers have their own prejudices, as their theological perspectives are formulated by their particular religious experiences, intellectual and theological training, and personal life experiences. Preachers bring their own preunderstandings or theological perspectives as "colored glasses" to the process of biblical interpretation and see reality through them. However, as theological perspectives of the preacher-as-interpreter do not always function positively in the interpretive process, she needs to examine whether they function positively or negatively in creating new meanings out of the text to become the word of God for her contemporary listeners.

What, then, are the criteria for evaluating theological perspectives? At least two criteria should be used. First, the preacher's theological perspectives must be based on her reflection on the communal experience of her listeners, the congregation. The preacher-as-interpreter is not a private, independent reader of a biblical text but a representative of a community of faith that is eager to hear the word of God in its particular context. When a preacher reads a biblical text on behalf of the congregation, she is supposed to interpret the text with theological perspectives that reflect not only on her own personal experience but also on the communal experience of the congregation. In order to develop such an inclusive, communal theological perspective, the preacher must live her daily life as a member of the community of faith and experience directly and indirectly the reality in which the congregation lives daily.

The second criterion for evaluating a theological perspective is its openness. The preacher's theological perspectives should be neither static nor absolute, but be open-ended to the internal and external changes of the congregation's environment. The preacher's theological perspectives are supposed to function as a lens through which she recognizes God's revelation in human history and interprets it in light of the biblical text to give spiritual direction to the congregation. When the preacher's theological perspectives are not able to do this positive function, they must be shifted. Thomas Kuhn explains that in scientific research, when an increasing number of problems cannot be solved by the paradigm, a paradigm shift happens because the old paradigm should be rejected and a new one accepted (47). As such, when an existing theological perspective does not contribute to grasping the significance of a biblical text in our reality, a new perspective is needed. However, a shift in theological perspectives does not happen naturally but occurs only when the preacher is open to accept new experiences, information, and knowledge generated within the changing environment of the faith community.

In this respect, biblical hermeneutics for preaching is not simply a set of theories for decoding a text but a theological practice. As an ongoing theological activity, biblical hermeneutics for preaching constantly challenges the preacher to examine and renew her theological perspectives as the context for preaching changes, so that she will be able to function effectively rather than repeating old messages without critical reflection. Therefore, biblical hermeneutics for preaching is a never-ending spiral, allowing the past to inform the present and point to the future.

Based on this fundamental understanding of hermeneutics for preaching, our next concern relates to how the Bible has been used in Korean American preaching.

THE BIBLE IN KOREAN AMERICAN PREACHING

The Present Situation of the Korean American Community

Historically speaking, Korean Americans are latecomers to this country. Although Korea has had an official relationship with the United States since the 1882 Korean-American Treaty of Amity and Trade, over 80 percent of the one million Korean immigrants arrived after the 1965 Immigration and Naturalization Act. They have emigrated to the U.S. voluntarily, in search of a better world, due to the political repression and socioeconomic instability in Korea as well as the Korean government's policy of encouraging emigration (J. H. Kim: 7).

At the time of their entry, most Korean immigrants dream that the U.S. is a land "flowing with milk and honey," where they can easily obtain their goals of immigration. However, they soon realize that the identification of America as "the promised land" is only true from the perspective of white European Americans and that this new land is not a "sweet paradise" for Korean immigrants to pursue their dreams. Like other racial/ethnic minorities, Korean Americans experience their presence in the U.S. as permanent strangers and face an identity crisis in an Eurocentric American culture (C. Kim: 164).

Korean and other Asian Americans—either first-generation immigrants or those who were born and raised in the U.S. as second- or third-generation immigrants—have not been completely accepted into mainstream American society but remain relegated to the margins. This is not simply because of their language barriers but also because of the racial prejudices of the dominant racial groups in U.S. society. Asian Americans' different physical appearance and cultural heritage from those of the majority race make it impossible for them to assimilate completely within the existing social structures. Fumitaka Matsuoka, a Japanese American theologian, explains racism as follows:

> Racism is socially defined as a structural and systemic deprivation of the human rights and dignity of people of color by those who are in positions of dominance. Racism is more than that, however. It is the negation of relation and the absence of direction for a collective human life due to the devaluation of life generated within societal institutions functioning as powers and principalities in our communal life. In this sense, racism is an obstacle to the formation of a common peoplehood. The negation of relation and the absence of direction are evil not because of some conceptional notion of evil but because of a total attitude expressed in both life and thought. (58)

Korean Americans and other racial/ethnic minorities experience racism in their daily lives. This condition challenges Korean American preachers to ask such questions as, "Who are we in this racist society? How does the Bible help us to interpret our minority experience in the U.S.? What kind of future can we imagine for our community in light of the biblical witness?"

The Use of the Bible in Korean American Preaching

According to my review of the Korean American sermons that I collected, most Korean American preachers seem to recognize that their congregations experience suffering and pain in this foreign land, and attempt to give them instructions to survive the hardships of life in the U.S. These preachers regard the Bible as the solution to the immigrants' problems; thus, the preachers struggle to interpret the biblical text to respond to the situation.

However, most of the sermons that I read reveal that these preachers understand the problems within the Korean American community at a personal, private level rather than at a broader political, socioeconomic, and cultural level. More precisely, although all the sermons I examined differ from one another in degree or detail, over 90 percent of the sermons understand Korean immigration to be motivated by the possibility of personal prosperity in the U.S.; but once arrived, immigrants come under physical and psychological hardships to achieve this goal. As a result, their sermons aim to teach listeners how to achieve personal prosperity.

Interestingly, the theological perspectives based on such sermons are similar in the sense that they are associated with an ideology of blessing. In other words, preachers interpret biblical texts from the perspective of a present-centered, individualistic, and materialistic worldview that identifies worldly success with the blessing of God. The blessing of God is understood as the reward of an individual believer's personal devotion and faithful commitment to church activities. From this theological perspective, preachers encourage their listeners to accept Jesus Christ as their personal savior and to increase their faith by devoting themselves to Bible study, prayer, and other church activities. Biblical texts are often selected and interpreted superficially to confirm the ideology of blessing without historical-critical investigation or deep theological reflection. As a result, biblical texts are often misused as proof texts to illustrate the reward and punishment of God.

Sang-Kyu Kim's sermon, "The Secret of Blessings," is one example of the ideology of blessing. He uses Psalms 126–128 as his preaching text and explains in three points how to gain God's blessing. First, God's blessing is given to those who do not despair but rather continue to strive in their present lives. Second, God's blessing is given to those who trust in God's power. Third, God continues to bless those who worship God with awe. In the sermon, the biblical text is used as the proof text of God's promise to bless individual believers who are faithful church-goers. Without critical study, Kim simply applies the literal sense of the text to his individual listeners by identifying the expression of God's blessing in the text as the listener's desires and dreams for worldly success. In order to help listeners better understand how they can obtain the blessing of God, Kim refers to the life of a Korean immigrant family as an illustration:

> Fifteen years ago, I was an associate pastor in the Oriental Mission Church (in L.A.). One family immigrated to the U.S. with three children. They

worked so hard that they could become the owner of two gas stations and buy a nice house in a suburban area. In the beginning of their immigrant life, they devoted themselves to the church. They came to the church every Sunday and kept it holy. However, when they became financially stable, they preferred playing golf and going fishing to going to church. One Sunday, the father went fishing and collapsed because of hypertension. Although he was taken to the hospital immediately, he passed away.... The Bible stresses that the way to enjoy a blessed life is to obey God and worship God with awe. (54–55; translation is mine)

For S. Kim, the Bible is authoritative because it is a secret book containing both God's blessing and the ways to acquire God's blessing in this world. In the process of interpretation, the biblical text does not challenge him to expand his theological perspectives. Instead, his preexisting ideology of blessing plays a major role in developing the meaning of the text.

In my opinion, there are at least two reasons why the majority of Korean American sermons are based on the ideology of blessing. First, there is the influence of indigenous Korean shamanism, which appeals to the natural human desire of well-being and the life experience as a minority in the U.S. According to shamanism, the most blessed in the world are those who obtain five blessings from heaven: wealth, success, health, longevity, and many children at home. For Korean American Christians, the blessing of God is easily understood in association with their traditional understanding of blessing rather than in light of the biblical concept of the eschatological kingdom of God. In addition to this cultural assimilation of the Christian gospel, the motivation behind Korean immigration, which includes the desire for personal prosperity and higher education for the children, reinforces the ideology of blessing among Korean immigrants. Most Korean American preachers are also not free from the traditional shamanistic concept of blessing. They bring it consciously or unconsciously to their own theological interpretation of a biblical text.

The influence of the ideology of blessing on biblical interpretation for Korean American preaching can be divided into three aspects. First, theological perspectives based on the ideology of blessing drive preachers to reduce their understanding of Christian faith and life to a personal dimension and to overlook the intimate relationship between personal faith and communal well-being that the Bible emphasizes. This individualistic ideology of blessing makes the preacher-as-interpreter blind to the inevitable relation between an individual and the community to which the individual belongs. In fact, the ultimate concern of the Christian faith in the Bible is to build an identity for the community of faith. Individual believers are called to contribute to the maturity of the faith community by developing their Christian character, vision, and ethos so that believers eventually participate in transforming this world into the kingdom of God. This vision is eschatological, proleptic, and communal.

Second, preaching based on the ideology of blessing is in danger of distorting the essence of Reformed theology, which is based on the doctrine of *sola gratia*. The emphasis on personal devotion and faithful commitment to church activities as conditions of God's blessing leads the congregation to ignore the biblical message of salvation by grace. Moreover, the reduction of all biblical witnesses as either rewards or punishments by God prevents the preacher-as-interpreter from exploring a variety of theological and doctrinal concepts in the Bible.

Last, biblical interpretation based on the ideology of blessing tends to identify the blessing of God, which Christians must pursue throughout their lives, with materialistic worldly success and the Christian faith as the religion of winners. According to Paul the apostle, however, the true blessing of God given to faithful Christians is the fruit of the Holy Spirit, which includes "love, joy, peace, patience, kindness, goodness, faithfulness, gentleness and self-control" (Gal 5:22). This blessing is given not as a reward of personal piety and commitment to church activities, but as a gift to those who live by and with the Holy Spirit, even in the midst of suffering and pain. In sum, biblical interpretation based on the ideology of blessing does not pay attention to how the Bible helps believers find existential meaning in their present suffering and struggle for a communal future in light of God's promise.

The review above leads us to conclude that the Bible has been used in Korean American preaching as a series of proof texts to support preachers' preunderstood ideology of blessing. On the one hand, Korean American preaching based on the present-centered, individualistic, and materialistic approach to the Bible has contributed to encouraging individual listeners to live a "successful" life by having faith in God. On the other hand, Korean American preaching runs the risk of distorting the essence of the Christian faith, which is concerned with a future-oriented and communal well-being of everyone. Korean American preaching has not sufficiently responded to the unjust sociopolitical problems and prejudices occurring in the U.S. or challenged listeners with the liberating word of God to envision a future community in the promise of God. Korean American preaching needs to be renewed. A different hermeneutics of the Bible can help guide the communal journey of the Korean American community in the midst of a racist United States.

A Hermeneutical Proposal

Keeping in mind the weakness of Korean American preaching in relation to biblical interpretation, I ask, "What kind of theological perspectives and exegetical methods can help Korean American preachers interpret the biblical text in a new way?"

A Theological Perspective

In order to create a new theological perspective for Korean American preaching, we must take seriously three questions that arise after reviewing the present situation of the Korean American community: (1) Who are we in this racist society? (2) How does the Bible help us interpret our minority experience in the U.S.? (3) What kind of future can we imagine for our community in light of the biblical witness? The new theological perspective that responds to these three questions can be explored in three ways: (1) the Bible as the source of identity formation; (2) biblical interpretation as the voice of the congregation; and (3) the paschal mystery as a theological foundation.

1. *The Bible as the source of identity formation.* According to my analysis of Korean American preaching, many preachers read the Bible as a guidebook for individual listeners' moral behavior and personal piety, emphasizing the doctrine of reward and punishment by God. When preachers approach a biblical text, they usually aim to discover what lesson the text teaches regarding what individual believers *must do* to become more faithful Christians. However, when we read the Bible carefully and comprehensively, we realize that the primarily concern of the Bible is our identity formation, that is, *who we are* in the grace of God rather than moralistic exhortation for what we must do. The Bible calls us to *be,* that is, to grow in Jesus Christ to become a new humanity, a living parable of God's promise to the world. This mature life is the fruit of the Christian faith, and morality is only a by-product of this maturity. Biblical witnesses provide us with wisdom and insight into shaping our identities, not only personally but also communally. The Bible challenges us to change our worldviews, our attitudes toward our present life situations, and our expectations for the future by inviting us to see the world in a new way and to live out what we see. When we see the world in the biblical way, we aspire to live a life under the grace of God that is different from our old life under sin. We no longer support the established order or the world's standards of materialism, shamanistic idealism, and legalism. Instead, we see a visionary kingdom of God that God has promised us in the Bible, and we become inspired to live with the human responsibility for the humanness of life in this world.

Reading scripture in light of identity formation has actually been practiced in indigenous Asian cultures. Confucian, Buddhist, and Hindu scriptures have existed with authority as the sacred books within Asian and Asian American communities. These scriptures are authoritative in that they are believed to be true to life. That is, these sacred books are not merely the transmitted words of Buddha or Confucius, but a collection of writings conveying the truthful ways one needs to grow ethically and spiritually. These sacred books help readers shape their new identities and live truthful lives in their present situations. Once readers are enlightened to truth through the scriptures, they no longer need them (E. Kim: 78–83).

Given this context, it is important for Korean and other Asian American preachers to recover the way of reading scriptures in light of identity formation. When they read Christian scriptures for their preaching, the Bible is the authoritative and normative scripture because it has the enabling power to transform listeners' lives communally as well as personally. Remembering that Korean and other Asian American communities are diasporic communities seeking to negotiate an identity in an alien context, one of the tasks of Asian American hermeneutics is to interpret the Bible to illumine and shape a new identity for the community.

2. *Biblical interpretation as the voice of the congregation.* Korean and other Asian American Christians suffering from persistent racist and Eurocentric mentality often question what the Bible says concerning their existence and experiences in American society. When they listen to a sermon, they want to hear a truthful interpretation of their life experiences, including why they suffer and what kind of meanings their present suffering and pain have for the future of their lives. Given this context, Asian American preachers read and listen to the scriptures on behalf of their congregations. Their task is not simply to deliver the information and knowledge of a text based on historical-critical studies but to interpret the text with reflection on their listeners' experiences. When the biblical text engages the oppressed experiences of the congregation in a racist society, a new meaning that is created through the interaction between the text and the context represents the voice of a voiceless community.

The voice retrieved by dialogue between the text and the particular Korean or other Asian American context expresses the views and experiences of Asian Americans and affirms their rights. It will also have power to transform a society that is under the control of dominant ideologies. As Mary Hudson and Mary Turner describe in their book *Saved from Silence,* the retrieved voice of those marginalized from the mainstream of society

> calls attention to the pain of suffering of the individual and community; criticizes oppression; offers and demands solutions; cries out in passion, anger, and outrage; shocks and touches; changes attitudes, social customs, and practice; motivates reform; calls people out to radical and revolutionary action; and resists systems of injustice. (13–14)

Likewise, giving voice is not simply describing the present reality but provoking the passion for justice and evoking a radical vision for the future. The voice provoked by suffering and pain transgresses the boundaries of the dominant culture and represents the living God. God uses the voice of the marginalized people to draw the "new worlds" into the present and future of a society (Hudson and Turner: 52). Through the voice of the marginalized, God calls people into existence and liberates humanity not only for Korean and other minority immigrants but also for all Americans, majority and minority alike. Therefore, the goal of biblical interpretation for Korean and other Asian American preaching is to "contemporize" or "incarnate" the text in the world of the listeners to give them a voice. Through preaching, listeners hear what they want to voice and experience the presence and work of the living God in the midst of their suffering and pain.

3. *The paschal mystery as the theological foundation.* In spite of the evil structural power of racism surrounding the Korean and other Asian American communities, Asian American preaching should not be passive; nor should it merely lament the present reality. Instead, it should seriously and actively respond to the question, "What kind of future can we imagine for our community in light of the biblical witness?"

As an answer to this theological question, the Bible reminds us of God's eschatological promise for a new heaven and new earth and convinces us that God can and will bring life beyond death. This promise of God is revealed in the paschal mystery of Jesus Christ and becomes the foundation of the Christian faith. Our new future is possible because God has promised it through the resurrection of Christ Jesus, which is the first fruit of our hope. Therefore, we celebrate that "death and evil do not have final victory; the power of God does" (Hilkert: 116). God's promise in the paschal mystery is not about a remote future of another world after death. Rather, the power of the paschal mystery is already working in our present situation as transforming power. In our concrete political, social, and ecclesiastical structures that continue to impoverish, oppress, or marginalize God's people, the liberating Spirit of God has worked to make human life human.

Based on this paschal mystery, Korean and other Asian American communities of faith can envision their future. The proleptic view of God's eschatological promise revealed in the paschal mystery invites preachers to imagine the future of their communities. Through imagination, as Mary Hilkert states in her book *Naming Grace,* the preacher-as-interpreter is able to "reconfigure reality by seeing it through an alternative lens" (189). Through imagination, the preacher sees the human world in a new way and creates a vision for a new world in the promise of God despite the injustice of our reality. The Spirit of God abides with us in our wounded world and breaks through human evil as the source of hope for Korean and other Asian American communities.

Therefore, the ultimate task of biblical interpretation for Asian American preaching is to create hope for the community by pointing to the power of the resurrection in today's world. This is done by interpreting the concrete experience of the community through the lens of the paschal mystery. Having hope is profoundly connected with the ability to imagine the future and to find meaning in the relationship between God and humanity. Matsuoka describes the hope for the Asian American community as "the establishment of a just society and the recovery of the basic form of humanity" (24). In this vision, people have communion; they break bread together by welcoming one another and, thereby, transcending racial and cultural differences.

This hope connects Asian American Christians to other oppressed racial/ethnic minority groups in the world as well as in the U.S. By sharing their experiences, Asian American Christians recognize not only their suffering and pain but also the transforming power of the Spirit working as the source of hope in the midst of suffering. Biblical interpretation based on faith in the paschal mystery energizes preaching and invites listeners to struggle for the creation of a just society in which people are respected equally by one another as children of God and live harmoniously side by side.

Exegetical Strategies

To help Korean American preachers interpret a biblical text as the liberating word of God in the particular context of a congregation, I suggest that the preacher-as-interpreter read the text metaphorically. Metaphorical interpretation goes beyond searching for the literal meaning of a text toward creating a new meaning of the text, by relating the world of the text to that of the listeners. Metaphor has traditionally been regarded as merely an "ornament of discourse," a decorative word or phrase that does not influence the cognitive meaning of the discourse. However, in the last few decades there has been much progress in understanding the concept of metaphor differently in the field of theology as well as philosophy and literature. In this new understanding, metaphor is

> a semantic operation, a powerful way of generating new meaning by the creation and exploitation of linguistic tension. Metaphor is a linguistic strategy for extending meaning beyond what can be expressed literally.... The purpose of metaphors is not to be clever but to provoke the mind into deeper involvement with the subject matter of the discourse. (Schneiders: 20).

Metaphors usually have two parts, the "is" and the "is not." There is a tension between the explicit literal meaning of a word and its implicit symbolic meaning. Thus, metaphorical interpretation for preaching considers a biblical text as a metaphorical expression that involves both factual and imaginative meanings and aims to create a new meaning out of the text that goes beyond its literal meaning and in connection with a particular context of contemporary listeners.

Therefore, metaphorical interpretation is different from the traditional method of biblical interpretation. While the traditional method is a two-step procedure from explication to application, metaphorical interpretation does not separate explication from application but integrates them as a spiral from the beginning to the end of the interpretive process. Throughout the entire process, the preacher-as-interpreter looks at the reality *through* the text and creates its contemporary meaning.

How, then, can the preacher-as-interpreter practice metaphorical interpretation as a way to create a new meaning from a biblical text? I suggest three strategies for interpreting a text metaphorically. The first strategy is to read the text as a performative act. Reading the text as a performative act means reading it slowly, aloud, and repeatedly, with the imagination that a group of people is listening to the text. By using her imagination, the preacher-as-interpreter is immersed in the world of the listeners and hears the text as if she were standing in the shoes of the congregation. This imaginative reading makes it possible for her to feel the text empathically, as her congregation would feel it. The images, stories, and metaphors in the text often challenge her to remember the personal and communal experiences of the congregation and stretch her imagination to view them in a different way. When the preacher-as-interpreter reads the text this way, she can be responsive to the text as a member of the congregation.

The second strategy for interpreting the text metaphorically is to utilize modern and postmodern interpretive methods eclectically, including the historical-critical method, the "new literary criticism" (Segovia: 15–20), and "cultural studies" (28–31). The historical-critical method offers background knowledge of the text. However, it creates a broad gap between the text and contemporary listeners because its primary concern is to discover the ancient meaning, that is, what the text meant to the original readers. On the other hand, the new literary criticism—which evolves from narrative criticism, structuralism, rhetorical criticism, psychological criticism, reader-response criticism, and deconstruction—narrows that gap by emphasizing the contextuality of the text. Its basic premise is that the text exists not only for the original readers but contemporary readers as well. While the new literary criticism moves the hermeneutical concern from the author's intention to the reader's personal and existential experience, cultural studies goes one step further. Cultural studies is not limited to the individual reader's existential domain but extends to the sociocultural location of the reader's/listener's community. Cultural studies, which includes a liberation theological approach as well as postmodern and postcolonial strategies, leads the interpreter to recognize the ideologies and perspectives of the larger society to which the reading community belongs.² Metaphorical interpretation for preaching uses these diverse, multilevel approaches to the Bible eclectically as well as synthetically. It does not limit itself to one interpretive method.

A final strategy for interpreting a biblical text metaphorically is to link the world of the text and that of the listeners relationally. This relational link is based on the dynamic interaction between text and context, using a to-and-fro movement rather than a linear order that goes from text to context. Linking the different worlds of text and listeners relationally can be practiced by retelling or paraphrasing the biblical text. Retelling the text means more than simply repeating the original text. In the process of retelling the text, the preacher-as-interpreter locates the text in the life of the congregation and connects it with listeners' ordinary experiences. This is done by inducing certain events and leaving others out, based on the listeners' experiences from a certain theological perspective. In this way, the biblical text is transformed into a contemporary story of the congregation's.

Based on these three strategies, metaphorical interpretation goes beyond what the text actually meant in its original context or the author's intention and acknowledges the possibility of multiple interpretations. Thus, metaphorical interpretation is open-ended and flexible. At this point, some may ask how we can measure the validity of a newly created meaning through metaphorical interpretation. Are there any criteria for evaluating the validity of an interpretation? To this ethical problem of metaphorical interpretation, I regard Sandra Schneiders's answer as a thoughtful response:

> [T]here are criteria—such as methodological integrity, fruitfulness, consistency, explanatory power, compatibility with known data, and convergence of indices—and they must be applied in judging the validity of an interpretation. But the important point for our purpose is that these criteria are not restricted to historical facticity, author's intention, or the insight of the first-century audience.... we must wrestle with the text rather than merely submit to it as the fundamentalists would have us do, or attempt to dominate it as a pure historical-critical scholar might propose. (33)

Interpretation of Psalm 137

How, then, can we apply this hermeneutical proposal to Korean American preaching? This last section presents an example of the application by interpreting Psalm 137.

---

² For further explanation of the historical-critical method, new literary criticism, and cultural studies, see Segovia: 1–31.

While Psalm 137 is a well-known text in the Christian church, it is rarely preached in Korean American churches.[3] This is perhaps due to a large gap between the captive life of the ancient Jews in Babylon as described in the text and the contemporary life of Korean immigrants in the U.S. Indeed, it is not possible to directly correlate the world of the text to that of the listeners. However, when we interpret Psalm 137 metaphorically from a liberating theological perspective, the text has meaning in a new way for the Korean American community of faith.

In the process of interpreting Psalm 137 metaphorically, the first thing for the preacher-as-interpreter to consider is that the literary genre of Psalm 137 is a poem. Most poems are appreciated by contemporary readers emotively and imaginatively. Even though they were written in a particular historical context for the original readers, poems have new meanings that relate to the experiences and life situations of contemporary readers. Thus, appreciating a poem *as* poem is important in going beyond the poem's literal meaning.

According to biblical scholars, the historical setting of Psalm 137 is unclear. Whether it was composed during the exile period in Babylon or after returning to live in the ruins of Jerusalem is debatable because of the incoherent use of grammar and the rhetorical expressions in the poem (Mays: 421; Freedman: 187). In this ambiguity, when a Korean American preacher reads the poem, she will easily relate the poem to the particular experience of her congregation. It may be unjustifiable for Korean Americans to identify themselves as the exiles because their historical and cultural situation is not the same as that of the exiles in Babylon. Korean Americans are not prisoners of war or captives forced to move to the U.S. for political and ideological reasons. Instead, Korean Americans volunteered to live in the U.S. to improve their social and economic positions.

Nonetheless, some Korean American Christians remind us that Psalm 137 becomes the song of Korean American Christians beyond the boundaries of its original context because similarities exist between their world and the world of the exiles. The first similarity is that both Korean Americans and the exiles live in the margins of society. Although Korean Americans are legitimate American citizens, they are pushed to the periphery like aliens or strangers. Sang Hyun Lee, a Korean American theologian at Princeton Theological Seminary, explains that Korean Americans experience their lives in the U.S. as "perpetual aliens and strangers" who are not

---

[3] Among my collections of Korean American sermon books, only one sermon "Lent and March First," preached by Yoon (1997) used Ps 137:1–7 (along with Gal 6:11–18) as the basis. In the sermon, Yoon connected the text to the Korean situation during Japanese occupation instead of contemporary Korean immigrant life in the U.S. (Yoon, 1997:121).

being completely accepted by the majority group in American society because of its Eurocentrism: "if you are a non-white immigrant, such as an Asian American person, you are a perpetual stranger in this society whether you have just arrived from Asia or even if you were born here with names like Esther, David, etc." (78). In this situation, Korean Americans who experience severe racial discrimination in the U.S. empathically join the weeping of the exiles and sing together: "By the rivers of Babylon/there we sat down and there we wept/when we remembered Zion" (137:1).

Another similarity is that the country in which Korean Americans live is one of the most prosperous and powerful nations of the world, just as Babylon was. The cultural ethos of both superpower countries is rooted in materialism, militarism, and racial pluralism. The process of cultural assimilation present in both superpowers discourages minority groups from shaping their identities but encourages them to dilute their ethnic and cultural distinctiveness. The values, feelings, and morals inherited from the minorities' ethnic traditions and cultures are either neglected or regarded as an "exotic" or "esoteric" subculture within the majority society. This cultural imperialism is described in verses 2 and 3 of the poem. The exiles, when mocked by the captors to sing their traditional or cultural songs, refuse to sing:

> On the willows there
> we hung up our harps.
> For there our captors asked us for songs,
> and our tormentors asked for mirth, saying,
> "Sing us one of the songs of Zion." (137:2–3)

Korean Americans understand this brokenhearted feeling of the exiles through their experiences in the U.S. as a marginalized group and join the exiles in singing this psalm.

Here, it is worth noting the implicit meaning of "the songs of Zion." The songs of Zion is used synonymously with songs of mirth (137:3) and "the LORD's song" (137:4). These songs signify the hymns of joy or "hymns of praise to the Lord sung in the Temple at Jerusalem" (Mays: 422). Zion is not simply the homeland the exiles left behind. Rather, the temple mountain is a symbol of "the city of the great King" (Ps 48:1) and Yahweh's dwelling place (Willis: 297). John Willis further points out by quoting E. J. Hamlin that "in several songs of Zion, cultic gatherings at the Temple are seen as anticipations of the gathering of the nations and peoples of the earth to the shrine of Israel's God, who is over the nations" (302). In other words, Zion does not represent the exiles' geographical homeland. It remains not in their past memory but in their future vision for the reign of God. Consequently, when the exiles remember Zion (137:1), they are not merely expressing their personal homesickness or longing for familiar scenes and accustomed places from their hometown. Rather, they are yearning for the consummation of the sovereignty of God. In this sense, the songs of Zion are in conjunction with the eschatological hope of the people of God. They are not only the songs of old but also those of the vision of a future community. At this point, the exiles who have no hope for their future in Babylon ask themselves: "How could we sing the LORD's song in a foreign land?" (137:4).

Instead of directly offering some insights to this question in the following verses, the poem takes a somewhat different move in verses 5 and 6:

> If I forget you, O Jerusalem,
> let my right hand wither!
> Let my tongue cling to the roof of my mouth,
> if I do not remember you,
> if I do not set Jerusalem
> above my highest joy. (137:5–6)

Hans-Joachim Kraus interprets these two verses as a nationalistic vow that the exiles make to their homelands: "in a strange land I cannot sing joyful songs of Zion, but I will never forget Jerusalem, for me it is the best of all my joys" (503). However, the theological perspective centered on the paschal mystery leads Korean American preachers to understand these verses not as the crying of the exiles but God's responsive song to them. God neither leaves them alone in their strange land nor ignores their suffering and pain. Instead, God is present in the midst of their suffering and becomes involved in their pain.

Biblical interpretation based on faith in the paschal mystery is found in S. H. Lee's sermon "How Shall We Sing the Lord's Song in a Strange Land?" In this sermon, he says to the Korean American congregation that "[t]hose who embark on this journey are already at home because that journey is precisely the journey of God. God came into this world to build a loving community. But this idolatrous world did not welcome God. God, too, was made a stranger" (81). God's presence with the oppressed is confirmed by God's responsive song in verses 5 and 6. When the exiles weep by the rivers of Babylon, God has not forsaken them even in the foreign place but weeps with them, sharing their agony and pain in the strange land. Psalm 137, therefore, is not a monological song sung by one party but a dialogical one between the exiles and God. It is a song of responsive duet.

When God sings about Jerusalem in verses 5 and 6, the meaning of Jerusalem is more than literal. Jerusalem does not mean the exiles' geographical hometown but metaphorically represents God's promised land, the city of Zion. By singing these verses, God reminds the exiles that God does not forget the divine promise to them or leave them bereft of hope. Thus God's responsive song in verses 5 and 6 renews the promise between God and Israel.

The divine promise confirmed in God's responsive song is also the source of hope for Korean American Christians. With faith in "God with us," they are encouraged to remember their song of the vision of God's kingdom and to sing it again in the wilderness. As long as God doesn't forget the song, they won't either. As long as God is with them in their suffering and pain, they have courage to sing faithfully, believing that there will one day be justice and a setting right of all that has gone wrong.

The last stanza of Psalm 137 follows God's responsive song:

Remember, O LORD, against the Edomites
the day of Jerusalem's fall,
how they said, "Tear it down! Tear it down!
Down to its foundations!"
O Daughter Babylon, you devastator!
Happy shall they be who pay you back
what you have done to us!
Happy shall they be who take your little ones
and dash them against the rock. (137:7–9)

It has been considered problematic in the Christian church to preach these verses because of the harsh words and brutal images of vengeance. For instance, the Common Lectionary includes only the first six verses of Psalm 137, omitting verses 7–9. In the Revised Common Lectionary, the entire psalm is excluded. Indeed, when one reads these verses literally, one may feel that they are not to be preached because the vehement rage and brutality depicted in them go against the essence of the Christian gospel of love.

However, in my view, Korean American preaching should not exclude verses 7–9 for two reasons. First, Psalm 137 is one piece of artwork in which *all* verses form a network that becomes the design and structure of the artwork; the verses do not simply exist independently. The last stanza of the poem is the concluding part that makes the function of the poem clear. That is, the goal of the poem is not achieved without the final verses. The new reality is not evoked until the poem is sung in its entirety.

Second, this emotionally and eloquently described stanza can be interpreted differently from the conventional literal reading by reading it metaphorically. When the preacher-as-interpreter reads Edomites and Babylonians, she doesn't have to restrict their meanings as enemies of the exiles in the historical and original meanings. Rather, she can extend their meaning metaphorically to her listeners' contemporary experiences and link these groups in their consciousness with the contemporary evil powers existing in a racist America. In addition, "to dash babes against the city walls" can be interpreted not literally but metaphorically, in the sense that the evil powers will be conquered at any cost. Likewise, the graphic language of the poem has the potential of strengthening the empathy and solidarity among listeners who have had a similar experience to that of the exiles.

According to this metaphorical interpretation, the last stanza has meaning not as a voice of rage and resentment for marginalized people but as a hopeful voice that yearns for an alternative future. The subversive power of the language in Psalm 137 invites listeners to the vision of God's eschatological kingdom and calls the listeners to work as agents of God to fight against evil powers such as racism. The powerful and vivid expression of the last stanza gives Korean American Christians hope when the dividing walls of racism will fall so that the United States, where they are currently living, will be transformed from Babylon into Jerusalem, the eschatological city of God.

Therefore, interpreting Psalm 137 by using the proposed hermeneutical method provides new insight to the poem. Although biblical studies have traditionally categorized Psalm 137 as either "cultic lamentation" (Kraus: 502) or a "psalm of disorientation" (Brueggemann: 31), interpreting Psalm 137 metaphorically from a liberating theological perspective makes it possible to appreciate the poem as a renewed song of Zion that evokes hope for the community's future. The movement—from the weeping of exiles to God, God's responding song, and finally to the exiles' song of hope—reveals that Psalm 137 is not simply a nationalistic communal lament of the defeated but a song of the vision of God's kingdom.

Preaching Psalm 137 based on this interpretation focuses on how God, who is marginalized from the dominant culture of America, weeps with the marginalized people and begins building a new community on the margins. This kind of preaching invites listeners to enter into a new world by participating in the very life of God. Preaching Psalm 137 is a call to both the preacher and the Christian community to cultivate a new song for a new community in the future.

WORKS CONSULTED

Brueggemann, Walter
    1995   *Psalms: The Life of Faith*. Ed. Patrick D. Miller. Minneapolis: Fortress.

Chang, Jong-Chan
    1995   *Expand the Lot*. Seoul: Cumran.

Choi, Hyo-Sup
    1995   *The Joy of Love*. Seoul: Voice.

Council of the Korean American Church in New Jersey
    1995   *Those Who Crossed the Sea*. Seoul: Voice.

Council of the Korean Presbyterian Church in the West
    1994   *The Heavenly Door Is Opening*. Seoul: Word of Life.

Ferguson, Duncan S.
    1986   *Biblical Hermeneutics: An Introduction*. Atlanta: John Knox.

Freedman, David N.
    1971   "The Structure of Psalm 137." Pp. 187–205 in *Near Eastern Studies in Honor of William Foxwell Albright*. Ed. Hans Goedicke. Baltimore: Johns Hopkins University Press.

Gadamer, Hans-Georg
    1990   *Truth and Method*. Trans. Joel Weinsheimer and Donald G. Marshall. New York: Crossroad.

Gillingham, S. E.
    1994   *The Poems and Psalms of the Hebrew Bible*. Oxford: Oxford University Press.

Hilkert, Mary C.
    1995   *Naming Grace: Preaching and the Sacramental Imagination*. New York: Continuum.

Hudson, Mary L., and Mary D. Turner
    1999   *Saved from Silence: Finding Women's Voice in Preaching*. St. Louis: Chalice.

Kim, Chan-Hie
    1994   "Reading the Bible As Asian Americans." *NIB* 1:161–66.

Kim, Eunjoo M.
    1999   *Preaching the Presence of God: A Homiletic from an Asian American Perspective*. Valley Forge, Pa.: Judson.

Kim, Jung Ha
    1997   *Bridge-Makers and Cross-Bearers: Korean-American Women and the Church*. Atlanta: Scholars Press.

Kim, Min-Oong
    1995   *The Bread Sent Out upon Waters*. Seoul: Institute of Korean Theology.

Kim, Sang-Kyu
    1994   "The Secret of Blessings." Pp. 47–55 in *The Heavenly Door Is Opening*. The Council of the Korean Presbyterian Church in the West. Seoul: Word of Life.

Kirschner, Robert
    1990   "Two Responses to Epocal Change: Augustine and the Rabbis on Psalm 137 (136)." *Vigiliae Christianae* 44:242–62.

Kraus, Hans-Joachim
    1989   *Psalms 60–150: A Commentary*. Minneapolis: Augsburg.

Kuhn, Thomas S.
    1970   *The Structure of Scientific Revolutions*. Chicago: University of Chicago Press.

Lee, Dong-Won
    1995   *For the Sake of Joyful Life*. Seoul: Nachimban Ministries.

Lee, Sang Hyun
    1996   "How Shall We Sing the Lord's Song in a Strange Land?" *Journal of Asian and Asian American Theology* 1/1: 77–81.

Lee, Sung-Nak Paul
    1996   *Grace Which You See with Eyes.* Seoul: Kulmarum.

Lee, Young-Jae
    1993   *The Well Dug in the Wilderness.* Seoul: Star.

Lee, Young-Kil
    1998   *The Dance of Jacob.* Seoul: Kulmarum.

Matsuoka, Fumitaka
    1997   *The Color of Faith: Building Community in a Multiracial Society.* Cleveland: United Church.

Mays, James L.
    1994   *Psalms.* Interpretation. Louisville: John Knox.

Miles, Carol A.
    1994   "'Singing the Songs of Zion' and Other Sermons from the Margins of the Canon." *Koinonia* 6/2:151–75.

Ricoeur, Paul
    1976   *Interpretation Theory: Discourse and the Surplus of Meaning.* Fort Worth: Texas Christian University Press.

Schneiders, Sandra M.
    1993   "Scripture As the Word of God." *Princeton Seminary Bulletin* 14:18–35.

Segovia, Fernando F.
    1995   "'And They Began to Speak in Other Tongues': Competing Modes of Discourse in Contemporary Biblical Criticism." Pp. 1–32 in *Reading from This Place,* vol. 1. Ed. Fernando F. Segovia and Mary Ann Tolbert. Minneapolis: Fortress.

Sugirtharajah, R. S.
    1998   *Asian Biblical Hermeneutics and Postcolonialism: Contesting the Interpretation.* Maryknoll, N.Y.: Orbis.

Willis, John T.
    1997   "'Isaiah 2:2–5 and the Psalms of Zion." Pp. 295–316 in *Writing and Reading the Scroll of Isaiah,* vol. 1. Ed. Craig C. Broyles. Leiden: Brill.

Yim, Dong-Sun
    1996   *You Reap Whatever You Saw.* Seoul: Word of Life.

Yoon, Samuel Yoon
    1994   *Living the Prayer.* Seoul: Voice.

    1997   *Living the Faith.* Seoul: Voice.

BIBLICAL THEMES FOR PASTORAL CARE REVISITED: AN ASIAN AMERICAN REREADING OF A CLASSIC PASTORAL CARE TEXT

Peter Yuichi Clark
Seton Medical Center

ABSTRACT

Twenty years after its initial publication, William B. Oglesby Jr.'s book *Biblical Themes for Pastoral Care* still is consulted and used by seminarians and ministers who are interested in honing their caregiving skills by understanding how biblical texts can inform the processes of pastoral care and counseling. This essay revisits Oglesby's work and seeks to apply its insights to ministry with Asian Pacific American populations. The central theme of the Bible and five subthemes are identified by Oglesby and summarized in this essay, and then several additional subthemes are explained due to their relevance for APA women and men. Finally, to test the hypotheses advanced by Oglesby and expanded in this article, the written testimonies of fifty-two contemporary Japanese American Christians are examined.

Over the past twenty years, an intriguing trend has emerged in Christian theology. On the one hand, there has been a growing and laudable emphasis on interpreting theological issues and biblical studies from Asian Pacific American (APA)[1] perspectives. On the other hand, though, it is an open secret in the field of pastoral care and counseling that scant attention has been given thus far to its implications for the APA experience. The difference between the former, where vigorous dialogue is occurring, and the latter, where there has been a trickle of articles and book chapters but (to date) no major book on the topic, is striking. Yet the effect is that pastoral caregivers who desire to respond sensitively to APA concerns often must discover the specifics from more general sources. For the time being, we

---

[1] There is no consensus about this term. In fact, there is an ongoing debate about whether Asian Pacific American (or Asian and Pacific Islander American, or Pacific Asian North American, etc.) people even want to be grouped together under such a categorization. I am doing so because I believe there is a common set of psychodynamic and pastoral care issues that affects many, if not all, of these populations. However, all of my examples in this essay derive from Japanese American communities, with which I have a personal history, professional experience, and some research knowledge.

must consult books on pastoral care and counseling toward people within a particular developmental cohort, gender group, crisis or life situation, or non-APA population and then particularize or translate those insights into an APA context.[2] This is not intended as a disparagement of the field, by any means. I am simply observing that such translation is currently necessary—and offering a challenge to myself and other pastoral theologians to address this gap more intentionally with our own contributions.

However, given this reality, I suggest that we utilize this translation technique and apply it to an influential text in pastoral care, specifically, William B. Oglesby Jr.'s book *Biblical Themes for Pastoral Care*. Although Oglesby, who was professor emeritus of pastoral counseling at Union Theological Seminary in Richmond, Virginia, wrote the book twenty years ago and died six years ago, his voice lives on as recommended reading in seminary pastoral care courses and in Clinical Pastoral Education (CPE) programs. Further, his book is still cited frequently by other scholars in the disciplines of pastoral care, pastoral counseling, and pastoral theology. Since this issue of *Semeia* is focused on the Bible in Asian America, and since numerous APA Christian ministers have been exposed to Oglesby's work in their seminary training or CPE experience, it seems worthwhile to revisit this book on its twentieth anniversary and explore how it applies to ministers and laypersons who interpret the Bible and offer care within an APA context.

To structure my exploration, I will pursue three streams of thought. In the first stream, I will summarize the major lines of Oglesby's argument, laying the groundwork for our discussion. Then, in the second stream, I will accept his invitation and investigate some themes he mentions but does not emphasize in his text—themes that can have particular resonance and relevance for APA Christian faith communities. Finally, in the third stream, I will examine the written testimony of some contemporary Japanese American Christians and seek to apply our expanded version of Oglesby's theoretical awareness to their narratives.

My goal, therefore, is not to supplant Oglesby's book but rather to supplement it so that it can speak more helpfully to members of the APA community. Oglesby's method will become for us a useful springboard from which we can create more contextualized and healthful pastoral interventions.

---

[2] Perhaps the works that are most amenable to such translation address the subject of cross-cultural pastoral care and counseling. Augsburger remains the standard and is quite valuable, while van Beek provides a more concise presentation of some salient issues. Leslie's monograph is also helpful, though not widely available. Many pastoral caregivers and counselors, however, refer to Sue and Sue as their primary resource in this area, which then means that they must translate their clinical insights into more formal pastoral theologizing.

I

Oglesby begins by asserting his conviction that "a responsible use of the Bible is basic in the performance of constructive pastoral counseling and *can provide needed principles* whereby the minister may evaluate ongoing pastoral work and make constructive use of data that have emerged from the behavioral sciences" (1980:11, emphasis added). Clearly, Oglesby does not intend to expound upon a biblical perspective of anthropology or how the Bible may be employed in pastoral care. Rather, he affirms that there is a "sense in which biblical material informs process" (1973:309),[3] and it is that connection between the Bible and the process of pastoral care that draws his attention.

According to Oglesby, many, if not all, ministers[4] respond in one of three ways when a parishioner approaches with a crisis. The first way is influenced by insight-oriented psychoanalytic therapy and suggests that, if a person understands his or her often-hidden inner dynamics, then he or she can respond more creatively to life's circumstances: "Let's explore the meaning and impact of what is happening to you right now." The second way is influenced by behavior-modification theory and asserts that if a person can be motivated to act differently, then the inner tension that person feels will lessen: "Let's figure out some more effective responses to the situation you are facing." The third way is shaped by Rogerian relationship-oriented therapies and affirms that as a parishioner experiences a relationship of acceptance and regard with the minister, that person can move away from debilitating patterns toward more creative, meaningful possibilities: "You sound like you're having a really rough time and are not sure which way to turn." In each of these approaches, Oglesby contends, there is an emphasis on *right knowing* (awareness), *right doing* (changed behavior), and *right being* (personal transformation).[5] But what is critical is "which of these emphases is seen as primary, from which the other two derive" (1980:18).

Oglesby then pursues an exegesis of these three concepts in biblical texts and discovers that knowing gains priority only in the context of knowing and encountering God; what one knows about oneself and ultimate reality emerges only from within a trustful relationship with God. Doing, like knowing, is

---

[3] Oglesby's book is based in part on two articles he authored for *Interpretation*, a journal published by the seminary where he taught (see Oglesby, 1973, 1979).

[4] Oglesby employs the term "minister" throughout his book. Clearly he desires to assist professional clergywomen and clergymen in their provision of pastoral care within a congregational or institutional setting. However, what he offers also applies valuably to laypersons interested in providing pastoral care, as he himself acknowledges (1980:40–41).

[5] Readers interested in pursuing this line of reasoning are advised not to depend on the condensed treatment in Oglesby's 1980 text but to consult his more focused 1973 article instead.

derivative, and right doing is only possible because of faith. So in Oglesby's reading of the biblical material, it is in right being—a quality of "heart" and relationship[6]—that right knowing and right doing become possible:

> [Q]uality of life is primary to quality of thought or quality of behavior. It is the person who has experienced newness of life who now sees things in the proper perspective, and whose actions attest to the restoration that has been wrought in the experience of forgiveness and reconciliation. So it is that pastoral care and counseling that focuses on being without disregarding knowing and doing is consistent with the biblical perspective, which sees all three as essential but also is clear on the basic priority of being over knowing and doing. (1980:29)

Or, as he says in a playful and pithy mood, "The person is always more important than the problem, and the relationship is more important than the solution" (1980:41).[7]

While Oglesby does not make it explicit, he does favor a Rogerian approach as having the correct emphasis; yet he does not pause to gloat over this point. Instead, he moves from a focus on being and relationship to underscore what he perceives as the central theme of the Bible. He declares that the Bible, taken as a whole, contains a "quadratic emphasis" that informs us of God's character, human nature, sin, and salvation (1980:33). God is seen as just and holy, and yet as merciful and compassionate. Human beings are viewed as creative in our choices and created for relationship with self, others, and the divine. Sin emerges as human beings try to be more than we are and break the relationships we have with others, God, and ourselves, creating a separation and isolation that in turn produces fear and misery (cf. Oglesby, 1979:164); throughout the book, Oglesby equates "sin" with "hiding." Salvation arises as God reaches out in loving initiative to restore relationships and as people accept the opportunity to freely say

---

[6] This point is echoed by Asian American feminist theologian Rita Nakashima Brock, who—while not endorsing Oglesby's atonement-based interpretation of sin and salvation—expands on Oglesby's point by claiming that the primacy of Heart and relationality applies not only to human beings but to God as well (Brock). Oglesby and Brock also concur that "Heart" (or being, to use Oglesby's term) is not a static category, but one that involves interaction with others and entails mutual transformation.

[7] Elsewhere Oglesby asserts that "[i]n pastoral care, *who* the minister *is* has much more significance for his [*sic, passim*] people than *how* he goes about counseling. This is another way of saying that his *being* takes priority over his *knowing* and *doing*. If he truly loves his parishioners, then distortions in theory and practice can be overcome" (1973:326, emphasis original). Gender-exclusive terminology notwithstanding (he is more attentive to inclusive language in his 1980 book), Oglesby here inverts the Augustinian doctrine of *ex opere operato*. For Oglesby, the person of the minister *does* matter in the offering of grace-filled pastoral care, a point made quite eloquently for three generations of seminarians by Henri Nouwen.

"yes" to grace and life. This interplay of God, humanity, the "tragic flaw," and the offer of reconciliation constitutes the criterion by which ministers can interpret their own pastoral actions. Do my actions promote a better comprehension of this central theme? How does my pastoral care help people to live more faithfully and relationally with God and others?

This central theme, Oglesby contends, is elaborated in various interdependent subthemes, of which he proposes to examine five in detail. These themes, which he has expressed in pairings reminiscent of Eriksonian developmental crises, include initiative and freedom, fear and faith, conformity and rebellion, death and rebirth, and risk and redemption. His method in each chapter is consistent. He demonstrates how each subtheme appears in the biblical narratives (primarily the Yahwist materials), analyzes verbatim vignettes to illustrate how a specific subtheme is operationalized,[8] and then summarizes the implications of each subtheme for pastoral care.

The first subtheme that Oglesby addresses is *initiative and freedom*. By this phrase he means the divine initiative of covenantal love and the human freedom to choose how to respond to that initiative. He sees this theme illustrated in the Genesis narrative (3:1–21) wherein Adam chooses to misuse his freedom, God calls Adam to remain in relationship, Adam hides from God, and God participates in Adam's hiding (by making clothes for him) while simultaneously inviting Adam (and his descendants) to reconcile. The implication that Oglesby sees in pastoral care involves the minister's initiative in establishing pastoral relationships with people in need of care and those persons' freedom to accept or refuse the offer of help. On the minister's side, Oglesby underscores the importance of ministers reaching out to others on their own initiative and staying engaged by following the parishioner's conversational lead. On the parishioner's side, he notes that when assistance is accepted there exists a deep ambivalence—both a desire for help and "a relationship to overcome the isolation and aloneness," as well as a resistance to being helped because of "past experiences where closeness brought injury" (1980:77).

Acknowledging the ambivalence felt by the recipient of care leads Oglesby to his discussion of the second subtheme, that of *fear and faith*, in which his third major thesis emerges. (As a clarifying reminder, his first thesis was the priority of being over-knowing and doing; his second was the quadratic central theme of the Bible.) This third thesis involves a triadic movement that he discerns in all effective pastoral care. According to Oglesby, pastoral care begins when there is an acknowledgment of the

---

[8] Oglesby's analyses of these verbatim conversations are perhaps the richest material in his book. By their very nature, however, they resist synopsis, and so interested readers must go to the 1980 text to trace how Oglesby discovers these subthemes in records of pastoral encounters.

parishioner's situation—a statement that tells the truth, "*There you are*" (in your suffering, alienation, or crisis). It continues as the caregiver declares where she or he is: "*Here I am*" (with a different perspective, but also knowing that I too share this human predicament). Together these two statements voice "the word of judgment" (1980:85) that illuminates the parishioner's fear and brokenness. The word of forgiveness and grace and the culmination of effective pastoral care occur in speaking "*I love you*" (and I will stand with you as you face this situation). In response to the fear that leads people to hide themselves, this triadic movement embodies "the primary word of the Gospel, the Good News of God, [which] is simply, 'You no longer need to be afraid,'" because we are not ultimately alone (83).

The implication for pastoral care in the tension between fear and faith is that while fear is paralyzing, faith is a dynamic process that is transformative if it is not coerced into maturing too quickly or abandoned because it seems to be progressing too slowly. "Only an awareness of faith as process that continually struggles with doubt and fear can enable the minister to respond to the person where s/he is at any given moment in the sure conviction that this moment is ultimately the most crucial since it is the only point available for encounter," Oglesby maintains. "The goal, then, becomes not some fixed destination, but the capacity to live in an openness which requires fewer façades and in which the person is able to meet any situation creatively (Phil 4:13) because of the faith which is born of love and which overcomes fear" (113).

The two main obstacles that can impede this faith-based openness constitute the third subtheme, that of *conformity and rebellion*. In Oglesby's mind, "[a]lthough either conformity or rebellion tends to become the general characteristic of a person's stance toward life, neither is ever present without the other" (114). The conformist seeks to gain love and favor by hiding behind acceptable behavior, fearing that "if you knew who I am, you wouldn't love me"; Oglesby names this as the flaw of Cain's offering (Gen 4:3–7) and of the elder brother in the Lukan Jesus' parable of the two sons (15:11–32). By contrast, the rebel seeks to be known through her or his destructive behavior, but the fear is that "if I were myself, you would never know I exist" (this is the younger, prodigal brother). Despite their opposite approaches, however, both want to hide and hinder authentic relationship.

An attentive minister must therefore be ready with genuine acceptance, but with two different strategies to counter these styles of concealment. With a conformist parishioner, what is needed is acceptance of his or her personhood in the presence of failure. When the parishioner reveals an aspect of his or her self that is "negative" or less than "acceptable," the minister must facilitate an opportunity to face that "shadow" and to experience reconciliation rather than offering excuses, reassurance, or allowance for that person to blame others. With a rebel parishioner, the minister needs to communicate acceptance without excoriating the parishioner, simply focusing on the presenting problem, or assuming (or allowing the parishioner to abdicate) responsibility for her or his own choices and consequences. As a corollary, Oglesby warns, in anxiety-producing situations—such as intense pastoral encounters—ministers will tend to either excuse or blame parishioners because of their own hiding dynamics, and so there is an ongoing need for ministers to seek peer consultation and support.

But what is the fear that provokes such tenacious patterns of hiding? Oglesby understands it as the fear of dying, that "whoever finds me will slay me" (Gen 4:14b). This leads to the fourth subtheme, which is *death and rebirth*. As noted earlier, when people seek help in times of crisis, there is simultaneously a desire to be whole, to find healing, and a resistance to doing what it would take to gain health. That resistance, if it is given up, means a "dying" to familiar, albeit damaging, patterns and the potential of "rebirth" into new life. Employing the narrative of Jacob at the River Jabbok, Oglesby shows how resistant Jacob was to the possibility of new life, which comes anyway as he strives with God, receives a new name, and is reconciled with his long-estranged brother Esau (Gen 32:1–33:11).

From this story Oglesby derives three implications for pastoral care. First, despite whatever pain or distress a parishioner's presenting problem creates, there is a level at which the person "needs" the painful behavior and will feel terrified at the prospect of surrendering it. Second, the unhealthy strategies and painful behavior that the parishioner describes as occurring elsewhere in his or her life will also manifest within the context of his or her relationship with the counseling minister. Only as the parishioner and the minister deal with those patterns in the "here and now" will healing take place. Third, it is vital (all puns intended, given this subtheme) that the minister resist "buying into" the parishioner's story and abdicating her or his own perspective on reality and that she or he also resist the temptation to "take over the reins" of the parishioner's life and rob him or her of the opportunity to act helpfully on his or her own behalf. In Oglesby's terms, the minister must be willing to say "Here I am": to tell the truth about where the parishioner is and then offer authentic confrontation, clarification, and support. If the minister chooses to accept this task, however, the risk is high. For both parishioner and minister, there is the potential for death and rebirth in a pastoral care event.

This acknowledgment of risk is key to the fifth subtheme that Oglesby examines, which is *risk and redemption*. Those men and women who would offer pastoral care must be "wounded healers," in Henri Nouwen's phrase—people who know their own vulnerabilities and are willing to risk their safety in order to serve others. Three threats to a minister's safety are identified by Oglesby: (1) the myth that people will always be glad to receive pastoral assistance and that success is inevitable; (2) the danger of depleting or eroding the self because limits are not set, the minister cannot clearly assess his or her strengths and liabilities, or the minister is caught in the parishioner's pathology; and (3) forgetting to seek consultation and support from one's peers. Knowing the risks, Oglesby contends, means that a minister can more capably enter into times of crisis and offer the counsel "There you are; here I am; I love you" with her or his whole self and with the hope of renewal and growth for all concerned.

From the preceding discussion, it is obvious that I affirm Oglesby's text as a valuable contribution to the field of pastoral care and counseling. In my own experience as a health-care chaplain, his insights and suggestions have been quite useful in ministering with a variety of people in critical situations because he continually invites me to be intentional with my pastoral goals and interventions.[9] Our focus in this essay, though, is to discern how Oglesby's work might inform pastoral care with a particular population—namely, APA women and men. Here is where the work of particularizing his insights is so necessary.

The five subthemes that Oglesby highlights have much to say to people who identify themselves within an APA sociocultural milieu, but I will lift up two particular points at this time that will help particularize his work. The first observation is that Oglesby offers us a gift in reminding us about the ambivalence that individuals may feel about receiving care. From an APA perspective, though, as we shall see in the next section, it will be important to recognize when ambivalence is rooted not only in an individual's psychodynamics but also in a familial and cultural context. The other nuance I would add to Oglesby's work concerns his assertions about conformity and rebellion. He notes that both conformity and rebellion are forms of concealment, and he equates "concealment" and "hiding" with sin. Working with APA parishioners and clients, though, requires that we be careful about what receives the label of "concealed." While the dynamics of conformity and rebellion certainly exist in many APA families, we will see in the next section that there is a distinction between the social roles that one must fulfill and one's own emotional life and inner dynamics. In those cases, it may be a premature pastoral diagnosis to assume that a particular APA individual is "hiding" without a more intensive assessment.

However, simply nuancing these subthemes is not quite enough. Certainly we have discovered, though in a telegraphic way, that these five

---

[9] Critical reviews of Oglesby's book have been uniformly positive. The only major critique I could find came from Donald Capps, who observed that the book tends "to *under*emphasize the fact that the Bible consists of different literary forms that influence the way its themes are represented.... What are the implications of this inseparability of forms and themes for a Biblical understanding of the counseling process? Answers to this question would strengthen Oglesby's already excellent proposal" (1981:220–21, emphasis original).

subthemes have applicability to an APA context. Yet at this juncture it is as important—if not more so—to learn if there are other subthemes that might illuminate the psychological and spiritual dynamics faced by APA men and women. Now that we have a sense of Oglesby's line of thought, we can move into our second stream of thought by exploring three biblical subthemes that might be utilized helpfully with APA parishioners needing pastoral care.

II

Given my summary in the previous section, a reader might assume that Oglesby believes that he has been definitive in his survey. Actually, quite the contrary is true. To his great credit, Oglesby takes pains to underscore that he has not written a comprehensive catalog of biblical subthemes. From the beginning he acknowledges that his list is not exhaustive (1980:37), and in his epilogue he identifies other themes, such as the significance of naming and being named, dependence and independence, and individuality and community, that could easily have been explored if not for utilitarian considerations (222–23). Indeed, he invites others to embark on that exploration in dialogue with him—a dialogue that, unfortunately, he is no longer alive to sustain.

Yet Oglesby's spirit of inquiry and conversation survives in his book, and it is in that spirit that we now venture into an all-too-brief examination of the very subthemes he mentions in the epilogue of *Biblical Themes for Pastoral Care*. I find it intriguing that the three themes he would note are three that have special resonance for APA groups. Hence we will start with those three, and what we will find, I believe, is that attending to these other subthemes will concretize some of the insights about APA care recipients that we inferred from the five subthemes lifted up in Oglesby's text. Thus we will attempt an expansion or advancement of the book, to make it even more relevant for our purposes.

The first subtheme that Oglesby suggests in his epilogue is that of *naming and being named*. In his book, Oglesby mentions a number of individuals in the Hebrew Bible who receive new names. Abram ("exalted father") becomes Abraham ("father of a multitude," Gen 17:5), Sarai becomes Sarah ("princess," Gen 17:15), and Jacob ("he takes by the heel" or "he supplants") becomes Israel ("he strives with God," Gen 32:28), for example. What Oglesby notices is that the Hebraic perspective attributes a name with a power, the power of one's self, and so when people receive new names, those mark a new relationship with God and consequently with others.[10]

---

[10] While this pattern generally holds, there are several exceptions in the Hebrew Bible that involve grief. While dying in childbirth, for example, Rachel names her last son Ben-oni, or "son

Generations of Jewish men and women, for instance, have recited at the harvest festival, "A wandering Aramean was my father" (Deut 26:5–9), thus identifying themselves with Jacob and his descendants—and their God of deliverance—by voicing that tribal name. Names convey identity, and identity entails a sense of personal power ... or powerlessness. Our names can carry multivalent connotations from our personal stories, which can be experienced as blessing (one may be named for a beloved ancestor or an admired historical figure) or as curse (one may carry the name of an abusive or neglecting parent or feel the burden of "living up to" one's name). How we hear and wear our own names helps to shape who we are.

This point is where I see a clear parallel to the life experience of APA populations in the United States. As with the ancient Israelites, the name one bears can have great significance, not just for oneself but for one's family and racial group. In the Japanese language, it is no accident that the common words for "name," *seimei* and *namae*, both contain the *kan'ji* character *mei*, which denotes both "name" and "reputation." The name one holds indicates one's relationship with others, especially one's family, and an individual must act so as to bring *sonkei* (respect and honor) rather than *haji* (shame) upon one's family and one's name (cf. Lebra).

From a pastoral care perspective, this reminds us that it is important to understand the APA individual seeking care as a participant within his or her familial and cultural context. Part of that context, however, is a long history of being the recipients of institutionalized racial discrimination within this country (Takaki) and living with a societal structure wherein "[w]e utilize race to provide clues about *who* a person is.... We expect people to act out their apparent racial identities; indeed we become disoriented when they do not" (Omi and Winant: 59, emphasis original). Often this situation engenders ambivalence about one's ethnic, cultural, and racial identity, a crisis that Erik Erikson aptly called "identity vs. role confusion" (1968).[11] It can affect how others view and interact with APA people. This can be seen

---

of my sorrow," but Jacob renames the boy Benjamin, or "son of the right hand" (Gen 35:18), and Naomi ("pleasant") calls herself Mara ("bitter") after she returns from Moab following the deaths of her husband and two sons (Ruth 1:20–21), although other characters in the story seem to ignore her new self-appellation.

11 Erikson's writings demonstrate that the term "identity" bears four connotations. First, it is a conscious sense of being a unique and separate individual; second, it indicates a feeling of "inner sameness and continuity" over time; third, it is the wholeness achieved through the synthesizing functions of the ego; and fourth, it is a sense of accord or solidarity with the self-definition and ideals of a group that in turn affirms the person's own identity. Within the context of this essay, I concentrate mainly on Erikson's fourth connotation but, as readers shall soon see, I implicitly question the validity of the first connotation if it is construed to imply a separative self.

when members of non-APA groups construct cultural tropes about what it means to be "Asian" (cf. Ong), and it can be noticed when Japanese people distrust and ridicule Japanese Americans because of the latter's ambiguous identity (Lebra: 25)—they may claim to be Japanese, but their behaviors are "Americanized" and even their *Nihon'go* (language) is antiquated. Such is ambivalence about *being named*. Yet this ambivalence also can be internalized toward oneself, as evidenced by the intrapsychic struggle of many children of interracial Japanese American marriages. Are they *hapa* (a Hawai'ian word meaning "half") because they do not belong fully in either of their parents' cultural frames, or are they really "double" because they have access to two rich cultural traditions?[12] This illustrates an ambivalence about *naming* oneself. The challenge for pastoral caregivers along this subtheme lies in three questions. How can I as a minister hear the crisis of meaning that arises in an APA person seeking spiritual care when she or he feels conflicted about being identified (being named) as Asian American or about identifying herself or himself as Asian American (naming)? In Oglesby's terms, this is the question of indicating "There you are." How can I encourage and challenge APA parishioners and clients to claim the richness of their ethnic and racial heritage (naming)[13] and to actively define how others view them (resisting the damaging side of being named), so that they can move toward the developmental virtue or ego strength Erikson calls fidelity? This is the question of saying "Here I am." And how can I honor the ambivalence I hear in these people's voices and souls? This is the question of embodying "I love you." The *how* lies within me—my own way of being a person and being a minister. Yet these questions must be asked by every spiritual caregiver who would work with APA populations.

Related to this theme of naming and being named, at least in an APA context, is the tension between dependence and independence. Oglesby perceives this tension as indicative of the struggle for maturity and inner

---

12 This sentence poses a loaded question, I admit. While I do use the term *hapa* to describe myself (I am the child of a Caucasian American father and a Japanese "war bride" who became a naturalized U.S. citizen), I definitely believe that I did not receive "half" of the culture of either of my parents. In this sense I am indeed "double," which carries its own blessing (I benefit because I have multiple cultures with which I can connect) and burden (I can be conflicted in my behavior and thinking because I am negotiating multiple cultural values). This awareness in myself is an awareness of the ambivalence I am describing above. We also should note that how an APA individual labels cultural elements as either "Asian" or "American" conveys a great deal about the meaning-making and identity-making processes that he or she employs (see Yanagisako).

13 Thus I am encouraging pastoral caregivers to nurture a function that religion has frequently served in immigrant communities: to oppose and counter the experience of discrimination and "wholesale assimilation into American life" by reinforcing generational and racial-ethnic ties through a conscious exercise of religious identity (cf. Yoo: 38ff.).

authority and locates this struggle in the early object relations of a child with his or her parents. Based on the way Oglesby frames this subtheme, the applicable Eriksonian developmental crisis would involve autonomy versus shame and doubt, and the appropriate ego strength to be cultivated would be will.

From an APA perspective, however, positing a tension between *dependence and independence,* as if one side must prevail, represents a false dichotomy. For that matter, Erikson's emphasis on autonomy and the development of will as an ego strength may also not fit an APA cultural worldview. Both dependence—stereotyped as an "Asian" way of being—and independence—often characterized as a "Western" trait—are polarities, extreme positions that cannot be held too rigidly if one desires health and wholeness. The goal may be neither independence and autonomy nor dependence and passivity, but rather "*interdependence* in social responsibility and solidarity with significant others" (Augsburger: 88, emphasis added). Framed in this manner, the Eriksonian developmental crisis that seems predominant is not autonomy versus shame and doubt, but instead that of intimacy versus isolation, in which we become more fully ourselves by discovering that "*We* are what [and who] we love" (Erikson, 1968:138, emphasis original; cf. Kasulis).

This subtheme, which I would call *the myth of independence or dependence and the reality of interdependence,* is present from the Genesis creation narrative throughout the biblical texts. One way of interpreting Adam's disobedience, for instance, is that he broke the connections he enjoyed with God, the earth, and his fellow creatures by ignoring the relativity of his autonomy, and the result of this lapse is that "cursed is the ground because of you; in toil you shall eat of it all the days of your life; thorns and thistles it shall bring forth to you" (Gen 3:17–18 RSV). The consequences of Adam's choice affect all creation, so much so that the apostle Paul will say that it is groaning for God's deliverance (Rom 8:22). Calling upon another of Oglesby's favorite examples, Jacob, allows us to see that Jacob's intent in his schemes against Esau and Laban was to become independent of them at their expense—in other words, to use his dependence upon them to gain the "upper" independent hand against them. As he grows older, Jacob learns that this independence is an illusion. Ultimately he must acknowledge an uneasy interdependent truce with Laban (Gen 31:43–54) and seek reconciliation with Esau (Gen 33:1–11). Indeed, in his old age Jacob must accept that he and his clan cannot grow enough food for themselves, so he must buy food from the Egyptian government, and he learns that he cannot control the destiny of his beloved sons Joseph and Benjamin, much as he desires to do so. In the end, it is propitious that he could not control everything and be self-reliant, for ultimately it is when Jacob and his sons are compelled to acknowledge their interdependence that they are reunited with Joseph, who himself has had to learn this lesson: "I am your brother, Joseph, whom you sold into Egypt. And now do not be distressed, or angry with yourselves, because you sold me here; for God sent me before you to preserve life" (Gen 45:4–5 RSV).

In terms of providing pastoral care to APA men and women, this subtheme both reinforces the implication we discussed above for naming and being named—that is, the need to be aware of people's sociocultural and familial contexts—but also assists caregivers in their goals and stance. It means, on a macro level, that ministers and other pastoral caregivers in the United States need to claim our prophetic voices and call our more individualistic brothers and sisters toward an inclusive and interdependent vision of our selves and our communities. On a micro level, it entails helping people negotiate between their individual autonomy and their links with the larger community. With a Japanese American parishioner, for example, the minister or pastoral caregiver should seek to help that person strike a balance between her or his inner emotional life and her or his social roles so that both can be honored (and not confused); this balance is what psychiatrist Takeo Doi describes as living with *tatemae* and *honne* (cf. Leslie). Pastoral care interventions can be structured so that individuals are given the room to make their own choices, as well as the space to examine and experience the consequences of their decisions. Together these "rooms" form two of the statements Oglesby insists are vital to pastoral care: "There you are" and "Here I am." Finally, though, the statement that must be expressed and embodied in pastoral care, according to Oglesby, is "I love you." In this circumstance, however, I believe that affirmation requires a slight revision. Rather than singling out the individual caregiver, it is crucial to redirect the focus toward "You are loved" or "We love you," so that the APA recipient of care can regain her or his basic orientation, which places "a primary emphasis on preserving and enhancing intimacy ... [in which] we are most human when we form bonds of belonging with nature, with each other, with our nation [and with ultimate reality, I would add].... We are most ourselves not when we know the world, but when we feel at home in it" (Kasulis: 439, 447).

Framing the discussion of the second subtheme in this light, however, involves and implies the third subtheme that Oglesby suggests, which is *individuality and community*. For Oglesby, this subtheme touches on the issues of space and distance, and it highlights the need for corporate as well as individual involvement. We have just dealt with this insight above, but from a biblical perspective the aspect that demands attention here is how God often relates with *individuals* as members of a *people*. An example of this tendency, although a harsh one, comes from the Deuteronomic code: "I the LORD your God am a jealous God, visiting the iniquity of the fathers upon the children to the third and fourth generation of those who hate me, but showing steadfast love to thousands of those who love me and keep my commandments" (5:9–10 RSV). In the Pentateuch, God is as good as this word: while Korah and his entire family are destroyed in an earthquake as punishment for his rebellion against Moses (Num 16:20–35), the faithfulness of one person, Abraham, predisposes God to make a covenant with all of Abraham's descendants forever (Gen 17:1–9). This focus on future generations highlights what I believe is a vital developmental issue for many APA persons: what Erikson has called the tension between generativity and stagnation. The fundamental challenge here is to realize an excess of procreativity, productivity, and creativity over a pervading mood of personal inertia or self-absorption.[14] Such a realization or resolution results in the blossoming of the ego strength of care, defined as "the widening concern for what has been generated by love, necessity, or accident; it overcomes the ambivalence adhering to irreversible obligation" (Erikson, 1964:131).

There are two different foci for this developmental crisis or tension, at least when one considers members of Japanese American communities. The first is a phenomenon that has been very evident because Japanese Americans have often defined themselves by generational categories (*Issei* for first generation, *Nisei* for second generation, *Sansei* for third generation, *Yonsei* for fourth generation). Simply put, it is a sense of pessimism about the persistence of the cultural community. In my ethnographic fieldwork as well as in more everyday interactions with Japanese Americans, particularly Nisei elders, I have heard a number of people mention their concern that succeeding generations will not preserve the traditions and heritage of the community. While many subsequently qualify their statements by expressing their confidence in their own children or grandchildren, the fact that it is mentioned merits our pastoral scrutiny as a manifestation of existential anxiety or "generativity chill" (cf. Snarey: 23). The caregiver who hears a statement along these lines could listen for further notes of fatalism and for

---

[14] Working from a Geertzian perspective, Alexander et al. criticize Erikson for being too focused on biological procreation and argue that his concept of generativity is embedded in the American cultural value of individualism—that is, people invest in others because they unconsciously are seeking to create an enduring, continuous self that transcends death, so generativity is a culturally sanctioned form of self-absorption. While I concur with both these points, I do not believe that either is the major theme that Alexander et al. asserts it to be. Erikson's definition expanded over the years to include other dimensions of generativity, and—as I have seen in my own interview-based research with elderly Japanese Americans—generativity from an individualist American cultural perspective lives in a negotiated, creative tension with a more group-oriented Japanese understanding of the self. (Significantly, Alexander et al. cite the example of a ninety-three-year-old woman who sponsored two Japanese American women so that they could leave the internment camps during World War II and find work.) Simply put, because generativity presumes a context in which the self finds meaning in relating with and helping others, I find the term useful for the analysis I am attempting here.

actions that demonstrate an abdication of care or investment in younger generations. At that juncture, the care recipient would need encouragement and challenge to reinvest and help create a milieu in which future generations can contribute to the maintenance of the larger community.[15]

The second, which applies more generally to Asian Americans, involves a reluctance to seek mental-health treatment because of the stigma that it carries for the family of the "identified patient," that is, the one seeking and/or needing help (Fujii et al.; Sue and Morishima). Here the pastoral caregiver needs to shift the generative focus toward a family-systems perspective in order to address the ambivalence that people feel toward receiving assistance (which Oglesby noted; see above). While an Asian American family may desire their member's well-being, it also may be swift to associate a member's mental illness with stigma and shame for the family, and it also may be reluctant to examine how it as a system must undergo change in order for the "sick" family member to recover (cf. Friedman). A sensitive pastoral caregiver must confront this systemic tendency toward ambivalent homeostasis and urge the participating family members to activate their generative impulses toward the person who is seeking help by cooperating with the plan of care or counseling. The keys to ensuring that this strategy succeeds lie in the caregiver's ascribed status (the initial respect that the family feels toward the caregiver), the caregiver's ability to normalize the stress, a strong assurance of confidentiality, and the minister's competence in "gift giving"—that is, providing a direct benefit to the patient and her or his family almost immediately (Sue and Zane; Tempo and Saito). From a biblical perspective, this form of pastoral caregiving in an APA context rebuts the Deuteronomic warning. While one person's error (or sin) would be borne by successive generations, one APA generation's caring could mean the difference in the healing trajectory of an individual in that family—if the pastoral caregiver can gain the trust and sustain the confidence of the involved parties.

From this cursory elaboration, it should be evident that there is rich potential in Oglesby's subthemes for ministers and other pastoral caregivers who serve APA groups. Understanding and exploring these threads can yield more effective and specific spiritual care for APA parishioners and clients. However, in considering these three "incidental" subthemes, a fourth subtheme emerges for our recognition. While unmentioned by Oglesby, this subtheme, I will contend, has great significance for how the Bible is read and utilized for pastoral care in Asian America.

---

[15] For more attention to this topic, readers should consult Fugita and O'Brien.

III

In emphasizing Oglesby's three evoked subthemes, I believe that there is still one major subtheme that has thus far eluded our attention. This is the tension—often violent in the biblical narratives as well as contemporary historical experience—between *oppression and liberation*. The paradigmatic biblical example of this subtheme is, of course, the Exodus narrative of God's deliverance of the Hebrews from Egyptian slavery under the leadership of Moses, Aaron, and Miriam. For many people this event is paired with the later Israelite experience of Babylonian exile and the hope, expressed by such prophetic gestures as Jeremiah's purchase of the field at Anathoth (ch. 32), that God's protective love will endure and that there will be restoration.

The subtheme of oppression and liberation is not an unfamiliar motif within the history of the United States. For example, among African American men and women from antebellum days through the modern civil-rights movement into the present, the imagery of the Exodus event has served both as inspiration and challenge for the recognition of basic human rights and dignity. It has been a powerful metaphor that has permeated the larger U.S. culture as well. Today American Christians of many different races can be heard singing the gospel song, "Go Down, Moses," with an appreciation of the subversive abolitionist hope at the heart of its melody.

As we indicated above, many APA individuals can identify with this subtheme[16] and with its historical connection because of their own experience of discrimination and oppression within American society. Among Japanese Americans, however, it holds particular resonance because of the internment of approximately 120,000 Issei and Nisei by the War Relocation Authority and the U.S. Department of Justice, under the executive order of President Franklin D. Roosevelt, during World War II. Enduring the often harsh conditions of the camps, they survived, resisted the infringement of their constitutional rights,[17] proved their loyalty to the United States

---

[16] One cursory example of this identification would be the title of Mike Masaru Masaoka's autobiography, *They Call Me Moses Masaoka*. Masaoka was national secretary of the Japanese American Citizens League from 1941 through 1943 and then served in combat with the U.S. Army through the end of World War II. He subsequently resumed his service with the JACL until 1972 and died in 1991. His role in the evacuation and internment—specifically, whether his support of U.S. governmental policies helped or hurt the Japanese American community—makes him a controversial figure even now. There has been a heated public argument, for instance, about the placement of a statement by Masaoka on the National Japanese American Memorial, which opened in late 2000 in Washington, D.C. Regardless of personal opinion about the merits or flaws of Masaoka's character and choices, however, I find the reference to Moses quite telling.

[17] There were four major challenges to the constitutionality of the internment that were heard by the U.S. Supreme Court during World War II. Gordon Kiyoshi Hirabayashi was

(notably through the valor of the U.S. Army's all-Nisei 442nd Regimental Combat Team), and—in a feat of grassroots support and political power—eventually won an official apology and reparations from the United States government in 1988.[18] Theirs is a story of oppression and liberation.

Based on my comments thus far, it should be no surprise that I consider the primary psychological dynamic within this subtheme to involve what Erikson described as the tension between basic trust and mistrust. Hope is "the enduring belief in the attainability of fervent wishes, in spite of the dark urges and rages which mark the beginning of existence" (Erikson, 1964:118). Phrased more formally, the capacity for hoping is a constellation of perceptive-cognitive and affective responses to stressors or deprivations in one's life in which one believes that the future is filled with possibilities, and believes further that those possibilities that one desires can be realized (cf. Capps, 1995; Lester). It entails an openness to experience that is implied by the *kan'ji* characters for the word "hope," or *kibo*, whose pictograms illustrate a hand arranging cloth while one looks into the distance, thus implying planning and acting in the present while expecting a future.[19] Phrased even more

---

convicted in 1942 for refusing to register for evacuation and for curfew violations; Fred Toyosaburo Korematsu was convicted in the same year for violating the military order that excluded persons of Japanese ancestry from designated areas; and Minoru Yasui was also convicted in 1942 for curfew violations. All three cases were appealed to the U.S. Supreme Court, which upheld the convictions. See *Hirabayashi v United States,* 320 U.S. 81 (1943); *Korematsu v United States,* 319 U.S. 432 (1943) and 323 U.S. 214 (1944); and *Yasui v United States,* 320 U.S. 115 (1943). Mitsuye Endo filed a habeas corpus petition to challenge the legality of her detention based solely on her race, and the Supreme Court unanimously found in her favor without addressing whether her constitutional rights had been infringed; see *Ex parte Mitsuye Endo,* 323 U.S. 283 (1944). The texts of these opinions are available on the World Wide Web at the URL http://www.findlaw.com/casecode/supreme.html. Korematsu's conviction was vacated in 1983 and Hirabayashi's convictions were vacated in 1986 and 1988 on the granting of writs of error *coram nobis* (literally, "error before us"), a legal process that can be invoked only after defendants have been convicted and released from custody and only to raise errors of fact that were knowingly withheld by prosecutors from judges and defense attorneys. Yasui's conviction was vacated in 1984, but he died in 1986 before his case could be fully resolved. These four people are viewed as civil-rights champions within the Japanese American community; indeed, I have heard references to Endo as "our Rosa Parks."

18 The list of writings that address the internment experience is lengthy, attesting forcefully to the Japanese Americans' desire that this event not be forgotten. For an accessible illustrated description of life within the camps, see Okubo; and for information about the camps from a historical and archaeological perspective, see Burton et al. To understand the impact and consequences of the internment, see the thorough Report of the U.S. Commission on Wartime Relocation and Internment of Civilians. For an incisive analysis of the Japanese Americans' campaign for redress and how it embodies an ethic of repentance and forgiveness as understood in the Christian tradition, see Shriver.

19 It is also implied by the linguistic structure of spoken Japanese, in which there is no clear distinction between the active present and future tenses of verbs. Inflection and context determine the chronological frame of a statement more than conjugation.

conceptually, the ability to hope involves what philosopher Ernst Bloch calls an "anticipatory consciousness" at the core of human selfhood that is grounded in a trust that grows from one's childhood experiences of caring for others. Building upon these assertions, I would suggest that the capacity to hope is vital to the survival of an oppressed people and a major factor in their endurance of trauma and in their search for liberation.

But does this hold true in an APA context, and what ramifications does it have for pastoral care for these populations? To discern some answers to these questions, we will turn to the written testimonies of fifty-two Japanese American Christian men and women,[20] collected by the Japanese-American Internment Project in an anthology entitled *Triumphs of Faith* (Okada). I have selected this text as a resource for our inquiry for two reasons. First, it provides us with convenient access to a sizeable group of APA Christians who have given implicit permission for this analysis by publishing their accounts.[21] The group is not a representative sample: Many of the participants were acquaintances of the project director, and so it is a convenience sample, with clergymen making up 31 percent of the total authorship and over 50 percent of the male representation. However, it is almost evenly balanced between men and women, and the book makes no pretense to be a quantitative study—it is more like a collection of transcribed oral histories. Second, these contributors' reminiscences of the camps as well as beyond the internment experience were solicited and compiled because their Christian faith was invaluable in sustaining their lives. It seems reasonable to infer that their use of biblical texts will assist us in learning what motifs (or, to use Oglesby's language, subthemes) are important for them. What they emphasize in their writings will, I contend, help validate or correct the emphases that Oglesby has made and upon which we have expanded.

Obviously, I do not have the space here to do justice to the richness contained in Okada's anthology. What I would like to do, however, is to briefly note what seems to recur in the testimonies that are included. Based on my count, the most frequently cited biblical books are Isaiah (6:1; 9:6; 41:10; 43:2; 55:9), Romans (5:3–5, 20; 6:1–2; 8:28), the Psalms (23:5; 90:1–9; 121:1–2; 139:1–6), and variations of the so-called "golden rule" of the Gospels

---

[20] One of the contributors was not Japanese American by birth, but had married a Nisei Christian minister.

[21] This is a premise I have accepted in other instances of Japanese Americans' written testimonies (see Clark). I am aware of the danger of "reading" my own values and assumptions into these texts, but even with that possibility I still believe it is a valid use of the material presented in anthologies such as Okada's. I also feel that it is a way in which I can take seriously and honor what these people have endured and are relating in their stories.

(Matt 22:35–40; Luke 6:27–31), with the passages mainly serving as texts of assurance about God's providence and the importance of faith. When biblical figures are mentioned, they tend to be from the Pentateuch: Abraham (though in the context of Heb 11:8–12, 17–19 rather than the Genesis narrative), Joseph, and Moses. However, also specifically cited are the prophet Jonah and Jesus of Nazareth, though the latter is addressed primarily in terms of the contemporary author's conversion and personal relationship with the risen Christ rather than from the Gospel accounts.

In my reading of the anthology, furthermore, I was struck by three themes that kept appearing in the various authors' testimonies and that resonate with the expanded version of Oglesby's paradigm we have constructed here. The first theme involves exile, diaspora, and deliverance, which correlates to the subtheme of oppression and liberation I mentioned above. Exile is explicitly mentioned by the Rev. George Aki, a United Church of Christ minister who recalls being ordained while confined in the Tanforan Assembly Center just south of San Francisco:

> In every way, this event was the turning point of my life, for it brought into focus what God wanted me to do with my life. I also learned the following: that Christians would gather amid danger for Christ and His church, that they would never cease to pursue the noble adventure of faith, and that though dreams may be shattered, God will see to it that they are built anew. *I learned that the church may go into exile, but it would never die.* (Okada: 2, emphasis added)

Clearly Aki sees a parallel between the historical experience of the ancient Hebrews being led to Babylon and the internment camps, which Hazel Morikawa echoes as she describes the postinternment years of herself and her husband Jitsuo, an American Baptist minister who is well-known among Japanese American Christians even today:

> In retrospect, Jitsuo and I saw our lives as being caught in an explosive diaspora. We were being carried in the belly of a whale like Jonah and spewed out onto the shores of Chicago, many miles from the place we once called home. We may never have chosen this course if left on our own, but we were landed first in Chicago, then in New York, Pennsylvania, and finally Michigan. Out of this deliverance, we can say that the ways of men [*sic*] cannot contain God's love and peace. (Okada: 80)

And, in his foreword to the anthology, United Methodist bishop Roy Sano connects this theme to the experience of the early Christian church: "If the blood of the martyrs is the seed of the church, hardship and humiliation made the Risen Christ come alive for thousands of Japanese Americans in the concentration camps" (in Okada: viii). So for these Japanese Americans, the biblical frame of exile/diaspora and deliverance has become a guiding metaphor for interpreting—and coping with—the trauma of the internment and its aftermath.

How these people survived can be linked to the second theme, a major theological assertion that they make repeatedly in this text. It ties explicitly into Oglesby's subtheme of fear and faith. It is the good news of God—"do not be afraid." On Pearl Harbor Day, Marian Maruko Kadomatsu recalls, she asked herself if God would protect her and her family from their enemies (whether she means the Japanese military or American racists, she is unclear), and the answer came in remembering a passage from Isaiah: "*Do not fear, for I am with you;* do not be dismayed, for I am your God; I will strengthen you and help you; I will uphold you with my righteous right hand" (41:10, in Okada: 48, emphasis added). The Rev. Ren Kimura heard this same declaration in the response of his parents to frequent searches and harassment by police and federal agents: "Do not fear," they would say, "for God is with us. He [sic] will guide us wherever and whatsoever. Keep hoping and praying" (Okada: 64). This admonition to not be afraid, as Oglesby notes, allowed Ms. Kadomatsu and Rev. Kimura to be flexible and open to possibilities in the midst of trying circumstances. In other words, it allowed them to have faith.

The response of faith in the internment years leads to the third theme, another theological declaration that keeps emerging in the Okada anthology, which involves the connection between endurance and hope. The anthology project's director, the Rev. Paul M. Nagano, links these two together by citing the apostles Paul and James and then contending that the internment was a test of faith:

> Someone has written, "Nothing significant would ever be accomplished without the aid of anxiety." Was this not what the Apostle Paul meant when he wrote, "We also boast of our troubles, because we know that *trouble produces endurance, endurance brings God's approval, and His [sic] approval creates hope.* This hope does not disappoint us, for God has poured out His [sic] love into our hearts by means of the Holy Spirit, who is God's gift to us" (Romans 5:3–5). In addition, James said, "Consider yourselves fortunate when all kinds of trials come your way, for you know that when your faith succeeds in facing such trials, the result is the ability to endure ... so that you may be perfect and complete, lacking nothing" (James 1:2–4). Here was a real test of faith. (Okada: 86–87, emphasis added)

Nagano understands that the capacity for hope is nourished by endurance. Such endurance is highly praised in Japanese culture (*gaman*), but for these Christians it is not paired with the fatalism that is often expressed in the Japanese phrase *Shikata ga nai*, "It cannot be helped." Rather, it is grounded in a trust in divine providence, as William Hohri poetically notes in his reminiscence:

On April 4, 1942, the remainder of our family went by bus under armed guard to the Manzanar War Relocation Center. The next day was Easter, which we celebrated outdoors in the early morning at the foot of the mighty Sierra Nevada and its inspiring Mount Williamson. At the same time, the disorder and desolation of concentration-camp existence were beginning to engulf us. We were living a parable whose meaning it would take the rest of my life to understand: the reign of God is here, within us, in our midst, for us to enact in our own lives and history, just as Mount Williamson stood in its majesty alongside our disorder and desolation. (Okada: 28)

This expression of faith in God's care, even despite much evidence to the contrary, carries through even beyond the internment years to more present-day crises, as we can hear in the testimony of Rhoda Iyoya, who comments on her son's suicide nearly twenty years ago:

When we live through a crisis, we do not survive intact. We experienced a death of part of ourselves in the death of Bodie. *But we were not destroyed. We were in fact made strong.* Those who prayed for me, cared for me, forgave and nurtured me in Christ's name helped me grow through suffering to *a vital and living faith that gives my life trust, meaning, and hope.* I have been enabled to become a more open channel for the healing love of God to flow through into the hurting and brokenness that are all around me. I have been able to learn how to laugh at myself and with others, to celebrate with aliveness and joy the gift of life, with all its mystery and wonder, pain and joy. (Okada: 45, emphasis added)

Returning to our Oglesby-informed perspective, Mrs. Iyoya's stance could be seen as her *freely chosen* response to the *divine initiative*, a response that calls her to *faith over fear* and *beyond hiding* toward the openness of being compassionate toward others. The *death* has been painfully real, as she has had to grieve the premature and self-inflicted death of her son; but she also has experienced a *rebirth* of her faith, facilitated through the care of her *community*. By including this story within her testimony about the internment, she is making the linkage between her experience of *oppression and liberation* in that time—in which, I would maintain, she had to endure and hope—and the endurance and hope she is living in the present. Thus we witness the interlacing of multiple subthemes in her life experience, all of which point to the quadratic emphasis of God, humans, suffering, and grace that Oglesby maintains is the central theme of the Bible.

Hence, while I do not offer conclusive proof of the validity of Oglesby's insights on APA pastoral care situations, my reading of these Japanese American Christians' stories leads me to believe that his text, with additional contextualizing, can be of great help to ministers and other pastoral caregivers working with APA populations. Given this admittedly anecdotal evidence, the biblical themes (or subthemes) that he highlights, with the extensions I suggest here, do seem to be present in the life experiences of APA men and women. As with any pastoral care text, the proof of its value lies in its application, specifically in the intervention strategies that it suggests. Yet I am convinced that, since it seems "on target" with its understanding of the issues affecting these groups, this enhanced version of Oglesby's model will demonstrate its utility in promoting the health and wholeness of APA people who receive pastoral care. However, we must await another anniversary to answer this question definitively. Like Oglesby himself, I will look forward to that continued dialogue.

WORKS CONSULTED

Alexander, Baine B., Robert L. Rubinstein, Marcene Goodman, and Mark Luborsky
    1991   "Generativity in Cultural Context: The Self, Death and Immortality As Experienced by Older American Women." *Ageing and Society* 11:417–42.

Augsburger, David W.
    1986   *Pastoral Counseling across Cultures.* Philadelphia: Westminster.

Beek, Aart M. van
    1996   *Cross-Cultural Counseling.* Minneapolis: Augsburg Fortress.

Brock, Rita Nakashima
    1988   *Journeys by Heart: A Christology of Erotic Power.* New York: Crossroad.

Burton, Jeffery F., Mary M. Farrell, Florence B. Lord, and Richard W. Lord
    1999   *Confinement and Ethnicity: An Overview of World War II Japanese American Relocation Sites.* Tucson: Western Archeological and Conservation Center, National Park Service, U.S. Department of the Interior.

Capps, Donald
    1981   "Review of *Biblical Themes for Pastoral Care* by William B. Oglesby, Jr." *Pastoral Psychology* 29:219–21.

    1995   *Agents of Hope: A Pastoral Psychology.* Minneapolis: Augsburg Fortress.

Clark, Peter Yuichi
    1998   "Faith and Identity in Nisei Self-Narratives." *Princeton Seminary Bulletin* 19:279–93.

Doi, L. Takeo
    1985   *The Anatomy of Self: The Individual versus Society.* Trans. Mark A. Harbison. Tokyo and New York: Kodansha.

Erikson, Erik H.
    1964   *Insight and Responsibility: Lectures on the Ethical Implications of Psychoanalytic Insight.* New York: Norton.

1968   *Identity: Youth and Crisis.* New York: Norton.

Friedman, Edwin H.
1985   *Generation to Generation: Family Process in Church and Synagogue.* New York: Guilford.

Fugita, Stephen S., and David J. O'Brien
1991   *Japanese American Ethnicity: The Persistence of Community.* Seattle: University of Washington Press.

Fujii, June S., Susan N. Fukushima, and Joe Yamamoto
1993   "Psychiatric Care of Japanese Americans." Pp. 305–45 in *Culture, Ethnicity, and Mental Illness.* Ed. Albert C. Gaw. Washington, D.C.: American Psychiatric Publishing.

Kasulis, Thomas P.
1990   "Intimacy: A General Orientation in Japanese Religious Values." *Philosophy East and West* 40:433–49.

Lebra, Takie Sugiyama
1976   *Japanese Patterns of Behavior.* Honolulu: University of Hawai'i Press.

Leslie, Robert C.
1979   *Counseling across Cultures.* New York: American Baptist Churches (USA) Educational Ministries.

Lester, Andrew D.
1995   *Hope in Pastoral Care and Counseling.* Louisville: Westminster/John Knox.

Masaoka, Mike Masaru, with William (Bill) Hosokawa
1987   *They Call Me Moses Masaoka: An American Saga.* New York: Morrow.

Nouwen, Henri J. M.
1972   *The Wounded Healer: Ministry in Contemporary Society.* Garden City, N.Y.: Doubleday.

Oglesby, William B., Jr.
1973   "Pastoral Care and Counseling in Biblical Perspective." *Interpretation* 27:307–26.

1979   "Implications of Anthropology for Pastoral Care and Counseling." *Interpretation* 33:157–71.

1980   *Biblical Themes for Pastoral Care.* Nashville: Abingdon.

Okada, Victor N., ed.
1998   *Triumphs of Faith: Stories of Japanese-American Christians during World War II.* Los Angeles: Japanese-American Internment Project.

Okubo, Miné
1946   *Citizen 13660.* New York: Columbia University Press.

Omi, Michael, and Howard Winant
    1994   *Racial Formation in the United States: From the 1960s to the 1990s.* 2d ed. New York and London: Routledge.

Ong, Paul M., ed.
    2000   *The State of Asian Pacific America: Transforming Race Relations: A Public Policy Report.* Los Angeles: LEAP Asian Pacific American Public Policy Institute and UCLA Asian American Studies Center.

Shriver, Donald W., Jr.
    1995   *An Ethic for Enemies: Forgiveness in Politics.* New York: Oxford University Press.

Snarey, John R.
    1993   *How Fathers Care for the Next Generation: A Four-Decade Study.* Cambridge: Harvard University Press.

Sue, Derald Wing, and David Sue
    1990   *Counseling the Culturally Different: Theory and Practice.* 2d ed. New York: Wiley.

Sue, Stanley, and James K. Morishima
    1982   *The Mental Health of Asian Americans.* San Francisco: Jossey-Bass.

Sue, Stanley, and Nolan Zane
    1987   "The Role of Culture and Cultural Techniques in Psychotherapy: A Critique and Reformulation." *American Psychologist* 42:37–45.

Takaki, Ronald
    1989   *Strangers from a Different Shore: A History of Asian Americans.* Boston: Little, Brown.

Tempo, Phyllis M., and Ann Saito
    1996   "Techniques of Working with Japanese American Families." Pp. 109–22 in *Ethnicity and the Dementias.* Ed. Gwen Yeo and Dolores Gallagher-Thompson. Washington, D.C.: Taylor & Francis.

U.S. Commission on Wartime Relocation and Internment of Civilians
    1997   *Personal Justice Denied.* Washington, D.C., and Seattle: The Civil Liberties Public Education Fund and the University of Washington Press. [Reprint of U.S. Government Printing Office publication originally issued in 1982–1983]

Yanagisako, Sylvia Junko
    1985   *Transforming the Past: Tradition and Kinship among Japanese Americans.* Stanford, Calif.: Stanford University Press.

Yoo, David K.
    2000   *Growing Up Nisei: Race, Generation, and Culture among Japanese Americans of California, 1924–49.* Urbana and Chicago: University of Illinois Press.

"THE BIBLE TELLS ME TO HATE MYSELF": THE CRISIS IN ASIAN AMERICAN SPIRITUAL LEADERSHIP

Leng Leroy Lim
Harvard Business School

ABSTRACT

In this short essay, I will share stories from my years ministering in Asian and Asian American contexts to explore when the Bible is useful in spiritual growth and when it is not. I will pose the metaquestion of why the Bible ends up having such a prominent place in the lives of believers, situating this logocentrism in the context of European history and East Asian cultural privileging of texts. I will then argue that experiencing God is central to the Christian life, and finally suggest what might then be other tools or means for experiencing this other than the Bible.

My first job after ordination was as the assistant chaplain at the University of California, Los Angeles. Because of the overwhelming number of Asians, UCLA was sometimes mischieviously referred to as the University of Caucasians Lost among Asians. I would set up my table next to the many other tables advertising other campus groups in the middle of Bruins Walk, an open stretch of pavement in the middle of campus. Shortly thereafter, a Korean American sophomore from the Campus Crusade table walked up to me and gazed quizzically at the sign I had posted: The Episcopal Church Welcomes You. This ubiquitous banner for the Episcopal Church had a tag line that I had inserted: *As You Are.* I meant to say that at the Episcopal Chaplaincy, our hospitality would be unconditional, since unconditional acceptance was a key feature of Jesus' ministry. Intrigued by my tag line, he asked if the Episcopal Church accepted everyone? I said we weren't always good with doing that, but yes, because Jesus did so.

"But what about the Pharisees? Jesus rejected them!" he countered.

"Okay, let's say he did. Who do you think the present-day equivalents of the Pharisees are?" I asked.

"They are the unbelievers," he replied.

I wondered who made up this group of modern-day Pharisaical unbelievers. His following questions gave me a clue.

"What does the Episcopal Church believe about abortion?" he asked.

I started to reply, talking about how in the Anglican tradition we assess truth claims based on reason, tradition, scripture, and experience. I then commenced on a brief exegesis of different biblical passages he had alluded to and tried to tie them to a feminist context. But before I could finish, he then asked me about divorce, and then he cut my exegetical response and asked about homosexuality. Finally he asked: "Do you believe that the Bible is the Word of God?"

I didn't know whether to look hurt, insulted, or incredulous! Somehow, my previous responses had given him an impression that I didn't believe in the Bible.

"No," I purposely said, "the Bible is *not* the Word of God." He looked startled. I had his attention.

I continued, "Jesus is the Word of God. In Jesus, we know who God is. The Bible is just the faith record of how the people of God experienced God's salvation."

"But to believe in Jesus, you must believe in the Bible," he argued.

I wondered to myself why folks don't just call themselves Holy Biblians instead of Christians.

I said, "We can keep on discussing what the Bible is or is not, but I am more interested in who Jesus is to you." Looking startled a second time, he replied, "*The Bible says* that Jesus is God's son, who came down to earth, died on the cross for our sins, rose from the dead, and then went back up to heaven to be with God the Father." Sounded more like a Gnostic heresy to me, but I kept that comment to myself.

"Okay, that's what the Bible says. But what do *you* say?"

For the next minute, he repeated what he had just said to me, word for word, sounding like a modern-day version of the Nicene Creed. Each time, I pressed him to share something about himself as a person, and each time he repeated his creed. Then, perhaps because he had had enough of me, he abruptly stood up and left.

This was not the last time I was to have such a conversation with a student at UCLA or UC Irvine, two schools that I served. The students, both white and Asians (of which there were many at these schools), almost invariably wanted to know if I believed the Bible to be the Word of God. That was always a starting question, prior to any other subsequent topical question. It is a real curiousity that no one has ever asked if I love Jesus. If indeed we even have the right to test someone's faith and devotion, why not ask other questions?

Despite all the talk among these evangelical/fundamentalist students about a personal God and personal Savior, they were themselves unable to speak about their own persons. What do you love? What does your heart say to you? Who is Jesus to you? These questions were invariably met with canned answers, and the mark of individuality that one expects of university-age students was strangely missing. I wondered what lay at the heart of their singular focus on the Bible.

Then one day a student came up to me and launched into one of those questions again. This student had recently been "saved," and he wanted to know what I thought about divorce. He had said to me, "when I find the woman of my life to love, we are going to live together forever." This was soon followed by questions about homosexuality and the Bible as God's Word. (Meanwhile, I couldn't help but wonder if there was some internal dam about to collapse around the pressure created by girlfriend, divorce, *homosexuality,* and God.) The questions about what I thought of these topics came in rapid fire. At the same time, there was no interest in what I had to say. What was he trying to figure out about me? I didn't know, and there wasn't time. How could I reach him through his juxtaposed questions?

I said, "Look, I won't try to convince you of anything. You seem to have your mind made up. But I do have one thing to say to you, as one brother in Christ to another. Ultimately, I don't think that God cares what you do or what you believe. God only cares that you come to love yourself as unconditionally as God loves you."

He paused, then said, "But I can't do that. *The Bible teaches me to hate myself.*"

I

In America today, though perhaps at other times as well, our private convictions and our public discourse both invoke the Bible. Someone points to a part of the Bible and says: the Bible teaches that slavery is okay. Abraham owned slaves. King David too. Hey, even St. Paul says that a slave ought to obey his master. Then someone else points to another part of the Bible and says: slavery is not okay. The story of the Exodus is about God setting slaves free.

Throughout the ages, any topic *de jour*—abortion, divorce, homosexuality, tax cuts, military service, etc. etc.—could be simultaneously supported or refuted by passages from the Bible. Those outside the Christian tradition see what we don't see: that there is a *person,* who teaches the Bible, regardless of what the Bible actually says. It's a bit like the Wizard of Oz: a little person behind the curtain pushing the buttons and creating the steam and fire that on the outside of the castle look incredibly threatening and powerful. Our equivalent of this Wizard in Christianity is sometimes the single pastor of an independent church on a street corner. Sometimes it is the collection of such individuals organized as a presbytery, council, committee, convention, or papacy. Whether Protestant, Catholic, or Orthodox, human agency is involved in every instance in which truth claims are derived from the Bible. Even if we were to stick literally to believing that the Bible is a divine oracle, a human agent is still involved in at least communicating the contents of that revelation.

So why is it that we don't notice the fingerprints of human teachers? In fact the opposite is true. Whenever the Bible is invoked, we completely don't see or hear or notice the very presence of the human person making those assertions. Why is it that the student at UCLA who told me that the Bible tells him to hate himself doesn't say: John Doe my youth ministers *tells* me that the Bible tells me to hate myself? Why are the various John Does who inhabit the left and right of the theological spectrum never identified in all of the controversies?

The Catholics are a bit more honest—though just a little bit—when they make claims about doctrine and truth. They say, the pope says so. They admit a human agent (though really, as the vicar of Christ, that makes him almost divine). Protestants cannot do that, because our tradition was a refutation of the papacy's role in dictating truth claims in favor of Martin Luther's cry of scripture only. Except that we never really did get rid of human agents in interpreting scripture. They just stopped wearing embroidered garments and instead left the Vatican for Main Street, whether in the U.S. or in any other country. They buckle into suit and ties and simply say: scripture says. Like a Las Vegas ventriloquist show, one doesn't notice the human mouth articulating such convictions.

What I have just described is fairly discernible in fundamentalist factions. But those of us who come from the liberal/rational tradition are not absolved of this sleight of hand. Indeed, those of us trained in the higher-critical methods are taught to investigate biblical texts objectively, using the rational/scientific methods of textual, historical, redactional, and literary criticisms. We do to the Bible what archaeologists do to soil and what historians do to events, by using the methodology of the Enlightenment: dispassionate and reasoned search for truth, without human bias. But the biblical scholar, as a human agent, *chooses* the passages he or she will explore. Show me any Ph.D. candidate in biblical studies, and I will show you a process in which that person's very choice of exegetical passage for research is bound in the politics and personalities (and oh yes, high drama) of academia. A committee of professors (and these days they are *not* just white males) with very real egos that are patiently hidden behind veils of rationality, sit to vet, critique, and approve biblical projects.

Those familiar with Friedrich Nietzsche and Michel Foucault will know the argument I am making, that hegemonic truth claims become exercises in power. However, I am not going to go in the poststructuralist direction of more teeth grinding. As a pastor, and as a practitioner in the action-oriented world of business, power is not a literary abstraction. Power is very real. Power does things, implements decisions, changes and transforms relationships. Power is more phenomenal (i.e., an expression of energy) than moral. The most important thing to note is that power resides in leaders.

What we must bring to the forefront of discussion about Asian Americans and the Bible (or for that matter any other topic) is the role played by the leader. And if today we are floundering in biblical exegesis, or community organizing, or meeting the pastoral needs of our people, the crisis is one of leadership. The question is not about finding out which passages of scripture are relevant to Asian Americans, but what kinds of leaders and leadership qualities are needed by Asian Americans.

II

At St. Mary's Episcopal Church in Los Angeles, a one-hundred-year-old Japanese parish whose members had been rounded up and interned in various desert camps during World War II, the parishioners often say to me: "Father John used to say to us that our internment was like what Israel experienced in the Exodus." Father John, now regrettably deceased, was the long-time rector of the parish. He and his father (also a priest) and the rest of the Japanese community in Los Angeles had been rounded up by the U.S. government and imprisoned in internment camps. They, and other American citizens of Japanese ancestry, were considered national security threats. Father John's use of the Exodus story was an application of a biblical story to a real-life situation. (That's what those of us who are pastors do. We find passages that are of *use* to our people.) Father John used the stories in the book of Exodus to help his people survive the internment. He said that just as the children of Israel had left Egypt to wander in the desert for forty years and God did not leave them, but instead stayed with them and fed them manna from heaven, so too was God now watching the Japanese people of St. Mary's. This application of a biblical story so impacted their ability to survive as a community that when they returned after the war, they had a stained-glass window made of Moses and the Exodus to remind them of their own Exodus.

What Father John did was great leadership. His funeral was one of the most moving outpourings of gratitude by the Japanese American community in the U.S. But may God forgive me for criticizing a deceased man, because his biblical exegesis and application were flawed. The Exodus story is about a people who had been enslaved in Egypt, and who were then led to freedom by Moses to enter a promised land. That they were delayed in the desert for forty years had to do with their disobedience. As such, the Exodus story is *not* analogous at all to the Japanese Americans for whom the U.S.A. was already *the* promised land and for whom their internment was a betrayal by their adoptive country. In fact, it is the story of the Babylonian exile of the Jewish people that most fits the Japanese American internment experience.

And that was what I tried to do, teach the story of the exile and of the return from exile. The return from exile, found in Ezra and Nehemiah, is particularly interesting because the returning Jews were asked to let go of their foreign spouses. The reconstituted nation, freed by the new Persian overlords, was particularly conscious of racial purity. I felt that the exile story was therefore a good departure point to talk about the completely different tack that Japanese Americans took after their return from exile: cultural assimilation and intermarriage to non-Asians. But my effort at drawing parallels with the Jewish exile didn't work that well. Folks were simply too unfamiliar with the exile story. (Perhaps if Charlton Heston had made a sequel to the *Ten Commandments,* things might be different.) One simple reason is that it is very hard to tell the story of the exile and the various destructions of the Jerusalem temple. Those stories are not found in a particular book in the Bible. Furthermore, Ezra and Nehemiah are a bore to read for many people! Although I can no longer confirm with Father John, I suspect that exegesis wasn't what he cared about. Rather, ministering to his people in the most appropriate and powerful way was key, and his decision to use the Exodus story to teach spiritual lessons was an exercise in leadership rather than exegesis.

The crucial issue facing us all is, what then is good leadership? The UCLA student who believes that being a good Christian involves hating himself because the Bible tells him to do so has been told a lie. His spiritual teachers *abused* him. Now that's a strong statement *I* have made. Some other pastors may challenge me. Okay. This raises a macro question: How are we going to adjudicate the veracity of the instructions of leaders? If all the Wizards of Oz, including myself, now come out from behind the curtain (if you are missing this metaphor, do go watch this American classic!), who is the better leader? Or the truer teacher? It's a question of biblical proportions, about discerning who the true prophet, or the Good Shepherd of the Sheep, is. And the answers are fraught not only with controversy but danger, for historically this is how Christians have killed each other. Of course, we can appeal to a higher force and ask, so what does the Bible say about good leadership? But then, we end up in a circular argument: a good leader interprets the Bible well, and the Bible tells us who a good leader is.

Here I want to suggest that we step out of our colonized mindset. The universe is not just Christianity and the Bible. All things good and beautiful are not to be found in America alone, or in the Christian tradition (though there is much of goodness and holiness there). Asian is a broad category, and Asian Americans hail from many ancient cultures, with their own wisdom (and folly) about what good leadership is. Therefore, we must look into this much more deeply and extensively. We do not just come from cultures of despots (as the press is liable to portray, though half the time it's true). We come from some of the most veritable birthplaces of spiritual insight, from India to China to Japan.

This topic of Asian American leadership is extensive and beyond the scope of this essay or anthology to cover. However, I suggest two frameworks going forward.

First, regard truth or insight like a bird landing on your hand. Don't grasp. This framework of nonattachment to truth appears in many traditions. Zen has a saying that "when you see a Buddha on the road, kill it." In Christianity, we have Jesus responding to someone who has just called him good with the saying, "don't call me good, only God is good" (Mark 10:18; Luke 18:19). In the Jewish tradition, Moses asks God for God's name, and God says, "I am that I am" (Exod 3:14). All these traditions are saying, don't make your experience of truth into an idol. Your attempt to concretize truth, to make it *your own* (and nobody else's) that you will defend with guns, money, and books, will end up an ironical and tragic repudiation of your own spiritual insights.

We see this grasping of a fragment of truth and thereby the making of it the whole truth so evident in the splintered denominationalism of Protestantism. For example, the Methodists, Baptists, and charismatics, as well as those sometimes derogatorily called cults, like the Mormons and Christian Scientists, have all had leaders who had some mystical or ecstatic insight. All have reified and codified these insights, albeit with different degrees of flexibility. All have had others react to this codification with either affirmation or disdain. All scramble to define orthodoxy. The drama is slightly hysterical if you ask an outsider to observe. Even upper-class and dignified denominations like my Episcopal Church are not free from the anxiety of needing to grasp tightly onto the Dove that has landed on one's hands.

It is a good practice to hold truth lightly, simply because IT is larger than us.

Now, truth or insight, if it is held lightly sometimes seem to be dispensed with altogether. This is my second point: the corrective is that truth must be practiced, and practiced somewhat silently. It was Jesus who said that we are to go into a closet to pray (Matt 6:6). I think this is good advice for our age. Less rhetoric and more results. If it works, okay, continue with it. If it doesn't work, it may not be bad, but at least it is not for you. But practice it. Then, what I would like to see is that we come together to share notes of how the truths we have grasped have worked for us. What worked to help us out of depression when a loved one dies? What works for us in prayer to be more centered? What works for us to keep our relationships passionate and committed? And finally, we bring these stories into conversation with the Bible.

These two frameworks I have just described are found throughout different religious traditions, including our own Christian one. It is also embedded in the twelve-step program of Alcoholics Anonymous. However, I would be negligent if I did not say that in modern America, their clearest articulation is to be found in the Buddhism that has come to the U.S.A. Nonattachment and mindfulness are key teachings in Buddhism and may be found, among others, in the writings of the Vietnamese Buddhist monk, Thich Nhat Hanh, in the meditation instructions of Vipassana and Zen, and in the writings of the Tibetan and Zen Buddhist teachers.

For Asian American leaders, including religious practitioners and pastors who find resonance in some of the thoughts I have articulated here, the time has come for us to do an important work. We must integrate our experience of Christianity and the risen Christ with the ancient wisdom practices of our forefathers and mothers. As we have discovered, but must now say more publicly: the canon of scripture is not closed. It is not closed because the gospel is being written in our individual and collective lives now. We might be called heretical for doing so. But let us also remember that *heresy* has its root in the word *to choose*. What we are choosing is exercising leadership and insight.

Part III
Response

AT THE TABLES OF AN ASIAN AMERICAN BANQUET

Jung Ha Kim
Georgia State University

Being invited to celebrate the banquet table full of multivoiced (re)readings of the Bible in Asian North America is to acknowledge the privilege and the risk it enlists simultaneously. This banquet gathers and uplifts Asian North Americans who are wrestling with the text(s) to discern what and how biblical stories are at work in their own individual and communal lives. Such an occasion substantiates both the course and the purpose of the banquet. Essays in this volume clearly represent a collective effort that goes beyond seeking access to the conventional religious and/or academic interpretations of the Bible and parochial theology. They instead offer Asian North American life narratives that have been informed, intersected, and integrated with contributors' own (re)reading of the text. That is to say, they offer an alternative interpretive paradigm. To partake and learn from such a community-enhancing banquet is, indeed, a privilege. By placing biblical stories and Asian North Americans' immediate life situations side by side, however, this banquet also challenges the long-assumed centrality of the Bible in Christianity and in the field of biblical studies. In other words, the issue(s) and question(s) pertaining to what the Bible says about Asian North American lives is no longer considered to be primary, but what Asian North Americans say about the Bible and how they (re)read the text have been articulated as the main menu of the banquet. To participate in a banquet that weaves together people's situated lives and their own (re)reading of the Bible, and to make the claim that human life—not the Bible—takes first place, are therefore risky.

In order to sort out and respond to the in-between and in-betwixt feelings of such privilege and risk-taking, I relied heavily on two closely intertwined perspectives: as a sociologically trained reader, and as an Asian North American woman seeking life-enhancing stories both in the Bible and in the community. As a sociologist, I am aware of my own tendency to raise questions regarding rather functional aspects of the "reality," such as "what *does* (re)reading the Bible do *for* and *to* the people?" rather than questions like "what *is* the Bible?" and/or "what does the Bible say?" And as an Asian North American woman who reads the Bible to understand life lessons, my primary concern is to address questions such as "how does the particular truth speak to me as an individual and as a member of the community?" and "what are the ways of reading the Bible that enable life to be enhanced and love to flourish?" Since both sociological training and membership in Asian North America encourage me to accept the invitation to participate in this banquet that puts lived experiences at the center and celebrates life foremost, I wholeheartedly welcome the occasion and attempt to share what I have learned from its abundance. First, I will highlight multifaceted functions that the Bible and the (re)reading of the Bible play in Asian North America; and second, I will uplift various ways of (re)reading the text in Asian North America that are life-enhancing. By dividing my response largely into two, I am also in consort with the two-course design of this special *Semeia* banquet. My response highlights the very act of *(re)reading of the Bible* as the main feature of the first course, and probing of the particularities of *Asian North American-ness* in the (re)reading of the Bible in the second course.

(Re)reading the Bible in Asian North America

> Unfortunately, her Chinese silent treatment backfired. The doctors thought Kwan had gone catatonic.... The doctors diagnosed Kwan's Chinese ghosts as a serious mental disorder. They gave her electroshock treatments, once, she said, then twice, she cried, then over and over again.... "All that electricity loosened my tongue so I could no longer stay silent as a fish. I became a country duck, crying *gaw-gwa-gwa!*—bragging about the World of Yin.... The ghosts branded me for having two faces: one loyal, one traitor. But I'm not a traitor! Look at me, Libby-ah. Is my face loyal? What do you see?" (Amy Tan: 15–16)

The complexity and richness of the first course of the banquet lie in (re)reading the text in ways that speak the truth(s) to and about everyday lives of Asian North Americans. As such, the banquet celebrates heterogeneity of social locations and voices that re-present struggles and issues pertaining to the survival of Asian North Americans. In this section, I offer selected highlights from the contributing authors' (re)reading of the text by probing a deceptively simple twofold question: "How do Asian North Americans (re)read the Bible?"; and "What functions do such (re)readings play in their own individual/communal lives?"

Fernandez offers his (re)reading of the tower of Babel as "a symbol of imperial praxis" (30) and the Pentecost story as "a vision of what it means to live together in a pluralistic society" (29). By juxtaposing his (re)reading of the tower of Babel with the European American founders' claim of the U.S. as God's "chosen people" with the call to fulfill the "manifest destiny," Fernandez warns against attempts to master the world—both in the Bible and in the U.S. His (re)reading of the text clearly favors promoting respect for the particularities of cultures to bring about the truly pluralistic "kin-dom" of God on earth.[1] Bundang, Moy, and Sano also advocate the rich heterogeneity and plurality of God's kin-dom through critical examinations of their own situated lives. Bundang, for example, demonstrates how the exile—both in its spiritual and in its physical sense—can be viewed as a form of judgment, "yet turn out to be a gift, revealing yet another face of the sacred that was never gone in the first place" (99). The core of Bundang's (re)reading arises from understanding Asian North Americans' everyday practices of religion as both dynamic and creative, as they negotiate various challenges to survive in exile. For Moy, examining a history-long maxim in Chinese/Chinese North American communities, "one more Christian, one less Chinese" (61), enabled him to (re)read *Youxue Zhengdaohu* as an alternative institution for Chinese Christians in nineteenth-century San Francisco to embrace both their religious and ethnic identities at the same time. By liberating Christianity from Western bondage and by embracing "both/and" perspectives in the process of forming identities, Moy lifts up the wisdom of Chinese Christian ancestors in tactically separating themselves as a way for Asian North Americans to actively participate in God's pluralistic kin-dom. Both Bundang's and Moy's (re)reading of the text and situated lives of Asian North Americans, then, point to the importance of human agency in negotiating identity formation and community survival. In Sano's work, the dynamic process of shifting the "canon within the canon" in Asian North America is tied to "our" negotiating and surviving the macrohistorical changes in the past half century in the U.S. By arguing that "no individual or community of faith can fully grasp the totality of the Bible" (116), Sano demonstrates how a particular community's attempt to accommodate and/or advocate necessary social changes can lead to "different" readings of the Bible. This contextualized (re)reading of the Bible makes it plain that Asian North American interpretations of the Bible are influenced not only by their shared culture/ethnicity but also by history.

While Fernandez, Moy, Bundang, and Sano's (re)readings of the text elucidate the pluralist thesis from without, the next set of work points to the richness of plurality within Asian North America. Uriah Kim, for example, examines the politics of naming by (re)reading the story of Uriah, Bathsheba's (first) husband. By highlighting the Gentile origin of Uriah the Hittite, the fate

---

[1] The term "kin-dom" is used by Ada María Isasi-Díaz and Yolanda Tarango to describe the community of struggle among Hispanic women. In their own words, "*kin-dom* makes it clear that when the fullness of God becomes a day-to-day reality in the world at large, we will be sisters and brothers—kin to each other" (116). The word "kin-dom" also is a corrective to the sexist assumption that God is male and that God's realm is hierarchically reigning people as in kings ruling over their subjects.

of Uriah and his wife have been renarrated. Both explicit and implicit in U. Kim's discussion of Uriah's story are the deeply gendered phenomenon of the so-called "out-marriage rate" and the contested terrain of gender dynamics in Asian North America. Both seem to be crucial lenses through which U. Kim (re)reads the text. Complementing the complex gender dynamic, Cheng discloses another layer of contested terrain: the notion of human sexuality and the politics of heterosexual privilege in Asian North America. He places a premium on "multiplicity present in the Bible" by (re)reading the story of the unnamed concubine in Judges 19 and argues how the story is akin to the social location of Asian North American queers as "radical sexual and geographical outsiders" (129). Warning against the tendency of Bible readers to "reduce such narratives into one-dimensional stories or lessons" (ibid.), Cheng calls for a critical remembrance of multiple fragmentation, oppression, silencing, and naming, both in the Bible and in Asian North America.

Race/ethnicity, gender, and sexual orientation are not the only salient identity-claimers that can shed much light on how Asian North Americans (re)read the biblical text. Foskett's and Rietz's work disclose yet another complexity and richness of the plurality within. Reclaiming Moses as an adopted son of an Egyptian princess, Foskett offers a dynamic (re)reading between the lost identity and the newly gained identity via the process of adoption. The story of Moses' adoption and his bicultural socialization triggers painful memories of more than fifty thousand people who were adopted from Korea as children, as well as thousands of Chinese daughters who have entered into the U.S. since 1991.[2] By retelling Moses' story as an adoptee's struggle to come to terms with his own identity and purpose in life, Foskett problematizes the complacency and amnesia that Asian North Americans suffer from their missing or lost members. As Asian North American adoptees negotiate their own identities (as Moses), Foskett also pushes us to remember the love and sacrifices of people who enable adopted lives to flourish: their biological mothers, sisters, and the mothers who raised them. Rietz's reflection on a *hapa* identity also discloses a painful truth about the politics of identity formation in Asian North America. By challenging "whose identity is being privileged by the category of Asian [North] American?" (151), Rietz argues for an understanding of identity construction that "emphasizes particularity

---

[2] Korean children who were adopted into "American" homes in a wave that began in the 1950s are now in their thirties and forties. Because they came into the U.S. during the days of secrecy and sealed files of the adoption process, it has taken decades for open discussions to take place. While the kind of open discussion of bicultural socialization has existed from the beginning for adopted daughters from China, Asian adoptees go through tremendous hardship in constructing self-identities. For further readings, see Felicia Law; Karen Evans; and Dele Olojede.

as the basis for community and communication" (152). By offering (re)readings of the Bible by often silenced and invisible members of Asian North America, Foskett and Rietz aptly demonstrate that identity formation is not necessarily a matter of inheritance, but of politics.

With its abundant plurality and complexity, the first course of the banquet celebrates a collection of liberating good news created and proclaimed by the people whose presence and voices have been marginalized in the history (of biblical scholarship) recorded by the dominant culture. This banquet, then, is about celebrating how Asian North Americans came to reclaim their own "re-storied" lives in light of (re)reading the text (Joan Laird). When editing *Stony the Road We Trod* as a collection of African American (re)readings of the Bible, Cain Hope Felder articulated a keen sense of dissonance between what African American biblical scholars know and what they are taught in academe. I think this dissonance is akin to the sentiment shared by contributing authors in this banquet. Felder argues that a liberatory breakthrough "comes when scholars no longer bury what they know in submission to the traditional 'experts,' [and] they begin to question the subtle biases and the very management of the departments and guilds of biblical scholarship" (5). He also asserts that people who read the Bible "must use the training that we have received, but we must also argue with and correct such training, so we can apply our tools, language, and theological sensitivity to those realities that we were not taught to take seriously academically" (8). I believe the first course of this banquet that celebrates Asian North American (re)readings of the text has accomplished just that: applying what they know from living Asian North American lives to restory the text and their own lives. Put differently, (re)reading functions as both the means and the end to restory biblical stories and Asian North American lives.

Having learnt much from the contributors' life-sustaining act of putting the Bible and their own situated lives side by side, I offer a small reminder about the possible consequences of telling the truth, which was narrated by Kwan in Amy Tan's *The Hundred Secret Senses*. For the crucial matter in front of us is no longer discerning a choice between keeping silent or speaking about what we know, but preparing for possible consequences of telling the truth from both within and without Asian North America. "The ghosts branded me for having two faces: one loyal, one traitor. But I'm not a traitor! Look at me.... Is my face loyal? What do you see?" (Tan: 15–16).

The Life-Enhancing Ways of (Re)reading the Bible in Asian North America

The Bible is very important in the life and growth of grassroots communities. But its importance must be put in the right place. It's something like the motor of an automobile. Generally the motor is under the hood, out of sight.... Way back when the first cars came out, the motor was huge. It was quite obvious and made a lots of noise.... Today the motors are getting smaller and smaller. They are more powerful, but they are also quieter and better hidden.... Much the same is true about the Bible and its function in the life of Christian communities. The Bible is supposed to start things off, to get them going; but it is not the steering wheel. (Carlos Mesters: 197–98)

When naming a vantage point of the reader of the text as "Asian North American," what exterior and interior vantages are privileged? What are the ways of (re)reading texts that enable Asian North American lives to flourish? In this second course of the banquet, I encounter adroit use of life-enhancing sources that are both Western and Eastern, both Christian and non-Christian, as well as both racially-ethnically specific and universal, to address the foregoing questions. While several authors have drawn specific stories and interpretation of the text from an ethnic community, most authors address Asian North American life experiences and (re)reading of the text in a pan-ethnic fashion. And regardless of various life-enhancing sources that the authors have drawn from, they seem to be in consort with elucidating the mystery of how universal truth(s) are paradoxically present in the particularities of Asian North American life.

In the second course of the banquet, Iwamura, Matsuoka, and Lim openly challenge the much-assumed notion of the (closed) canon, and the authority of the Bible, by placing Asian North American experiences at the center of their studies. Iwamura, for example, names Joy Kogawa's *Obasan* as the "manna" of re-membering the traumatic Japanese Canadian (and Japanese American) internment experiences and points to the important function that such naming of lived experiences plays in the everyday life of Asian North Americans. Since a name is "no mere label, but an essential expression of its personality and being" (171), the main function of naming is not to constrain, but to liberate people to reflect and to accommodate changes in life. As Asian North Americans encounter and experience different "manna" in their lives, they also come to see that the Bible is an open canon. In Iwamura's own words, "the imperative of God's love figures the Bible not as a closed text, but rather as something that is continually being revealed and rewritten" (176). While Iwamura offers the power and responsibility of naming contemporary Asian North American experiences as various kinds of "manna" that witness the ongoing canonization process, Matsuoka and Lim provide discussions of fluid and nondoctrinal permutation of Asian North American spirituality that informs their own (re)reading of the text, as well as use the legacies of their own ancestors as sources for life-enhancement.

Drawing upon Japanese American (re)reading of the Bible as "literature that helps enrich both the joy and the sorrow of an everyday life" (181),

Matsuoka offers another understanding of the authority of the Bible in Asian North America. For Japanese Americans, biblical truth claims are not perceived as authoritative doctrinal truths, but as truths that need to be discerned in light of their own experiences of life. Thus, the Bible can be "authoritative to the extent that it illumines the experiences of a given community with insights that would sustain through the pain of life and provides joy in it" (188). By comparing and contrasting the logocentrism in the European context with the cultural privileging of texts in the East Asian context, Lim also argues that "the canon of scripture is not closed" (322). Remembering Jesus—not the Bible—as "the Word of God," Lim asserts that "truth must be practiced, and practiced somewhat silently" (321). For Lim, life-enhancing sources come from two practices: (1) how Jesus lived his life; and (2) learning from the "ancient wisdom practices of our forefathers and mothers" (322). By continuing on the legacy of the good news that has been written in Jesus and our ancestors' lives, Asian North Americans come to know for certain that the word/text is an open canon.

The importance of Asian North American self-identity and how such self-understanding shapes the (re)reading of the text are discussed by Jeung, Alumkal, and Tseng. Identifying the two main institutional logics in pan-Asian American churches (in the Bay area, California) as (liberal) mainline and evangelical, Jeung provides concise definitions of Asian American identity. To mainline pan-Asian American Christians, Asian Americans are "a racial minority group with a common history of cultural oppression and racism"; and to evangelical pan-Asian American Christians, Asian Americans are "a spiritual consumer target group made up of personal networks and lifestyle affinities" (212). These two different institutional logics not only shape self-understandings of Asian North Americans but also determine their interpretation of the text. (Re)reading the text from distinct institutional perspectives, then, pan-Asian American Christian communities can come together either to promote tolerance and social justice in multiracial North America or be bound together by their common mission to evangelize others. While Jeung offers pan-Asian North American self-understandings and the relationship between self-identity and the (re)reading of the Bible, Alumkal and Tseng take generational differences in two ethnic communities seriously to offer their own (re)reading of the community life. Alumkal, for example, makes a claim that second-generation Korean American Christians "have accepted mainstream American evangelical theology as synonymous with 'Christianity'" (239), to a large extent. Giving much-needed attention to generational differences among Chinese American evangelical Christians, Tseng elucidates the dynamic process of identity construction among ABC (American-born Chinese). On the one hand, ABC are reacting to "the perceived immigrant ethnocentrism akin to that of the 'Judaizers' in the New Testament church" (260); and on the other hand, ABC are also responsible for raising questions honestly about "how white evangelical norms have shaped their own perspectives," and "how structural racism operates in white American evangelical circles" (263). By discussing processes both of assimilation and racialization, Tseng argues that Chinese (and other Asian) North American cultural identity "should not be viewed as a fixed reality" (257) and that people must "make the gospel contextually relevant to each new culture it reaches" (256).

By reading critically Oglesby's *Biblical Themes for Pastoral Care* from an Asian North American perspective, Clark offers yet another double-layered dialogical model of reading and rereading the text. From reading Oglesby's text, Clark identifies a distinct way of obtaining "needed principles" (293) in the Bible to assist parishioners (in general) with crisis. Rereading critically the insights that he gained from reading both Oglesby's and the biblical text, Clark further explicates the in-between subtleties of both implicit and explicit messages that may be of assistance to Asian North American parishioners. Clark's involvement in the oral-history project enables him to name Japanese American experiences of life crisis as exile, diaspora, and deliverance. In order to appropriately assist people with these crises, one needs to reassess both "needed principles," and the context in which pastoral care is experienced. While Clark offers Japanese (and other Asian) North Americans' understanding of both Oglesby and the biblical text in the context of pastoral care, Eunjoo M. Kim examines the usage of the Bible in Korean American preaching. Drawing upon insights from Gadamer, Ricouer, and her own experiences in the Korean American church, E. Kim argues that the main role of the preacher as "an interpreter" is to bridge "the world of the text and that of the congregation" in order to create "a new meaning contextually" (272). In order to (re)read the text "by reflecting its truthful meaning relevant to the contemporary reader" (ibid.), she warns against privatizing the Bible to "proof text" one's own political stances and personal needs. Instead, E. Kim argues for (re)reading the text as the main source of identity formation and to give heed to a specific, biblical interpretation as "the voice of the congregation" (278).

My Yearnings for More

I learned long ago in seminary what David Tracy identifies as two principal sources for doing Christian theology: (1) Christian texts; and (2) common human experiences and languages (43). Certainly and clearly, this second course of the banquet delineates the intricate relationship between the text(s) and commonly shared experiences and language of Asian North Americans. I would also argue that the banquet goes beyond Tracy's understanding by elucidating how neither the texts nor human experiences and language are constant. Thus encountering and intersecting these two dynamic processes necessitate critical assessments of how certain lives may be privileged in a particular historical context and by a particular cultural (re)reading of the text. These contributors' insistence on Asian North American particularities in their (re)reading of the text also makes it clear that they believe that the God of the Bible does not speak uniformly in a universal language to all human life circumstances. By making available an alternative interpretive paradigm that is methodologically and theologically grounded in lived experiences of Asian North Americans, this banquet extends an invitation to all those who are concerned with dismantling hegemonic attempts to canonize theological orthodoxy in the reading and the readership of the Bible.

To further encourage others to uplift various life-enhancing ways of (re)reading the text, I especially yearn for another abundant course of the banquet that offers the following yet-to-be-heard voices in Asian North America.

First, the effect of radical democratization within Asian North American faith communities. Many Asian North Americans claim their (Christian) religious identities not so much as an inherited faith but as their own chosen faith. In fact, multigenerational people often find themselves belonging to the same faith community as first-generation Christians. While highlighting the generational difference between the first-generation immigrants and their predominantly English-speaking offspring in the context of their own ethnic community is important, more nuanced documentation of how the radical equalizing of generational difference is managed and experienced in the community is needed.

Second, biblical scholars, such as Walter Brueggmann and Daniel L. Smith, have commented on the centrality of "land" in biblical religion(s). The "lure of sacred space" and the notion of "home" are especially strong among the homeless and the dis-/relocated. If Asian North Americans are another dis-/relocated people *en route* to God's "promised land" or "exile" of sorts, paying more attention to documenting their relationships and experiences of "land" and/or "home" (both physical and spiritual) may be meaningful.

Third, well knowing that Asian North American women are too broad and diverse to be considered as a single readership of the Bible, I long for more gender-specific ways of (re)reading and experiencing the good news. The various ways by which Asian North American women search for healing messages and develop survival strategies in light of their own (re)reading of the Bible need to be acknowledged and celebrated. When conducting a study about never-married Korean American women's life narratives, for example, I learned that women's shared marital status also shapes their (re)reading of the Bible. Let me offer two such "Ah-ha" moments of contextualized (re)reading of the Bible here (Kim, forthcoming):

Have you ever heard a pastor preaching about Jesus's marital status? [Pastors] sometimes mention the fact that Jesus was single [and that] he was often misunderstood and rejected by his own people. The Bible clearly states that Jesus was often alone and felt utterly lonely. But pastors never spell out Jesus as a never-married man. He wasn't just a single man.... I mean I have zillions of questions about why he was single. If Jesus was fully a man and fully God, why don't we talk about his human side in the church? Rather than picking on *no-cheu-nyeu* [literally, "an old maid" in Korean] like myself as an exception, people should ask serious questions about themselves, [such as] why they got married if they are serious about imitating Jesus's footstep.

I think Jesus was able to care for so many people because he was single. If he was married and had a wife and children, he probably could not do all those things he did for the people.... And when I compare Jesus's life with mine, I take comfort in knowing [that] God understands what it means to live a life as a single person. Just as Jesus relied on those women [who are mentioned in the Bible] to help him, I rely on many people for their kindness and friendship.... I think people who discriminate against single people don't really understand why God made Jesus to live alone in the first place.

All in all, if one of the important purposes for conducting any systemic study is to bring a fuller knowledge of human experiences to strengthen contexualized understanding and to enhance human life in general, the paucity of celebrating Asian North American (re)readings of the Bible points to a serious knowledge gap. This banquet with its two distinct courses attempts to bridge such a knowledge gap. And to take a part in such an attempt is, indeed, a privilege I do not take lightly. As a small token of my thanks for what I have learned from the banquet, I offer two tables based on my own rereading of the banquet. Besides, what good is a sociologist without her tables and figures?!

Table 1: *(Re)reading of the Text* in Asian North America

Author	The (biblical) text(s)	The function of (re)reading the text(s)
Fernandez	The story of Babel and the Pentecost	Critique of imperialism and promoting pluralism
Moy	Missionary texts and Chinese American migration history	*Youxue Zhengaohu* as a model of tactical separation and an alternative model for embracing both racial-ethnic identity and religious identity simultaneously

Uriah Kim	The story of Uriah the Hittite	Politics of naming and the reflection of interracial/ethnic unions and gender dynamics
Bundang	The story of exile in Babylon	Exile as a gift and yet another face of the sacred
Sano	(The shifting nature of reading) The Bible and history of the U.S.	Influence of history for understanding the community's shifting "canon within the canon"
Cheng	The story of the unnamed concubine in Judges 19	The Queer Asian North American as a radical sexual and geographical outsider par excellence and promoting multiplicity (by resisting reduction and simplification of the text)
Foskett	The story of Moses and adoption as *telos* in Romans 8 and 9	The lost and the newly gained identity of (Asian North American) adoptees and remembering people who enabled other lives to flourish
Rietz	Autobiographical narratives and the Dead Sea Scrolls	*Hapa* identity and the politics of identity in Asian North America

Table 2: (Re)reading of the Text *in Asian North America*

Author	The (re)reading of the text	Life-enhancing experiences in Asian North America
Iwamura	Kogawa's *Obasan*	Contemporary Asian North American "manna" that names and remembers the past as part of the present and as the ongoing process of canonizing the sacred text(s)
Matsuoka	The Bible in Japanese American communities	Authority of the Bible is not assumed but earned as the text illuminates the truth of lived experiences and inspires to sustain life

Liew	Kogawa's rereading of the Bible and Asian American literature	"Wonky" and "random" reading of the Bible to facilitate the work of love
Jeung	Pan-Asian faith communities	Institutional logics shape both self-identities and (re)reading of the text
Alumkal	The intergenerational Korean American church	Influence of mainstream evangelical theology among second-generation Korean American Christians
Tseng	The intergenerational and evangelical Chinese American church	ABC (American-born Chinese) against immigrant ethnocentrism and ABC critiquing structural racism in white American evangelical circles
E. M. Kim	The usage of the Bible in the Korean American church	Preaching the contextually relevant good news (rather than "proof texting" the Bible for private use)
Clark	Oglesby's *Biblical Themes for Pastoral Care* and the oral history of Japanese Americans	Rereading between the lines to obtain "needed principles" to assist Asian North Americans with life crises
Lim	The logocentric culture of Europe and the text-oriented culture of East Asia	Remembering Jesus (not the Bible) as the word of God and to learn from ancient wisdom practiced by ancestors

Works Consulted

Brueggemann, Walter
    1977   *The Land*. Philadelphia: Fortress.

Evans, Karen
    2000   *The Lost Daughters of China: Abandoned Girls, Their Journey to America, and the Search for a Mission Past*. New York: Putnam.

Felder, Cain Hope, ed.
  1991 *Stony the Road We Trod: African American Biblical Interpretation.* Minneapolis: Fortress.

Isasi-Díaz, Ada María, and Yolanda Tarango
  1988 *Hispanic Women: Prophetic Voice in the Church.* San Francisco: Harper & Row.

Kim, Jung Ha
  Forth- "The Restoried Lives: The Everyday Theology of Korean American
  coming Never-Married Women." In *Mapping Korean American Religions.* Ed. David K. Yoo and Ruth Chun.

Laird, Joan
  1989 "Women and Stories: Restorying Women's Self-Constructions." Pp. 427–50 in *Women in Families: A Framework for Family Therapy.* Ed. Monica M. Goldrick, Carol Anderson, and Froma Welsh. New York: Norton.

Law, Felicia
  1993 "Transracial Adoptions, A Case of Colorblind Love or Cultural Genocide?" *McNair Journal* 1:21–31.

Mesters, Carlos
  1994 "The Use of the Bible in Christian Communities of the Common People." Pp. 197–210 in *The Challenge of Basic Christian Communities.* Ed. Sergio Torres and John Eagleson. Maryknoll, N.Y.: Orbis.

Olojede, Dele
  1998 "Chinese Woman Fights Family Planning Laws." *Newsday,* Nov. 30.

Smith, Daniel L.
  1989 *The Religion of the Landless: The Social Context of the Babylonian Exile.* Bloomington: Meyer-Stone.

Tan, Amy
  1995 *The Hundred Secret Senses.* New York: G. P. Putnam's Sons.

Tracy, David
  1995 *Blessed Rage for Order: The New Pluralism in Theology.* Chicago: University of Chicago Press. [Orig. 1975]

www.ingramcontent.com/pod-product-compliance
Lightning Source LLC
Chambersburg PA
CBHW021933290426

44108CB00012B/825